JAGUAR

SPORTS RACING CARS

C-TYPE • D-TYPE • XKSS • LIGHTWEIGHT E-TYPE

JAGUAR

SPORTS RACING CARS

C-TYPE • D-TYPE • XKSS • LIGHTWEIGHT E-TYPE

PHILIP PORTER

Technical Consultancy by CHRIS KEITH-LUCAS
Edited by MARK HUGHES
Special Photography by PAUL DEBOIS
US Consultancy by TERRY LARSON

In association with PORTER & PORTER LTD

FRONT COVER
The greatest of the C-types? Driven by Duncan Hamilton
and Tony Rolt, XKC 051 won Le Mans in 1953,
fitted with pioneering disc brakes.
Today it is owned by Adrian Hamilton, Duncan's son.

TITLE PAGE
The full-width windscreen shows this D-type
to be one of the six long-nose cars built
for the 1956 season. This car, XKD 606,
is actually the last D-type built.

BACK COVER
The conclusion of the story. Perhaps the most original
of the Lightweight E-types is chassis number 11,
owned briefly by Neil Corner in the 1960s
and now back in the same family being raced by
his son, Nigel, in historic events.

Published 1995 by Bay View Books Ltd
The Red House, 25-26 Bridgeland Street
Bideford, Devon EX39 2PZ, UK

Revised edition 1998

© Copyright 1995, 1998 by Philip Porter

ISBN 1 901432 21 1
Printed in Hong Kong

CONTENTS

INTRODUCTION

Few cars excite the enthusiast more than Jaguar's sports racing cars of the 1950s and 1960s. Few cars have been so significant in the evolution of the racing car. To many car enthusiasts they are possibly the ultimate sports racing cars, and to Jaguar enthusiasts they certainly are. Their style is still entrancing, their international successes unquestioned, their performance sensational and their charisma intense. They are thrilling motor cars.

The C-type was arguably the first pure sports racing car, and it influenced design in that field for a decade or more. The D-type was even more innovative. Between them these cars pioneered features that are still in use on racing cars today, and some that are now standard practice on production cars worldwide. Such developments included disc brakes, dry-sump engine lubrication, alloy wheels, bag fuel tanks, fuel injection, automotive aerodynamics and monocoque construction for two-seater bodies. The Lightweight E-types, while not really sports racing cars and not ground-breaking in the same way, were nevertheless the ultimate form of a brilliant production car derived directly from the Le Mans D-types.

In this book I look first at the XK120's development and baptism in the harsh reality of the competition world in more detail than has previously been offered. I then trace the related design and development of the competition version, the C-type, which built on the inherent qualities of the XK120 and its superb engine. Having described the C-type's specification, I follow the history of the works cars as they took up the ultimate challenge of Le Mans and other events. In many instances the drivers, such as Stirling Moss, are quoted, and throughout the book there is considerable comment from Jaguar's legendary team manager, F.R.W. 'Lofty' England.

After looking at the activities of the production C-types and ex-works cars racing in several continents, I move on, via the curious but highly significant low-drag car, to the D-type, once more tracing design, development, specification, the works cars and the production versions, together with the XKSS. Again these chapters are spiced with quotes and anecdotes. In my books I always try to convey memories from people who were involved at the time in the hope that these give an added dimension. It has also been my desire to capture some of the humour of motor racing in those days. The book review I treasure most was written by the late Innes Ireland, who said of my *Jaguar E-type: The Definitive History* (Haynes, 1989) that one of

'Lofty' England's stories, 'had me rocking with laughter; so vividly was the tale told I could imagine the whole scene'.

The birth, back in the mid-1950s, of the brilliant E-type as both a racing car and a production sports car is examined and its course of development unravelled. The early racing exploits that led, gradually, to the development of the Lightweight, which would regularly vanquish the legendary Ferrari 250GTO, are described, together with a history of the cars in competition.

This story of these three racing models is followed by a uniquely detailed history of the individual cars by chassis number. This section starts on page 161 and has a separate introduction.

These Jaguars were so much more than just racing cars, as 'Lofty' England made clear when once addressing a meeting of the Institution of Mechanical Engineers. He gave five reasons for a company going motor racing: national prestige was raised by racing successes, the company's reputation was enhanced, free and widespread publicity was obtained for its products, engineering development was accelerated, and the workers' interest was increased.

Bill Heynes, who, together with his team of engineers, was responsible for creating these cars, made a number of very telling points in various papers he composed over the years.

On the C-type: "Up to that time, nearly all sports cars or semi-racing types had a spidery chassis and cycle wings, and the C-type with its complete envelope was to become the pattern of design which has been followed by the majority of sports cars since that date."

On keeping abreast with contemporary developments: "It is true to say that competition cars, specials, GT cars and racing sports cars are the prototypes where most new developments are tried out, so that it behoves the designer of a sports car to keep well up to date with all that is going on in his field. He must also keep up to date in what is happening with motorcycle development and, to some extent, aircraft development because there are quite a number of items and ideas that can be borrowed from these sources."

On using a production-based engine: "The fact that we have always kept our racing engines as close as possible to our production engines has been of considerable advantage in carrying out development work. As our engines are based chiefly on production components, we can test them to destruction if necessary without too great a financial loss, a form of testing our rivals cannot

ABOVE **The C-type helped considerably to further young Stirling Moss's career at a time when he was not enjoying much luck in Grands Prix – today he still has a high regard for the Jaguar.** FACING PAGE **Stirling Moss at the 1953 Le Mans, a race won by a disc-braked C-type. Bill Heynes said this success "changed the whole conception of brake design in this country".**

afford with their specially-built power units costing several thousand pounds."

On disc brakes: "These were a joint development with the Dunlop Company and there is little question that the outstanding success of these brakes in the Le Mans race of 1953 has changed the whole conception of brake design in this country. There is not the slightest doubt that the rest of the automobile world will have to follow."

On the benefits of racing: "That the participation in the Le Mans race has been a very strong incentive there is no question at all. Not only has it made it necessary for us to increase the power, but it has also made it necessary for us to increase the reliability and durability of all component parts of the engine, transmission, axles, brakes and all the other various components on the car. It has made it necessary to work up to a standard of perfection, both in design and manufacture, far in excess of the needs of the general public."

On pioneering work: "We have often not originated an idea but we have pioneered an idea and assisted in the development of it in quite a lot of cases, examples being Dunlop tyres, the Dunlop disc brake and Lucas fuel injection. The major part of the spade work has all been done by the company concerned but in these cases I think we can take the credit for having seen the light and collaborated in the development of these items to an extent that they have influenced the trend of design throughout the industry. On these and other projects there have been brilliant engineers who have worked with us as so much a part of our own team that we hardly regard them as having a separate existence."

This book is a tribute to the engineers under Heynes, to the drivers led by Stirling Moss and Mike Hawthorn, to the dedicated mechanics and backroom boys, and to 'Lofty' England, who stage-managed the successes on the world stage. All worked under the shrewd captaincy of Sir William Lyons, who appropriately named his first boat the Sea Type! One man, though, played perhaps a greater role than any other.

The Jaguar sports cars succeeded at Le Mans for various reasons, but indisputably their good aerodynamic shape allowed them to compete with, and beat, more powerful cars. The man who effectively introduced the aircraft art of aerodynamics to racing cars was Malcolm Sayer. This remarkable man, who was universally liked and admired, and who hated to be called a stylist, used the principles of Computer Aided Design without a computer.

In creating the D-type, his masterpiece, he uniquely blended science and art to produce an effective shape of timeless beauty. He brought science to the art of racing car design, and scientifically created a work of art.

Philip Porter
Knighton-on-Teme, Worcestershire, May 1995

ACKNOWLEDGEMENTS

As one of the world's greatest experts in the field, Chris Keith-Lucas has played a leading role in helping to create this book. For 20 years he has run Lynx, a company that has probably rebuilt more D-types, C-types and Lightweight E-types than any other. He has contributed to the technical chapters, suggested cars that should be photographed, checked the manuscript, and contributed very significantly to the individual chassis histories. My first discussions about this book were with Chris several years ago, and he has put an enormous amount of time and effort into bringing this complex project to fruition. The Lynx files also yielded helpful information and illustrations.

I am also indebted to all the people I have interviewed over the years and who contributed first-hand accounts of events they were involved in. I am particularly grateful to Stirling Moss, my hero since childhood, with whom I conducted a fascinating interview specially for this book – he could not have been more helpful.

Malcolm Sayer's daughter, Kate, kindly provided copies of her father's papers. Julian Ghosh, late of Jaguar, supplied copies of some of Sayer's original workings, a unique feature of this book, and drawings that he rescued many years ago during a clear-out at Jaguar. Doug Nye provided me with the benefit of his encyclopaedic knowledge when discussing innovations in racing car design, and could not have been more generous with his time. Martin Morris on two occasions provided hospitality, a plethora of information and a run in his most historic C-type and D-type (OKV 3). Willie Tuckett provided much information, and again allowed me to remind myself what a very exciting car a good D-type is to drive.

It would be churlish not to acknowledge the debt that fellow enthusiasts owe to the late Andrew Whyte. It is inevitable that more and more information becomes available as times goes on, but Andrew's research was the sturdy foundation on which I and others have been able to build.

I would like to thank the owners of the cars specially photographed for this book for their generous co-operation and patience. They are the Rt Hon Alan Clark (production C-type), Adrian Hamilton (works C-type, 1953 Le Mans winner), Martin Morris (ex-works short-nose D-type), Alan Lawson (alloy-framed D-type), Nigel Dawes (production D-type), Allen Lloyd (XKSS), Robert Brooks (long-nose D-type) and Nigel Corner (Lightweight E-type). Paul Debois's photography speaks for itself and it has been most rewarding to work once again with one of Britain's top car photographers.

'Lofty' England took such great interest in this book, but sadly died just after it had been despatched to the printers. Late in life he remained razor-sharp and had a remarkable memory. Not only did he entertain me at his lovely Alpine retreat for several days while we talked through the subject extensively, but he also checked the manuscript and, in characteristic manner, did not hesitate to say if he thought others were talking a load of rubbish! While I was writing he was the only person still alive who had played a leading role throughout the period, and I remain more than grateful to him for immeasurably enhancing and giving credibility to my work.

CHAPTER ONE

XK120 BACKGROUND

What attribute or achievement has made the Jaguar company so successful and the name so famous throughout the world? Was it the XK engine with its unique spread of versatility ranging from world-beating sports cars to armoured fighting vehicles, from Le Mans winners to silent executive saloons built some 30 years after it was first designed? Was it Sir William Lyons' sound and cautious business ability, combined with his pre-eminence in the field of automotive styling? Was it the superb team of engineers, led by William Heynes, and a loyal and dedicated workforce who developed and produced a fine range of stylish sporting cars? Was it simply the quality of the products? Or was it the company's success in international sports car racing?

The answer, of course, is a combination of all these factors, and more. Indeed, all relied upon each other. Successful cars depended on a brilliant engine, which could not have been created by anyone other than the finest engineers, who could not have been retained by a company that was not well run, and so on. However, one factor – motor racing – contributed more than any other to making the company internationally known, leading to considerable expansion and the blossoming of Jaguar into one of the great names of the British motor industry. By winning Le Mans in 1951 and four subsequent years that decade, Jaguar promoted itself from being a company of promise and pretension to one of international renown and perceived quality. There are certainly no doubts about the significance of motor racing for F.R.W. 'Lofty' England, who was Jaguar's Service Manager from 1946, Competitions Manager from 1951, Service Director from 1956 and Assistant Managing Director from 1961.

"From 1949 I used to go to the USA reasonably often. Until we won Le Mans, people didn't know what Jaguar was. If you were driving one, they would pull up alongside and ask, 'Say, Mister, what's the auto?' 'Jaguar.' 'What's Jaguar?' 'Fine British car!' In fact at the first motor show I attended over there we had the 3½ Litre. People asked what these 'lighters' were. 'A lighter is a litre, 1000cc.' 'What are cc?' 'Spanish for yes!'"

Bill Heynes, the most influential man at Jaguar after Lyons himself, described Le Mans as, "...the

ABOVE **Jaguar's sensational XK120 on its launch at the Earls Court Motor Show in 1948. The C-type would evolve directly from it.**

longest and most arduous of all races in the world. The stakes are high – but then so are the prizes. The winning drivers take in prize money alone over £3500 which with bonuses, etc, may total up to £4000 or £5000 between the two of them. The value to the company cannot be assessed in pounds, shillings and pence – it gives a world prestige to the winning car that no other race or sequence of races can confer and is without doubt the most sought-after hallmark in the motoring world, and the only European or British race that receives front-page publicity in the USA."

Pre-war the company was just one of many British car manufacturers. Although it had carved out a niche for itself in Britain, it was barely known abroad and indeed was unknown in the US, a market of vast size and enormous potential. From humble beginnings in Blackpool in 1922 making motorcycle sidecars, the Swallow Sidecar Company had progressed remarkably in the pre-war years. It had begun making stylish versions of the ubiquitous Austin Seven in 1927, meted out the same treatment to several other makes – most

ABOVE **The XL sports car styled by William Lyons in 1946-47 was the starting point for the XK120 prototype, which was built in just a few weeks before its first public appearance.**

notably Standard – and gone on to produce its own SS cars with Standard engines. As a response to the need for a suitable model name, the appellation SS Jaguar was adopted in 1935 and progress was only halted by the outbreak of war in 1939.

While the company was undoubtedly successful and enjoying increasing stature, its progress had been built on style, image, value for money and imitation more than innovation. The pre-war cars aped Bentleys of the period but cost considerably less. These SS Jaguars showed Lyons at his most shrewd because they appealed to two very different sectors of the market: those who aspired to own a Bentley but could not yet afford one, and those who used to own such cars but could no longer afford them because of the Depression. An SS Jaguar suited those on the way up and seemed less of a comedown for those on the way down. As for performance, the long bonnets promised much but delivered little until the advent of the 3½-litre SS Jaguar 100.

If the company was to join the big time, it needed its own engine and its own image. Thus the stage was set for the XK engine.

BIRTH OF THE XK ENGINE

Car production ceased with the outbreak of war and the company turned to military work: aircraft components, manufacturing sidecars for military use, carts to be drawn by mules, and various development projects like working on lightweight Jeeps that could be dropped by parachute. War work had the incidental benefit of introducing the company to aircraft industry techniques that would later influence some designs.

Furthermore, everyone employed at the SS factory had to spend one night each week on fire-watching duty, looking out for incendiary bombs falling on the factory or the surrounding neighbourhood. As the bombing of Coventry was largely over by 1943, the sessions were not unduly taxing. Lyons, keen to make use of the time, organised matters so that he, Bill Heynes, Claude Baily and Wally Hassan would be on duty together on Sunday nights. They discussed post-war plans and exchanged ideas in these brainstorming sessions.

Even during the blitz Lyons had continued to create prototype body styles with the assistance of Fred Gardner, who ran the sawmill, and Cyril Holland, who had been with him in Blackpool. He intimated his desire for a new engine, which would be more powerful, refined and advanced than the Standard power units used previously. He was taken with the idea of a twin overhead camshaft engine partly because it would look glamorous – style was of paramount importance to him. Like Ettore Bugatti, Lyons wanted his cars to be not only very fast but also works of art.

During the war it was not easy to undertake non-essential engineering work and progress was slow. With the prefix 'X' for experimental, the first five projects, XA to XE, were concepts only, so the first engine to be built was designated the XF. This 1360cc engine was followed by the XG, which was heavily influenced by the pre-war BMW six-cylinder engine. Then came the XJ, which, unlike the earlier designs, was freed from the constraints of having to use as much as possible of the existing tooling. A family of engines was envisaged with four-cylinder and six-cylinder versions largely sharing the same tooling. Detail design work began in 1945 and engines were running the following year.

"This engine," stated Bill Heynes, "was one of the first twin overhead camshaft engines to be put into large-scale production. This design had previously been by-passed by engineers because of its higher cost, but the inherent reliability of this unit has well repaid the extra expenditure on tooling and machining costs. The use of overhead camshafts was chosen for the light weight of the reciprocating valve parts and because the direct thrust from the camshafts on to the valve tappet eliminates wear and the necessity for tappet adjustment.

The new XK engine in cutaway view, showing its twin overhead camshaft layout.

"The design of this engine and the addition of twin overhead camshafts and a hemispherical head was severely criticised by the leading engineers of the day who had far more experience, design and production-wise, than I. Had it not been for the enthusiasm and encouragement, and the insistence of my Managing Director, Sir William Lyons, that we must have something that would anticipate the competition for 10 years ahead, I think we might have been discouraged, even though we had complete faith in the principles we had adopted."

Meanwhile, Lyons had been working on a new body design for a large saloon, and Bill Heynes and Bob Knight had been designing a new chassis with independent torsion bar front suspension. Due to the cost of developing the engine, the company could not afford to introduce the new car immediately. It had resumed production of the pre-war cars with the cessation of hostilities and introduced the Mark V model in 1948 as a stop-gap until the new car was ready.

The story of the thinking behind the XK120 sports car is well-known. With the engine ready, Heynes was keen to put it into production. Lyons felt that it was wrong to blunt the impact of its introduction by fitting it in the rather staid Mark V, but the company had no sports car in production. Lyons, however, knew the publicity value of sports cars and decided to build such a car for the

1948 Motor Show, which was just a few weeks away. The new chassis could be cut down to suit, the powerful new engine would be ideal, and the more tolerant enthusiast buyers of this low-volume car could help to evaluate the engine.

Lyons had already built a prototype sports car called the XL and this new project was not too dissimilar. He created a sensational shape in a very

BELOW **The first public demonstration of the XK120's remarkable performance was at Jabbeke, Belgium, in 1949. Ron 'Soapy' Sutton achieved 132mph in the prototype.**

10

RIGHT **The start of the Production Car Race at Silverstone in 1949. Peter Walker's red XK120 has all but disappeared but is followed by Leslie Johnson's white car and Prince Bira's car in his traditional Siamese colours of blue with yellow wheels.**

BELOW **For the Production Car Race at Silverstone in 1949 three cars were lent to leading drivers. This one, Leslie Johnson's, was the eventual winner.**

short time, and the car, fitted with the XJ 3.2-litre engine, was the sensation of Earls Court, even though it had never run. This car, of course, was the legendary XK120, its title taken from the engine designation – the final 3.4-litre version was called the XK – and an estimate of the top speed.

A smaller-engined version, the XK100, was listed but only one was ever produced. There were various reasons: the four-cylinder engine exhibited secondary vibrations, demand for it was likely to be low because the six-cylinder engine had been received with such enthusiasm, and the company was unlikely to make a profit on it.

"After some discussion," stated Heynes, "it was agreed we would make about 200 sports two-seaters and put them on the market in an effort to get some customer miles on the new engine before changing over our main production. It was thought that a car of this type would have a limited market only..." However, "It was obvious right from the time of its introduction that the demand, particularly in the US, was far in excess of what we had visualised, and as a result of this we had to take steps to put the car into reasonable series production."

DEVELOPING THE XK120

Clearly the XK120 was not ready for production and development testing began in earnest. Ron 'Soapy' Sutton reported to Heynes and Baily on the initial tests on 10 December 1948. The first was simply a run up the Keresley Road. The third involved running up to maximum speeds and 102mph was the highest that could be achieved. The rear wheels were fouling the bodywork, the brakes were described as 'entirely inadequate', 'cornering cannot be considered satisfactory', a great deal of water was being lost through the overflow during braking, and there was a tendency for the car to 'swing when decelerating from high speeds. This can be counteracted by opening up momentarily'. It did not sound a very good start...

In March 1949 Wally Hassan issued a three-page report entitled 'Points requiring design or improvement before release for customers or demonstration purposes'. A number of fundamental items still had to be resolved. Dunlop was developing new high-speed tyres and Lucas was designing new headlights. It was also impossible to build right-hand drive cars due to the steering column fouling the rear carburettor.

In April Sutton took the prototype to Belgium for a series of high-speed runs on the Jabbeke motorway, where Lt. Col. Goldie Gardner had been setting records. With the car in standard specification and the hood down, he achieved the magic figure of 120mph on his first run. An undershield was then fitted and the speed improved to 123.25mph. Still with the undershield but with the hood erected and side curtains in position, he managed 125mph. With the windscreen removed he clocked 131.3mph. For his fifth and final run a tonneau cover was fitted over the passenger area and the XK held a steady 135mph. These speeds were, of course, tremendously impressive for a production car in 1949.

Having proved that it could be done, a public demonstration was set up a month later to be witnessed by a party of journalists flown over for the occasion. It was a splendid publicity stunt and established the XK120 as the fastest production car in the world. Heynes later commented that the car was standard apart from, "fitting tyres with a slightly thinner tread for safety at this speed. These tyres were the predecessor of the present Dunlop Road Speed".

From Jabbeke Wally Hassan and Tom Wisdom took the car, registered HKV 500, on a 'Continental Test Run' with the dual aims of determining further development work and assessing the car's chances on the Alpine Rally. They drove to Brussels, into Luxembourg and on to Switzerland. Here they tackled several passes including the Col de Galibier. Conditions were difficult and they were hampered by a snow storm that reduced visibility to a few feet. "The climb was abandoned," reported Hassan, "at about 6500ft and the descent began. Times were taken over the sections which were climbed in reasonable conditions, and Mr Wisdom expressed the opinion that the car had a fair amount in hand over the average speed required. He also remarked on the stability under acceleration in lower gears enabling full throttle to be used without tail slides."

Hassan has since stated that he and Baily were always aware of the tuning possibilities which had been incorporated in the XK engine during its

design, but that there had never been an intention to use it as a competition engine even though it looked the part. Those who had dismissed Jaguar's claims for the XK's top speed as exaggerated publicity had been silenced by the Jabbeke demonstration, but question marks still surrounded the car's all-round ability. The perfect opportunity to prove the car comprehensively came when the BRDC and the *Daily Express* combined to host a race meeting at Silverstone in August 1949. The inclusion of a race for production cars was an innovation.

"We had to prove," stated 'Lofty' England, "that the car would go round corners, as well as go quickly in a straight line. Sir William said we would compete if an example could be driven for three hours non-stop under the lap record without breaking down. We had no racing drivers, only a couple of chaps called England and Hassan. So we did the driving. I tried to go quickly and Hassan tried to break it. Being in the Experimental Department, it was his job to break things. He always believed there was something wrong if he couldn't break it!"

Hassan also recalled the day vividly. In attempting to go faster and faster to beat the lap record he "went through the bales several times and ended up with a bashed bonnet with straw all over it!" He also remembered that, "Bill Lyons said he must try it for himself, called Bill Rankin to join him and set off. As they approached the first corner, Lyons

TOP **Bira led initially at Silverstone but then spun off, leaving Johnson (seen here) in front, despite a fracas with another competitor, with Walker a close second.** ABOVE **Johnson takes the chequered flag at Silverstone to mark the start of the XK120's remarkable and highly versatile competition career.**

turned to his passenger and said, 'Rankin, I've left my specs behind, indicate which way to go and thump me on the back when I must brake'." When they returned to the pits, Lyons noticed the look of fright on Rankin's face and "laughed like hell". Bill Rankin was the company's PR chief and the man who did so much to build the image of SS and Jaguar. He covered advertising, exhibitions, press relations and public relations with help from only one secretary. He set the standard of exhibitions which made Jaguar outstanding at motor shows.

Useful lessons learned from the Silverstone tests contributed both to competition preparation and general development. The brakes were found to be wearing too quickly, so wider shoes were used and air scoops were provided for the rear brakes. The master cylinder on this left-hand drive car, probably the only XK to have been built at this stage, overheated owing to its proximity to the exhaust downpipe, so it was moved rearwards.

Oil was found to be leaking from the nearside of the axle onto the brakes. 'It seems,' stated Hassan's report, 'that due to all the bends being right-handed and two being of long duration the oil is thrown along the banjo tube in large quantity and with some force, which is more than the seals can cope with. It is suggested that baffles be fitted either side of the differential assembly inside the axle casing.' The offside wheel was found to be losing adhesion very easily on these right-hand bends, resulting in excessive wheelspin. 'There appears to be no easy method of overcoming this trouble. The right-hand drive car will be better than the left-hand one as the weight is better placed. A self-locking differential of ZF type might be considered and should be tested some time, and as a future project the de Dion type axle should be considered.'

As tested, the car was fitted with a 3.54:1 axle and reached 4600rpm in top gear: 'These short circuits with straight portions of no more than a mile require acceleration more than maximum speed'. At 25cwt the XK was considered heavy, due to its all-enveloping bodywork that was unusual for the period and certainly heavier than the rudimentary bodywork of most sports cars. Additionally the over-engineered chassis (borrowed from the heavier saloon) and an engine that was no lightweight contributed to an overall weight which compared unfavourably with the 17-20cwt typical of the competition. It was considered essential, therefore, to use all the XK engine's power and a 4.1:1 axle: in a reference to the XK100 this ratio was 'quoted in the catalogue as being for the 2-litre only but should be made available for the 3½-litre'.

The water temperature caused some alarm by rising to 96° C within five laps, so the thermostat was removed. The oil temperature also gave concern by rising to 140° C within a further five laps, but 'it is thought that this must be accepted and will not cause any trouble'.

Interestingly the seating, which has never been one of the XK's strongest points, received comment in Hassan's report: 'There is no doubt that the seats are much improved from a driving point of view with the addition of low arms or pads each side. It should be possible to devise some such armchair type of seat which will have the desired appearance as well as the comfort and freedom of movement given by this type of seat.'

RACING THE XK120

With this test considered to have satisfactorily proved the XK120's ability, the decision was made to lend three cars to leading drivers of the day for the debut in the One-Hour Production Car Race at Silverstone in August 1949.

"It was decided," recalls 'Lofty', "that Hassan could prepare the cars and some old boy called England could be pit manager or something". The three cars, respectively painted red, white and blue, were lent to Peter Walker, Leslie Johnson and Prince 'Bira', drivers who had been selected by 'Lofty'. The race was a fine show of superiority by the new Jaguars. Initially 'Bira' led Johnson and Walker until Johnson hit a spinning Jowett Javelin, causing the XK also to spin and drop back to fifth. 'Bira' then spun off and his race was finished, as 'Lofty' explains: "That body on HKV 455 was a bit of a lash-up – the tyre wall fouled on the wing strut and wore through". However, Johnson and Walker went on to record an excellent one-two, and the XK engine's illustrious competition career had begun in the finest fashion.

Initially the production cars were to be made in the traditional coachbuilt manner with aluminium panels over an ash frame, but with production needing to be raised considerably from the initial estimates it was realised that pressed steel bodies were required. This took time and the first 240 or so cars were built in aluminium. In 1949 no sales were recorded on the home market and just 62 were completed for export. It has always been stated that the change to steel bodywork was purely for production reasons, but in fact Jaguar was also concerned about the weight of the car.

On 12 October 1949 Bob Knight wrote to Heynes enclosing a report entitled 'Weight Reduction on XK120'. In it he wrote: 'The attached weight analysis was compiled in order to find reasons for the excessive weight of the XK120, and provide a basis for a systematic reduction of that weight'. Although steel panels would be heavier, the use of structural wood would no longer be required and Knight estimated that the weight of the finished car could be 1¼cwt lighter if all his suggestions were followed. In reality not all of his thoughts were adopted and the resulting steel XK120 was 3 per cent heavier than the previous 'lightweight'. However, the steel cars would not be ready until well into 1950 so a trickle of alu-

minium cars continued to be produced, the majority for export.

The car driven by Peter Walker at Silverstone, chassis number 670001, was shipped to the US in time for a round-the-houses race at Palm Beach Springs, Florida, in January 1950. Driven by Johnson, the car won the production class. Experimental Department mechanic John Lea attended the event and reported, 'The conditions at Palm Beach were wet, windy and sandy. Water and sand gained entry into the brake drums at the front, and the mixture had the effect of accelerating the wear very considerably. Our car finished with no linings and with the steel shoes bearing on the brake drums.'

Meanwhile, a few days earlier the Experimental Department had issued its first report on another XK120 model, one that would not be introduced until 1951. It is interesting that the Fixed Head Coupé was created many months before the changeover to steel bodies began.

In early 1950 it was decided to build five XK120 two-seaters for competition – these were chassis numbers 660040-660044. On 7 February a list was drawn up entitled 'Five Competition Cars: Desirable Modifications', this document stating that the chassis numbers 'have all been drawn from production as frames, parts being drawn as required. The engines have all passed production engine tests, and will now be stripped for examination'.

The modifications to the engines included the fitting of lead-indium bronze bearings, 'ports in cylinder head to be modified to Silverstone standard', and the fitting of 8:1 pistons. As for the brakes, various linings were to be tried and new

ABOVE **Five XK120s took part in the 1950 Production Car Race at Silverstone and Peter Walker led the field home in JWK 977, one of the works-prepared competition cars.** RIGHT **In 1950 the BRDC invited** *Il Maestro,* **Tazio Nuvolari to compete at Silverstone. Seen here with William Lyons, he practised in a works XK120 but was too ill to compete.** FAR RIGHT **Most XK120s were exported to the US, where some allowed drivers like Phil Hill and John Fitch (seen here) to cut their teeth. Unfortunately the signature cannot be identified.**

drums made up with steel back plates containing cooling holes. On the chassis, all suspension and steering attachment points were reamed for better fit and all bolts were split-pinned. Specially built shock absorbers were on order. The rear axle was fitted with an 'oil baffling scheme', and 'single fuel line dual pumps finally decided upon'.

Other snippets we learn from this paper include: 'Outside filler of sufficient size and adequate venting, 4in bayonet type from Derringtons, Kingston.

Tanks to be made by Abbey Panels. Special jacking methods required (Smiths hydraulic). Centre lock wheels – Dunlop investigating possibility of producing wheels.' An interesting clue to policy was given in a statement on headlights: 'Removable covers for first periods in 24 hour races'. With the journey to the circuits presumably in mind, the instruction 'Racing Windscreens' reads, 'fit two until practice begins then remove the passenger's screen'.

A further specification sheet on these cars was sent by Phil Weaver to Bill Heynes on 26 April 1950. A sixth chassis had now been added to the list and the cars were allocated to the following drivers: 660040, L. Johnson (White); 660041, L.H. Haines (Opalescent Green); 660042, P. Walker (Olive Green); 660043, M. Biondetti (Red); 660044, I. Appleyard (White); and the additional 660057, T. Wisdom (Apple Green). As Biondetti's first name was Clemente, one presumes the initial 'M' was an error.

Biondetti's XK120 was completed first so that he could take part in the 1950 Targa Florio. Until approximately half-distance the Italian was lying a brilliant second overall on this most gruelling of courses and was headed only by a young Alberto Ascari. With this one exception he was leading all the Ferraris, and then a connecting rod broke. All the Ferraris gradually retired as well, and the Jaguar was blamed for pushing them so hard that they destroyed themselves.

The next event was the equally legendary Mille Miglia, on which Biondetti was attempting to achieve his fourth win in a row. He was joined by the XKs of Haines, Wisdom and Johnson. The last-named was to finish an impressive fifth overall but unfortunately Biondetti was delayed by relatively minor ailments and did not figure in the top placings at the end.

The next major event was the Le Mans 24 Hours. Three of the semi-works cars were entered, these being the Johnson example with Bert Hadley as co-driver, Nick Haines together with Peter Clark, and the Walker car to be driven by his great friend Peter Whitehead and John Marshall. This race has often been described as merely an exploratory exercise, but a good deal of preparation went into it. On 7 June, Nick Haines wrote to 'Lofty' England with a list of suggested spares and the comment, 'Please make every effort to ensure a really good set of lights for the car, those at present on it are hopelessly inadequate'. A comprehensive list of spares was drawn up by England under two headings – those to be carried in the car or in an accompanying lorry.

"The three cars which were entered for Le Mans," commented Bill Heynes, "were probably the most standard that have ever been run in that race." As to whether they had much chance, 'Lofty' was doubtful: "Not really. We'd never done it before. We very generously lent them one mechanic each. They did very well and the Johnson/Hadley car, if it had kept going, might even have won, or at least come second or third. But they ripped the clutch centre out, which I think was Johnson's rough handling. He was using the gearbox to stop it rather than the brakes."

Bill Heynes makes the point that Johnson's XK after 21 hours, "was lying in third place averaging 93.8mph while Rosier's Talbot which led the race was only averaging 85.9mph" – but the car retired

at 1.05pm. The Clark/Haines car finished 12th and the Whitehead/Marshall car 15th.

It has often been stated that Lyons went to Le Mans in 1950 and gave the go-ahead there and then to produce a competition car. 'Lofty': "Only Bill Heynes and I went to Le Mans in 1950 – nobody else. We went just for the race with the Dunlop people in a Rapide aeroplane and came to the conclusion that there was not much serious competition. We felt that our standard mechanical units put into a lighter chassis with a decent aerodynamic body would do the deal. Nobody was using aerodynamics. But it took until December to convince the Old Man."

"This race," stated Heynes, "debunked the tradition of the tuning wizard with a life of experience on the track and a special gimmick in his tool box. I realised that a car could be built by two or three of us in the factory, that could win the race comfortably, given reasonable luck, and opposition of the same standard it was in this year 1950."

Meanwhile, no fewer than five XK120s contested the 1950 Production Car Race at Silverstone and once again they finished first and second, Peter Walker this time leading home Tony Rolt. Later in the year Walker, a Herefordshire farmer,

ULSTER T.T. 1950.

took his car to Shelsley Walsh hillclimb in neighbouring Worcestershire and won the over 3-litre class from Sydney Allard.

The famous Tourist Trophy was revived in 1950 and held at Dundrod, Ulster, because, it was stated at the time, 'of the lack of a suitable road course east of the Irish Sea'. Tom Wisdom wrote about the event some years later: 'I was taking high-octane refreshment in the Steering Wheel Club, London's mecca of motor sporting folk, when a fresh-faced, curly-haired youngster whom I already knew slightly, Stirling Moss by name, came alongside, drew up a bar stool and dropped a broad hint. He'd noticed that I'd filed two entries for the forthcoming Tourist Trophy...so what were my plans for whichever car I didn't drive myself? An hour later I found I'd accepted, subject to his father's okay, the persuasive Stirling's proposition that he should drive my XK in the TT, leaving me to handle the works-owned Jowett Jupiter that its makers had entered.

'Moss had never driven an XK120 when our TT pact was made, but the makers sportingly put one at his disposal for pre-Dundrod familiarisation drives on the road. I say sportingly because I think they were beginning to kick themselves for not having offered the boy a TT drive themselves. They had turned Moss down as too young and inexperienced.' Moss himself says: "You could only get Jags if you were important or press."

Moss set fastest time in practice in the dry, but on race day the heavens opened and the track was drenched – 'non-stop, gale-driven torrents of rain,' was one press description. These conditions were particularly tricky for drivers of open cars such as Moss, Whitehead and Johnson in the XKs – the drivers of the closed Astons were spared the worst of it. Frank Rainbow, who worked in Engine Development and was one of the racing mechanics, remembers the day with great merriment.

"I have never seen so much rain in all my life. But it was hilarious. On the opposite side of the road to the pits was a beer tent. All the good souls were watching the racing with pints in their hands – Guinness and so forth. The rain came and the wind blew. Then suddenly this marquee collapsed. It was the funniest thing in the world to see people clambering out, still clutching their pints!"

Johnson led initially in JWK 651, but soon young Moss caught and passed him in JWK 688. At the two-hour mark Moss led Peter Whitehead by 2mins, with Johnson a further 27secs down. The race was a handicap based on engine capacity, but Moss, in spite of the conditions, was averaging an amazing 76.02mph. This equated to 98 per cent of his target speed so his father gave him the 'Slow' sign from the pits. 'Works teams management,' recalled Wisdom, 'was in the hands of 'Lofty' England...During the TT he left his official post at the Jaguar works pit from time to time to give us horse's mouth advice for relaying to Stirling.'

Towards the end a rumour began to spread that Bob Gerard in the swift Frazer Nash was actually ahead on handicap. So, with just one lap to go, Stirling's father hung out the 'Flat Out' sign and his son calmly responded in the increasing gloom by putting in a last lap at 77.61mph, a Dundrod TT record. This brilliant victory, the day before his 21st birthday, led to Lyons offering him a works drive for the following year. Moss has not forgotten the importance of that race to his career.

"That was my first big, big opportunity in motor racing," he told me many years later, "because I had asked a lot of people at that time if they would let me drive their cars in the TT but none of them would trust me. They thought I was going too fast for my experience, and if I was going to have an accident and kill myself, they didn't want me to do it in their car. So none of the companies, including Aston, Jaguar, MG and many of the lesser ones, would let me have one. I was very grateful to Tommy Wisdom for fixing it up so that I could borrow his. Sir William came up to me that evening and asked if I would lead the team following year."

In October Moss found himself once more in an XK when he and Johnson took JWK 655 to Montlhéry and averaged 107.46mph for 24 hours, with a last hour at 112.40mph and a fastest lap at 126mph.

Ian Appleyard had already enjoyed some fine successes in international rallying with SS100s, including his famous one registered LNW 100, and the registration of its replacement was to become even more famous. Teamed with his wife Pat, one of Lyons' two daughters, he took NUB 120 to a famous victory in the 1950 Alpine Rally, proving once again the versatility of the XK120. To this triumph he added a win in the Tulip Rally early in 1951.

The XK120 had shown itself to be a remarkable machine. But one motor racing peak, the highest of them all, remained to be conquered – Le Mans.

BELOW **That the XK120 was more than just an effective racing car was proved by Ian Appleyard with NUB 120, a combination of car and driver destined to be one of the most successful and famous in rallying history.**

CHAPTER TWO

C-TYPE DESIGN & DEVELOPMENT

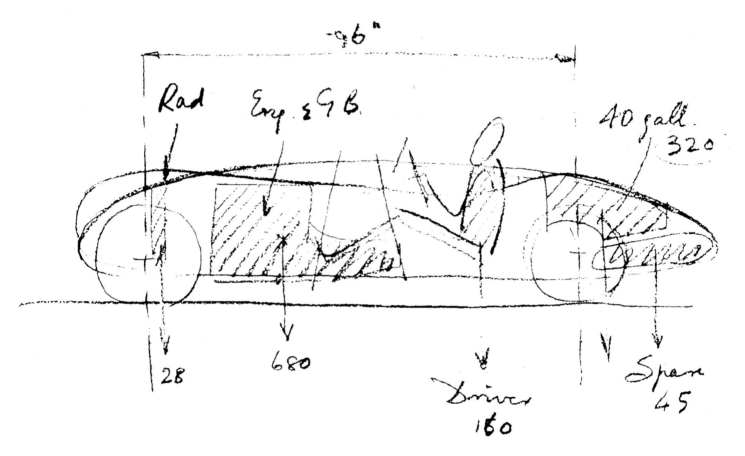

Bill Heynes and 'Lofty' England had returned from Le Mans in 1950 convinced that they had the basis of a Le Mans winner in the XK120. Greater priorities, however, kept William Lyons' mind from contemplating for the time being the creation of a pure competition car. The XK120 was only just starting production in its steel-bodied form and, even more important, the Mark VII was being finalised for launch that October. This model was to be the company's main source of income and had to come first. However, once the Mark VII had been launched serious thought could be given to the new competition version of the XK that would be specifically designed for just one purpose – victory at Le Mans.

A little before the 1950 Earls Court Motor Show the first thoughts concerning specification were put on paper, probably by Bill Heynes – but the document is unsigned. As will be seen, the initial ideas were very different from the car that would be built. First and foremost, the name was

different – it was designated XK150. However, this is entirely logical when one remembers the reasoning behind the XK120 title: clearly a top speed of 150mph was being envisaged even at this early stage. The report ran as follows:

GENERAL SPECIFICATION FOR XK.150 ON THE BASIS OF MODIFICATION TO THE EXISTING XK.120

1) Wheel Base 8' 2".
2) Track 4' 2".
3) <u>Power Unit</u>. Optional power units will be catered for under the following headings: (a) XK.120 standard 8:1 compression unit, giving 160bhp; (b) 3½ litre petrol engine, 9:1 compression ratio, special high lift camshaft giving 190bhp; (c) 3½ litre engine, Methanol, 12:1 compression ratio, special high lift camshafts, larger valves, lead-bronze bearings, magneto ignition, giving 250bhp; (d) Standard XK.100 4-cylinder 2 litre engine, 8:1 compression ratio, giving 110bhp; (e) 2 litre 4-cylinder XK.100 engine, 9:1 compression ratio, racing cams, giving 125bhp; (f) 2 litre XK.100 4-cylinder engine, 12:1

ABOVE **Bill Heynes and colleagues set out to enhance the proven qualities of the XK120's mechanical components by designing a lighter structure and a more aerodynamic body. Here are the origins of the C-type...**

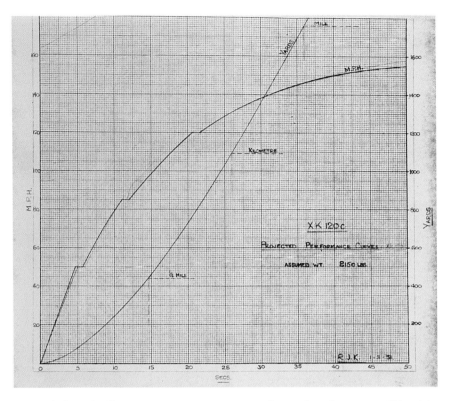

ABOVE **Before the first car was completed, Bob Knight computed the new XK120C's projected performance.**

RIGHT **Bob Knight, who would achieve a pre-eminent position in his profession, designed the XK120C chassis frame and the innovative rear suspension that was designed to improve traction.**

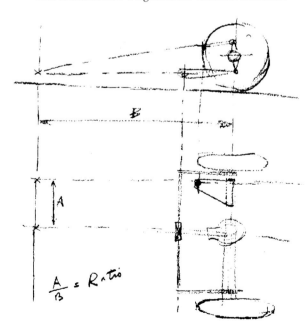

compression ratio for Methanol, giving 150bhp; (g) Another possible engine is the 2 litre 6-cylinder engine modified from the 3½ litre XK.120 with 12:1 compression ratio, from which it may be possible to get horsepower figures in the neighbourhood of 180bhp. This would be subject to the crankshaft permitting speeds between 7000 to 8000rpm to be obtained.

4) Gearbox. The present gearbox, but modified with close ratio gears.

5) Clutch. Borg & Beck with solid centre plate.

6) Rear Axle. (a) Normal solid type axle. (b) Fixed axle centre with de Dion axle. This latter is considered desirable if a weight below 15cwt is achieved.

7) Frame. Tubular type frame with two main basic tubes and basic front cross member and rear cross member. Tubular centre cross member and tubular upper frame side members would be suitable either for the body to conform to the International Sports Car Regulations, or with straight tubes which would permit the construction of a monoposto body.

8) Front Suspension. Transverse wishbone type, approximately 11" lower wishbone and 9" top wishbone, with provision for Thornhill strut suspension.

9) Rear Suspension. With solid axle would be of BMW type, long lower link either side and a single triangular link in the centre. De Dion type rear axle, Salisbury fixed centre, embodying brake drums, wheels carried on single torque arm either side connected by a de Dion tube with a centre guide.

10) Wheels. Rudge type wire spoked onto an aluminium rim.

11) Tyres. Normally the car would be supplied with 6.00×16" road racing pattern. Alternative equipment 7.00×16", 6.50×16" or 6.50×17". Also twin tyres for hill climbs.

12) Brakes. Two-leading shoe type front and rear, hydraulically operated by two master cylinders. Drums to be situated away from the centre line of the wheel so that better cooling is obtained. Internal drum diameter 12" × 2¼" ('self adjusting is essential' added in handwriting). The system would have to incorporate a small transmission hand-brake to make this cover the legal requirements, or alternatively two 8" internal expanding brakes operated by the hand lever might be incorporated in the rear drums.

This fascinating document yields some interesting details and gives an indication of the thinking at the time. Clearly the reference to the 2-litre engine suggests that there were thoughts of entering more than one class. The mention of the smaller six-cylinder, as opposed to the 'four', pre-dates the later 2.4-litre XK engine by several years.

Of particular interest is the early thinking about the chassis frame. It was proposed to use a twin tube method of construction similar to Ferraris of the period, but this was soon to be changed for a rather more advanced structure. It is noteworthy that a de Dion rear set-up was once again proposed, but this would not be incorporated until the latter days of the D-types, and then only experimentally. As for the Thornhill strut suspension, 'Lofty' England explains: "Peter Thornhill worked with Lockheed having joined them after he had designed the Aeroleg suspension for aircraft. His car suspension was on the same basis and was fitted to the first V16 BRM cars. It was pneumatic/hydraulic." Clearly braking was predicted to be an area for concern and improvement.

But perhaps of greatest interest is the reference to a monoposto body. Was Jaguar seriously considering building a single-seater Grand Prix car? We know the company gave it some thought later, but how interesting that it was on the agenda as early as this.

In September 1950 Heynes recruited an aerodynamicist who had previously worked for the Bristol Aeroplane Company. His name was Malcolm Sayer and he was to become one of the key figures in the Jaguar story over the next 20 years. His pioneering aerodynamic work would contribute enormously to Jaguar's successes and he would win the respect and affection of all his colleagues.

'In September,' stated Sayer in his Curriculum Vitae, 'I started to design for Jaguar a car to resemble their XK series, and using the same mechanical parts, but capable of winning the Le Mans 24-hour race. I was responsible for general layout, body and frame.'

Phil Weaver, who had also been at Bristol, where he had met Wally Hassan and Malcolm Sayer, was the Service Department's representative based at Henly's in Brentford. When Hassan left to join Coventry Climax, Weaver was 'borrowed' by Heynes, on what turned out to be a permanent basis, to share Hassan's former job with Jack Emerson, an engine specialist. Weaver would eventually take charge of the Competition Shop.

By December the specification had changed considerably and was largely as the car would be built. A report dated 22 December was headed 'XK.150 PROVISIONAL SPECIFICATION', but 150 had been crossed out and 120C written above. It reads as follows:

ENGINE. 3½ litre 6-cylinder twin overhead camshaft, 83mm bore × 106mm stroke = 3442cc.
FRAME. Tubular, of triangulated construction.
TRANSMISSION. 4-speed single helical synchromesh gearbox. Optional wide or close ratios.
CLUTCH. 10" Borg & Beck single plate.
PROPELLER SHAFT. Hardy Spicer needle roller bearing.
REAR AXLE RATIO. 2.8, 3, 3.6, 3.9, 4.1 or 4.3 to suit customers' requirements.
SUSPENSION. Front – transverse wishbone type. Rear – controlled longitudinal link type.
BRAKES. 12" diameter with full hydraulic control.
STEERING. High efficiency type.
WHEELS AND TYRES. Knock-on Rudge type wire wheels (first four words crossed out and 'quickly detachable' written above). Tyres 6.00-16, 6.50-16 or 7.00-16 to suit customers' requirements.
ELECTRICAL EQUIPMENT. Either coil or magneto ignition. 12 volt battery, dynamo and starter.
BODY. Open or closed two-seater body.
DIMENSIONS. Wheelbase – 8ft. Track Front – 4ft 3in. Track Rear – 4ft 2in (but 2 changed by hand to 3). Dry weight, fully equipped – 16cwt (and written across the bottom is 'Ring Allard re Prototype for Le Mans').

The most significant change was to the method of chassis frame construction. The twin tube idea had been dropped in favour of a fully triangulated spaceframe. One wonders if this was an influence from Sayer's aircraft-based experience, but Bob Knight, the Project Engineer, played the leading

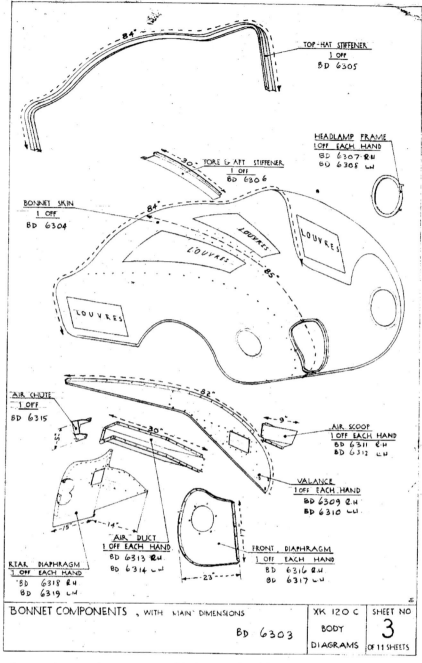

role in chassis design. He added considerable strength to the structure by using sheet steel attached to the frame in the bulkhead area, and to this day he refers to this as 'monocoque construction'. It was a method that Colin Chapman would apply very effectively at Lotus 10 years later. Another to play an important role in the creation of the new competition Jaguar was Tom Jones, who carried out some of the detail design work.

The other facts of significance in the new specification are the wheelbase being 6ins shorter than the XK120's and the reference to open or closed body styles. Clearly the closed body would create less drag, but it would have a larger frontal area than an open car with aero screens. The reference to customers is also interesting: this suggests either that the factory had no intention of running the cars itself or that there were embryonic plans even

ABOVE **Malcolm Sayer, who had been with the Bristol Aircraft Company, was engaged to design a body which would be aerodynamically superior to the XK120's but still retain a family likeness. Removing the headlamps from an XK120 front end makes it appear akin to the C-type's bonnet.**

RIGHT **A remarkable man, Sayer did not design cars in the conventional way but used mathematical co-ordinates to define a shape, just as computers would do several decades later. These are his figures for the C-type body shape – pattern-makers then used them to create the bucks on which the bodies were built.**

XK 120 C   BODY   ORDINATES.   SHEET 1.

STATION	£	4	6	8	10	12	TOP 14	16	18	20	22	24	26	28	30	MAX. WIDTH	AT (INS. ABOVE DATUM)
13	20.22		17.7	17.24	17.66	18.8	19.85	20.74	21.42	21.96	22.34	22.48	22.18	20.7		29	16.5
20	25.08			23.58	22.75	22.5				24.05	24.56	25.	25.54	23.65		30	
30	27.5	27.35	27.1	26.7	26.18	25.7	25.62	26.05	26.54	27.00	27.34	27.6	27.75	27.2	23.5		-
38	28.34	28.2	28.06	27.82	27.48	27.06	26.58	26.3	26.4	27.05	27.6	27.95	28.04	27.52			
46	28.92	28.84	28.78	28.66	28.42	28.02	27.44	26.86	26.74	27.05	27.4	27.8	27.96	27.5			
54	29.36	29.3	29.2	29.05	28.82	28.5	28.06	27.45	26.96	26.9	27.2	27.45	27.5	27			
62	29.64	29.58	29.46	29.3	29.06	28.76	28.32	27.68	27.06	26.7	26.75	26.9	26.85	26.2			
70	29.88	29.84	29.74	29.6	29.36	29.04	28.58	27.94	27.18	26.55	26.4	26.3	26.22	25.76			
78	30.08	30	29.88	29.75	29.52	29.2	28.68	28.04	27.24	26.44	25.96	25.66	25.45	24.9			
86	30.2	30.12	30	29.84	29.64	29.28	28.76	28.08	27.24	26.3	25.6	25.06	24.7	24.1	20		
100 / 112 DOOR REAR	30.1 / 29.55				29.5 / 29.07		28.7 / 28.3		27.1 / 26.85	26.05 / 25.9	25.05 / 25.0	24.18 / 24.5 / 24.62	23.7 / 24.2 / 24.42	22.95 / 22.6 / 23.82	19.5 / 20		
126	28.28	28.2	28.1	28	27.82	27.56	27.2	26.74	26.1	26.02	26.52	27.12	27.3	26.74	23		
134	26.95	26.88	26.82	26.72	26.58	26.35	26.08	25.64	25.2	25.3	26.05	26.65	26.8	26.2	20	30	
142	24.8	24.76	24.72	24.6	24.54	24.34	24	23.5	23.2	23.45	24.1	24.5	24.5	23.8	-	29.82	20
150	21.2	21.16	21.12	21	20.85	20.6	20.16	19.6	19.4	19.6	20.2	20.55	20.16	18.25	-	18.83	12
158	15.3	15.26	15.2	15.05	14.7	14.25	13.65	13.05	12.65	12.5	11.8					22.7	10
													STN. 152 154	28.1 27.0			

13 GENERAL 150			←	2.38	2.39	2.46	2.66	2.98	3.59 .16	4.45 .75	5.72 1.64	7.58 2.98	11 5.16 6.35
158 EXH. RECESS.							4.42 3.5	5.6 6.55	7.7 7.6	8.26	9		

DIST. OUTBOARD FROM £ CAR, INCHES.

	0	4	6	8	10	12	14	16	18	20	22	24	26	28
FWD OF STN. 10				1.47	2.18	2.88	3.48	3.92	4.21	4.26	4.05	3.46	2.06	-.066
AFT OF STN. 160	2.48	2.43	2.33	2.15	1.90	1.56	1.16	.71	.04	-.72	-1.65	-2.83		

COCKPIT

DIST. OUT FROM £	0	10	16	20	22	22	20	18	16	10	0	COCKPIT ½ WIDTHS:					
STATION DIM.	89.17	89.21	89.33	90.1	96.8	113.87	117.2	119.35	120.63	121.11	121.18	STN.	90	94	100	112	120	102
												½ WIDTH	19.78	22.85	23.8	22.36	17.16	3.84 (MAX)

at this early stage to make more than a handful of works-run cars.

"I well remember," stated Phil Weaver, "Sayer drawing the C-type full-size on the floor in chalk."

"He started," recalls Bob Knight, "from basic sketches, from a notion of what he had to clothe, which is the starting point for anybody designing anything, and then he would develop the notional lines mathematically from that point onwards. He claimed he had been taught the system of complex curved surface development in the desert in Iraq by some German as they sat in their tents! He was a very able bloke. He had developed this dimensioning system and the remarkable thing was that the skin drawings he produced were found to be accurate dimensionally."

Cyril Crouch, who was then in the Body Drawing Office, recalls Sayer "using mathematics to calculate all the shapes, as one would do on a computer now". Bill Jones, brother of Tom and a skilled pattern maker who made Sayer's wind tunnel models, remembers that he always had "loads of foolscap paper covered in calculations".

"There was one thing in particular that everyone liked about Sayer," remembers Weaver. "If you make drawings of some of these obtuse shapes, which were aerodynamically perfect, you could produce a drawing with dimensions on it, but then a woodworker had to try to translate all those dimensions into shapes, which wasn't easy. It's a specialist job and the body makers at Jaguar, although they could make the framework of a wooden body and formers, weren't exactly slide rule experts."

"You wouldn't receive normal drawings from him," explains Harry Rogers. "He did a lot of figures and you got it in book form. There were water lines and body lines, and each intersection had a dimension from a datum." Body lines run across a car and water lines from front to rear.

Sayer's brief was to design a body but within certain constraints, as 'Lofty' England explains: "Malcolm Sayer was brought in to produce an aerodynamic shape but still keep it resembling a Jaguar in some way. This is probably why the wing line swept up and down rather than being straight." He also remembers Heynes constructing a mock-up of the chassis with matchsticks...

The body shape for the new XK120C, as the company designated the competition model, had a frontal area of 11.80sq ft, which was only marginally less than the standard XK120's 13.86sq ft. However, drag was considerably improved: to propel the car to 100mph took only 53bhp instead of 68bhp for the production car, an improvement of 22 per cent.

Apart from reduced drag, other design aims were to reduce weight, improve braking, increase power and improve handling. The weight factor was improved by the use of the new chassis (described in detail in the next chapter) and by constructing the body skins in aluminium.

TOP **With his background in the aircraft industry, Sayer used wooden models in wind tunnels and smoke tunnels to check his designs, and paid particular attention to problems like the airflow around the driver (note the bubble canopy).** ABOVE **Sayer's later experiments included different louvres and enclosed rear wheels, which, although beneficial to the shape, were detrimental to brake cooling.**

"Three of us built the first C-type frames," recalled the late Joe Sutton, who worked in the Experimental Shop. "Everything was laid out in pencil on two 6ft × 6ft sheets of plywood. Every angle was cut by hand and filed to the angles of the frame drawn on this plywood. The fellow who brazed the frames was quite a good lad, because heat and metal tend to fight each other. So it was a matter of brain work as to where and how he did the brazing."

Engine development work was done by Jack Emerson, whom 'Lofty' England rates very highly and feels has never received proper recognition: "In his younger days he had been an ace tuner of motorcycles, and I believe he was the first man to ride 80 miles, and then 100 miles, in one hour. He used to produce three engines which were within two horsepower of each other. So there was never any argument that one car had a better engine than another. Old Jack was brilliant."

Engine modifications included fitting larger exhaust valves, enlarging the exhaust porting, fitting higher lift cams, widening the timing and increasing the compression ratio. The carburettors were fed with air from a balance box which was itself supplied through ducting from the front end, so they received cool air with some ram effect. The exhaust system benefited from the new chassis frame and body layout because the manifolding could project straight from the engine before bending at some distance from the head, whereas the manifolds on the XK120 had to bend sharply due

to the constrictions of the body and chassis. These various modifications raised power output from 160bhp to 200bhp.

Braking was improved by the adoption of the latest Lockheed development. The two leading shoes on the front brakes were self-adjusting and the use of wire wheels considerably assisted cooling for the drums.

The first C-types, as the cars soon became known, at least outside the factory, were built at the old Swallow Road works at Foleshill, prior to the company's move to Browns Lane. Phil Weaver, who supervised the construction, makes the point that this small, highly-skilled team in the Experimental Shop could turn its hand to almost anything. A typical example was the prototype for the C-type steering wheel: "I drew it and sawed it out myself in my office!"

Aiming for Le Mans in June 1951 gave barely six months to complete the designs, build three cars and test them. The first test was carried out by 'Soapy' Sutton in April, but he then left to join Alvis and further testing was continued by 'Lofty' England in the evenings and at weekends.

"He took the car to MIRA," states 'Lofty', referring to Sutton testing at what was then known as Lindley. "The only complaint was a loss of oil from the gearbox breather. Then we had no test driver and this is where I came in. There wasn't much wrong with the first car except that it oversteered a bit. Then we got the second car built quite quickly, and I remember one Sunday morning Bill Heynes wanted to make sure it would do the speed it should. It wouldn't, so we had to find out what was wrong.

"This second car oversteered very badly. I screamed off in it just as I'd done in the first car. I nearly lost it at the first corner – and I thought, 'England, you're losing your touch'. At the second corner I nearly lost it again, but when this happened yet again at the third corner I decided the problem wasn't me. So we had to sort that out. But the interesting part of this lack of speed was the fact that oil built up at the back of the sump when you put your clog down, and the crank would dip. Altering the sump baffling cured it.

"Apart from that, we tried to improve the brakes, which were basically the same as on the XK120. We tried things like Alfin drums." Knowing how quickly drums can fade on a circuit, I asked 'Lofty' about this: "To be very honest, I have never been much of a brake user! I never had any problem."

'Lofty' was often assisted in testing by Peter Walker and Peter Whitehead who, he remembers, never asked for payment but were rewarded with fish and chips for supper! Moss also did some testing, he and Walker recording virtually identical times, the latter 0.1sec faster. Criticisms were relatively minor: the dipstick was difficult to read, the pedal layout was not good for heeling and toeing,

ABOVE **Initially the prototype competition car was constructed without louvres in the bonnet top and with bonnet straps positioned on the sides. These straps would be moved to the bonnet top to enable one person to undo both from one side of the car, saving valuable seconds during pit stops. The bonnet was at first constructed with the so-called letterbox louvres projecting internally.**
RIGHT **With time pressing before the XK120C's debut at Le Mans in 1951, the prototype was revised and the familiar louvred panels were added to the bonnet top, together with innovative faired-in headlamp glasses, a feature first used by Sayer on the Gordano sports car.**

the bonnet release could be improved, and 'Lofty' suggested stiffening the rear suspension.

Moss recorded in his diary that he went up to Coventry on 16 May and saw the 'new Le Mans car' for the first time. He met Johnson and Walker and they took it to MIRA. He found that it was very rapid, capable of over 150mph, but suffered from oversteer that was thought to be caused by a

problem with the shock absorbers. He found that the brakes were rather poor, but noted that they did not suffer any fade.

A third car was completed, according to Heynes, "a bare six days before the cars left the country". With a minimum of testing behind them, the three secret new cars were driven to Le Mans for their ultimate test.

CHAPTER THREE

C-Type in Detail

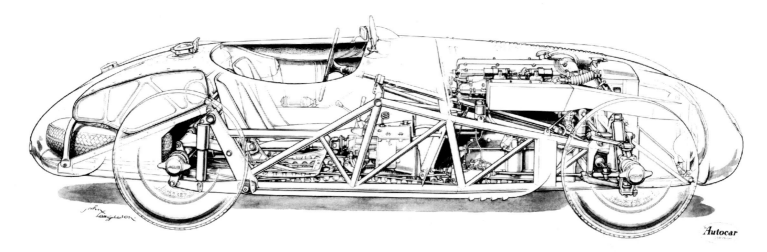

It is often stated that the C-type was closely based on the production XK120. However, with the major exceptions of the engine and front suspension principles, this is not really the case. The novel design and construction of the chassis and body, and the design of the rear suspension and steering, were all totally different from XK120 practice.

The chassis frame was probably the most radical departure from normal Jaguar design. Multi-tubular spaceframe construction was chosen for weight-saving reasons, but to give the necessary rigidity there was considerable triangulation and some welding of sheet steel sections to the framework. The frame was constructed in 16 swg steel tubing of varying diameter and various square and folded sections. It consisted of three main structures – a main central frame, a detachable front subframe and a detachable rear subframe.

The main frame was constructed virtually as a rectangular box of arc-welded, circular-section tubing, sub-divided and triangulated for stiffness. The front of the chassis terminated in a rectangular frame somewhat akin to the later E-type 'picture frame', made of folded and square-section tubing and containing the necessary brackets to support the front suspension and shock absorber mountings. The chassis number was stamped on the right-hand shock absorber mounting.

At a central position in the chassis, sheet steel flanges were welded to the tubular frame to provide attachment points for the bulkheads of the centre section bodywork. This enabled the bodywork to be removed leaving all the main mechanical components in place within the rolling chassis.

The unusual rear bulkhead consisted of a rectangle comprising folded vertical members at either side, and circular-section tubing top and

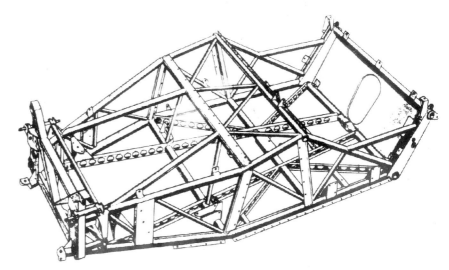

bottom. Between the four sides a 22 swg sheet steel diaphragm was welded to give stiffness to the structure and to provide the lower part of the firewall. The lower tube was a heavy 10 swg section with a central anchorage welded in to secure the rear suspension torsion bar located inside it. Pressed-in bronze bearings at either end of this tube provided location for the rear trailing arms.

"Originally the car was designed with a tubular frame taking the load," recalled Heynes, "as was current with nearly all competition cars of this date. The built-up bulkhead, which was welded to the tubular frame, showed an increase in frame stiffness of over 100 per cent from end to end and contributed very largely to the satisfactory operation of the chassis. This really set a basis of the stressed bulkhead and stressed skin design, which was elaborated on in the D-type and E-type cars."

The body, in 18 swg aluminium, consisted of two main sections and several minor ones. The traditional bonnet and separate front wings of the

TOP **Cutaway drawing from The Autocar reveals XK120 ancestry with many of the mechanical components shared with the production car.** ABOVE **First thoughts on the chassis design had followed contemporary practice, but then much more innovative ideas prevailed and Knight designed this multi-tubular spaceframe with considerable triangulation.**

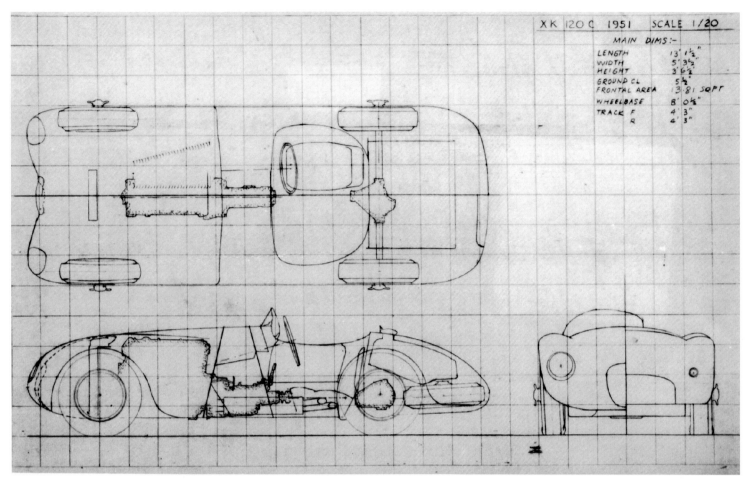

XK 120 C   1951   SCALE 1/20

MAIN DIMS :-

LENGTH	13' 1½"
WIDTH	5' 3½"
HEIGHT	3' 6½"
GROUND CL	5½"
FRONTAL AREA	13·81 SQFT
WHEELBASE	8' 0½"
TRACK F	4' 3"
R	4' 3"

ABOVE **Sayer's drawing of the 1951 C-type shows that his shape was very clean and simple, yet retained a Jaguar feel to it, being clearly related to the production XK120.**

XK120 were replaced by a complete one-piece structure which hinged forward to give excellent access to the engine and other mechanical components. Making this large section of bodywork into a single complex panel also saved weight. The early works cars were distinguished by a symmetrical triangulated pattern of louvres on the upper surface of the bonnet and four large 'letterbox' louvres on either side. Production cars, however, had two symmetrically placed rectangular panels of louvres on the top surface and a panel of sloping stamped-in louvres on the sides, for ease of manufacture.

The centre section of the bodywork was a stressed skin structure and consisted of two main bulkheads which had multiple attachments to the outside of the chassis, with the intention of further increasing chassis rigidity, there otherwise being no bracing of the bulkhead area within the chassis. Sill members, also bolted at several points to the chassis, formed part of the skin and extended between the front and rear wheel arches, a style repeated on the E-type. A shallow door was fitted on the driver's side. A fairing was provided for the centrally mounted rear-view mirror and the driver had a small Perspex aeroscreen.

The rear of the car was clothed by another large section of bodywork which could easily be removed. Within this was a small removable access panel to the spare wheel stowage area. The

last C-types of 1953, the so-called 'lightweight' cars, had a prominent central stiffener to support the tail skin, within which a Marston rubber fuel tank cell was suspended.

Lightweight aluminium undertrays ran the full length of the underside of the body and chassis to give the cleanest possible aerodynamic shape, the only apertures being for access to the sump, gearbox and differential.

The independent front suspension was by top and bottom wishbones, telescopic shock absorbers and longitudinal torsion bars anchored in the scuttle area. These principles were shared with the XK120, but the lower wishbones were shorter and wider than those fitted to the production car, and the torsion bars themselves formed the axis about which the lower wishbones rotated. The rear suspension was completely different from the road car. A Salisbury axle, with offset hypoid bevel final drive, was attached to the rear of the chassis frame by trailing links.

On the right-hand side an 'A' bracket, or reaction plate, was fitted above the axle housing and connected to the rear upright of the chassis. This was designed to have a dual purpose. The first was to provide solid lateral location of the axle within the car. The second was to avoid and harness the rotational forces exerted to the rear axle under heavy acceleration. In fact this reaction member translated the forces into downward pressure on the axle, improving adhesion. Additionally the tendency for weight to be transferred from the offside to the nearside rear wheel during fierce acceleration from rest or low speed was avoided by positioning the reaction member a specific distance from the centre of the axle, the downward pressure thus equalling the weight transfer. The result was reduced wheelspin and a lessening of the tendency of the offside wheel to lift and spin when accelerating away from corners.

With further development, and the advent of the limited slip differential, most production cars were later modified to have a simple single top link fitted in place of the 'A' bracket, with a Panhard rod running diagonally from the left-hand side of the chassis to the right-hand side of the back axle, giving lateral location. The very last, lightweight C-types were further modified to have a pair of top links, one each side, running parallel to the lower links in a system which was copied for the subsequent D-type. The conventional propeller shaft was fitted with Hardy Spicer needle roller bearing universal joints and the springing medium was provided by a single transverse torsion bar with Newton telescopic shock absorbers.

Unlike the XK120, but more like the later XK140, the C-type was fitted with Jaguar-designed rack and pinion steering which gave a more precise and lighter feel than the XK120. Like the XK120, the 17in Bluemel 'C' steering wheel had telescopic adjustment, with the additional bonus of height adjustment.

As for braking, new Lockheed self-adjusting hydraulic 12in drum brakes were fitted on the front and the more usual manually-adjustable drums on the rear. A tandem master cylinder was used in conjunction with separate front and rear hydraulic circuits. The use of wire wheels saved weight but perhaps even more importantly assisted with brake cooling and minimising fade. Furthermore, with their knock-off fixings, they were around four times faster to change than the solid five-stud steel wheels used on the XK120s in the 1950 Le Mans. The Dunlop 16in wire wheels had aluminium rims with 54 spokes for production cars and 60 spokes for the lightweight cars. Dunlop racing tyres of 6.00×16 (front) and 6.50×16 (rear) section were used.

The tinned steel 39-gallon fuel tank was situated in the tail area and mounted onto the rear bulkhead above the spare wheel. The tank sat at its front edge on two rubber mountings and to its rear on a single central mounting on a tubular bridge piece over the spare wheel. This gave a three-point mounting which prevented any torsional strain being transmitted to the tank from chassis movement. Two SU electric fuel pumps were fitted, drawing from either side of the tank, and, by way of a 'T' union, amalgamated into a single line running forward to the engine.

The XK engine developed for the competition

LEFT **This later production car (XKC 013) shows the bulkhead panel which was attached to the chassis tubing, considerably increasing stiffness. This was a first step in the evolution towards monocoque construction.**

LEFT **Wire wheels had several advantages: they saved weight, assisted brake cooling and allowed quick wheel-changing during pit-stops.**

car was not greatly dissimilar to that of the standard XK120. Indeed Bill Heynes once said that "finished crankshafts and cylinder blocks and all engine parts except the head and pistons were taken at random from the production line". In fact a few more parts were special to the C-type engines, but the principle remains that the engine was lightly modified rather than re-designed.

ABOVE **The XK engine used 1½in SU carburettors for Le Mans in 1951, but these were soon changed to the familiar 2in sand-cast SUs which today are simply known as 'C-type carbs'.** RIGHT **The front suspension, in principle, was unchanged from the XK120, and employed double wishbones, telescopic dampers and longitudinal torsion bars.**

"From the comparative power curves," stated Heynes in his paper on the design of the XK engine given to the Institute of Mechanical Engineers in 1953, "it may be seen that the modified engine gives a fairly substantial increase in power over the standard touring unit, but on the other hand none of the changes made to this unit for racing is of a major character or even beyond the capabilities of a private owner who is experienced in these matters. Much of the special material which has been used by the company for racing has been duplicated and made available not only to the owners of XK120Cs, where it is fitted as standard, but also to owners of the XK120, and in certain respects Mark VII owners as well." It is extraordinary to think, in this day and age, of engine modifications

designed for a Le Mans winner being offered on a current luxury saloon...

The standard cylinder head was fitted with 1⅝in exhaust valves rather than the production valves of 1⁷⁄₁₆in. The inlet valves and porting were unchanged but the exhaust porting was enlarged by ⅛in to 1⅜in. New camshafts were adopted which gave ⅜in lift as opposed to ⁵⁄₁₆in. Various pistons were employed depending upon the compression ratio. Originally this was to have been 9:1 but was later changed to 8:1 for the 1951 Le Mans race due to doubts about the quality of the fuel to be supplied. For this race the standard twin 1½in SU carburettors were used but shortly after they were substituted by the familiar sand-cast H8 2in SUs, often referred to as C-type carburettors. Cold air was ducted from the front of the car into a balance box which fed the carburettors. The lightweight cars were fitted with triple 40DCO3 Weber carburettors and a more developed cylinder head.

"We had for some time been experimenting," stated Heynes, referring to the Webers used in 1953, "with the use of carburettors giving one choke per cylinder, and this year for the first time we used three twin-choke Weber carburettors of 40mm size, and although these only gave approximately the same power at 6000rpm, we gained a very useful increase between 3500rpm and 5500rpm, the maximum being about 30bhp from 4000rpm to 5000rpm. This gave us very much improved acceleration. We have found that for sports car racing acceleration in the upper middle ranges has proved all-important. The maximum

power developed by this engine was 220bhp at 5000rpm."

It is interesting that this engine was not only capable of giving more power, but also that the basic design could withstand the increased stresses. The crankcase, for example, proved its inherently good design and the effectiveness of the internal webbing on the standard power unit. The bottom end was unchanged apart from the fitting of indium-coated lead bearings. A special hammer-head sump pan was fitted to all C-type engines, the purpose being to increase the cooling area of the sump surface and slightly to reduce its overall height. Whereas the XK120 under-bonnet layout and chassis frame dictated sharp bends in the exhaust manifolds, the C-type frame allowed a gentler curve and a twin system was used. In order to reduce drag to a minimum, the expansion boxes were sunk into the nearside sill area, exiting just ahead of the rear wheel.

The cooling system comprised a large Marston radiator with an integral header tank, and was mounted vertically within the front subframe. The engine had no fan, but there was a relatively efficient water pump. For modern traffic conditions, it is not surprising that many original cars have now been fitted with auxiliary electric fans.

The gearbox was basically a standard XK120 'box of Jaguar manufacture with a special short top cover to move the gear lever position forward.

ABOVE **Side view of the prototype shows the exhaust exiting in the sill area so as not to interfere with the shape of the underside. Detail changes had been made by this stage: the bonnet side louvres now project externally and the straps have been moved to the top of the bonnet.**

LEFT **As on the car's front firewall, the principle of adding strength but not weight to the structure was employed on the rear bulkhead.** RIGHT **The mandatory spare wheel was slung under the fuel tank in the tail.** FAR RIGHT **Steering differed from the XK120, with the XK120C using a rack and pinion arrangement that would later be adopted on the production XK140.**

ABOVE **After several months of intensive effort, three examples of the exciting new XK120C were ready just in time for their debut at Le Mans in 1951. Compare this shot with the one on the facing page: the bonnet straps are back on the car's flanks and an aero screen has been fitted.**

Incidentally, 'Lofty' England states that all close-ratio 'boxes were made by Jaguar and had separate gears splined to the mainshaft, whereas the Moss 'boxes had a cluster layout. The C-type 'boxes contained a dipstick for rapid checking of the oil level and a take-off for an oil breather, which ran to a mushroom-shaped outlet fixed high on the front bulkhead. The 10in Borg & Beck single-plate dry clutch had a solid centre and linings, riveted and cemented to the plate to cope with racing starts, and a lightened flywheel was fitted.

The dashboard was fitted with a 160mph speedometer, a 6500rpm rev counter with the red sector between 5700-6500rpm, an ammeter, fuel gauge, and combined water temperature and oil pressure gauge. The seats were a pair of aluminium buckets, generally covered in cloth rather than leather. The passenger seat was somewhat higher and contained a built-in tool box under the hinged base. The gearbox tunnel was covered in silver Hardura of a ribbed pattern bound in silver Ambla. The side panels of the cockpit and the passenger side of the dashboard were also covered in Ambla. A tonneau cover was fitted on the passenger side, fixed permanently to the bulkhead behind the seat and to the front edge of the cockpit. At a distance of about 4in from the front edge the tonneau cover was divided by a zip, which allowed the main portion to be stowed neatly behind the passenger seat.

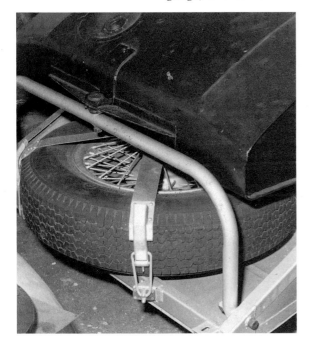

CHAPTER FOUR

WORKS C-TYPES IN COMPETITION

The existence of the new XK120C cars was a well-kept secret and nobody outside the factory knew the real story. Even *Autosport* magazine was in the dark. In previewing the race in its 22 June 1951 issue it expected to see a team of XK120s: 'In spite of rumours as to the existence of a much-lowered and larger-engined Jaguar, it seems pretty certain that the Coventry concern will pin its faith on the well-tried XK120 model, with the high-compression head permitted by the use of 80-octane fuel. At the time of going to press, no details had been issued as to modifications (if any) to the Le Mans cars.'

In fact William Lyons had not been convinced that the new C-types would be ready for Le Mans and had issued instructions for three special XK120s to be prepared and held in reserve. With the 1951 race rapidly approaching, the first two XK120Cs were tested at MIRA and Silverstone by all the drivers except Biondetti. The pairings were

to be Stirling Moss/Jack Fairman (XKC 002), Peter Walker/Peter Whitehead (XKC 003) and Leslie Johnson/Clemente Biondetti (XKC 001).

THE 1951 LE MANS CAMPAIGN

'Lofty' England has this to say about the choice of drivers: "Johnson had driven for us before, and we wanted to give Biondetti a run. Walker had driven at Silverstone, while Whitehead had raced in the TT and was a fast, reliable, experienced driver. Moss requested Fairman as a partner, and he drove quite smoothly. In those days I used to try all these drivers myself, riding with them round a circuit – brave wasn't I? You could soon tell if a bloke was a rough handler or a smooth handler."

"I would think," states Moss, attempting to recall his reason for choosing Fairman, "that I took Jack along because I already knew him, and because he was a consistent, steady driver, if not

ABOVE **The C-type's finest hour. Under the ever-watchful eye of 'Lofty' England, who stands on the pit counter to Duncan Hamilton's right, Tony Rolt takes over XKC 051 to resume progress towards a famous Le Mans victory in 1953.**

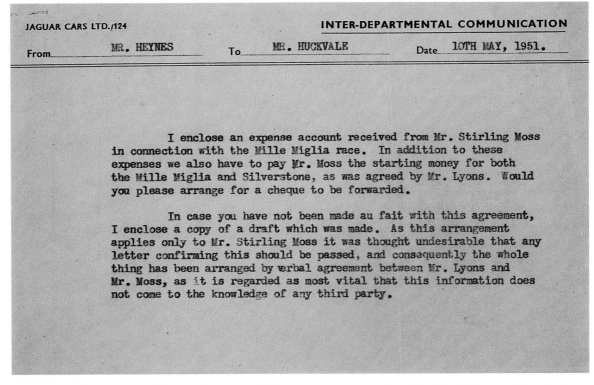

JAGUAR CARS LTD./124   INTER-DEPARTMENTAL COMMUNICATION

From____ MR. HEYNES   To____ MR. HUCKVALE   Date____ 10TH MAY, 1951.

>   I enclose an expense account received from Mr. Stirling Moss in connection with the Mille Miglia race. In addition to these expenses we also have to pay Mr. Moss the starting money for both the Mille Miglia and Silverstone, as was agreed by Mr. Lyons. Would you please arrange for a cheque to be forwarded.
>
>   In case you have not been made au fait with this agreement, I enclose a copy of a draft which was made. As this arrangement applies only to Mr. Stirling Moss it was thought undesirable that any letter confirming this should be passed, and consequently the whole thing has been arranged by verbal agreement between Mr. Lyons and Mr. Moss, as it is regarded as most vital that this information does not come to the knowledge of any third party.

particularly fast. He would do as he was told: he wouldn't go off the road trying to do funny things and he wasn't out to prove that he was better than me." Moss had been signed by Jaguar after his brilliant drive in the 1950 TT, and a company memo dated 22 December 1950 confirmed the basis on which he was retained.

'£100 per drive plus reasonable personal hotel expenses in the case of British and Continental races. In the case of American races, or races that necessitated exceptional expenses, special arrangements would have to be made. Prize money and bonus money would be retained by the driver.

'Entry to be made by the driver, on the company's instructions, in any race of the company's choice. On the other hand Mr Moss will agree to give us priority of his services as a driver in any race open to sports cars in which we may wish to participate. This would, of course, not preclude Mr Moss from taking part in formula racing or 500cc racing with other makes of vehicle.

'The car to be raced would be loaned to Mr Moss as his property, but would remain in the control of the company at all times other than when actually participating in events.'

The third car was finished only two or three days before this great team – just five people! – was due to leave for Le Mans. Jack Emerson drove one car, Phil Weaver the second and 'Lofty' England the third. John Lea and Joe Sutton travelled in a 30cwt Bedford van carrying the spares. A young man called Bob Berry was seconded to the team during practice, and would go on to play a leading role within the company for many years.

"Berry was studying at Cambridge," recalls 'Lofty', "and wrote to say that he went to Le Mans every year – but I think he'd actually only been once! He said his mother was French and he could speak the language, and that he would be only too pleased to be a member of our team. I wrote back saying it was a jolly nice offer but we had our own staff for this sort of thing – it's very amusing looking back. But I also said he was welcome to call by and see us, and by the time he and his sister turned up I had come to the conclusion that they could do a job of work – timekeeping.

"Meanwhile we'd had a few troubles. On the first night's practice a plug electrode fell out on Biondetti's car and wrecked the engine, which had to be rebuilt and needed a new piston. On the second night Moss hit somebody up the back, so we had a rather flat-fronted C-type which I had to repair myself. The headlights were also hopeless. We'd been given what were supposed to be the very best Marchal competition headlights – in those days you had to use approved French lights and Lucas weren't approved – but they turned out to be the wrong ones. Bill Heynes had arrived by that time and did most of the sheet metal work to make new back shells. So between us, with his help, we actually got three cars on to the circuit on the Saturday."

On the Wednesday night, Walker had smashed the record with a lap of 104mph, but only after he had received a little advice from 'Lofty': "He came in complaining he couldn't go any faster. He was using some strange tinted goggles so I told him to put on some clear ones – he went out and broke the lap record!". Walker's time was 4min 50sec (4min 46sec according to *Autosport*), but the other drivers apart from Moss recorded times over the 5min mark – Moss reckoned he was saving his brakes and recorded 5min dead. Moss felt his team manager was satisfied with this, but he was even more pleased with the 5min 11sec he recorded in rain and mist.

The car Moss hit on the Thursday evening was an Aston Martin DB2 driven by Mort Morris-Goodall, who recalls the incident well: "The track was very wet and at about midnight I went out to see how the brakes would work in the rain. Coming round the fast right-hand bend over the brow of the hill which drops you down to the notorious White House Corner, my headlights picked out grass and mud on the road. A split-second later I saw the track 100 yards ahead half blocked by an overturned car, the other half being occupied by two gentlemen violently waving yellow flags. Asking St Christopher's forgiveness for past sins, I trod on those brakes and found out all right whether they worked, coming to rest about a quarter of a millimetre from where the two gentlemen had been standing half a second earlier. Then, to my horror, I saw in my mirror the glare of headlights approaching very rapidly.

"I whipped the gear lever into bottom and stamped on the loud pedal even harder than I had on the brakes. The Aston seemed to gather speed so slowly and then I heard the shrill scream of tortured tyres close behind me. However, thanks to the cool head of that brilliant young driver, Stirling Moss, and the wonderful brakes on his Jaguar, and also the fact that the Aston eventually responded nobly, all I felt was a nasty bump. In the words of an eye-witness, the Aston showed acceleration which was remarkable, even for a DB2! Luckily the front of the Jaguar and the rear of the Aston suffered superficial damage only, but it might have been much worse. Herr Sauerwein, the unfortunate Porsche driver who had attempted to go round the corner too fast and overturned after running off the road, suffered a broken leg and cheek bone.

"After the impact I slowed to let the other car past – I still had no idea who it was but I recognised Stirling when he drew level. I stopped at my pit and walked up to the Jaguar pit to see if Stirling's car was badly damaged. Stirling, not unnaturally, was hopping mad because he thought that I'd merely stopped to look at the accident, but after explanations and apologies all round everyone fell to congratulating one and all upon a very lucky escape. I returned to my pit, had a quick brandy and went out to do another lap just to show I hadn't been frightened, a process which fooled no-one, not even me!"

Moss reckons he was travelling at two miles a minute and describes the accident as "quite a close thing". And how did the C-type feel in comparison with the XK120? "A much tighter car, much better – the XK120 was just a touring car that went rather quickly."

"After the second practice," recalls Jack Fair-

man, "Stirling and I were in complete agreement about almost everything – which gear to use at which corner, when to lift off and braking points. But we couldn't agree about the approach to Arnage, which is through a forest. After discussion, we decided that a certain tree was the place to lift off. The question was, how do you identify a tree when it's dark? So Stirling had a brainwave. He rushed off to a local farmhouse and borrowed a bucket of whitewash with which he painted the tree." This occurred during the Thursday night, but Fairman was not convinced. He felt the chosen tree was far too close to the bend, and the point could not be settled on Friday as practice was wet.

ABOVE **A contrast to today's motor racing teams. The Jaguar entourage for Le Mans in 1951 consisted of six drivers, two mechanics, an engine specialist, Phil Weaver, 'Lofty' England, Bill Heynes, William Lyons (who flew out), three C-types and a Bedford van!**

ABOVE **After the retirement of the Moss/Fairman and Johnson/Biondetti cars, Jaguar's Le Mans fortunes rested with the surviving Walker/Whitehead C-type (XKC 003). Here Walker climbs aboard during a pit-stop, with team manager 'Lofty' England (far right) looking on.**

LEFT **Despite his youth, Moss was team leader for Le Mans and thrilled the large crowds with a splendid performance in XKC 002 to head the field and break the opposition.**

But Moss assured him it would be all right...

The opposition at Le Mans was led by Fangio and Gonzalez in the 4½-litre Talbots, thinly disguised Grand Prix cars that had thrashed the field in 1950. The Ferraris were also a major threat, and Briggs Cunningham had brought over a team of Chrysler-engined cars from the US. 'Lofty' gave the drivers strict instructions about the lap times they were to maintain and Moss was given the job of breaking the competition.

The cars lined up for the traditional Le Mans start in order of descending cubic capacity, so the Jaguars were midway down the field with Moss starting in 22nd place. He was very quick on his feet for the sprint across the track, and over the years he would make a speciality of fast Le Mans starts. His first Le Mans experience was no exception and he passed 14 cars before anyone moved. He soon picked off the remainder and took the lead going down the Mulsanne Straight. At the end of the straight he was out-braked by Gonzalez but passed him again shortly after. He could have pulled away but chose to play a cat-and-mouse game, allowing Gonzalez to out-brake him into the corners and overtaking him again on the straights. Within five laps the Talbot's brakes were ailing and Gonzalez dropped back.

Stirling then built up a huge advantage in spite of using only 90 per cent of full revs, some 5700rpm, down the straights. Thanks to Sayer's superb aerodynamic work he found he could still reach 150mph on half throttle. On his 31st lap he set a new record at 4min 46.8sec, and after three hours he was 12 miles ahead of the leading Talbot, which was followed by Biondetti and Walker in close formation. Moss was motoring so rapidly that he soon lapped Walker, who was driving to instructions. After four hours the Jaguars held the first three positions with Moss two laps ahead of Walker and Biondetti, who were on the same lap.

Moss was taking the two right-hand bends between Mulsanne and Arnage completely flat and saving the brakes by not using them at White House and the Dunlop Curve. Or so it appeared: "As you come up to a corner, you want everybody to think you're taking it flat, so I was rolling back on the throttle for the Dunlop Curve way before the pits, then going through the pits with it hard on the floor. I appeared to be going flat out, but the point was that I'd dropped 2-3mph!"

After Fairman took over from Moss, he came up behind Fangio in the Talbot. *Autosport* noted there was great cheering from the crowd as 'the British driver passes the Argentinian crack. Fangio must have been astonished. A 'GP' Talbot being passed by a British sports car – well, well!'

"For the first two or three laps," remembers Jack, "I tried to lift off at the white tree and found myself going much too fast. I thought this young fellow Stirling really must be a wizard, and started lifting off 100 yards before it." Fairman, who had driven superbly to maintain the lead in very wet conditions, handed over once more to Moss. As the young man roared off into the darkness, Jack was handed a note his co-driver had written him: 'White tree much too late. I am braking 50 yards after curve past Mulsanne'. The Jaguar pit was said to be aflame with invective for 10 minutes. Meanwhile Moss was still pressing on and it was noticed, due to the absence of brake lights, that his was the only car not to brake for the Dunlop Curve, or so it appeared! However, it was all too good to be true...

Biondetti, very much an engineer, noticed the oil pressure drop but managed to nurse his car to the pit without running a bearing. However, there was nothing the mechanics could do because the rules stated that only tools and parts carried in the car could be used. Moss's valiant run also came to an end around midnight when he lost all oil pressure.

'Lofty': "It was pouring with rain and Stirling didn't notice the pressure go, so the engine put a rod through the side. By that time we had asked ourselves what was happening to cause two similar failures. We found that the oil delivery pipe had broken off and thought that a slight vibration period at about 5200rpm was responsible. Fortunately the Walker/Whitehead car had a big enough lead for them to keep the engine below this limit.

"Bill Heynes had been working pretty hard with this big team of ours, so he went off for a sleep somewhere. Mr Lyons didn't arrive until just after Moss dropped out: he'd come on the Dunlop 'plane, which had landed somewhere else because of the bad weather and he'd had to take a taxi to get to the circuit. Heynes re-appeared looking a bit bleary and talked to the Old Man, who then spoke to me: 'Mr Heynes has worked it out – we're not going fast enough'. I said we were in front by three-quarters of an hour. 'No,' he said, 'if anything serious goes wrong he won't have time to put

ABOVE **With the opposition at Le Mans broken by Moss's early pace, Walker (driving here) and Whitehead could afford to slacken their speed in the surviving C-type, its nose now battle-scarred, and avoid the oil loss problems that had eliminated their team-mates.**

it right'. I replied that if anything serious went wrong he wouldn't be able to put it right!

"He spoke to Heynes and came back: 'Mr Heynes is quite adamant that we're not going fast enough – you'd better signal them to go faster'. Bloody hell! I didn't want us to lose the whole lot, so I put out a signal that didn't look any different from 'OK'. 'Don't think they can see that signal, England,' said the Old Man, so then I did as I was told. On the next lap, of course, Walker's time was about 20 seconds quicker. 'That's too fast, he'll break it,' said the Old Man. So I put out a 'Go Slow' signal. 'That's too slow now'.

"I'd had enough of this. Peter Whitehead was about to take over, so I gave him a stopwatch and told him to time himself going past the Hippodrome on the straight, and to ignore all my signals unless they said 'stop' or 'go like bloody hell'. And that's what he did. 'They aren't paying any attention to your signals, England'. 'Aren't they, Mr Lyons? Very difficult to see you know!' In later years I don't think I ever did own up to the Old Man about this..."

Naturally there was considerable tension in the Jaguar pit, although 'Lofty' remained as cool and calm as ever. Joe Sutton was allocated to the Walker/Whitehead car and has an interesting memory to illustrate how the team operated on a shoestring: "My mechanic was one of the drivers. If Whitehead came in, he was my mechanic until Walker took over."

The XK120C held together to give Peter Walker and Peter Whitehead one of the great race victories of all time. The winning Jaguar comprehensively broke the distance record, actually exceeding the previous record in the 23rd hour. Amid all the celebrations the British National Anthem was played no fewer than three times. Almost overlooked in all the excitement, a virtually standard (apart from its wire wheels) XK120 driven by Robert Lawrie and Ivan Waller finished a highly creditable 11th.

Towards the end, when victory looked likely, John Lea was given a rather unusual task: "There was no champagne or anything in the pits. I was sent to buy champagne and glasses from a stall on the other side of the track so that we would have some ready for the drivers when they finished."

The victory brought tremendous rewards. It was headline news everywhere and suddenly the Jaguar name was famous throughout the world. Jaguar had arrived internationally, the true calibre of its products unquestioned. *Autosport*'s editorial stated that 'the result will raise British prestige to an undreamed-of height'. Quite rightly the magazine paid tribute to William Lyons' courageous move, 'to the designers and mechanics, the last-named working under the capable direction of 'Lofty' England, who has done more than most to see that the new Jaguar had all possible things done to ensure its development'.

On a more mundane level, 'Lofty' England, who had stayed at his post throughout the race, recalls being totally exhausted. He persuaded Jaguar's West Coast US importer Chuck Hornburg, who had a suite at the Hotel de Paris where the team was based, to let him use his bath and promptly fell asleep in it. Hornburg had to pour cold water on him to wake him in time for the celebratory meal. "I dozed off during the soup and again during the fish – and then I gave up. I went and sat in the car outside and fell asleep!"

Later Claude Baily was quoted in the *Daily Mail* as saying that the XK120C is "practically in production and assured of an enormous sale. Almost every one we turn out will be for export".

OTHER RACES IN 1951

The next event for the factory team was the classic Tourist Trophy at Dundrod, scene of Moss's success in an XK120 the year before. The three Le Mans cars were rebuilt and were to be driven by Moss, Walker and Johnson. Unfortunately it was not a particularly strong field, partly because the Italian GP was due to take place at Modena next day. Moss (XKC 002) took the lead and was shadowed by Walker (XKC 003), with Johnson (XKC 001) following but not able to maintain the pace.

"Johnson's health was getting a bit ropey," says 'Lofty', "and frankly he wasn't very good anyway. Tony Rolt was there as reserve driver for Nick Haines with his XK120 but Haines shunted it in practice – so Rolt didn't have a drive. I let him do one or two laps in practice as reserve driver, and then in the race Johnson wasn't very well so I stopped him and sent Rolt out. We had to move the steering column up to get him in. In spite of all that he went off and beat the lap record. So that's how he got into the Jaguar team..."

BELOW **Peter Walker (left) and Peter Whitehead, close friends since schooldays, celebrate a great victory for Jaguar.**

In spite of the fact that the TT was a handicap event, the Jaguars finished first, second and fourth. Moss took his second TT victory (he was only the third driver ever to achieve this), Walker was a dutiful second in spite of having to wear a form of galosh after sustaining a burned foot in a V16 BRM, while Rolt drove superbly but a stop to change drivers was sufficient to allow Bob Gerard's rapid Frazer Nash to split the Coventry cars on handicap.

Behind the scenes things were not quite as serene as they appeared. Heynes was in the US visiting various companies in Detroit and Lyons wrote to him there on 21 September: 'I do not know whether you have yet seen the Salisbury axle people. If you have, you may already be aware of the trouble we ran into with the TT cars with the lower axle ratio, 3.54. Three of these failed on test at Lindley after approximately 150-180 miles, the trouble apparently being caused by a breakdown in the film strength of the lubricant. We then ran a fourth axle with the SAE140 oil, which stayed put, but we had only time to do 110 miles at Lindley.

'Unfortunately, this was on the Friday before the cars had to leave on the Monday and, although I was very disturbed at the idea of running on the higher axle ratio, it appeared to be the only safe thing to do, as the short test was not conclusive that we should not have trouble in the race. However, England took two of the lower axle centres, which I told him to risk if we were hopelessly over-geared. Fortunately, although the drivers did complain of being over-geared, the cars seemed to be fast enough to win.'

Lyons went on to talk of receiving complaints of camshaft noise, something he had 'predicted for a long time', and asked Heynes to determine the delivery situation with Borg Warner as Moss Gears could not supply sufficient 'boxes and 'gearboxes are going to be a limiting factor in our production'. He concluded, 'As we thought, Johnson was well down on the others, and actually fell to eighth or ninth position. He came in and handed over to Rolt, who...went like a bomb, but could not do better than pull up to fourth position. Two or three laps more, and he could easily have been third.'

The XK120C made its English debut at Goodwood a couple of weeks later. Moss, who was entered in five events that afternoon, was down to drive the 'C' in two sports car races. In the first, in which there were no fewer than eight XK120s entered, including cars driven by John Coombs and Michael Head (father of Williams designer Patrick), and three more among the reserves, he won as he pleased with no opposition. The second race was a handicap but again there was no stopping Moss, who sailed off into a large lead, breaking the lap record in the process. In an earlier race another young man by the name of Mike Hawthorn had gone cross-country motoring on the first lap.

This completed the C-type's first season and on 27 December 'Lofty' England sent Lyons, Heynes, Baily, Rankin and Weaver a copy of official speeds issued by the RAC over the timed kilometre during the TT. Walker's car was the fastest at 128.20mph, followed by Moss at 127.60mph and Rolt at 127.40mph. Fairman in an XK120 was recorded at 115.60mph, Macklin in the fastest of the Astons (a DB3) at 114.90mph, a 2.6-litre Ferrari at 121.20mph, the Allard of Collins at 110.30mph and Gerard in a Frazer Nash at 109.10mph.

Three days later Malcolm Sayer reported to Heynes on a number of wind tunnel tests he had conducted during the month on the XK120C: 'Tests have been made in a closed tunnel to measure total drag and differential lifts of various versions of the model under still air conditions (car running straight)'. The features with which Sayer had experimented included closing off the radiator aperture in varying degrees, fairing in the rear wheel arches, various louvres open and closed, the exhaust silencer faired over, the front wheel 'faired to permit full lock', and the driver's compartment both open and covered with a 'dome'. His report read as follows:

A. DRAG
1. A total reduction of 15½% was possible by using a 'dome', rear wheel fairings, and closing the bottom louvres and half the top louvres. This reduction represents 6.7hp at 100mph, or 35hp at 165mph, and is made up thus:

    Dome 8% (3.4hp at 100mph)
    Rear wheel fairings 6.9% (3hp at 100mph)
    Louvres 0.6% (0.3hp at 100mph)

2. No advantage resulted from fairing the exhaust silencer.
3. Fairing the front wheels completely, to provide the same steering lock, caused an increase in drag.
4. Reduction of radiator intake area caused 2-3% increase, due to lateral compression of the air before entry. This does not mean, however, that an improved bonnet shape would not permit a reduction in intake area with a decrease in drag. It is likely in fact that the only chance of any appreciable further reduction in drag lies in lowering the radiator block so that this shape can be achieved. This would entail changes in the cooling system (such as the use of a remote header-tank) which would require investigation.
5. As drag was slightly reduced by closing the bottom louvres and front top louvres, and as smoke tests showed that these were also most inefficient as louvres, their elimination seems desirable (the top front louvres have already been deleted for production).
6. With radiator grille and louvres blanked off, as for short record attempts, a further reduction of 1.9% took place, making a total of 17.4%.

B. LIFT
Accurately checked figures are not yet available, but it is apparent that they are most satisfactory under all degrees of modification tested, in that in all cases there was a moment turning the nose of the car down, accompanied by a slight overall lift. Thus the steering of the car should not deteriorate with speed increase, and as the centre of the moment is very far behind the centre of gravity, stability is assured.

C. SMOKE TUNNEL
These tests were of value chiefly in locating inefficient louvres and points of disturbance and breakaway. The most serious disturbance is in the region of the front wheel aperture, as would be expected. This may have been falsely exaggerated by the lack of hollowness in the wooden wing of the model. A possible method of reducing this turbulence is by reshaping the wing in front of the wheel aperture in an endeavour to even the pressures across the gap and hence soften the vortex; though this is a slight hope, it is not difficult to try.

FURTHER TESTS
A. DRAG
1. Tests with engine compartment undertray open and closed, in conjunction with smoke tunnel tests. These link with tests on sump cooling methods.
2. Tests on a further model (using as much of the existing model as possible) with a new nose line based on the assumption that the radiator block can be lowered.
3. Tests on the possibility of reshaping the front wing as mentioned above (C).
4. Tests on a new model having completely modified lines, with lowered scuttle, possibly lowered wing crowns as in C (2) below, and new nose line.

B. OTHER WIND TESTS
Cross wind tests to establish the effects of the modifications upon stability.

C. SUGGESTED TESTS NOT IN WIND TUNNEL
1. To discover the adverse effects of fairing the rear wheels on disc and drum brakes.
2. To discover the actual maximum bump of front

ABOVE **Driving later in 1951, Stirling Moss followed up his great TT victory of 1950 with a second success at the bumpy, dangerous Dundrod course in Northern Ireland, driving XKC 002.**

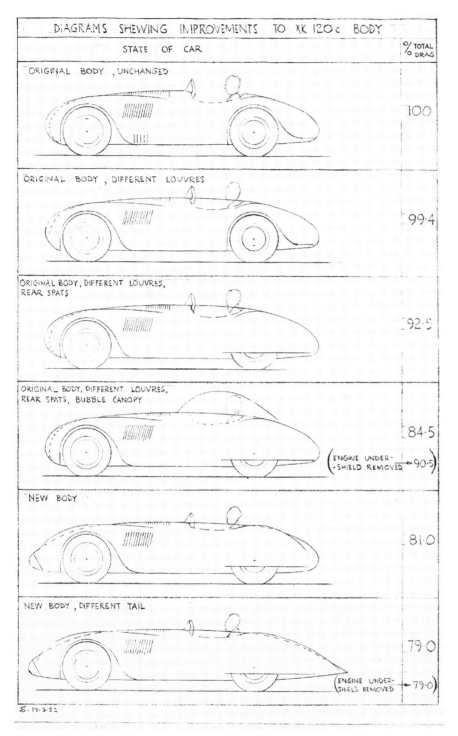

DIAGRAMS SHEWING IMPROVEMENTS TO XK 120c BODY

STATE OF CAR	% TOTAL DRAG
ORIGINAL BODY, UNCHANGED	100
ORIGINAL BODY, DIFFERENT LOUVRES	99·4
ORIGINAL BODY, DIFFERENT LOUVRES, REAR SPATS	92·5
ORIGINAL BODY, DIFFERENT LOUVRES, REAR SPATS, BUBBLE CANOPY	84·5 (ENGINE UNDER-SHIELD REMOVED → 90·5)
NEW BODY	81·0
NEW BODY, DIFFERENT TAIL	79·0 (ENGINE UNDER-SHIELD REMOVED → 79·0)

S. 19·3·52

ABOVE **This fascinating document shows how Sayer's thinking was developing in March 1952, with consideration of a bubble canopy (actually the beginnings of the D-type head fairing) and first thoughts of the extended nose and tail treatment that would be seen on the Le Mans cars that year.**

and rear wheels, in an attempt to lower the wing crown and thus reduce frontal area.
3. Tests on sump cooling methods.
4. To find the minimum acceptable size of 'dome' with a lowered seating position, using templates for clearances.

This report throws up a number of points. It is interesting that a 'dome', a throwback to Sayer's aircraft background, was being considered. Of particular note is the fact that he was already thinking of a revised and lowered nose line. As we shall see shortly, such a revision would briefly be adopted but in controversial circumstances. It has

always been assumed that this was last-minute thinking.

Meanwhile it had been a perfect first year for the C-type. The car had won the race it was designed for and its other outings had given it an unbeaten record. Writing at the end of the season, Moss had nothing but generous praise for the new Jaguar but in previewing the 1952 season he expressed some trepidation about the challenge from a works-entered team of Type America Ferraris which were 'understood to be giving the colossal output of 240bhp...On the other hand, Mr 'Bill' Lyons of Jaguars has already dropped a hint in public about the possibilities of scaling up the sports-racing XK to 4½ litres, a development which, provided it didn't entail more than a slight weight increase, would result in a truly fantastic all-round performance.'

DISC BRAKES FOR 1952

During 1951 important collaboration had begun between Jaguar and Dunlop to develop the disc brake, which had been designed for aircraft prior to being adapted for automotive use. Jaguar had been without a test driver since Sutton had left, but this was rectified when Norman Dewis joined the team early in 1952.

"When I first joined," recalls Dewis, "the big push was for disc brakes and that was my first project. I knew the people at Dunlop and we had a good tie-up. There was a good team build-up between Jaguar and Dunlop, and Mr Heynes said to me 'You've got the car, get on with the development'. The first trial disc brake was put on the XK120 by Dunlop. In those days it wasn't a great big empire, and there were probably only about five people involved. It was just a matter of test, test, test until we got it right.

"There were problems right from the start. Nobody had any idea of what temperature the discs would run at, or the pad material, because aircraft brakes and car brakes are entirely different things. The unit was inside the wheel and we hadn't realised what sort of airflow or ducting we needed to cool it, so all that was done by trial and error. We were seeing temperatures after a few laps of 500-600 degrees C, and I could finish up with the disc glowing dull red and the fluid almost bursting into flame. First we fitted wire wheels to get air from the outside, and then we had ducts in the front to bring air to the inside of the brake, and gradually we got the temperatures down to a sensible level.

"We did most of our testing at Perton, a disused aerodrome just outside Wolverhampton which Dunlop hired from the Air Ministry. We used to go there every day, seven days a week, and it was nothing to knock up 600 miles in a day. We used to be there at 8.30 in the morning and stay until it got dark at 7.00 in the evening. We did thousands of miles, but it was the only way to get the job done quickly."

The other important area of co-operation between Jaguar and Dunlop was with tyres, as Bill Heynes explained: "Our strong appeal to the Dunlop Rubber Company on the question of racing tyres brought immediate results. The knowledge of how to produce racing tyres was already in the company although it had not been put into effect. During late 1951 and 1952 a tremendous number of hours were put in by our drivers in conjunction with the Dunlop Rubber Company on experimental C-type cars and as a result of this test work and the technical work carried out by the tyre manufacturers, a completely new outlook on tyres was obtained. In addition to the life factor apparently having been increased by three times, it should be remembered that the speed of the cars has gone up considerably..."

Dewis's disc brake tests during March were with XKC 001. It had covered 1705 miles when he noted the following in his log for 7 March: 'Disc brakes refitted and bled, discs hard chrome plated, special non-shear front engine mountings fitted, bonnet louvres modified, handbrake assembly fitted to transmission, gearbox cover modified to suit'. Brake testing transferred to Lindley and on 29 March Dewis noted: 'Brakes still unsuitable for high-speed braking'. The rear suspension was causing concern and would soon be changed, and on 9 April Dewis wrote: 'Rear subframe removed & Panhard rod fitted, re-assembled and prepared for test'.

Meanwhile XKC 003 had also had disc brakes fitted and was entered for Moss at the Easter Goodwood meeting. The star of the day was to be a blond-haired young chap called Hawthorn in a Cooper-Bristol, Moss having a less happy day. He drove the 'C' in a handicap race that was much publicised as a duel between champions on two and four wheels – Moss and Geoff Duke. This was Duke's first race in a car and he had a DB3 Aston. Moss was on scratch and had to give 25secs to Duke. Although Stirling set fastest lap, the traffic was too much and in a six-lap race he finished 10secs behind Duke, who in turn finished behind two XK120s.

Dewis was out testing again in XKC 001 at Lindley a few days later and on 17 April he noted the various temperatures and pressures after 28 laps: water, 75°C; sump, 130°C; axle, 120°C; brake fluid, 65°C; oil pressure, 20-35lb sq in. The next day Bob Knight issued a report on aspects other than braking that had been explored in the XK120C's development. Although he stated that body development was not his concern, he felt it desirable to show the improvement in performance which resulted from lower drag coupled with increased power. He prepared graphs to show the results of a 20 per cent reduction in wind drag combined with the use of a 220bhp engine.

'It can easily be seen that the drag saving contributes most to the increase in performance, especially under Le Mans conditions where most of the running takes place at speeds above 100mph. At 140mph the acceleration is increased by 60%, and the maximum speed is increased by about 10mph.' Knight went on to comment on 'the rather unfortunate conditions which arise from the present gearbox ratios'. He proposed lowering third gear and raising first to make the ratios closer. With regard to suspension, 'the damper settings which were hastily arrived at ten months ago were reasonably satisfactory on smooth surfaces, eg Le Mans, but considerable trouble was experienced at Dundrod. The latter course has a choppy surface which caused the cars to slide considerably, especially at the rear axle. The writer considers that the trouble was wheel bounce due to an inadequate high-speed setting of the rear dampers'. He went on to suggest a solution based on experience gained on 'the bumping machine at Rubery Owen & Co'.

As for the rear suspension, he believed that the existing means of locating the axle transversely by a top link had two disadvantages, one of which was weight transfer: 'Due to the fact that the roll centre of the rear end is at the height of the top link (16in above ground), the majority of the weight transfer on corners takes place at the rear end. Assuming a 0.75g cornering force the conditions are: front transfer, 185lb; rear transfer, 385lb; total 570lb. The weight on the rear axle with 30 gallons of petrol and driver is 12cwt. This means that the weight on the inside rear wheel on a 0.75g corner is less than 300lb. Therefore the latter wheel spins if much power is used in the corner. When Peter Walker last drove the car at Lindley he wore the NS back tyre right through to the breaker strip as a result of this defect.

'The writer has proposed the use of a transverse link which locates the axle below the centre line of the rear wheels and which lowers the rear roll centre by 6in. As a result of this change, 75lb less weight is transferred across the rear wheels, and 75lb more weight is transferred across the front ones. This assists in promoting understeer, and reduces the tendency to spin the inside rear wheel when using throttle on a corner.'

Initial tests of this revised rear suspension gave encouraging results. The car was more stable on the straights and in corners the driver had 'far more latitude for changing his mind'. It was 'much more difficult to cause the inside wheel to spin when using power in a corner' and 'slides can be countered much more easily'.

THE 1952 MILLE MIGLIA

The second event of 1952 for a factory C-type, and the international debut for the disc brake, was the Mille Miglia, and Norman Dewis was to be in the

RIGHT **In 1952 Stirling Moss, together with Chief Test Driver Norman Dewis (who took this photograph of XKC 003), gave the disc brake its international debut on the Mille Miglia. Despite a valiant effort and several hairy moments, a broken steering rack mounting eliminated them from fourth place.**

RIGHT **Moss and Dewis completed most of the course, as the stamps at the various time controls show.**

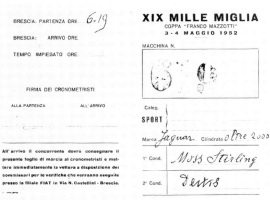

thick of the action after all his work on the new brakes: "We went to the Mille Miglia with a brake which we knew very little about. But we thought it was the right sort of race, with the distance to be covered, for us to see (a) just how the brake would perform and (b) what the pad life would be. Stirling Moss, for whom I co-drove, knew all the work we'd done, and of course he was very interested because to have something that your competitors don't have is worth quite a lot in a race. Fortunately, we didn't strike any great problems with the brake. It was certainly a very great feature when we were racing against Caracciola in the Merc. We caught him and stayed with him for probably 60 or 70 miles, and we were able to out-brake him every time. He couldn't understand it at all and we could see him looking at us every time we went past. We would go by flat-out when he started to brake and then put the brakes on in front of him. He said it was incredible and several times he thought our car wasn't going to stop."

Moss also has distinctive memories of the Mille Miglia: "Actually the disc brakes in their early days were prone to all sorts of problems, knock-off, vaporisation and goodness knows what else, but we learned an awful lot about them. They were really powerful, but the trouble was that each time you used them you had to wait quite a while for them to cool down again because of the fluid vaporisation."

At the time Moss was quoted as lamenting the fact that Jaguar was less prepared for the event than Mercedes: "The whole Mercedes team, with mechanics and spare cars, was out in Italy months before the race. The drivers all did two or three trips round the circuit, and picked out places to set-up refuelling and servicing stations. We weren't even allowed to do one lap! 'You're going to do it on the day. Why bother before? You'll wear the car out.' That was the attitude."

The event for the intrepid duo and XKC 003 began in rain and Dewis likened the first hour to "motoring on ice", but at least the brakes did not boil in these conditions. After two hours they had passed Piero Taruffi in the 4.1-litre works Ferrari and Rudi Caracciola in the new Mercedes-Benz 300SL Coupé, but then the offside rear tyre threw a tread on one of the high-speed sections. Moss skilfully avoided disaster, but changing the wheel cost valuable time. Karl Kling in another works 300SL shot past while they were stopped, but Moss and Dewis caught him again by the next control. After Ravenna the C-type's discs allowed Moss to overtake Kling under braking, but then the exhaust pipes split in their flexible section. Fumes in the cockpit affected Dewis and then Moss went off the road, giving them both such a fright that Dewis "used a whole box of matches to light a cigarette"! By the time they reached Rome, they were lying seventh but by now the rear shock absorbers were tired and the petrol tank had sprung a leak. Nearing Siena they took a bridge at 120mph when 80mph would have been more appropriate.

'In Siena,' wrote Dewis in a contemporary article in the Jaguar Apprentices' Magazine, 'Biondetti's Ferrari had caught fire during refuelling leaving us no choice but to drive through the flames that had spread across the roadway. Once through the flames, I leaned backward over the rear of the car to assure myself that our leaking tank had not ignited and, giving Stirling the thumbs up sign, it was not long before the rev counter was showing 5500rpm again.' Later, '...arriving rather too quickly at the Shell pit we struck the door of a competing saloon which had been left open and tore it from its hinges. Nipping out smartly I retrieved it for the owner, who snatching it from me, proceeded to scream in his best Italian who he thought my ancestors were, and my knowledge of Italian being what it was, I could do no more than smile and agree with him entirely!' A week later Jaguar received a letter from the unfortunate owner saying that his Fiat had been 'striken by your race-car'...

The heroic drive continued with Moss and Dewis battling through worsening weather. They were in a secure fourth place, with a chance of third, and the finish was comparatively close when the C-type's front end slid into a hard piece of scenery, damaging the steering. They found that the rack mounting had broken, and that was that.

Autosport felt that Jaguar should have entered more cars: 'Surely one C-type was rather a case of putting all the eggs in one basket'. Jaguar had viewed it more as an exploratory run, but there were ramifications which would be felt later. Moss stated at the time: "I was doing about 150mph on the Ravenna straight. It was pouring with rain, and there was a nasty cross wind which made it very difficult to keep the car on the road. The mechanic had his head down – said he daren't look! – and as a matter of fact I was frightening

myself stiff. But at least I thought I was pressing on as hard as anyone could – when a Mercedes went past me! I managed to overtake it again later, but I can tell you it shook me". The Mercedes drivers had the advantage of being in a closed car in the dreadful conditions, but this experience so concerned Moss that he telegraphed Jaguar after the event: 'Must have more speed at Le Mans'. 'Lofty' England feels, incidentally, that Moss may have been overtaken by the Mercedes just after he had had his frightening moment, and as a consequence may not have been back up to full steam.

Meanwhile the *Daily Express* meeting at Silverstone in May turned out to be a day of mixed fortunes for Jaguar. In the main race three C-types were fielded for Moss (XKC 002), Tony Rolt (XKC 001) and Peter Walker (XKC 011, a new car) – a very strong line-up. What should have been total domination despite strong Aston Martin representation, however, nearly turned to disaster. Walker had to pit very early on with no brakes and Rolt's offside rear hub failed near the end. Luckily Moss's car behaved and he took a good win.

During this period the production C-type, covered in the next chapter (page 56), was being developed and a trickle of deliveries began in May.

In 1952 the Monaco GP was held for sports cars and the factory entered a single C-type (XKC 003) for Moss. Having started from pole position and led initially, he was dicing for the lead when, at about quarter distance, he and his sparring partner Manzon, in the leading Gordini, both hit Reg Parnell's DB3 Aston, which had been busy pirouetting on its own oil. Tony Crook (of Bristol fame) and others helped Moss bend the damaged bodywork clear of the wheels to enable him to depart from the mêlée. He motored round to the pits where 'Lofty' England and Frank Rainbow carried out a more proper repair and re-entered the race. He was later black-flagged and disqualified for outside assistance, but Rainbow reckons it was because he was catching a Frenchman!

"The 2-litre Gordini was very quick," remembers Moss, "because it was virtually a GP car with a little body. I would think it was only two-thirds, if that, of the Jaguar's weight. It had quite a good, free-revving engine and we were at a circuit where, even with the Jag, I wouldn't think we were doing more than 105mph. I would think the Gordini also probably had better ratios. On the C-type we used to change the back axle, but the idea of changing intermediates didn't enter into it. Manzon was a quick driver anyway and I hadn't a hope in hell."

FAILURE AT LE MANS IN 1952

Three cars were again entered for Le Mans with the driver pairings of Moss/Walker, Rolt/Hamilton and Whitehead/Stewart. "Good driver, Peter Walker," says Moss, who thinks that sharing with

ABOVE **Although Sayer had not proceeded with his work on a revised C-type body and it had certainly not been evaluated in full size, three new bodies – intended to increase straight-line speed – were hurriedly fabricated for the 1952 Le Mans entries after Moss cabled William Lyons to express his concern about the maximum speed of the Mercedes 300SLs.**

Walker was probably his choice as they were the quickest drivers. "Pete was an easy sort of guy to get along with and certainly competitive, and would want to have a go."

Duncan Hamilton had already done Le Mans the previous year with Rolt in a Nash-Healey, he had been campaigning an XK120 with enthusiasm, and he had just taken delivery of the first production C-type. Ian Stewart was a young Scot who had also impressed with his handling of an XK120. The cars were largely to the previous year's specification, with one important exception. Panicked by Moss's reports of the Mercedes' straight-line capabilities, Sayer had hurriedly designed a new body with a longer, lower nose and a longer tail – but as we saw earlier he had already been thinking in this direction some months before. The new bonnet required a lower radiator, so a system with a remote header tank mounted on the scuttle was designed, with plumbing carried out by Roy Kettle. The revised cars would also run on drum brakes as England felt that the discs were not yet ready for 24 hours of racing. Like the front brakes, the rears were now self-adjusting.

'Lofty' has no doubts about the reason for these late changes, which turned out to be so disastrous, and holds Moss responsible: "It was his fault for

sending a stupid cable to the Old Man. I didn't know about it because I'd gone to Monte Carlo". After various problems on the journey home with this C-type, England had dropped it off at Le Mans and continued back to Coventry with Rainbow in a Mark VII saloon.

"I got back to the factory late afternoon on Thursday to find absolute chaos – they'd had this telegram from Moss. The Old Man thought Moss was wonderful, so they were trying to give him the extra speed he wanted. Sayer had done this long-nose thing and Abbey Panels knocked the bodies up in about five minutes. They ran one car at MIRA and the temperature must have gone up by the end of the straight, but no-one noticed. So the car was supposedly all right and was taken to pieces again."

This car was XKC 011 and on the day 'Lofty' returned it was fitted, according to Dewis's log, with 'latest type header tank'. Meanwhile XKC 001 had been fitted with disc brakes. England explains what happened next.

"When I got back on Thursday night, Bill Heynes said, 'I think you'd better take over'. There were no cars built at all – not one. We had previously built the cars which were intended for Le Mans and they were the '51 cars, in effect, with 2in carburettors and a few more horsepower. They had ⅜in brake linings instead of ⁵⁄₁₆in and a transmission handbrake. So from Thursday night until Sunday morning, we built and painted three cars."

From Dewis's invaluable notes, we learn that XKC 012, another new car, was fitted with the 'new type header tank' on the Friday and completed a few laps with Jack Emerson at the wheel. The same day Duncan Hamilton's new production car (XKC 004) was also being tested and on the next day, 7 June, XKC 002 was run in readiness for Le Mans duty. From this we learn that 002, 011 and 012 were the cars taken to Le Mans, and presumably 001 was not used as it was fitted with disc brakes. However, with Le Mans on Saturday 14 June, four new cast aluminium sumps were flown out by Dunlop 'for the three Le Mans cars in France'. The front calipers were also removed from 001 'by Dunlop reps'.

"So off we went," recounts 'Lofty', "and drove the cars to Le Mans – they ran very cold on the road. The first thing we did when we arrived was to check the headlights down the Mulsanne Straight. I tried the first car and at 110mph on the straight it weaved. So I tried the other two – and they were the same. They were unstable because of this rear end change. So we sorted that out a bit by altering cambers and things, but the cars were a disaster when we got to first practice. The plumbing system was quite ridiculous and the cars overheated badly. Apparently Marston Excelsior had advised on the cooling system, and I was later told they had done the same for the Aston Martin that had also had overheating trouble at Monaco."

Besides the overheating problems, Moss felt that disc brakes should be fitted after that first practice session. Bob Berry was dispatched to collect the parts from an airport at Dinard – this probably explains the reference in Dewis's notes to Dunlop men taking the calipers off 001. In an effort to deal with the overheating fears, the old-style radiators were removed from the car that 'Lofty' had left at Le Mans after Monaco (XKC 003) and Hamilton's new production C-type which he happened to have brought with him (XKC 004). 'Lofty' beat the bonnets with a copper hammer to enable the radiators to be fitted.

The three Jaguars started the race but with little hope of success. The Stewart car, without the benefit of the old cooling system, retired after 16 laps. Moss's car held second place and ran perfectly well ("it had the one remaining decent cylinder head," remembers 'Lofty') with no signs of overheating, but then it lost oil pressure – a fragment broke off the timing chain tensioner spring and jammed open the relief valve – and had to retire. The Rolt car lasted long enough for Hamilton to take over and he tried to nurse it by getting a tow down the straights from slower cars, but it was to no avail and he retired at his next pit-stop.

"Jack Emerson was in charge of the engine

side," recalls Frank Rainbow, "and told me to put in some water. Eventually he said, 'I think that's enough, Frank'. I asked him why. 'My shoes are full already!' He was standing by those short exhaust pipes..."

These 'Series II' C-types (as Bill Heynes entitled them) were nicknamed the Kettle Specials, but

ABOVE **As well as showing the three ill-fated 1952 cars with their revised bodywork, this Le Mans newspaper confirms how well Moss could sprint – he was invariably the first away.** LEFT **The Moss/Walker C-type, with the old radiator and the last spare head fitted, was not afflicted with overheating like its team-mates, but lost its oil pressure due to a strange quirk of fate when a fragment broke off the timing chain tensioner spring and jammed open the relief valve.**

ABOVE **After dreadful overheating problems caused by deficient plumbing manifested themselves in practice for Le Mans in 1952, the old-style taller radiators were re-fitted to two cars and necessitated a spot of expedient panel-beating – the bulge can be seen above the number roundel. Here Moss follows a Cunningham through Mulsanne Corner.**

they were not very special. They had an identical frontal area to the 'Series I' cars and their engines developed only 203bhp, while their weight of 2100lb was the same as the '51 cars. The irony was that the Mercedes were not that fast at Le Mans and the '51 C-types could have won easily...

OTHER RACES IN 1952

Moss, who was having a bad year after agreeing to drive the ill-fated BRM that seemed to non-start more than it raced, was keen to race for Jaguar as often as possible, partly because Mike Hawthorn was clocking up a large number of points towards that year's BRDC Gold Star. So it was that he persuaded the factory to enter a car for him in the Reims Grand Prix sports car race. Presumably because no factory cars were in a fit state, the Wisdom/Cannell production C-type (XKC 005) was commandeered and run, to all intents and purposes, as a factory entry. It was fitted with disc brakes and Dewis noted 'brakes very good' when he tested it on 22 June. For once Moss was the lucky one. Manzon, who had stormed into an unassailable lead in the Gordini, had a stub axle break, allowing Moss to record the first ever international win by a disc-braked Jaguar.

"It was stinking hot," recalls 'Lofty' England. "Moss was virtually overcome by the heat and near to collapsing at the end. Old Joe Sutton and I held him up while they played the National Anthem, and poured a bucket of water over him!"

On 5 August XKC 001 was taken to Silverstone for yet more disc brake testing. Some 27 laps were completed with a best time of 2min 10sec, but the conditions were described as 'heavy downpours of rain with bright intervals'. However, what made this test significant was the driver's name – Mike Hawthorn.

The racing season as far as the works cars were concerned concluded with the Nine Hour Race at

Goodwood. The driver pairings were the same as at Le Mans and, according to Dewis's testing records, the cars to be used were XKC 002, XKC 011 and XKC 012. This was not Jaguar's year and it was to be another frustrating race. The early part of the race was wet and the quicker Astons led, but as the circuit dried Rolt led the field, followed by Moss and Whitehead. Then Whitehead (XKC 002) made a rare mistake and joined the scenery at Madgwick Corner. With less than three hours to go, Hamilton (XKC 012) had a breakage which allowed a rear wheel to separate itself from the rest of the car. Meanwhile the Moss/Walker car (XKC 011) had a healthy lead until, with an hour to go, the rear suspension 'A' bracket broke. Rainbow and Dewis valiantly changed it but the task took over 30min and Moss could only finish fifth.

"As I was coming round the back of the circuit," Duncan Hamilton told me just before he died in 1994, "I was looking across to the infield. We were racing in the darkness and the headlights weren't much good. Anyway, as I was going down the straight I was looking at the lights way ahead of me, and the marquees and the grandstand. Then, for no apparent reason, everything started to move. The lights all went round to the left, traced a circle and re-appeared again. They did that about three or four times before I could work out what was going on. I realised it was me spinning down the straight, not the blinking grandstand going round and round!"

'Lofty' England recalls the moment: "It had been announced that Duncan had gone off the road, and everyone was waiting for him to arrive back. All of a sudden the people at the back of the pit, waiting to see him arrive at the front, parted and Duncan arrived on foot carrying the wheel, with the hub still attached to it. 'Here, old boy, 755 bottles of gin that cost me!' He calculated everything in bottles of gin..."

To round off his own season Peter Walker took

LEFT **Although often as quick as his regular team-mate Moss, and occasionally even quicker, Peter Walker was an amateur driver and farmed in Herefordshire, not far from Shelsley Walsh hillclimb where he set a new sports car record with XKC 011 at the last 1952 meeting.**

XKC 011 to the Shelsley Walsh and Prescott hillclimbs, setting new sports car records at both. The C-type's season was completed when Moss, in Wisdom's XKC 005, and Rolt, in XKC 011 (which was to have been driven by Hawthorn had he not been injured), contested a five-lap sprint at Goodwood. Rolt's car had the new Panhard rod arrangement at the rear end which may have helped marginally, or he may have made a better start. Whatever, he won the race from Moss. Shortly after, England sent Heynes a memo quoting Rolt on the handling of the car.

'The car had the Panhard rod, and once again I can only say that it makes the car far nicer to handle. There is, admittedly, slightly more wheelspin when coming out of corners, but on the fast swerves the car has none of the tendency to oversteer that the normal C-types suffer from'. England also attached a note of the BARC's lap times, 'from which you will note the only lap which Moss was slower than Rolt was the first lap which, as far as I can understand, came about through him going through the corner much too slowly'.

On 23 September Dewis tested XKC 012, to which a 3.3:1 axle was fitted, in preparation for a continental road test by *The Motor*, whose plans included record attempts on the Jabbeke autoroute in Belgium. On 25 September Rankin issued a report entitled 'Operation Jabbeke', detailing the car's schedule. Dewis drove it to Dover the next day and took a ferry to Ostend. Breakfast cost him 3/6 (17p) and the crossing on the *Prince Charlotte* was £1 16s (£1.80)! On the Sunday and Monday evenings Dewis 'telephoned Madame'. This would be Madame Bourgeois, Jaguar's redoubtable Belgian importer. After the gentlemen from the maga-

zine had carried out various tests, Tuesday was scheduled for the high-speed record attempts. Norman's log runs as follows: 'Tuesday 30-9-52. Arrived Jabbeke 8.15am. Control van, recording aparatus (*sic*) & police already there. Delay owing to shortage of battery for electrical timing. By now it had started raining. Radiator blanked off to obtain 60-65 C Rad Temp. Madame arrived very late. By now there were plenty of journalists and officials. Attempt was now made over the measured mile in pouring rain. Maximum run before measured mile was 2 miles approx at either end. Wheelspin encountered at 5000rpm in 3rd. Maximum rpm in top in the wet 5600.'

Shortly after the occasion Bob Knight issued a report to Rankin: 'NW RUN. Mile – 144.5mph. Kilometre – 144.5mph. SE RUN. Mile – 143.0mph. Kilometre – 138.8mph. It would appear that the mean terminal velocity of the car would have been about 150mph had there been an adequate run-in, despite the wet road. Under dry conditions, with high tyre pressures, it is considered that the car would be capable of a mean speed of nearly 155mph.'

Jaguar's Competition Department was strengthened in late 1952 by the appointment of 'Mort' Morris-Goodall as Competition Manager. It would not, he recollects, be a very easy year for him because 'Lofty' England continued to exercise control over most aspects of the job: "Bill Lyons thought it was getting too much for 'Lofty' England to be Service Manager as well as Competition Manager. So I went up to see Bill Lyons and he put me on to Mr Heynes. It was agreed that I should start and they wanted me to write up a complete dossier on each of the racing cars – what engines

OPPOSITE TOP **In late 1952 a Panhard rod was fitted to the rear suspension of the C-type used by Tony Rolt for a Goodwood sprint race and his favourable report, underlined by the fact that he beat Moss in a sister car, led to its adoption on the '53 cars, with a reaction arm superseding the 'A' bracket arrangement.**
MIDDLE **Power output of the revised 1953 C-types increased when three twin-choke Weber carburettors replaced SUs. A bonnet scoop provided rammed air and ducted it evenly to the three carbs.**
BOTTOM **The single biggest change on the 1953 Le Mans cars was the adoption of disc brakes, which in their earliest form had no fewer than six pads in each front assembly.**

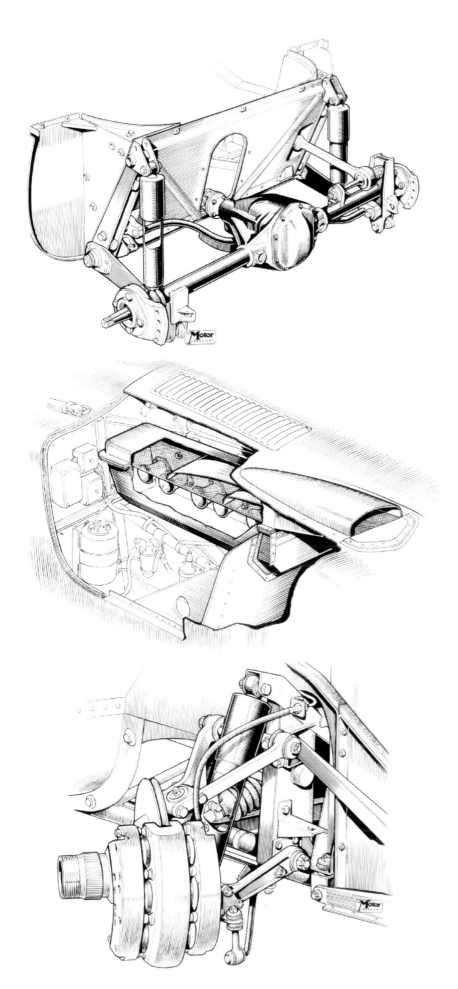

were in them, the axle ratios, the whole lot. But I had nowhere to sit, nowhere to write and no-one to talk to about it. So I had a very difficult job to do even that, and I never did start it. As for the team management, 'Lofty' wouldn't let go – he was still team manager. But I did a lot of work with the rally team and things like that."

INTO 1953

XKC 001 was prepared for further testing in late February with, according to Dewis's log, '1952 Le Mans radiator and bonnet fitted, new radiator header tank made up and fitted'. In early March it was used for disc brake testing, with '89 stops made at 2-minute intervals from 118-120mph, discs in very good condition'. On 6 March the notes record a 'one-piece metal deflector screen fitted, angle setting 45 degrees, wind pressure hit face above bridge of nose, also vision obscured'. On 16 March Rolt, Hamilton and Walker tested the car at Silverstone, Rolt posting the fastest lap at 1min 18sec: 'Brake fluid boiling every 10 laps approx'. Salisbury axle tests were carried out on 25 March: 'O/R wheel came off – slight prang'. Someone had fitted the axle the wrong way round and the spinner undid itself; the wheel was found about a mile away down an air raid shelter! At the end of the month a booster was fitted to the rear brakes, and an aluminium radiator and some new light alloy wheels were tried.

On 30 March three cars were taken out to Jabbeke – a C-type, a supposedly standard Mark VII saloon and an XK120. Jack Emerson had prepared the engines and the one fitted to XKC 012 was giving 214bhp on the test bed. The standard engine in the Mark VII was not thought to be giving sufficient power so a '1951 Le Mans type head' was fitted, resulting in 185bhp. The XK120 had a C-type engine with a 1951 Le Mans head. The Mark VII achieved 121mph, the XK120 141mph and the C-type 147mph – the C-type's speed was the same with normal and long-nose bonnets. Dewis noted: 'All records broken. The Mark VII gave marvellous results. The XK120C very disappointing'. When the cars returned Emerson put the C-type's engine on the test bed and reported: 'Comparison shows a loss of only 5bhp, which would have very little bearing upon the discrepancy in the maximum road speed obtained during the test'.

On 28 April Dewis visited London Airport 'in connection with the Ministry of Supply' and made 'six runs along the runway at 120mph, two runs made on wet surface, brakes tried on the wet, stopped in 150yds approx'. Next day he was testing a new car, XKC 037, which was being prepared for Silverstone.

The one works C-type entered for Jaguar's first race of 1953, the Mille Miglia, was supplemented by five production cars. Moss, teamed with Morris-Goodall, had XKC 011 and the factory once again borrowed XKC 005 from Wisdom for Rolt and newly-recruited mechanic Len Hayden to share. Leslie Johnson drove his own car (XKC 008) to which John Lea, who had now left Jaguar and set up on his own near Prescott, had fitted an overdrive unit. Unfortunately Moss retired early on with rear axle problems and Johnson was also one of the first to bow out with a split fuel tank. Rolt and Hayden maintained a good average speed until a big end seized near Pescara.

The factory entered three cars for the *Daily Express* meeting at Silverstone in early May – XKC 037 for Moss, XKC 012 for Rolt and another new car, XKC 038, for Walker. Moss was fastest of the Jaguar drivers in practice but Hawthorn was faster still in the works 4.1-litre Ferrari. However, Stirling had a rather big incident in practice, as 'Lofty' recalls: "Moss went upside down. He came through a curve in a big drift, but part of the track had been resurfaced and the tyres suddenly gripped. Old father Moss was there when the incident was reported on the public address. 'Can't be the boy's fault,' he said. I suggested we went to have a look. There was the car upside down and Moss had been carted off. Just as I was talking to his father, Ian Stewart did exactly the same thing, except that he didn't lose it. 'There you are, you saw that,' I said. 'That's it, not the boy's fault,' he replied. So we took the car back to the factory, changed the body and painted it – of sorts – overnight, and came back next morning."

Stirling, on the other hand, has no doubt about the cause of the accident: "It was my fault. In practice we were not quite fastest, but I was convinced I could squeeze a bit more by taking Abbey Curve flat. I came into it and there was a Frazer Nash, or something, in the way and I had to start one car's width out. I couldn't quite do it and I remember turning the car over and it landing on top of me – but I wasn't hurt. 'Lofty' was very good about it. I should have backed off and tried to go flat on the following lap, but I was impetuous."

The C-types had a poor day in the race. With drum brakes and 2in SU carburettors, they could not stay with Hawthorn or the Astons, finishing fifth, sixth and seventh.

As his car had been damaged in the Mille Miglia, Wisdom was lent XKC 011 by the factory for the Targa Florio. 'This,' wrote Wisdom, 'became a case of 'those in danger on the C' when, on striking a patch of wet clay left by peasants' boots as they crossed the course, I spun out and dived into a ditch. The peasants made amends, though, by hauling us out of our hole and back onto the road'. He kept going and, despite failing brakes, finished 17th, for which he was awarded a gold medal as the first foreign entry to complete the course.

In late May Dewis tested XKC 011 with Weber carburettors, the latest steel subframe, a rubber

fuel tank and a triple-plate clutch. Meanwhile, back at the factory, Jack Emerson was evaluating the benefits of Weber carburettors and attempting to determine why the Le Mans engines that were being built up were not showing the expected power. It was concluded that 'the flow characteristics of the cylinder heads we are now receiving from the Weslake establishment must be principally the contributory cause of the power loss'. He was also building an engine 'for Mr Swaters' Le Mans entry', this the Ecurie Francorchamps C-type for Laurent and de Tournaco.

"This was the first year the Belgians had a car," recalls 'Lofty', "but it had SU carburettors on it. We had three race cars with Webers, and a fourth which also had Webers but retained the old drum brakes. But the Old Man still had to be convinced that this Weber thing was better than the SU thing. So Dewis and I had to give him a demonstration with two cars side by side, me driving the Belgian one, Dewis the Weber one with drum brakes. We set off from a standing start to see which finished up in the lead at the end of a mile or thereabouts of runway – and obviously the Weber car was quicker. Then the Old Man said, 'I think I'd like to try this car, England'. So we gave it him, forgetting to tell him that it only had drum brakes. Next thing I know, he's gone down the road and is coming back at absolutely full crack, and suddenly I'm worried that he isn't going to stop. The runway was being extended and there was a drop at the end. But he pulled up, came back and said, 'these brakes are very good, aren't they?'."

Three new cars were built for the 1953 Le Mans. Although visually similar to the original '51 cars, they differed in many ways under the skin – and the skin itself also changed because the body was now constructed in 22-gauge MG.5 aluminium to reduce weight. Further weight was saved by using a rubber bag fuel tank (a first on a racing car, according to England), lighter electrical equipment and thinner gauge steel for some of the chassis tubes. The weight was 19¼ cwt with five gallons of Shell Premium petrol, oil cooler, spare wheel, tool kit, fire extinguisher, jack and handle, and 4lb mallet. Engine power was increased by various modifications but most notably by the adoption of three triple-choke Weber carburettors, which helped to raise output to 220bhp but, more importantly, improved mid-range torque. The rear suspension was improved by replacing the 'A' bracket with a Panhard rod and an additional pair of trailing arms. But the most significant change to the cars was the decision, finally, to run at Le Mans with disc brakes.

A SECOND LE MANS VICTORY

The works line-up for Le Mans of Moss/Walker (XKC 053), Rolt/Hamilton (XKC 051) and White-head/Stewart (XKC 052) was supplemented by the

RIGHT **Three lightweight works C-types were supplemented at Le Mans in 1953 by a private Belgian entry. The factory also took a spare car – note the two number 18s – and its use in practice nearly led to the exclusion of Rolt and Hamilton from the race.**

ABOVE **Peter Whitehead and Ian Stewart were given orders to conserve their car (XKC 052); the damage visible just behind the front wheel was probably caused during the usual mêlée at the start.**

works-prepared Ecurie Francorchamps entry (XKC 047) of Laurent/de Tournaco. The entry list was the strongest ever seen with cars from Ferrari, Alfa Romeo, Lancia, Talbot, Gordini, Pegaso, Nash-Healey, Cunningham, Porsche, Aston Martin, Frazer Nash, Bristol and Allard – only Mercedes was missing. Most GP drivers of the time were entered. This was the race that everyone wanted to win.

All three works C-types beat the lap record during Thursday night's practice, so 'Lofty' England decided to give everyone a rest by not practising on the Friday night. There was, however, a minor

drama when Norman Dewis, the reserve driver, went out to do the five laps required by the regulations. He was sent out in XKC 012, the spare car which carried the same number 18 as the Rolt/Hamilton entry.

"Dewis took the spare because we didn't want to give him one of the proper cars," says 'Lofty'. "Morris-Goodall got a bit over-enthusiastic and pushed it out on the circuit before the Rolt/Hamilton car had come in, so we had two number 18s on the circuit at the same time. Somebody protested and suddenly we were threatened with disqualification – big drama. 'I leave it to you, England,' the Old Man said."

'Lofty' knew the officials well and discussed the problem with them. After they had deliberated for some time, they told him that Jaguar was in the wrong and the penalty would be a fine of 100 francs. This is a little different from the 10,000 francs mentioned in a rather apocryphal account, and the whole business also happened on the Thursday night and Friday morning, not, as seems to have become myth, the night before the race. Hamilton and Rolt, who believed they had been disqualified, went out on the town to drown their sorrows. Dear old Duncan would exaggerate a little in later years by claiming that this binge occurred the night before the race, and that he started the race with a hangover!

Soon after the start Moss moved into the lead, followed by Villoresi's 4½-litre Ferrari with Rolt a close third, while Whitehead drove to conserve his car rather than join the leaders. The pace was frenetic. 'Villoresi in a Ferrari had a wrecking mis-

'sion,' Moss later wrote. 'With a big-engined Ferrari he was detailed to crack up the Jaguars. He did not succeed. For all his 4½ litres he could make no impression on us'.

Stirling described to me in a recent interview what it was like braking at the end of the Mulsanne Straight: "You'd brake a good hundred yards later than anybody else, and a hundred yards when you're at maximum speed is quite something. This was where we really ate up the other cars. We were going faster than most of them anyway, and if you're still going at 155mph when another car lifts off you catch it very quickly. I was not at all used to being able to brake this late, and the drivers of other cars were quite staggered."

Autosport likened the race to a Grand Prix rather than an endurance event. When Sanesi broke the lap record by some 7sec in his Alfa, the magazine's report stated, 'This is going to be the race of the century!' But the pace was telling and cars started to fall by the wayside. The Hawthorn/Farina Ferrari was disqualified for taking on hydraulic fluid too soon, Parnell went off in his Aston, and Fangio's Alfa succumbed to suspected piston problems. And then the gremlins attacked one of the Jaguars.

Moss came in with his engine misfiring. The plugs were changed but the stop took 4min 11sec. Two laps later he was back in the pits and this time he lost 6min 49sec while the trouble was traced to a blocked fuel filter. Meanwhile Rolt had increased his pace and taken the lead, lapping at 107mph. Moss, who rejoined the field in 21st place, hauled himself up to 17th by the end of the third hour. During the fourth hour the first scheduled stops took place, Hamilton taking over from Rolt in the leading Jaguar and Ascari from Villoresi in the second-placed Ferrari. The two remaining Alfas were

up to third and fourth places with a Gordini fifth and the Fitch/Walters Cunningham sixth.

Le Mans regulars could not believe this pace could be maintained, but the race did not slacken. During the seventh hour the Whitehead/Stewart car moved up to sixth and Moss/Walker were seventh. In the small hours of the morning the two remaining Alfas retired and so the order became Jaguar, Ferrari, Cunningham, Jaguar, Jaguar. With 12 hours gone the leading Jaguar's race average was faster than the previous year's lap record...

Soon after 4.00am a heavy mist descended on the course and visibility in places was reduced to less than 100 yards. Hamilton, though, continued to lap within 3sec of his daylight times. With 16 hours gone, the Belgian C-type was in an excellent 10th place and the Moss/Walker car was up to third, and closing on the second-placed – and unhealthy-sounding – Ferrari. During the 19th hour the Ferrari retired and the order became Jaguar, Jaguar, Cunningham, Jaguar.

"Our third car, Whitehead and Stewart," maintains 'Lofty', "would have been in third place but for the fact that its bonnet louvres started breaking up. My friends, the organisers, wanted Mr Cunningham to do better, I think, and so they stopped us to do something about it."

Four Jaguars started and all four finished, in first, second, fourth and ninth places. The distance covered was raised considerably and the winners averaged over 100mph for the first time. The supremacy of the C-types was unqualified. With their superb body design, complete reliability, mid-range power advantage and, above all, the new disc brakes, they destroyed the opposition.

In his autobiography, *In The Track of Speed*, Moss described it as, 'the most hotly contested marathon and the most amazing day-and-night

ABOVE LEFT **Moss and Walker were frustratingly delayed by misfiring, eventually traced to a blocked fuel filter, and dropped to 21st position. But after some spirited driving and a generous number of retirements they completed the 24 hours in second place.** ABOVE **Weary but worthy victors. Duncan Hamilton gives his great friend Tony Rolt, and mechanics Len Hayden and Gordon Gardner, a lift after they had defeated possibly the strongest entry ever seen at the French classic. The aero screen had been smashed when Hamilton hit a bird at high speed.**

PRIZE AND BONUS MONEY - LE MANS.

Gen. Category.	1st.	2nd.	4th.	Team & Class etc.	TOTAL.
Index of Performance.	4th.	5th.	7th.		
Prize Money.	£ 2,200.	£ 706	£ 125		£ 3,031.
Lucas.	75	50			125.
Champions.	100	50		T.30, C.10.	190
Girlings.	30	20			50
Dunlop.	250	150		T.50.	450
Shell.	100	-		T. 100	200
Mintex.	60	30		C.10	100
Totals:-	£ 2,815.	£ 1,006	£ 125	£ 200.	£ 4,146.

Also due to the Drivers in respect of Starting Money and Retaining Fees. (Due 1st July).

	Retaining Fee.	Starting Money.	TOTAL.
Stirling Moss.	-	-	
D.C. Walker.	£ 200	£ 100	£ 300
P.R. Rolt.	200	100	300
M. Stewart.	100	100	200
D. Hamilton.	100	100	200
N. Whitehead.	100	100	200
Totals:-	£ 700	£ 500	

ABOVE **The 1953 Le Mans was lucrative for the drivers, those occupying the top two positions also sharing the bonuses paid by various suppliers.**
RIGHT **William Lyons went motor racing for the publicity potential, and this American advertisement shows Jaguar was not slow to capitalise.**

chase ever recorded. The French were wild with enthusiasm...It was Coronation year, and there were demands for the famous Le Sarthe circuit to be re-christened and called the Elizabeth circuit. There were shouts of Elizabeth, Everest, Jaguar – Everest had recently been conquered and the emotional French just couldn't help linking the three great events of the year.'

The *Daily Telegraph* was moved to describe Jaguar's victory as 'Britain's greatest motor racing triumph'. *Autosport* magazine paid tribute with a special green cover and the editorial declared that this victory 'had gained the admiration of the whole world...no praise can be high enough for all concerned'.

At the late Duncan Hamilton's Memorial Service in 1994, Raymond Baxter concluded his address with a charming anecdote. As the BBC's motor racing commentator, Baxter was the voice of British motor racing for many years.

"I will end with a tale I have never told in public before. It was at Le Mans in 1953. At about 03.00 hours I went over to the pits. It was just before first light. Wisps of mist on the circuit, and headlights still on. Duncan Hamilton and Tony Rolt were thundering their way to what was to be an historic victory but these, of all times, were to be the critical hours. I went to the entrance to the Jaguar pit and stopped. I saw Angela Hamilton and Lois Rolt, 'Lofty' on the pit counter, various others of the team around the pit. It was silent – the tension was palpable. 'Oh hello, Raymond,' said Angela brightly. 'Would you like a cup of tea?'

"To this day, I find that recollection deeply moving. It epitomised for me what we then all knew it was all about. Curiously like the war. Stiff upper lip. Do what one has to do. Make a joke. Don't make a fuss. Get on with it – and by all means have a helluva party afterwards."

OTHER RACES IN 1953

Jaguar sent a single car (XKC 011) to the Isle of Man for the BRDC Empire Trophy race. On a twisty circuit and with a non-lightweight C-type on SU carburettors, Moss could only manage to finish second in his heat and fourth in the final.

The factory decided not to enter the Reims 12 Hours, so Peter Whitehead borrowed XKC 012 and entered it for himself and Moss. They planned to play a tactical game against quite a strong field and for a time lay in fourth place with, according to Moss, plenty in hand. After four hours the order was Ferrari, Cunningham, Gordini, Jaguar. Then the leading Ferrari was disqualified, the Cunningham crashed and the Gordini succumbed to mechanical maladies, leaving the C-type to lead for the final six hours and win by four laps.

Again just a single works car (XKC 052) contested the next event, the sports car race at the British GP meeting at Silverstone. Hamilton prac-

LEFT **The 1953 Le Mans win came to be judged as one of the great sporting achievements of the decade. A month after the race Hamilton (driving) and Rolt demonstrated their winning XKC 051 at Silverstone during the British GP meeting.**
RIGHT **The works team decided not to contest the Reims 12 Hours in 1953, so Peter Whitehead borrowed XKC 012 from the factory and, with Moss as co-driver, took an excellent win on a fast course that always suited the Jaguars.**

LEFT & RIGHT **The original 1953 Le Mans winner (XKC 051), driven by Duncan Hamilton and Tony Rolt, is today owned by Duncan's son, Adrian. It may seem curious now that Jaguar did not retain the great 1953 Le Mans winner, but at the time it was just a redundant racing car and was sold to Ecurie Ecosse in 1954.** BELOW **The chassis number was stamped on the front damper top mounting and indicates that this is indeed XKC 051, the illustrious 1953 Le Mans victor. Not all original C-types, however, were stamped with their chassis number.**

tised but he was not fully fit after his recent Oporto adventures when he hit a pylon head-on at 125mph, so Rolt took his place. He enjoyed a good dice for the lead with Parnell in an Aston until the C-type retired with piston problems. Once again a singleton entry was made by the factory for the next race, the Lisbon GP. Moss drove XKC 053 and managed to finish second despite the very bumpy course.

The team was back up to full strength for the Goodwood Nine Hours. Moss/Walker had XKC 012, Rolt/Hamilton used XKC 052 and Whitehead/Stewart were allocated XKC 053. It all looked too easy after eight hours with the Moss car in the lead, the Rolt car in a secure second and the Whitehead car fourth, taking it easy as instructed. 'Lofty' England is still peeved about what happened next.

"Hamilton and Walker decided to have a race on their own, much to my consternation. I knew bloody well what was going to happen – the oil temperatures rose alarmingly. We were nearly in trouble with this at Le Mans but fortunately the straights there are so long that you have a cooling-

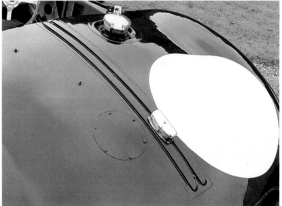

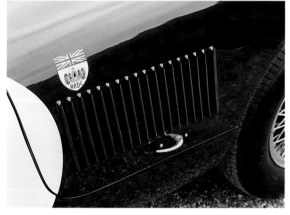

ABOVE **After its brief but glorious works career, XKC 051 enjoyed a very active and generally successful life with Ecurie Ecosse for a couple of years.** FAR LEFT **An innovative feature of the 1953 C-types was the fitting of an aircraft type flexible bag tank. As a consequence the rear bodywork was strengthened with a spinal member.** LEFT **The bonnet side louvres on the 1952 and '53 cars were rather more plentiful and subtle than the 'letterbox' style of '51 versions.**

off period. But at Goodwood, of course, there's no cooling-off period. In spite of all my signals, they just ignored me. One put a rod through the side and the other retired about two laps later, the oil having gone up in smoke. So I wasn't very pleased. This is when I rewrote the contract for drivers – disobedience of the pit manager's signals will result in being chucked out."

The TT at Dundrod was another disaster. Luckily a private entrant in an ex-factory C-type (XKC 037), John Manussis, highlighted the problem in advance. 'Lofty': "By good luck he decided to learn the circuit before we got there and had hired a car from some unfortunate bloke in Belfast. By the time we arrived, he had worn out two sets of tyres and the rear axle had quit. They had re-sur-

faced the circuit and it was as though the track was made of granite diamond cutters – you could hardly walk down to the front of the pits without wearing out your shoes! We started practice and did five laps before the tyres were worn out. The maximum we managed on a set of tyres was seven laps – 35 miles. So we had Dunlop flying backwards and forwards for more tyres. Even worse, that year you had to use the jack carried in the car to change a wheel. All this drama anyway, and then we had one gearbox go in practice and all three went during the race."

A combination of the abrasive surface and the normal vagaries of the tortuous Dundrod course put such a strain on the transmissions that the keyed constant pinion gears broke. For this event

ABOVE **Adrian Hamilton acquired XKC 051 in 1984 and had it restored by DK Engineering. It now has a stronger replacement body in the interests of durability, but the original lightweight body has been retained.**
RIGHT **The 1953 TT was not a happy race for Jaguar. As Stirling Moss takes over the task of refuelling XKC 053, Duncan Hamilton (in jacket), who had already retired, stands to the right of 'Lofty' England (white cap), Phil Weaver stands hunched on the pit counter, Claude Baily is behind the scaffolding pole, Tony Rolt (in sunglasses) is behind Moss, and Peter Walker crouches on the counter ready to spring into action.**

the drivers, as usual, were Moss/Walker (XKC 053), Rolt/Hamilton (XKC 051) and White-head/Stewart (XKC 012). Rolt was out within five laps, Stewart lasted until half distance and the third car failed towards the end, but not before Walker had set a new lap record. Moss waited on the line for the finish and coaxed the stricken C-

type across when the flag dropped, so he and Walker were classified as third on distance and fourth on handicap.

In a recent interview I asked Stirling Moss to reflect on the C-type's three-year career. He talked first about testing. "We did quite a lot of testing – mostly on the brakes. But I can never remember

LEFT **The interior of the C-type, as you would expect of a competition car, is basic, but far from cramped. There was plenty of room for the Hamilton arms and elbows to flail around as that great character pressed on.**

doing a test with Jaguar to improve the handling."

What sort of work would have been done to improve the cars during practice for an event? "Tyre pressures – it wasn't very sophisticated in those days. Maybe one would try a different roll bar, but it would be a pretty big move to do that. You have to remember that with teams like Jaguar, and even with Maserati and others, you just didn't change the car before a race. When they gave it to you, that was it. You see, when you had a car in those days set up properly, just changing the tyre pressures by 2lb altered the handling quite a lot. The Jag was fairly neutral. Another thing to remember about those days is that one adapted one's driving to the car. If you had a car that oversteered, you'd drive it in a very understeering fashion, and vice versa. That was the style then really, because so much less was known."

How did the personnel within the team operate? "We had 'Lofty' England, who was only service manager to start with but very powerful. The reason he was powerful is that Bill Heynes was a bit of a ditherer, but a nice guy. Lyons was more involved in styling and so on, so when something had to be decided he'd ask Heynes, 'What do you reckon?' And Bill would say, 'Well...' and then have a think. But 'Lofty' would come in decisively and say, 'Only one thing to do – this.' And so things would start happening. 'Lofty' got a tremendous amount done because he knew what he wanted.

"It is very difficult for people in the modern world, used to the sophistication of working with computers, to imagine how amateur even a factory

team was. But the C-type was built for the job and was pretty good. It must have been quite a good team to design a car on paper and make it work straight out of the box. The C-type really was an exceptionally good car."

How does he look back on Le Mans? "I really wanted to win Le Mans, but we were restricted in revs and you had to keep to that very carefully. But I would drive myself very hard in the car – use the brakes and all that sort of thing. But Le Mans wasn't a proper race, which is why I didn't like it very much as an event – but because I went in for it I naturally wanted to win."

Did the fact that Moss was always asked to be the pacemaker reduce his chances at Le Mans? "It was never that I was asked specifically – I was the fastest in the car and that's the way it happened. They said we're going to go to 5000rpm, or five-two, I can't remember now, but we were considerably restricted. There were no special instructions

ABOVE LEFT **The spare wheel sat below the fuel tank and was reached through a small panel in the tail.** ABOVE **The dash-mounted plaque needs no elaboration...**

RIGHT **The adoption of three twin-choke Weber carburettors helped boost the power output of the 3.4-litre engine fitted to the ultimate C-types to 220bhp. Air was fed to the cold air box from a new bonnet scoop.**

BELOW **The 1953 C-type's disc brakes, developed jointly by Dunlop and Jaguar, have often been described as the car's single greatest weapon in destroying the opposition at Le Mans.**

for me – I wasn't told I could go to maximum revs. The cars were very high-geared so you weren't likely to over-rev anyway, but I can remember that on the straights we could get up to our maximum and would have to lift off. I never really worked out whether it was better to ease off slowly and then put your foot down again, or just lift off sharply, give a breath and then back down."

A Moss speciality was the traditional Le Mans start, where the drivers had to sprint across the track to their cars. How did he manage invariably to be first away during his career? "I practised it time and again. I'm a fast runner, a sprinter rather than a long-distance guy, so I can get away quickly. I remember considering having a starter button fitted beneath the front wing so that you could save time by starting the car before you climbed in. But the trouble with this idea was that the gearbox had to be in neutral, and quite often it's more difficult to select first with the engine running. A good start at Le Mans was important, not for the outcome of the race but in case there was a shunt at the first corner – it was worth getting clear in case anything happened."

In late September Peter Walker took XKC 051 to Prescott and, according to *Autosport*, 'drove brilliantly to achieve 49.69sec – fastest sports car of the day'. That sounds like a good epitaph for the XK120C because this was the last event for a factory-prepared C-type. Although the car had its fair share of failures, two victories in three attempts at the world's most famous sports car race was an overwhelming endorsement of the C-type, probably the world's first pure sports racing car.

The achievements with the C-type in 1953 were officially recognised. Early in 1954 Jaguar was presented with the Ferodo Trophy by the Duke of Richmond and Gordon for the outstanding British contribution to motor racing during 1953. In accepting the award, William Lyons said that everyone in the Jaguar organisation would consider that a hall-mark had been placed on Jaguar cars by means of the magnificent Ferodo Trophy. The RAC also awarded Tony Rolt and Duncan Hamilton the Malcolm Campbell Memorial Trophy for the most outstanding competition performance in 1953 by British drivers in a British car.

CHAPTER FIVE

PRODUCTION C-TYPES

Following the great Le Mans victory in 1951, some people were keen to acquire XK120C replicas to race both nationally and internationally. Not surprisingly, many of these sporting drivers had been campaigning XK120s with success. The XK120C ironically contributed to shortening the competition life of the standard XK120, not only by being its obvious successor on the tracks, but also because it encouraged Jaguar's competitors to build sports racing cars rather than merely tune their production cars. Strong demand also came from the US, where enthusiasts were racing Ferraris and where Jaguar needed to compete on more equal terms. As in Britain, building a production XK120C would ensure that XK120 owners remained loyal to the marque and would continue to drum up valuable publicity.

There was nothing particularly exotic about the C-type because it used many production components, so it was not difficult for Jaguar to lay down

plans for a modest production run – but space was a constraining factor. Jaguar was fast outgrowing its factory at Foleshill and was unable to obtain planning permission to expand on adjoining ground, so it negotiated a lease on the former Daimler shadow factory (with one million square feet) at Browns Lane, Allesley. The company began a gradual move, which took a year to complete, in the autumn of 1951. With more space available, an area was established for C-type production, which was to be organised by Phil Weaver and Bernard Hartshorn.

Another cause of delay was the problem of obtaining sufficient parts and materials, partly due to the re-armament programme of that period. This certainly affected the supply of chassis tubing, but other parts such as splined hubs were difficult to obtain. On 9 January 1952 Claude Baily sent the following memo to Messrs Whittaker, Heynes, Blumson, Weaver, Cook and Siviter:

ABOVE **The 13th production C-type to be constructed is in remarkably original condition and belongs to the former Defence Minister, the Hon Alan Clark, who has also owned an XK120 since acquiring it new in 1950 while at Oxford.**

HUBS FOR KNOCK ON WIRE WHEELS
C.6020/1 FRONT, C.6022/3 REAR – XK.120
CARS

Mr Turner can provide 22 sets of Front and Rear hubs ex XK.120C finished stock, for the building of twelve XK.120 cars and ten XK.120C cars. These hubs are made from some stampings which they had in stock (not Jaguar) and in the case of the front hub an additional ring had to be welded on to make up the required length. The new dies and stampings are said to be still some twelve months away, so that a further covering order is necessary to bring up the total quantity of these hubs to the fifty sets for the XK.120C cars, and including our further anticipated requirements on the XK.120 cars.

This memo contains several interesting points. It confirms the intention to build a batch of 50 C-types. Indeed, 'Lofty' England states, "The reason for building 50 C-types, and later 50 D-types, was that when entering a prototype at Le Mans the manufacturers had to give a certificate that the car entered was the prototype of a car of which at least 50 examples would be built. I think we were the only company that in fact made 50!"

The memo also anticipates a delay in obtaining these vital hubs. It was to be, in fact, early October before Jaguar had completed 12 more cars, but the delivery situation must have improved on the forecast because the company built more C-types in October and the succeeding months, unless the company used hubs allocated for XK120s, in which case it would have run out in late November! What the memo further illustrates, as an aside, is that the vast majority of XK120s manufactured up to the end of 1952 must have left the factory originally with disc wheels.

The production cars did not differ significantly from the three 1951 Le Mans cars, but there were minor changes. They were fitted with 2in SU carburettors and the cylinder heads were modified from the production castings by having gas-flowed ports. The heads were fitted with 1⅜in exhaust valves, longer valve springs and ⅜in lift cams. In this form the engines produced 200bhp at 5800rpm. Later cars were fitted with a Panhard rod to locate the rear axle rather than the previous 'A' bracket. With road use in mind, some concession was made to comfort with basic trimming of the cockpit. A horn was required by law.

When the *The Motor* road tested XKC 012, which was essentially a works production C-type, the magazine quoted the top speed as 143.711mph, 'timed under very adverse conditions' (see page 44). The standing quarter-mile was completed in 16.2sec, 0-60mph took 8.1sec and 0-100mph took 20.1sec. The engine's excellent power range, flexibility and torque is illustrated by the fact that in third gear the C-type managed 20-40mph in 5.5sec and 60-80mph in 5.9sec, the same increments in top gear taking just 6.8sec and 7.9sec respectively. Maximum speeds in the gears at the recommended limit of 5700rpm were 48mph in first, 82mph in second and 119mph in third. Fuel consumption worked out at 16-18mpg.

RIGHT **Although the C-type was only intended to have a very limited run, Jaguar went to the trouble of producing a brochure for the production version, deliveries of which began in May 1952.**

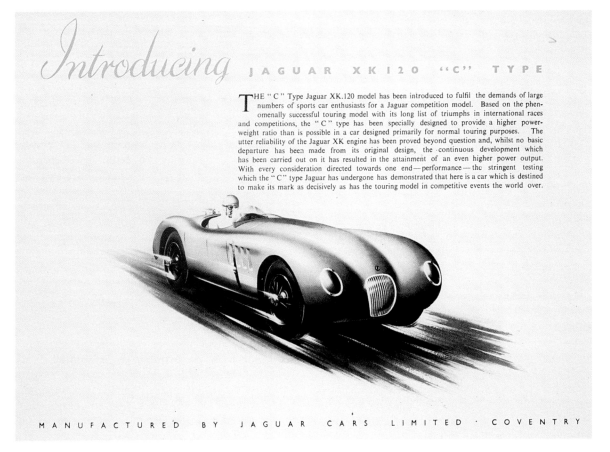

Introducing JAGUAR XK120 "C" TYPE

THE "C" Type Jaguar XK.120 model has been introduced to fulfil the demands of large numbers of sports car enthusiasts for a Jaguar competition model. Based on the phenomenally successful touring model with its long list of triumphs in international races and competitions, the "C" type has been specially designed to provide a higher power-weight ratio than is possible in a car designed primarily for normal touring purposes. The utter reliability of the Jaguar XK engine has been proved beyond question and, whilst no basic departure has been made from its original design, the continuous development which has been carried out on it has resulted in the attainment of an even higher power output. With every consideration directed towards one end — performance — the stringent testing which the "C" type Jaguar has undergone has demonstrated that here is a car which is destined to make its mark as decisively as has the touring model in competitive events the world over.

MANUFACTURED BY JAGUAR CARS LIMITED · COVENTRY

ABOVE **Many C-types have, not surprisingly, been rebuilt over the years and, although to original specification, may no longer be fitted with all the original components. This car is an exception.**

However, under the heading 'Maintenance' it was noted that you would have to take your C-type to your local garage for 12 points to be greased every 2500 miles...

The price was fixed at £2327, including purchase tax of £832 – but obtaining a C-type was not easy. The majority would be exported and a customer had to be very special to acquire one in Britain. The best way to secure a C-type, or indeed any early Jaguar sports car, was to have a strong enough track record to persuade 'Lofty' England that you intended to campaign it, regularly and competently.

In 1952 just two C-types left the factory in May, followed by one in July, four in August, one in September, nine in October, five in November and one in December. Into 1953 eight cars were completed in January, two in March, four in April and one each in May, June, July, August, September and October. The cars were not completed, or at least despatched, sequentially by chassis number. Together with 10 works cars, the 43 production cars made a total of 53 C-types manufactured by

Jaguar. Of the works cars, however, XKC 038 was never raced by the factory.

Duncan Hamilton fitted all the qualifications for ownership. He had been racing his XK120 vigorously, he had the means to back up his enthusiasm, he was keen to race far and wide, and furthermore he had just joined the works team. He managed to acquire the first production car which, with the numbering remaining in sequence with the '51 cars, was therefore XKC 004. His friend Tim Seccombe collected the car and shipped it via Liverpool to the Isle of Man. Hamilton flew in from Germany where he had been racing at the Nürburgring and saw his new C-type in the pits for the first time.

'The car went fabulously well in practice and, despite a wet track, broke the sports car record for the circuit by seven seconds,' wrote Duncan in his book *Touch Wood*. Unfortunately the bumpy Douglas course, a full tank of fuel and Kavanagh's Bridge caused the 'A' bracket to break after five laps and that was that. Hamilton decided to drive the car home and managed to collect five sum-

ABOVE **The C-type makes an extremely good road car, being entirely practical (except in rain) and totally docile. Initial acceleration is not shattering, but the car goes on pulling well right up to its maximum of nearly 150mph.**

monses on the way back! It then went to the factory shortly afterwards for, on 6 June, in the middle of testing the 'long-nose' cars built hurriedly for Le Mans in 1952, Norman Dewis also ran in a new gearbox on Hamilton's car.

After Le Mans Dewis ran the third production car (XKC 006), which was destined for Ian Stewart, and reported, 'improvement on previous prod. XK120Cs'. Meanwhile the second car (XKC 005) had been purchased by Tom Wisdom and Bill Cannell and collected by the former in May. Wisdom had also been involved in disc brake research with his XK120, and later wrote: '...old friend Joe Wright of Dunlop asked me whether I proposed to press on with the disc brake experimental and development work. I agreed readily and we all got busy...' As described in the previous chapter (see page 43), Moss and the factory borrowed the Wisdom car after the Le Mans debacle in 1952, took it to Reims and achieved the first ever victory by a disc-braked car. 'I think it can fairly be claimed,' stated Wisdom, 'that the modern disc brake, as fitted to millions of regular passenger cars, owes

something to the pioneer work of Moss and my small team in those far off days'. From Le Mans Hamilton went to Oporto where his car had been shipped for the Grand Prix but unfortunately he retired with mechanical trouble.

Ian Stewart's car (XKC 006) was delivered in July in time for the Jersey Road Race. Although owned by Stewart, the car was entered under the Ecurie Ecosse banner. This subsequently famous band of Scottish enthusiasts had formed their team at the beginning of the year, Stewart, Bill Dobson and Sir James Scott-Douglas racing their XK120s under the guiding influence of David Murray, with preparation by 'Wilkie' Wilkinson. The Jersey Road Race proved to be an excellent debut with Stewart winning his heat and the final after Oscar Moore's 3.8 HWM-Jaguar had retired.

In August the first three C-types to be exported went to the US and Leslie Johnson acquired XKC 008. At Boreham for the 100-mile race that month, Stewart spun off at the first bend, Hamilton finished second and Moss (XKC 005) won. In early September future World Champion Phil Hill

ABOVE **Like the great majority of C-types, XKC 013 was exported to the US and was supplied from New York by Max Hoffman.** LEFT **With no works cars available, the factory borrowed the second production car from Wisdom and Cannell for the 1952 Reims GP sports car race. Moss donned a natty defence against the intense heat, but 'Lofty' England is not amused.** BELOW **The bonnet badge on the C-type is identical to the one fitted to the XK120.**

ABOVE **Part of the reason why XKC 013 survives in a superbly original state is that it led a fairly quiet life, not figuring significantly in racing exploits.** RIGHT **At Reims Moss benefited from good fortune for once, XKC 005 clocking up the first ever victory by a disc-braked car.** BELOW **A Monza-type quick-action petrol filler cap was an obvious aid to rapid pit-stops in long-distance races.** BELOW RIGHT **Ecurie Ecosse had to endure a little teasing from** *Autosport* **magazine...**

ABOVE **The XK120C's interior is very different from the XK120's, with no attempt to hide the chassis and vastly improved bucket seats to assist fast cornering.**
FAR LEFT **A car's original chassis plate does not always guarantee a completely original entity, and some historic cars have been constructed around nothing more, but clearly this is not the case with XKC 013.**
LEFT **The engine number is stamped on the front face of the cylinder head – the '8' denotes the compression ratio.**

debuted Chuck Hornburg's car (XKC 007) at Elkhart Lake and took a splendid win, beating Phil Walters in a Ferrari; Max Hoffman's car (XKC 009), driven by George Weaver, finished third. A longer race the next day was not so successful and Hill, slowed by stupefying gases from an exhaust leak, followed home three Cunninghams and fourth-placed Weaver.

At Watkins Glen John Fitch drove Hoffman's car and took an excellent win in the first race of the day, with Lyons and England in attendance. The Hornburg car started the next event on the programme. "This second race," recalls Lofty,

"was abandoned because Mr Wacker's Allard-Cadillac went over the kerb. This was the main street in Watkins Glen and spectators were standing on the pavement. The car knocked down quite a few people, and sadly killed one or two. The Highway Patrol went round the circuit the wrong way on motorcycles, stopped the race and the ambulances came out. The injured people were taken to hospital and then the public address announced: 'Everything's OK folks, none of the drivers have been hurt. Now we've got a wonderful treat. James Melton is going to sing'. Famous baritone. And he sings 'God Bless America'!"

TOP **In September 1952 John Fitch won the Seneca Cup at Watkins Glen in a newly imported C-type (XKC 009) belonging to East Coast Jaguar distributor Max Hoffman.** ABOVE **Giuseppe Farina, the 1950 World Champion collecting XKC 032 in Brussels. Ferrari is believed to have examined this car closely.**

In early September Stewart and Hamilton took their cars to Ireland for 'two races in one' at the Curragh – a handicap race for the O'Boyle Trophy and a scratch race for the Wakefield Trophy. In practice Hamilton set a new lap record but Stewart's car ran its bearings, caused, according to 'Wilkie' Wilkinson, by oil surge. He and a couple of mechanics worked through the night and rebuilt the engine, having welded baffles in the sump. The start was actually delayed 10min because the job was not finished and 'Wilkie' tightened up the sump bolts on the grid. On the second lap Hamilton attempted to pass a slower car in a high-speed 'S' bend, lost the tail, struck a lamp-post and wrecked the car, but walked away relatively unscathed. Meanwhile the XK120 of Scott-Douglas and Stewart's C-type were fast working through the field. In the closing stages Scott-Douglas took the lead only to be passed by Stewart at Ballymaney Corner on the very last lap, within sight of the finish. It was a good day for Ecurie Ecosse because he won the scratch element of the race as well.

At Castle Combe in October Moss was entered in a C-type but was a non-starter, so the field was left clear for Stewart to win easily, his race average faster than the old lap record by 3mph. Later in the

month the two were pitched against each other at Charterhall, Stewart driving brilliantly to beat the maestro by 15.4sec.

At the end of October, at Motor Show time, Jaguar took over the cover of *Autosport* with a colour advertisement which featured a rather strange yellow-coloured XK120 and the following words: 'Enhancing British prestige by its achievements in the field of International Competitions, Jaguar has during 1952 brought to Britain no less than Ten Million Dollars as part of its great export earnings'. Jaguar was, in fact, the highest dollar earner of all imported makes.

Of the nine cars delivered in October, one (XKC 018) was for Fangio although he immediately sold it to the Jaguar distributor in Buenos Aires. Norman Dewis tested most of the production C-types at Lindley, and into 1953 he tried two cars ordered by Ecurie Ecosse, XKC 041 and XKC 042, respectively on 23 February and 20 March. Over the following weeks there were some interesting observations in his test log. On 9 April he tried XKC 044: 'Head removed to check valve seats, heavily pitted. Lindley circuit accused – cement dust'. The car would not be delivered until September. Next day he noted: 'Early morning run on the Bicester-Oxford road with T. Wisdom's XK120C, J. Gammon observer. Several runs made 130-140mph for cooling test'. The following Tuesday he wrote: 'XK120C 044 re-test at Lindley with new valves, etc, fitted. A piece of tape fixed to the front air box gauze smeared with syrup, only the average dust collected. I rule out Lindley as the cause of pitting the valve seats'. Next day he assessed 'Mr Lyons' 2-seater special. Tested on the by-pass'. This was the car which would become known as the 'Brontosaurus'...

In February John Rutherford (XKC 014) clocked 134.53mph over a flying mile at Daytona Beach and in March it was announced that young Lance Corporal Jimmy Stewart would be driving for Ecurie Ecosse in 1953 – and Scott-Douglas acquired XKC 046 so that three C-types would run under the Scottish banner. Meanwhile in the US two C-types were entered for the International 12 Hours Sports Car race at Sebring: Dave Hirsch led away and eventually finished, with B. Green, in fourth place behind the Fitch/Walters Cunningham, the works Aston DB3 of Parnell/Abecassis and Feverbacker's C-type driven by Sherwood Johnston and Robert Wilder. Giuseppe Farina, the 1950 World Champion, also took delivery of a C-type (XKC 032) in March, seemingly for Ferrari to examine. At Goodwood Graham Whitehead in a C-type, probably the car run by his half-brother, Peter, won a handicap race from Tommy Sopwith in an XK120.

No fewer than six C-types contested the 1953 Mille Miglia. There was a works car (XKC 011) for Moss, Wisdom's car borrowed by the factory for Rolt, Leslie Johnson's production car (XKC

008), Tadini and Cortese in XKC 045, Descollanges and Ugnon in XKC 016, and Heurtaux and his wife in XKC 035. Despite this weight of numbers, it was not a happy event for the Jaguars. The Heurtaux C-type was the only one to finish, two and a half hours behind the winning Ferrari. Descollanges had a serious accident in which he was badly hurt and co-driver Ugnon sadly died shortly after admission to hospital.

At Silverstone Graham Whitehead could only manage fifth in XKC 039, but on the Dieppe Rally Heurtaux won his class and finished second overall. During a French hillclimb at Planfoy Heurtaux broke the record on his first run but crashed fatally on his second. At Charterhall the Ecurie Ecosse cars of Ninian Sanderson and Jimmy Stewart had to give best to the works Aston of Parnell after what *Autosport* described as 'a thrilling struggle', but the Scottish team was then rewarded with two wins at Thruxton. In one race Jimmy Stewart led Ian Stewart home, their C-types beating Poore in a works Aston, and the same happened in a later race except that this time Ian was driving a Connaught. 'The Aston Martin team were preparing for Le Mans,' wrote David Murray, 'and when we met once more a few days later at Snetterton they were thirsting for revenge' – but Jimmy Stewart won with Ian Stewart third and Reg Parnell's Aston was fourth.

Two C-types contested the Hyères 12-hour race in France, Peter Whitehead and Tom Cole in XKC 039 and Armand Roboly and John Simone in XKC 025. After the fastest Ferrari crashed, they took an excellent C-type 1-2 in both the overall classification and the Index of Performance. Following the great Le Mans victory, Hamilton went straight to Oporto for the Portuguese GP. During a tussle for the lead with an inexperienced Ferrari driver, Hamilton was hit and had a massive accident which he was lucky to survive, even by his standards – his car went into an electricity pylon head-on at 125mph. He was taken to a rather suspect local hospital and became desperate for some water, but there was a language problem. Finally an attending nun understood and said in broken English, 'Water no good. Contaminated. We have only port'.

The Isle of Man course did not suit the C-types and Parnell took the British Empire Trophy race in his Aston DB3S, Moss leading the Jaguars home in fourth place followed by Sanderson and Jimmy Stewart. Snetterton in late June was the venue for a 10-lap Jaguar race for the Bill Lyons Trophy. The XK120s were given a start of 1min 15sec over the C-types: Roy Salvadori's XK120 spun off on the second lap after leading, and Ian Stewart's C-type took the flag by just 2.2sec from Hugh Howarth's XK120 and John Lawrence and Jimmy Stewart in C-types. When Moss and Whitehead took their excellent victory in the Reims 12 Hour race, Ecurie Ecosse made its continental debut, Sanderson and

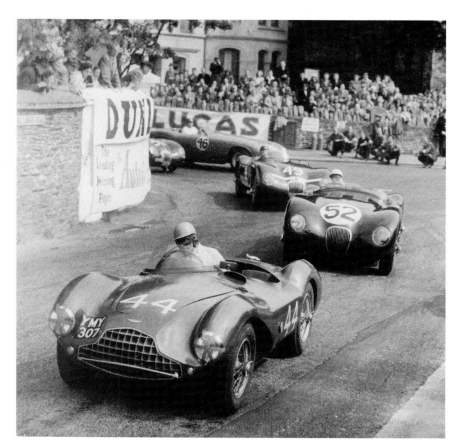

Scott-Douglas finishing fourth in XKC 046.

A strong field lined up for the SCCA's National Sports Car Races at Offut Air Base, Omaha, Nebraska, in front of 50,000 spectators, thought to be the largest ever crowd for an amateur club's event in the US. Masten Gregory brought his C-type home ahead of Carroll Shelby and Jack McAfee in the ex-Ascari 4.1-litre Ferrari, while John Urbas and Chuck Hassen were third and fourth in C-types. Tom Newcomer won the class for Production Sports Cars and Frank Larson was third in the class for Modified Sports Cars, both in C-types.

Ecurie Ecosse ventured abroad again in July for the Spa 24 Hours. The reward was an excellent second place for Sir James Scott-Douglas and Guy Gale behind Hawthorn's works Ferrari and in front of another Jaguar (XKC 019) driven by Hermann Roosdorp and Toni Ulmen, who *Autosport* said 'was making a reappearance in racing for the first time since he announced his retirement early this year'! At Shelsley Walsh Lord Louth also won his class in his C-type. When the works team failed to win the Goodwood Nine Hours with the two leading cars expiring after their indiscreet dicing, the remaining works car in third place was followed home by the Scottish-entered cars of Jimmy Stewart/Bob Dickson (XKC 041) and John Lawrence/Frank Curtis (XKC 042).

For its third and final foreign foray of the season, Ecurie Ecosse ventured to Germany for the Nürburgring 1000Kms. During practice Scott-Douglas came a cropper when he rolled his C-type,

ABOVE **In the 1953 British Empire Trophy on the Isle of Man C-types could not match the more nimble Aston Martin of Reg Parnell, who leads Stirling Moss in a factory car and Jimmy Stewart in one of three Ecurie Ecosse cars entered for the race.**

RIGHT **In their heat for the 1954 British Empire Trophy race, held at the new Oulton Park circuit, Tony Rolt initially leads in one of the Ecurie Ecosse cars (XKC 051), chased hard by eventual heat winner Duncan Hamilton (XKC 038).**

RIGHT **Ecurie Ecosse entered three cars for the 1954 British Empire Trophy. This one, XKC 052, finished sixth in the final driven by Jimmy Stewart. George Mangoletsi can be seen at far right and the man in the sweater looks suspiciously like 'Wilkie' Wilkinson, the Scottish team's chief mechanic.**

RIGHT **This is believed to be XKC 027, which was delivered in January 1953 to an American army officer based in Geneva and later sold to Jacques Jonneret, who contested the 1954 Geneva Rally.**

which luckily threw him out during its first somersault and then turned over twice more before coming to rest 100 yards below where it had left the road. Undaunted, he substituted his XK120 road car! During the race Ulmen (out of retirement again!) crashed his C-type twice within a few laps, but the Ecurie Ecosse entries proved reliable. Ian Stewart and Roy Salvadori took an excellent second behind Ascari/Farina in a works Ferrari, with John Lawrence and Jimmy Stewart sixth and Scott-Douglas and Sanderson 10th in the XK120. The XK120's disc wheels started to break up in the race, so wheels were borrowed from David Murray's Mark VII saloon to enable the car to finish. It was worth the effort for Ecurie Ecosse took the team prize.

C-types continued to be raced in club events for several years to come, with mixed results. In the winter of 1953/54 Ecurie Ecosse acquired the lightweight '53 Le Mans cars and raced them very extensively and successfully in '54, as detailed in the individual chassis histories (see page 161). Not everyone appreciated the C-type, however, as Jimmy Stewart indicated in an article in the Jaguar Apprentices' Magazine in 1957.

'It seems a funny thing, but I happen to be one of the few people who really enjoyed driving the C-type. Agreed, some of the earlier models were rather a handful, but later when we acquired the much faster and more stable ex-works C-types, I enjoyed the cars tremendously, and particularly the advantages of the famous disc brakes, which, putting it mildly, were a resounding success.'

CHAPTER SIX

D-TYPE DESIGN & DEVELOPMENT

The basis of the D-type, which would make its debut in mid-1954, was a curious prototype constructed a year earlier. This highly significant car was clearly an intermediate step between the C-type and D-type, and broke new ground in both shape and construction. Furthermore it was a foretaste of much to come, and even in the 1990s one can see its influence in the XJ220 supercar. This car was known, at various times, by a bewildering variety of names – XK120C Series II, XK120C Mark II, XP11, the D-type Prototype, the C/D Prototype, XKC 054 and XKC 201. But at the factory it was simply called the 'light alloy car'.

It has been wrongly stated that this car used a C-type chassis with different clothing, but its semi-monocoque construction was actually very similar to the D-type's. The fact that monocoque construction would not become the norm, even in Formula 1, for another 10 years shows just how advanced the thinking was at Jaguar. The company had come into contact with aircraft techniques during its war work, and Malcolm Sayer had an aviation background. Whereas the brief for the XK120C had been to retain a family resemblance in the shape, Sayer was now given a free hand to create the most efficient shape he could – in fact he described his brief as 'functional efficiency at all costs'. *Autosport* published a photograph of the car with the caption, 'Coventry Disco: a prototype 'Disco Volante' Jaguar, one of several new types built by the Coventry concern for sports car races'. Sayer had indeed been influenced by the dramatic and very advanced Alfa Romeo Disco Volante (flying saucer) of 1952, and had several photographs of this car in his possession.

Sayer gave a fascinating talk entitled 'The Shape of Cars' during which he expounded on the chal-

ABOVE **As engineering chief, Bill Heynes masterminded the D-type's design, which was principally in the hands of Malcolm Sayer, Bob Knight and Tom Jones. The brick beneath the exhaust pipes shows the prototype is not quite complete!**

LEFT **The first stage in the evolution from C-type to D-type was this multi-named prototype, known at the factory simply as the 'light alloy car'. The traditional grille has given way to an elliptical mouth, a Sayer theme that would be carried on through the E-type and XJ13 to the XJ220.** BELOW **Apart from its ultra-modern lines and smooth shape, the 'light alloy car', constructed in 1953, was remarkable for being largely of monocoque construction.**

lenges of designing a sports racing car. "The external shape is considered right from the start of the general layout. It is governed firstly by regulations, which are generally obeyed to the letter rather than to the spirit." He then illustrated his point by showing a photograph of a windscreen of regulation height that was completely obscured by a spare wheel...

"The general layout is evolved from the known data such as power units, tyre sizes, regulation fuel capacities and so on, and at the very earliest stages compromises have to be made – for instance the body man wants a nice narrow track and small frontal area for speed down the straight, whilst the chassis man wants a wide track and large tyres to increase the cornering force round the rest of the

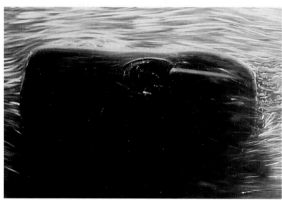

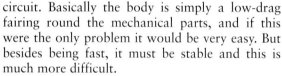

circuit. Basically the body is simply a low-drag fairing round the mechanical parts, and if this were the only problem it would be very easy. But besides being fast, it must be stable and this is much more difficult.

"Considering the car in side elevation, we must try to avoid lift, and what lift there is must act in the right place. The centre of lift must be kept reasonably far back and it must be kept reasonably stable. Its fore and aft position is altered by changes in attitude of the car, either when going over bumps, or when accelerating or braking, or under different fuel loads. It is also changed by crosswinds and by roll. So we have to try not only to keep the changes of lift centre small, but also to make them as gradual as possible, because it is the sudden changes in the car's characteristics which upset the driver.

"Similarly, in plan, we have to avoid total side force, to keep its centre back and as stationary as possible. This side force centre is completely independent of lift force centre, and moves back and forth and up and down. The amount of yaw which has to be catered for is quite large when you consider the case of a car overtaking a slower one and so meeting quite a violent sideways blast of air.

"So we have these two centres – lift and side-force – weaving about independently as the car is driven round the track. It makes rather a nonsense of these neat diagrams you see with one arrow attached to a blob in the middle of a car and labelled 'centre of pressure'.

"So far we have considered only the main shape; this has to be equipped with a series of holes to cool engine water, engine oil, rear axle oil, brakes, sometimes the battery or generator, supply air to the carburettors and to the driver. Just as the mechanically perfect design is supposed to disintegrate just after crossing the finishing line, so these holes should be just big enough for the job. But once again the requirements vary not merely from day to day but as the car circulates on one lap, so a compromise is necessary. Every duct can be considered as an air pump, consuming horsepower, and the same applies to body leaks. It is sometimes possible to get some of this horsepower back by strategic placing of inlets and outlets to improve the external flow. Some boundary layer control is possible but is uneconomic unless the duct is doing something else anyway.

"So much for the problems – the answers are arrived at by various means. The design cannot follow as precise a pattern as that for, say, an aircraft in nice laminar flow air because the car operates in turbulent air almost entirely, and near the ground – at least it should – which gives an entirely different set of conditions. But it is possible to evolve some basic rules and to apply mathematics to produce an overall three-dimensional shape which ought to behave itself. After that, the shape can be tested in model form – and I think it should be stressed that unless all the ducts and openings are reproduced it is rather a waste of time. Smoke tunnels produce very impressive patterns but are

ABOVE **These wooden models used in the wind and smoke tunnels show Malcolm Sayer's design evolving from the C-type (for which the brief was to retain strong visual clues to its lineage) to the D-type (for which the aim was pure functional efficiency). The D-type frontal treatment was first mated to a tail like a C-type's, with no head fairing. Then the tail was shortened and the distinctive head fairing was adopted.**

ABOVE **XKC 301 was nicknamed the 'Brontosaurus'. William Lyons thought this rather extraordinary device might have some record-breaking ability, but it also served to chivvy along the Engineering Department.**

misleading because of the slow speed at which they operate. In an ordinary wind tunnel forces can be measured and wool tufts observed, and I have had extremely accurate forecasts of the ultimate speed of cars by this means, though whether this was a question of errors cancelling themselves out is another matter.

"Once the prototype is built, development work can really begin. The full-scale tunnel is a great asset but has its limitations. The wheels are not rotating, the engine is not running, and I believe there is a five inch boundary layer. For sorting out duct sizes and stability, there is nothing to beat track testing. Thorough instrumentation, behaviour of wool tufts and of the whole car, using high-speed photography, can give a fairly complete picture of how the body is behaving.

"Now that race speeds are rising this is becoming increasingly difficult to carry out in this country, especially as frequent changes of regulations reduce the time available for this work and the weather reduces it even further."

As for the construction of the car, Bob Berry had this to say when giving a paper to the Society of Automotive Engineers, San Diego Chapter, on 25 August 1976. "The search for reduced body weight for both racing and production cars had led Bill Heynes to investigate the advantages of monocoque construction using magnesium alloys for such frame components as there were and, of course, for the body. The techniques for welding structures of this type were very much in their

infancy and to prove both the theory and the practice a guinea pig was built. This car proved almost too strong…"

"During the year," stated Heynes referring to 1953, "we had developed what was actually the prototype 'D' car. It was of light alloy construction throughout, the frame was magnesium tube welded by the Argon Arc process and a car was completed and tested well in time for the race in June. After the welding had been carried out, however, X-ray photographs were taken of all the joints, which showed that the welds of the joints were in a very porous condition and the recommendation of the experts who carried out these X-ray photographs was so damning that eventually we took the decision not to take a chance on the frame, as they were confident the welds would not hold. This car was put on test and in actual fact ran a far greater mileage on test work than any other racing car."

'Lofty' England recalls the 'light alloy car' being built. "It was made at about the same time as the 'Brontosaurus' thing which the Old Man got built – in fact there were various cars being built all round the factory. We must have been thought a bit slow in the Engineering Department, so the Old Man decided he would push everyone along – he was a wonderful character. So he got this damned Brontosaurus thing done by Fred Gardner. Then he also got Bert Hartshorn, one of the superintendents, doing one with a tubular backbone chassis with two C-type chassis back to back." This prob-

ably explains the fate of XKC 002 and XKC 003.

"I said to Sir William one day, 'I don't know, Sir William, everywhere I go somebody's building a new sports car. Do you think I should start?'

"'Not a bad idea, England,' he said," recalls 'Lofty' with much amusement.

The 'light alloy car' was fitted with engine number E1002-8, a Salisbury axle, rack and pinion steering and disc brakes. It was first run at Lindley on 13 May 1953 and weighed 19¼cwt with 20 gallons of fuel on board. Test driver Norman Dewis was not happy with the steering behaviour, and found that the axle was tramping, the clutch spinning and the battery was insecure. On 17 May a hub shaft broke. The car does not appear to have been run again until September, when Dewis carried out brake tests and lapped Lindley at 128mph. A few days later he tested what he described as 'the Lyons special'. This was the Brontosaurus, which was found to have 15 per cent less drag that a C-type. But on 28 September the Brontosaurus tests were curtailed, 'owing to the O-F wing valance shaking loose and falling off the car'.

In October the 'light alloy car' was being prepared for some high-speed runs at Jabbeke alongside an experimental Mark III XK120. The idea was, 'Lofty' explains, "to get some publicity before the Motor Show". A Perspex bubble had been fitted over the driver but on the day the 'light alloy car' seemed to suffer fuel starvation and would not pull cleanly at the top end. It still achieved a mean speed of 178.383mph but was rather overshadowed by the XK120, which clocked the quite remarkable speed of 172mph. "In comparison with the XK," Dewis recalls, "the

'light alloy car' was struggling at the beginning of the measured mile."

Sayer noted in his report that this car, 'was noticeably steadier, and the bow wave was all concentrated in a narrow strip about a foot from the ground. Stability was reported by the driver to be satisfactory'. The water temperature was found to be only 30°C and thus the air intake at the front could have been made smaller. However, Sayer was reasonably pleased with the behaviour of the 'light alloy car' at speed. He concluded: 'As this car is obviously sufficiently stable at higher speeds than those attained it appears feasible to reach them by the following modifications: a) A properly designed blanking frame on the radiator intake. b)

**A modified
XK120 also ran at
Jabbeke and recorded
the quite extraordinary
speed of 172mph. After
the run 'Lofty' England
congratulates Norman
Dewis, and Malcolm
Sayer can be seen over
England's left shoulder.**

A metal fairing to replace the rear half of the bubble, covering the filler cap and fairing properly
into the tail. c) Perhaps an attempt to obtain
rammed air to the carburettors by a positive scoop
in place of the louvres; and particularly if fuel starvation is found not to have occurred after all, this
is worth investigating.'

The head fairing mentioned by Sayer was to be
incorporated in the D-type design and would
become one of its most distinctive features. In
November 1953 the latest all-synchromesh gearbox was fitted, and SU carburettors replaced the
Webers. On 16 November Dewis was at Silverstone and reported, 'Tests carried out to try the
steering qualities of the car. The car will go
through a corner very well, indeed steering feels
quite good. The rear end bounces and really gets
wheelspin with full power on. This will have to be
investigated'. At Silverstone at the end of the
month Tony Rolt tried the car and Dewis noted,
'56lb weight fitted to the front of car. Rolt thought
that this improved the steering. My own opinion is
that it is B-awful. Rear wheel bounce is very
prominent and allows terrific wheelspin, but for
all this the car is very stable and controllable'.

"In October 1953," recalls Tom Jones, who was
a section leader in the Vehicle Design Office, "Bill
Heynes asked me to go down to the Motor Show
and that's where we set up our first meeting to do
the D-types for '54. We built them between October and the following June. In principle the car was
all aluminium, or MG7 as we called the magnesium alloy. It was 10 per cent manganese for the
frame and some of the panels too. The main structure of the panels was MG7 and MG4. Our experience from the war of making wing spans and so
on for the Short Sterling was relevant to the 'D',
and obviously we used aircraft practice for the fuel
tanks as well.

"I had a lot to do with the engine under Claude
Baily. I did the wide-angle head for it, under his
and Bill Heynes' direction. I did the chassis work,
under Bill Heynes, and all the suspension, cooling
system, exhaust system, and so on. Mr Heynes
used to come and see me every evening after his
day's work to check how far I'd got that day.

71

Sometimes he'd change things or he'd say, 'Oh yes, I like that idea'. We'd discuss things and he might say, 'Perhaps it would be better if we did it this way'. I'd do another scheme the next day and he'd have another look. Alongside planning the car on paper, we used to do mock-ups. When we were doing the sub-frames, we'd place tubes around the components to see how it would all go together – and I had to co-ordinate all this lot!"

On 16 December Claude Baily issued a Project Specification to Messrs Robinson, Sayer, Caine, Hayward, Knight, Emerson and Jones, with copies to Mr Whittaker, Mr Heynes, Mr Silver, Mr Short-ley and Mr Tattersall. It confirmed that individual responsibilities for project number ZX526/02 would be as follows: build of six prototype XK120C Le Mans cars (Bill Robinson); develop-ing body structure (Malcolm Sayer); developing chassis items, front suspension, rear suspension and fixed axle, brake layout, brake and pedal operation, accelerator layout, steering layout, exhaust system, radiator and pipes, petrol tank and fuel system, spares requirements (Tom Jones); electrical equipment (Bert Tattersall); oil cooler or tank (Bill Hayward).

Thus began the construction of what would, in time, become known as the D-type. During December Dewis tested a new type of Dunlop tyre on the 'light alloy car'. This would have been the Stabilia, which 'Lofty' claims was the first steel-braced, radial construction, low-profile tyre used in racing. On 28 December Hayward sent Baily, Jones and Sayer a memo headed, 'Series 4 XK.120.C Competition Car. The following are items which will require work done on them by members of the Engine and Chassis Sections of the Drawing Office before the design can be com-pleted'. Under 'Engine' the items included dry sump, special bell housing, special flywheel, inlet manifold (due to angle) 8½ degrees, exhaust mani-fold, engine mounting brackets, and oil cooler mounting and pipework. Under 'Chassis' it listed front suspension, front torsion bar anchorage, rear suspension, rear axle (narrow track), brakes, brake pedal and mechanism, clutch and pedal, throttle linkage and pedal, steering layout, exhaust pipes and silencers, radiator and pipework, petrol tanks and pipework, propeller shaft, rear engine mounting ('might mean a new gearbox exten-sion'), oil tank and installation (dry sump), battery mounting and brackets, and the handbrake.

On 4 January 1954 Stirling Moss tried the 'light alloy car' at Silverstone, and from Dewis's testing notes we discover: 'Chief complaints from Moss. Too much understeer. Pedal layout poor. Steering wheel position needs modifying. Total number of laps by Moss 17. Best lap 1-58. Continuation of Dunlop tyre tests by myself. Skated off circuit at Chapel Curve to the point of nearly overturning. B- fools of Dunlops swopped tyres without informing me!!!'

On 8 February 1954 this lengthy specification document was issued:

XK.120C LE MANS CARS
GENERAL SURVEY

ENGINE.
The engine follows closely on those used last year, and at the present time the variations from last year which are known and accepted as definite are given below.

The engines are being built to this specification as quickly as possible, but there are still a number of possible variations which may be brought in if they prove worthwhile on further bench and road tests which are still being undertaken. The present agreed specification is, therefore, as follows:

Cylinder Head Standard XK type with inlet valve increased to 1⅞", exhaust valve to 1⅝", not using salt cooled valves.
Pistons Brico 9:1, latest design.
Camshaft Wide angle timing, ⅜" lift.
Carburettors Three Weber 45 DCO with a special packing piece under the intake pipe to allow for the engine to be set over at 8½ degrees.
Cylinder Block The only change here is to the front bearing cap to permit the dry sump lubrication to be fitted, and slightly modified drilling on the rear face to suit the smaller clutch housing.
Lubrication Dry sump lubrication has been designed and the details are already in hand, and this is going to be one of the most difficult items to get clear and tested in time.
Clutch Housing A new casting required which will carry the starter motor on top of the gearbox. The detail for this is almost completed. A limited num-ber of sand castings will be made from temporary patterns.
Oil Radiator and Oil Tank A preliminary design is being arranged on the mock-up by Mr. Weaver, but the position of the radiator in the circulation is yet to be decided.
Clutch Triple plate clutch with a special flywheel ring to suit new starter position is being arranged for. Decision on the actual strength of the springs and counter-weights is still to be discussed with Borg & Beck, and a check must be made to be cer-tain that there is an adequate supply of these clutches available for our requirements.
Engine Mountings It is proposed to have the main engine mountings at the front and at the rear of the gearbox, with lower rated mountings adjacent to the rear face of the cylinder block.
Alternative Engine Specification 35/40 head with 9:1 compression ratio and normal valves or, alter-natively, with 10:1 compression ratio and salt cooled valves. This head can also incorporate ⁷⁄₁₆" lift camshafts, and the engine and various parts have been dispatched to Mr. Weslake, who is carry-ing out tests on these parts, and a decision on whether to use this head will have to be held over until his preliminary tests are clear. It is thought probable, however, that not more than one of these heads would be used unless a very material gain in power is found.

ABOVE **The 'light alloy car' was used extensively for testing and is seen here at Silverstone with Norman Dewis at the wheel. At one stage there were thoughts of running a team of these cars in 1953 in place of the C-types.**

Petrol Injection Both Messrs. S.U. and Messrs. Lucas have devised systems of petrol injection to suit this engine. In the case of the S.U. system this has already been bench tested and shown good results, and is now being tested on the road. Here again it will be necessary to show an improvement in performance or economy with the same performance if this unit, which is relatively untried so far as we are concerned, is to be employed. In the case of Messrs. Lucas, parts are still being made up to equip an engine, and bench tests have not yet been carried out. It seems doubtful whether sufficient bench and road testing will have been done in time for this to be employed in the actual race even if results are promising.

BODY AND CHASSIS.

Unit construction as employed for the light alloy car has been used. The structure is now well ahead. Outside skins have been put in hand with Abbey Panels and it is anticipated that the first body and frame can be completed before the end of this month.

The question of welding is being handled by Mr. Rippon in conjunction with Mr. Hanson of Dunlop, and the Argon Arc principle is to be employed.

The remaining outstanding items on design are connected with the rear structure carrying the tank and spare wheel, and the method of attachment of this rear end of the body onto the main frame. The method of support to the front out-riggers, which have to be used for jacking the car, is also not cleared, and the mounting for the radiator and the air duct and air box for the Weber carburettors is still outstanding.

Mr. Weaver is making a mock-up, which must be discussed with Mr. Emerson before acceptance. It is important that a long sealing joint of the type we had last year is avoided if possible.

Headlamp positions for the two main lamps have been established. It is now suggested that two further lamps should be arranged for inboard. Provision must be made for using glass fronts to the lamps instead of perspex as was used last year, owing to the loss of light through the scratched perspex window. Mr. Tattersall is to get in touch with Lucas immediately on this matter and obtain their assurance that they can get the necessary glasses through in time.

Bonnet louvres and general ventilation for the engine compartment are still to be decided.

Ventilation for the rear brakes is also undecided. It is suggested that ducts opening out on the top of the body could be designed.

Petrol Tanks Both petrol tanks will be of plastic construction by I.C.I. and it is important that the shape of these tanks is passed forward to I.C.I. at the earliest possible moment. A second smaller tank holding 3 to 4 gallons is suggested behind the rear diaphragm in the tail.

Front Suspension This is basically the same as used on the light alloy car and most of the parts are available. It will, however, be necessary to have new top arms with a greater spread, and the bottom arms will probably have to be re-splined on a slight angle to enable the torsion bar to be moved away from the driver's ankle. This is being set up by Mr. Weaver in the shop. It is important that information is released on this item to Alford & Alder as quickly as possible.

Rear Suspension This is basically the same as the suspension used at the latter end of the 1953 racing season, that is, with torque arms top and bottom at either end of the axle and a Panhard link for control. Details of the various parts are all nearing completion and it is not likely that any serious hold up will occur.

Hubs New hubs are likely to be required as it is proposed to abandon the wire wheel and change to a knock-on Aluminium wheel which is at present undergoing test. Rig tests are sufficiently advanced to indicate that this wheel has a considerably better life than the wire wheel or the small steel wheel, and there is no reason to think that there will be any change from this decision.

Brakes The brakes remain basically as used last year except that the Dunlop master cylinder will probably be used instead of the Girling master cylinder, but if this is to be so it is important that two or more of these cylinders are fitted to our own cars immediately for tests to be carried out to make sure that the pedal loss trouble is completely eliminated. Failing samples for test at an early date, it must be accepted that we shall move forward again with the Girling master cylinder, and units must be obtained from Messrs. Girling so that we are certain that these are available. The brake pedals are of the pendant type and hinged well forward, and will give a higher ratio than has previously been employed. It is hoped by this method to establish a better and more consistent pedal feel. The hand brake position and method of operation is still to be established.

Clutch Operation At the moment this is being laid out for hydraulic operation, and although this is the most convenient and suitable, in some ways direct rod operation would be preferable as it permits quicker adjustment for wear if necessary. Failing this, however, provision for quick adjustment must be incorporated in the push rod.

LEFT **As construction of the first D-type began, the pressure was on for the small team which had responsibility for the production cars as well as the competition side. The use of 1953 C-type rear suspension must have eased the workload a little.**

<u>Gearbox</u> At the moment the only completed scheme we have is the standard gearbox as used last year with the close ratios. We are, however, working on a 4-speed box which would give an additional usable gear ratio and possibly enable us to employ a direct 3rd and an overdrive top in the box, still leaving the two lower ratios basically the same. An alternative is being considered in the use of the Borg Warner overdrive, and contact is being made with Mr. Whittingham to see what is the maximum torque which they can cater for under these very exacting conditions.

<u>Prop. Shaft</u> Hardy Spicer type. Investigation is being carried out on a shaft which has been modified by Metalastik to give a certain amount of flexibility, but so far no practical tests have been made.

We obviously learn a great deal from this fascinating document about the thinking behind the D-type. The man who had to translate much of it into reality, with the colleagues who worked under him, was Phil Weaver, another with, significantly, a background in the aircraft industry.

"The tank on the dry sump owes its inception to the Bristol aero engine – all those radial aero engines were dry sump. This is how things evolved at Jaguar. When we were building the C-types and D-types, a lot was done by word of mouth which didn't come from the Drawing Office. For example, when it was known that a dry sump engine was being considered, the engine was simply produced, just like that. But the ancilliary equipment, like the tank and the pipes, was left to me. The principle of that tank was based on the Hercules aero engine dry sump, which was first installed in a Beaufighter, a fully aerobatic aircraft. Having had a lot of experience with dry sump in the Beaufighter, I knew the thing would work in the car.

The tank had to be triangular-shaped to fit in that part of the frame, but the inside, the baffling and everything, was exactly the same as in a Beaufighter tank.

"We were left to do it on our own. Had the job been left to the Drawing Office, they would have had to make all the details and fit them together. The tank had to be the right shape to fit, with the filler cap so that you could get at it in a race. I could say to old Len Hayden, 'Look Len, we'll do this, this and that', and it would just get done by blokes who knew exactly what was required. And it worked straight away. I knew the principle was right – we never had any trouble with the dry-sump system."

This was one major area in which the D-type differed from the 'light alloy car'. The use of a dry-sump set-up allowed the engine to be lowered, and so the frontal area of the body could be reduced. It was also stated at the time that the dry sump arrangement was employed to cure oil surge problems that had resulted from the efficiency of the disc brakes. Additionally Heynes stated that dry sump, "permitted higher engine speeds and greater bearing loads, and at the same time overcame the disadvantage of having a lot of loose oil floating about inside the engine".

When Sayer had completed his body design, he issued a long list of co-ordinates to Harry Rogers and colleagues, who then made up wooden formers on which Abbey Panels made the skin panels. Tony Loades, the present Managing Director of Abbey Panels, remembers a slight disagreement with Jaguar at the time: "A letter framed on my father's wall in the Isle of Man says, 'Mr Loades, £152 for this D-type Jaguar body does seem a little steep'!"

On 24 March new team driver Ken Wharton sampled the 'light alloy car' and two days later it was prepared for tyre testing at Reims with Dewis and Peter Whitehead. The chassis at this point was stamped XKC 201, probably for customs reasons. 'Lofty' England takes up the story.

"There was no test day at Le Mans in those days – I tried to get them to organise this. Until 1955 there was also no way of getting out of the circuit once you were inside for official practice, so you were stuck if you had trouble within five minutes of practice starting. But Joe Wright of Dunlop said he might be able to fix some test facilities for us through Monsieur Lallemont, Dunlop's racing manager in France, and the next thing we knew was that we had Reims for a week. A good friend of Bill Heynes, Joe Wright was responsible for pushing disc brakes through and for producing the new tyres we used at Le Mans in '54 – he was an excellent fellow.

"So we took a C-type with aluminium disc wheels, the D-type prototype [the 'light alloy car'] and some special tyres to try because we'd used too many tyres in '53. These were the first low-profile tyres and they were also steel-belted. We arrived on Sunday morning and asked Lallemont if everything was all right. 'Well,' he said, 'it's arranged but it's up to you to finalise things'. I thought we'd probably end up going back home after lunch...

"Anyway, next morning we went to see Monsieur Roche, an explosive little man who ran the Automobile Club de Champagne. He was delighted to see us and I asked if he could arrange things. 'Ooh, no,' he said, 'we'll have to go and see the Prefect of Police. The only problem is we have a new man, he's only been here a week, he's never been to a motor race, he came from Bordeaux'. So we went to see him and Roche explained how simple it was. He simply had to divert the traffic 25kms round – this was the main road from Paris – half a day, each day, for a week – morning one day, afternoon the next. The fellow looked aghast but Roche assured him it had all been done before and it was no problem. So he rang bells, sent for the Captain of the Gendarmerie, and gave him his instructions.

"Believe it or not, at 2.00pm that day the straw bales were up, the traffic was diverted, we'd got commissaires, members of the club, third party insurance – the lot. We started off the first afternoon with a few spectators, the next morning we had quite a lot of spectators, and the next it was all in the newspaper and television cameras had come from Paris! And these were our secret tyre tests!

"At the end of the week I asked how much all this had cost us – forty quid! It was incredible – but that's how things seemed to happen with Jaguar."

These tests were carried out to assess the suitability and durability of Dunlop's new Stabilia tyres for Le Mans. Dunlop's report indicates that Whitehead's times on the new tyres were similar to those for the previous year's tyres, but Dewis was 1-2sec a lap quicker on the new ones. As for wear, the Stabilia tyres outlasted the '53 type by a factor of nearly three to one. In general six tyres per car were changed in the '53 race, so it was anticipated that only two per car would be changed in '54.

Bill Heynes elaborated on the importance of these tyre developments: "The design of suitable racing tyres looked at one time as if it might be the limiting factor on the performance of the car, and a tremendous amount of credit is due to the Dunlop Company for the way in which they handled the problem and stuck to it until they had produced a tyre capable of running at speeds up to 200mph with a reasonable tread pattern and life, and quite a low power absorption.

"The latter point is one of great importance as far as the standing wave is concerned. It is well known that with a normal touring car tyre the standing wave, that is a wave deflection in the tyre shell, starts to take place at speeds around 100mph. Whilst the wave is small, no damage to the casing occurs, but as the wave grows a very considerable amount of heat is engendered in the tyre, and eventually tyre failure will take place by the tread stripping from its casing.

"At the inception of the standing wave in the tyre, the amount of power absorption rises very steeply. This is just the point where any saving in power is most important, and quite apart from the fact that the elimination of the standing wave in the tyre up to speeds over 200mph has made the tyre safe for the driver, it has also assisted in the attainment of these higher speeds by the elimination of power loss."

Bill Cassidy, Senior Foreman of the Experimental Machine Shop, remembers the construction of the D-types and some of the difficulties that had to be overcome in welding aluminium: "This was the inception of argon arc welding. I went over to Marston Radiators at Wolverhampton to get the first ones welded and a firm in Nuneaton called Freeman & Proctor had perfected this welding technique. We had them do all ours: we shipped their plant into the department to do all the welding for six cars.

"While we were building the cars for Le Mans the body fitters came along with the top skins. There was the centre section, with rivets every ¾in. Where the top met the bottom half and the door line, they had to be argon arc welded. While this 'U' section was open there were drawings in there and so many blokes around you couldn't see the car. They were round the back, under the car and putting the pedals in – you were stepping on men to get in the car. These body blokes came with the top skin with the two cockpits cut out, laid it on, put a couple of pins in, marked it, and took it away and cut some more off. They returned to try the top skin again and the pressure was on as time was running out.

"I remember Heynes coming into the shop while I was standing watching these men. They put the pins in and marked it. 'Bloody hell,' he said, 'they're not taking it off again: rivet it up'. So of course they got the rivets out and got the old guns going, riveting this thing up. When that was all done they carried this body in to be welded up. Meanwhile one of my blokes kept saying he'd lost his hammer. Anyway, the body was welded up and somebody happened to look down the hole for the steering column – and there was the ball end of a hammer!

"I didn't dare say 'don't weld' because Heynes and Claude Baily were in the shop. During the next couple of days I asked my boss and another fellow to help me split the weld and get the hammer out, but they were too scared to touch it. Finally, it got to the Friday and the suspension was on and the engine in. So I got a fitter and apprentice to come back at 8.00pm. We chiselled the weld off and drilled out the rivets. We got 18 drawings out, plus the hammer, a pair of Gilbow snips, a protractor, and so on!

"We couldn't weld it up again, and Heynes came in on the Saturday morning – you couldn't see anything except where the weld had been cut. 'Morning, Bill,' he said. 'How's car going? Has it been welded?' 'Well,' I replied, 'it had been, but it's going to be re-welded'. 'Oh! Did you find the hammer?' 'Yes, and 18 drawings, a pair of snips, a...'"

By 13 April the first new car was ready. It did not have a name initially and Dewis entitled his notebook on the car 'XKC – not registered – No. 1 car'. It was also termed the XK120C Series IV and the chassis number was XKC 401. Later the factory adopted the designation 'XK120D' or simply XKD, and today we call them D-types! It was

not an auspicious beginning when Norman tried the car that day: 'First test Lindley. Engine misfiring & banging. Returned to works. 15 laps on banking'. He returned the next day: 'More running obtained at Lindley, engine still misfires. Impressions obtained – 2nd gear jumps out on drive, steering very dicy, darts and kicks, seating arrangement very uncomfortable, elbow fouls rear panel when changing gear. Pedal layout very poor, feet are cramped. Clutch pedal very heavy to operate. Brake pedal very hard to feel'.

A day later Dewis was out again after some work in the shop: 'Distributor changed. Camber adjusted. Testing at Lindley, banked circuit. 103 laps completed at an average speed of 132mph. Fastest lap 138mph. No improvement on steering.

ABOVE **The design of the nose followed on from the 'light alloy car', but the frontal area of the D-type was significantly reduced by the use of dry-sump lubrication, which reduced the height of the engine.** BELOW **Sayer's idea of a head fairing to replace the rear half of the bubble used for the Jabbeke runs saw reality with the D-type.**

ABOVE **Norman Dewis chauffeured the Minister of Transport, A.T. Lennox-Boyd, in the unpainted D-type prototype to mark the official opening of MIRA.**

A few days later Dewis ran the car on Stabilia tyres and checked the feel with a full tank of fuel: 'Rear of car feels more stable, but steering still darts and weaves'. A gearbox seizure terminated that day's work but he noted, 'Rocker box breathers set alongside gearbox – these must be rearranged. Adjustable air ventilator required for cockpit ventilation'. He was, however, becoming more confident with the car and recorded a lap at 142mph.

While the gearbox was being refitted on 24 April, a pair of Mark VII top wishbones was modified and fitted, 'to give more adjustment on camber. Panhard rod removed and replaced by lower roll centre assy, as fitted to 120C 011'. Next day Dewis tried the low-speed circuit: 'Car now handles very well, big improvement made to steering, bags of understeer. Car is very safe handling'. He found it tricky to change from third to second, suspected that the rear dampers were bottoming on full bump and listed several items that he considered needed urgent attention: 'Gear lever to be cranked for ease of operation, adjustable seat, heel indentations in floor, and footrest for bracing driver when braking & cornering, rev. counter to be moved – covered by driver's left hand.' A couple of days later he was clocked at 158mph: 'Fumes very bad in cockpit'.

Test stopped owing to clatter from engine. Screen very good, it would appear that the air is now extracted from the cockpit by the amount of dirt on my face. Engine was running very well, no trace of misfiring. No. 1 ex tappet changed, worn through. Items for investigation: steering, 2nd gear, brakes – long pedal first app., vibration at 4200 to 5000rpm very bad on over-run, oil leaks from engine, plates supporting throttle linkage, breather on brake fluid container, centre of bonnet lifting, pedal layout, adjustable seat?, exhaust pipes flexes – already fatigued, crosswind affects steering, excessive end float both hubs, how can quantity of oil be checked in tank? Running temp at Lindley: ambient – 56 degrees F; water – 55 degrees C; oil 80 degrees C'.

Meanwhile Jack Emerson, who had built up a 2½ litre engine with Webers for assessment, was building seven dry-sump engines in preparation for Le Mans. Number 2001 had been 'installed in No. 1 XK.120CC. This is a test engine and will not be used for actual Le Mans racing, except at Silverstone' – so there we have yet another name for the D-type! As for the second engine, 2002, 'This engine has been used on the bench for testing the

RIGHT **Now painted, the prototype has had its supplementary driving lamp moved from its rather awkward position in the car's mouth. As the new car had yet to be called the D-type, the chassis numbers of the first examples were prefixed 'XKC'. Being a 1954 car, this one was designated XKC 401.**

oil tank. It is due to be released tonight to Mr. Weaver to go in car No. 2 XK.120CC'. The third was for the third car, the fourth was awaiting testing, the fifth was two-thirds built, the sixth had just been started and the seventh would be built if sufficient parts were available: 'It is imperative that we have a dry-sump bench engine which can be retained'.

Returning to the testing with the first car, on 3 May Dewis noted in his log: 'Testing at Silverstone. Conditions: wet morning, drying out a little late afternoon. Drove myself in morning. Drivers present after lunch – Rolt, Hamilton, Walker, Whitehead. Total no. of laps – 70. 16 galls of fuel used in 42 laps = 8 miles per gal app. Complaint from other drivers about the brakes – rears locking. Lap times not very impressive. Very bad water leaks in cockpit'.

Duncan Hamilton recalled his first acquaintance with the car coming one night at Gaydon. "I was a bit dubious. Bill Heynes suggested we put some oil barrels down the runway and said, 'You can drive it through and see what you think of it'. It was all over the place and felt most insecure. We had to change roll bars and all that sort of thing". Hamilton, incidentally, claimed to be the first person ever to spin a D-type!

On 3 May a document was prepared describing the new car, still entitled the 'XK120C Le Mans Car – 1954'. This description was probably put together by someone in engineering to form the basis of Rankin's press release, which was sent out two days later. It contains no surprises but the first sentence is rather interesting: 'On the new cars the frame and body are of unit construction and follow an entirely new patented principle, in which large box section members are formed integral with the stressed skin for the main centre section of the body'. It is curious that Jaguar was claiming to have patented this method of construction.

The sole D-type was then prepared for testing at Le Mans. The 3.54:1 axle was removed and replaced by one of 2.98:1. The cockpit was sealed to eliminate the water leaks, an air box was fitted to the carburettors and a longer gear lever used. With the Le Mans circuit using public roads, it was not normally possible to test there, but an opportunity presented itself when the road was closed for a few hours as a section on a French rally. Jaguar obtained permission to do a few laps and so the 'light alloy car' (fitted with SU petrol injection) and the new XK120D were taken out to France, where Dewis found himself deputising. 'Lofty' England explained how Jaguar came to make the most of this rare opportunity.

"A good friend of ours, Eric Adlington, who was Deputy Managing Director of Temple Press, had been a chum of the Old Man's since his motorcycling days. He'd been a reporter with *Motorcycling* magazine when Sir William was making sidecars. He had a good relationship with the Le Mans people and somehow found out about this rally, and we arranged to run between the classes.

"We took Tony Rolt and Peter Walker to drive, and they came over with Adlington and were met at Le Havre by Gerard Levecque. He was the Service Manager of Delecroix, our agents, and was our official refueller at every race at Le Mans, because you need a Frenchman to deal with the 'plombeurs' – this avoids any drama if you make a slight boo-boo! The only problem was that poor old Walker found his passport was several months out of date when he arrived at Le Havre. They wouldn't let him through, and as it was some sort of bank holiday he had to get the British Consul out of bed or something. He eventually arrived at Le Mans by taxi!"

Dewis therefore found himself in the driving seat. From his logbooks we learn how the 'light alloy car' performed: 'Driver N. Dewis. Total laps

LEFT **Sayer's D-type body design was an intoxicating blend of functional efficiency and pure beauty. Following a private Le Mans test, the addition of a fin on the prototype only strengthened the popular analogy that the D-type was an 'aircraft on wheels'.**

RIGHT **These self-explanatory diagrams, prepared by Bill Heynes to illustrate his talks, show the progress made between 1950-56 and the relative statistics of XK120, C-type and D-type models.**

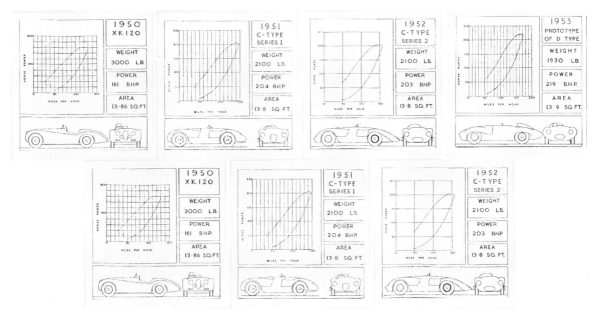

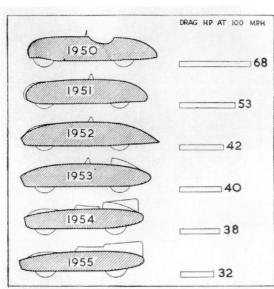

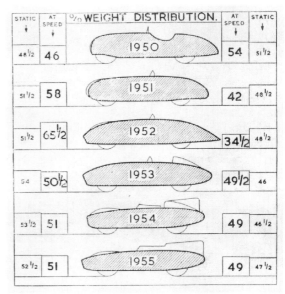

12? Strong crosswind during morning, impossible to hold the car on the straight above 5400. Brakes not fully bedded. Best lap Rolt 4-42. 5600 obtained down straight'. As for the new car: 'Driver Rolt. Clutch trouble on 3rd lap. Total laps 6? Best lap 4-22.5, new lap record (unofficial)'. Phil Weaver had had to change the clutch slave cylinder rapidly and Rolt, conveniently not noticing that the officials were trying to re-open the roads, covered one lap more than allowed. It was worth it for this final lap was 4.9sec faster than the record held by Ascari's 4½ litre Ferrari This not only gave the Jaguar team a boost of confidence, but also shook the opposition.

"My first impression in 1954," says Tony Rolt, "was that the car was astonishingly fast in a straight line – 170mph was no problem. It was quiet and comfortable, which must have been largely due to good aerodynamics."

In the haste to finish the new car the registration OVK 501 was painted on by mistake, which caused a moment's anxiety at customs on the way back. On its return to the factory, this was corrected to OVC 501.

A couple of days later Dewis was back at Lindley testing the second car's 'steering and cockpit ventilator with M. Sayer'. Next day he was checking fuel consumption but the test was brought to a halt when the gear lever broke. For the rest of May intensive testing continued at Lindley and Gaydon, although there was a brief break in the serious work late in the month when Dewis gave the Rt Hon A.T. Lennox-Boyd, the Minister of Transport, a run in the new car to mark the formal opening of MIRA's new facilities at Lindley. On 25 May Moss was involved in an evening test and two days later Rolt was filmed for television on the banked circuit at Lindley. With Le Mans rapidly approaching, two more cars were completed.

The original car would not be raced, but the subsequent three D-types were just about to face the ultimate challenge.

CHAPTER SEVEN

D-TYPE IN DETAIL

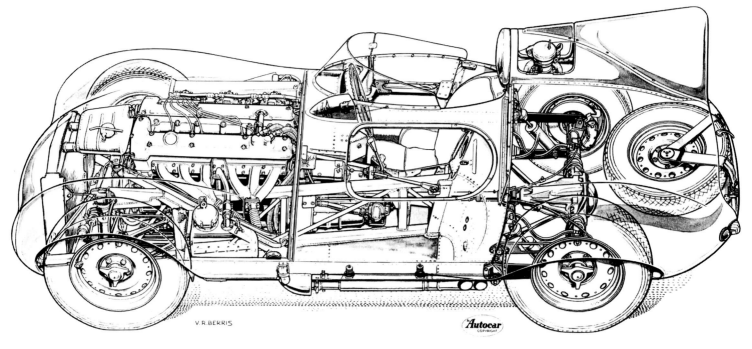

V.R.BERRIS
Autocar
COPYRIGHT

The design of the D-type shows the profound influence of Malcolm Sayer's aircraft background on the existing automotive technology at Jaguar. Aerodynamic influences are clear in the body shape, but other branches of aircraft technology were applied throughout the car. The most obvious example is the construction.

The revolutionary design of the structure, first evaluated on the 'light alloy' car, ran far ahead of contemporary sports car practice, and indeed ahead of any established terminology – what Jaguar elected to call the chassis would now be termed the front subframe. This was stamped with the chassis number and carried the basic identity of the car. The core of the car, the monocoque, was described simply as the centre section of the bodywork, and carried the body number. The monocoque's construction was akin to the way in which an aero engine is supported in a wing nacelle or a fuselage – indeed Bill Heynes used these aircraft terms in various lectures. In other words, it was a stressed skin structure with a system of bulkheads and strong points to which a triangulated tubular frame was attached, supporting the engine and mechanical components with even distribution of loads and great economy in weight.

The central tub was constructed mainly in 16swg aluminium and had an elliptical cross-section. This not only gave it great torsional rigidity, but also reduced the cross-sectional area – and hence drag. From end to end of the tub ran sill, or

pontoon, structures from floor level to the seam at the vertical centre point. The front bulkhead was formed by a sturdy compartmentalised box member some 6in deep and 11½in tall at its highest point, bridging the full width of the body. This lay directly on top of the pontoons and was connected to them by extensive patches of aircraft-style close riveting.

The lower half of the front bulkhead was formed by closing panels on the end of the pontoons which extended up the front face of the bulkhead to the top skin and enclosed the driver's and passenger's foot boxes. The token passenger foot box extended only 5in in front of the bulkhead, giving the passenger a very cramped seating position. These limited dimensions were dictated by the route of the exhaust manifold, which ran very close to the bulkhead and could cause a passenger's shoes to melt! The driver's foot box was considerably larger, giving reasonable room for any size of driver. It incorporated a heavy 12swg bracket for mounting the brake master cylinder and detachable brackets for clutch and brake pedals on the inside.

The rear bulkhead had the same elegance of design and fulfilled several functions. It closed the end of the elliptical structure of the monocoque, giving it great strength. It provided a firewall between driver and fuel tank, and the scalloped backs to the driver's and passenger's seats. Across the rear bulkhead ran two parallel 12swg channels with multiple riveting to the pontoons, seat backs

ABOVE **With aluminium welding techniques still in their infancy, maybe the Jaguar designers did not feel able fully to trust the integrity of the monocoque and chose to supplement it with the 'A' section frame. The 'light alloy car' continued to be tested exhaustively and was to prove conclusively the strength of the monocoque.**

and lower skin. These provided the essential strong points on which to hang the rear suspension, its subframe and practically the entire weight of the tail, complete with the fuel tank. This was a considerable load to attach to the back of a lightweight aluminium structure and explains the size and strength of these rear cross members.

The driver's cockpit was surrounded by a single wrap-around Perspex screen, and on the passenger's side a quick-release metal tonneau was fitted so that the car just qualified under the 1954/55 rules as a two-seater, rather than an offset single-seater. The monocoque had a single 18swg driver's door, initially 18.5in long, but the door length was extended on later cars to 19.7in (and a passenger door was fitted) to conform with Appendix C Le Mans regulations for 1956. These revised regulations necessitated other changes, as 'Lofty' England explains:

"The 1956 Le Mans regs required a full-width screen 25cm high with a windscreen wiper, and a hood which had to be furled in the car but only erected for scrutineering. In the previous year the regs didn't call for a door on the passenger side and we didn't have one, but at scrutineering it was claimed that a passenger entering from the driver's side had to be able to move across to the other side – but on the D-type the central strip joining the front and rear of the body prevented this. We refused to cut out this strip or to make a door on the left-hand side of the car, either of which would have reduced the structural strength. Finally we were told we must cut out the panel shape of a door and then bolt it back – it was a comic solution but we did it!"

The solid tonneau cover for the passenger side also had to be discarded to meet the new regulations. The central mirror fairing was superseded by a two-legged brace which supported the mirror and the new windscreen. On the passenger side the screen had a rolled top edge to which a Vybak tonneau could be attached, reducing the drag caused by swirl behind the screen. On the driver's side the screen remained straight to deflect air over the driver's head.

The removable tail section was secured to the back of the monocoque by just four ⅜ UNF bolts underneath and 12 mushroom-headed 2BA screws through the top skin. It took the form of an 18swg aluminium skin with a complex 16swg fuel tank cell spot-welded inside. This contained a Marston Aviation Division rubber bag tank initially with a capacity of 36.5 gallons (166 litres) for long-distance racing, but the size was reduced to 28.6 gallons (130 litres) to comply with the 1956 Le Mans regulations.

The bonnet was also constructed with an 18swg aluminium skin and 16swg internals. It carried internal ducting to supply cold air to the carburettors and, on the later long-nose cars, to the brakes. A striking feature of the production and long-nose cars was an asymmetric power bulge running down the centre of the bonnet, echoing the angle at which the engine was tilted. The long-nose styling, which appeared on the works cars from 1955, added 7½in to the overall length, improved aerodynamic penetration and arguably added to the elegance of the car. At the same time as the changes to the nose, the head-rest and fin were also revised so that the two became a single skin, thus saving some weight and cleaning up the shape aerodynamically.

The front subframe started life in the first six prototype cars as an all-welded frame constructed in aluminium alloy tubing and actually welded into the riveted structure of the centre tub section. This method was difficult to repair and unsuitable even for small-scale production, so for production cars and later long-nose works cars the subframe was made of rectangular section Reynolds 531 high-tensile steel tubing, with the joints bronze-welded. Perhaps lacking complete faith in their very strong monocoque, the D-type designers extended the front subframe right through the tub to the rear bulkhead.

The first five prototypes had chassis numbers retaining the XKC prefix and ran from 401 to 405, but an XKD prefix was introduced for the sixth car, XKD 406, and used for all subsequent cars.

In some areas the D-type chassis frame echoed the familiar C-type. For example, the front 'picture frame' was similar, as were the lower longitudinal members tapering together from front to rear. The rear subframe of the D-type was, in effect, the rear structure of the C-type chassis – torsion bar tube, folded upright sections and so on – bracketed and

RIGHT **Is it a chassis or a front subframe? The question would lead to bitter argument in later years. The ends of the vee-shaped part of the subframe attach to the front bulkhead of the monocoque body, with the tapering part continuing rearwards to supplement the tub.**

ABOVE **XKD 406 was raced by the factory in late 1954 and then loaned to Briggs Cunningham in the US, winning the 1955 Sebring 12 Hours with Mike Hawthorn and Phil Walters at the wheel. After its spell in the US, the car returned to the UK and was sold to Duncan Hamilton.** LEFT **On the five 1954 cars to be completed, the frame was constructed in aluminium alloy and attached to the tub, which proved to be highly impractical for a racing car that inevitably suffers accident damage from time to time.**

bolted to the monocoque in an equivalent position. However, the D-type was a more elegant and economical design. For example, the loads on the engine mountings were carried through to the suspension on a shared part of the structure, rather than being bolted to separate parts of a heavy chassis frame. This was typical of the advance in thinking embodied in the D-type.

The D-type's engine was based on the production 3½-litre block, but by now it was rather stronger. The pattern equipment had been altered

at the back of the inclined block to provide attachment to the vertical gearbox and bellhousing at an angle of 8½ degrees. Why was the engine canted over in this way? Many writers have repeated the statement that the inclined engine gave a lower bonnet line, but it only takes a moment with, say, a shoe box in the privacy of one's home to prove that rotating that shape 8½ degrees increases its overall height. Chris Keith-Lucas of Lynx Motors International believes that the answer lies in the carburettors and the inlet tract: "The designer was

ABOVE **The fin fitted to the D-types improved high-speed directional stability.** RIGHT **The 1955 and '56 cars – this is XKD 606 – had separate steel tubular frames bolted to the body structure. Many other detail differences from the earlier car can be seen.** BELOW **The chassis number stamped on the shock absorber top mounting indicates that this is one of the 1954 alloy frame cars. The fifth of the intended series of six '54 cars was not completed.**

simply after space for a sufficiently long inlet tract, including the inlet manifold, Weber 45DCO3 carburettors, bellmouths and cold air box. Even so, these run perilously close to the front wheels on full lock."

The cylinder head was a revised version of the casting first seen in the last C-types. It had larger diameter inlet ports and 1⅞in diameter inlet valves. As on the C-type, the camshaft gave ⅜in of lift but the design was now more efficient. The resulting improvement to the breathing gave a claimed

maximum of 245bhp at 5750rpm. Internally the engine employed 9:1 Brico pistons and conventional, but specially prepared, connecting rods, crankshaft and bearing caps. The front bearing cap supported a bronze skew gear which was driven by the distributor drive gear on the front of the crankshaft. The skew gear rotated on a small cross shaft which drove the scavenge and pressure oil pumps from either end.

The most important innovation on the engine side was the dry-sump lubrication system. The sump itself comprised two castings in magnesium or aluminium. The upper section was similar to the upper part of the C-type sump, but had a pad either side at the front to mount the scavenge and pressure pumps. The lower section was a fairly simple cover with fins to assist cooling, and inside an 'I' section baffle ran end to end quite close to the underside of the crankshaft. Through drillings in this baffle, oil thrown by the crank was drawn up by the scavenge pump and delivered via flexible braided hose to the remote oil tank. The capacity of the system was 28 pints.

By its remoteness from the engine, the tank provided an abundant supply of oil at the right temperature, without surge or air bubbles, for a full 24-hour race. As explained in the previous chapter (see page 74), this technology was largely borrowed from aircraft practice. The oil tank, located to the left of the engine, tapered to a point at its base to suit the curvature of the side of the body. Within the tank a stack of five baffles of decreasing size sloped in alternate directions. Oil was delivered to the tank through a fishtail orifice which spread it evenly across the top baffle, from where it flowed down over each baffle in turn, all the baffles being ribbed and drilled to encourage the oil to release its entrained air, and then to keep the oil and air separate.

The pressure pump drew from the base of the tank through a simple wire strainer. This then delivered the oil through a full-pressure aluminium Marston oil cooler straight to the cylinder block oil gallery. Surprisingly, no oil filter was designed into the system. Later an in-line Tecalemit filter became standard equipment on the XKSS and works D-types.

The cooling system showed the same level of innovation as the rest of the car. The water pump was of conventional design, although with a more efficient impeller and a cast aluminium casing for lightness. Its pulley was made in two halves, machined with a fine thread between the two. By rotating one half in relation to the other, the width of the vee for the drive belt could be increased or reduced, thus tensioning the belt by altering the pulley's effective diameter. This was not actually a Jaguar innovation as the same design was used on the Rudge Multi motorcycle of the 1920s, but the principle was later used in another technological milestone – the DAF automatic transmission.

After leaving the cylinder block and head, coolant passed via the inlet manifold to an aluminium header tank situated just in front of the engine, and positioned as high as possible to facilitate replenishment and de-aeration. Internal baffles ensured that an equal flow of coolant left the tank through two outlets feeding into either side of the Marston aircraft-style alloy radiator. This system distributed coolant equally across the full width of the core, preventing the normal situation where coolant tends to take the easy route down

one side from the delivery point at the corner of the radiator. At the bottom of the radiator a single central pick-up point was employed for the same reason. This cooling efficiency was essential because the D-type, like the C-type before it and in accordance with normal racing practice, had no cooling fan.

In line with more recent racing practice but a brave move for 1954, the engine was not fitted with a flywheel as such, but just an 8¾in diameter adaptor plate for direct mounting of the Borg & Beck triple-plate clutch. The clutch supported a small diameter, lightweight starter ring, and a specially designed Lucas starter motor engaged with this from behind, through a special mounting in the bellhousing. This low-inertia clutch and flywheel assembly greatly assisted acceleration while still providing a clutch strong enough to withstand 24 hours of racing. It is a great compliment to the six-cylinder design that the engine was nevertheless capable of ticking over smoothly at 700-800rpm, and did not have to be modified for the XKSS road-going version.

The D-type's gearbox evolved partially from the earlier Jaguar design, using virtually the same cast iron main casing and aluminium cover as the C-type, but internally it was completely redesigned and strengthened, retaining little of its predecessor. It had fairly close ratios, as follows: first 2.144:1, second 1.645:1, third 1.280:1 and direct fourth. Very significantly, this was Jaguar's first all-synchromesh gearbox, preceding the introduction of such a gearbox for the road cars by some 10 years. Other interesting points included a splined layshaft with removable gears to facilitate ratio changes and repair, and an externally fitted interlock system preventing the gear lever being moved in or out of second gear without the clutch being fully disengaged. Reportedly this was introduced following a fatal accident in which a driver had changed from fourth to first when attempting a clutchless downshift, causing loss of control after locking the rear wheels. In fact, according to

ABOVE **The engine in the D-type was mounted at an angle of 8½ degrees, supposedly to reduce overall height, but this cannot be true. A more likely reason was to provide extra space for the ram pipes feeding the three twin-choke Weber carburettors.**

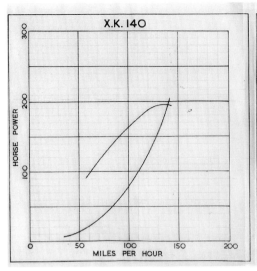

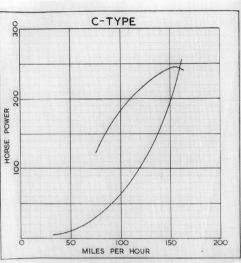

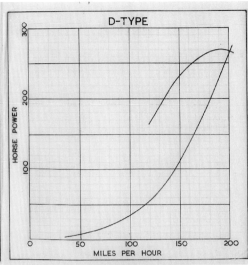

ABOVE **Comparison of D-type power output and speed capability compared with its predecessor and its production contemporary.** RIGHT **The dry-sump oil tank with its complex arrangement of internal baffles was copied directly from aircraft practice. It is also a good example of the practical design methods used at Jaguar, in that it was first built in the shop and then drawn up.** FAR RIGHT **The dry-sump tank, seen here fitted to XKD 601, had to be triangular in cross-section to fit between the front subframe and the sill.**

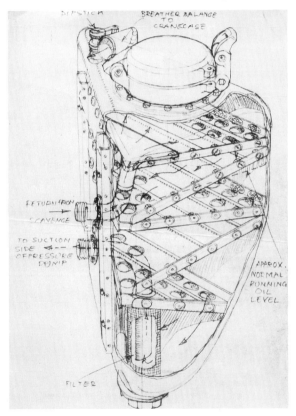

'Lofty' England this inter-lock system was intended to prevent the lever jumping out of second gear, a problem Norman Dewis repeatedly mentioned in his testing logs.

In the aluminium extension to the rear of the gearbox ran a small reciprocating oil pump feeding through the hollow main shaft direct to the gears. This extension also provided the mounting for the Plessey hydraulic pump which powered the brakes and was driven by its own worm gears, similar to the speedometer drive gears but considerably beefier.

The front suspension was again clearly evolved from the C-type design but refined to improve weight, geometry and strength. The first D-type built (XKC 401) gives an indication of the design progression in having a two-piece top wishbone, *à la* C-type or early XK. All subsequent cars were fitted with a forged blade which in turn became the prototype for the E-type wishbone. With the same uncompromised approach found in the entire car, uprights, lower wishbones and torsion bars were purpose-made for the D-type instead of being sourced from any existing model.

The rear suspension retained the transverse torsion bar and lower trailing arm of the C-type, but employed parallel upper trailing arms to improve axle location. Designed before the advent of the Rose joint, the arms were in spring steel to accommodate any twist caused when the car was in roll. The sturdy live axle was built for the car by Salisbury, using a Powr-Lok limited slip differential, thicker and stronger halfshafts, and peg drive centre-lock hubs to cope with the extra power – albeit at the expense of unsprung weight. Late works cars were fitted with ZF limited slip diffs which were so strong that Ron Flockhart was able to complete a race even though a half-shaft had sheared! To achieve the equal transverse location that the C-type lacked, the earlier Panhard rod was

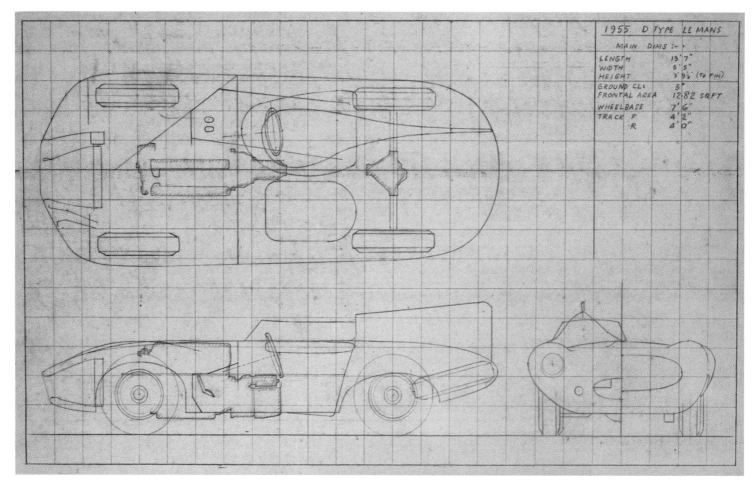

1955 D TYPE LE MANS

MAIN DIMS :—

LENGTH	13' 7"
WIDTH	5' 5"
HEIGHT	3' 3½" (TO FIN)
GROUND CL:	5"
FRONTAL AREA	12·82 SQFT
WHEELBASE	7' 6"
TRACK F	4' 2"
R	4' 0"

discarded in favour of a tubular A-frame which converged from either side of the rear subframe to a rotating joint under the centre of the back axle. This not only located the axle but also defined the low roll centre of the car.

Aviation practice again surfaced in the choice of wheels and brakes, supplied by Dunlop. First seen on the 1953 lightweight C-types, the advanced and powerful aircraft-derived multi-pot brakes were further developed for the D-type, with stronger pump drive and bigger diameter pistons. Twenty Mintex pads (twelve front, eight rear) in excess of 1in thick gave sufficient life to last a full 24-hour race. The light alloy wheel cylinders were spaced by an air gap from the pads and discs to avoid heat transfer boiling the brake fluid.

A compact master-cum-servo cylinder actuated only the front brakes, at the same time proportioning the available pressure from the constantly circulating fluid supplied by the gearbox-driven Plessey pump to front and rear brakes. In search of long-distance racing reliability, these systems were kept separate, so the driver would still be left with the non-servo front brakes in the event of the powered system failing. A larger, specially baffled fluid reservoir sat beside the master cylinder, again providing ample capacity while helping to cool and de-aerate the circulating brake fluid. Reversing the car caused the Plessey pump to run backwards: to avoid creating havoc in the braking department, a

ABOVE **In many ways the ultimate D-types were the single-seater 1955 long-nose cars, since new regulations for 1956 decreed full-width screens which increased frontal area. This drawing of a '55 car is by Malcolm Sayer.** LEFT **Following the great success of the revolutionary disc brakes on the later C-types, they were, of course, retained on the D-types. The rear calipers, seen here on XKD 527, had four pads per side.** LEFT BELOW **Another innovation on the D-type was 16in Dunlop alloy wheels. The extra length of the long-nose bonnet fitted on later cars can also be seen.**

TOP **The D-type cockpit was very different from that of the C-type. As this shot of XKD 406 shows, it was a much tighter fit.** ABOVE **The interior of the long-nose cars differed in detail. There were fewer instruments to save a few ounces and to reduce distraction.**

by-pass valve was included in the system to allow the fluid to circulate backwards in a closed loop, without affecting the rest of the system. This resulted in only the front brakes operating, so speedy reversing was not advisable...

Although they retained the 5in rim of the period, the distinctive 16in Dunlop pressed alloy disc wheels were a considerable improvement over the spoked wheels of the C-type, being lighter (15lb instead of 18lb), stronger and easier to change. The introduction of a peg drive system saved much fiddling in the pits as well as transmit-

ting the increased torque more happily than the old 52mm splines.

The D-type's interior was a big advance in ergonomic terms, although the word was barely known at the time. All controls fell to hand or foot naturally. Switches and instruments were clear and kept to a minimum – no fuel gauge was thought necessary because this was the concern of the pit crew. Instrumentation in production cars consisted of a combined water temperature/oil pressure gauge, an ammeter, a 180mph speedometer and an 8000rpm chronometric tachometer with tell-tale, red-lined at 5750rpm. In late works cars the speedometer was also deleted, removing another source of distraction.

Seat backs and squabs were quickly detachable to allow adaptation to different drivers, while both the steering wheel and pedal heights were adjustable, making more leg room available than was possible in the C-type. Fuse boxes and the RB310 voltage regulator were exposed on the left-hand side of the dash, facilitating electrical fault-finding and adding to the functional appearance of the cockpit. The interior finish was body colour or matt black, the only concession to trim a panel of Hardura glued to the gearbox cover. Dzus fasteners (another aircraft spin-off) made their first appearance as quick-release retainers for the transmission tunnel, and indeed for the Perspex covers over the special Lucas Le Mans headlamps.

CHAPTER EIGHT

WORKS D-TYPES IN COMPETITION

The secrecy surrounding the D-types was rather less intense than it had been with the C-types, and as early as February 1954 *Autosport* stated that at Le Mans 'Jaguars will have three brand new machines to defend their title'. But the opposition was not standing still either. It was rumoured that Mercedes-Benz was developing a 'hush-hush' 450SLR which might appear at Le Mans. The press also revealed that Aurelio Lampredi had developed a 5-litre Ferrari with 360bhp, a higher power output than any GP Ferrari, and that Cunningham had replaced the Chrysler V8 engine in the CR6, its latest Le Mans car, with a 4.9-litre Ferrari V12.

Two months later *Autosport* Editor Gregor Grant previewed the prospects for Le Mans and made one telling point of almost more significance than his description of the combatants: 'I cannot think of any other annual sporting event in Europe that attracts so many American press representatives'. Jaguar's chief opposition was considered to be the new Lancias, probably with 4-litre engines, the Ferraris, which had not won since 1949, and perhaps also the Cunninghams. It was thought the new Jaguars would be based on the 'light alloy car', and *Autosport* stated that during testing at Reims (see page 75), 'some remarkably fast laps had been achieved. Jaguar's team of drivers is probably the most talented collection of young men in modern racing'. Aston Martin would field both its 2.9-litre DB3S cars and its new 4½-litre V12 Lagondas, a policy that seemed excessively ambitious.

The unnamed new competition Jaguar was officially revealed to the press at Browns Lane in May. In its story in the 14 May issue, *Autosport* remarked that Tony Rolt had been at Le Mans the previous week for an 'unofficial try-out', lapping

ABOVE **Unlike the C-type, the D-type did not win Le Mans at its first attempt, but it came close. In 1954 Hamilton/Rolt finished second in XKC 402, just 105sec behind the winning Ferrari of Gonzalez/Trintignant.**

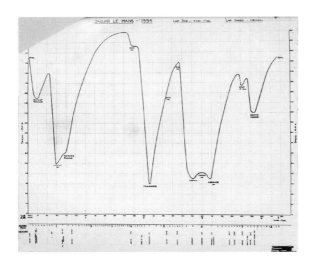

RIGHT **It was not possible to test cars at Le Mans because much of the circuit used public roads, so the engineers had to simulate a lap for engine evaluation.**

ABOVE **Professionalism increases. In 1954 Jaguar flew the D-types from Eastleigh to Cherbourg by Silver City Airways, although the onward journey on French roads provided some excitement.**

at 115mph and exceeding 170mph on the straight, speeds that would give the opposition something to think about! Indeed they did, for the next week it was reported that not only had Mercedes-Benz withdrawn its three-car team but also Lancia was to do the same because it was unable to prepare its large-engined cars in time. To rattle the competition a little more, *Autosport* also published a photo of Rolt at speed in the 'light alloy car' at Le Mans and an under-bonnet view showing its SU fuel injection. This was all good gamesmanship on Jaguar's behalf...

The drama of Jaguar's 1954 Le Mans campaign started before the team even reached the circuit, although this incident fortunately did not involve the three D-types. The factory had prepared one C-type (XKC 047) for Ecurie Francorchamps, and Frank Rainbow and Les Bottrill drove this car at the tail of a convoy through France led by 'Lofty'

England. 'Lofty', incidentally, had officially resumed the team manager's role, which he had never actually relinquished, after Mort Morris-Goodall left Jaguar to go to Austin-Healey.

"I was leading in a Mark VII," explains 'Lofty', "with the three D-types and the C-type behind me. In those days all the roads had high cambers and all the rises were covered in oil from lorries – it was like driving on ice. All Frank did was pull out to pass a car, put his foot down, the wheel spun and he lost it – he hit a double concrete telegraph pole. We reached a village called Montebourg just up the road and I saw that they were missing. So I stopped the whole lot and went back. Half the car was on one side of the road, half on the other, and these two blokes were walking around."

"We were all going along nicely at 55ish," recalls Rainbow. "I overtook a little family Renault and all of a sudden the car just flipped round. I got the wind on the back of my neck instead of my front. The car spun several times. The next minute, I'm picking myself up out of the road, looking around, and there's Les sitting up rubbing his elbow. Then I saw a wheel spinning round in the road and thought it must have come off the car, but it was the spare that had shot out of the back. Then I heard the engine still running. The car was across a ditch, so I went over and switched it off. I realised I'd only got one shoe on – my left shoe was still trapped underneath the clutch pedal!"

"Of course it's Whit Monday, usual thing, everything shut," continues 'Lofty'. "Anyhow I got the local garage man to bring his truck and drive the remains of this thing into his garage. We carried on to Le Mans seven up in the Mark VII – and it could still spin its wheels in top gear!" The team arrived at Le Mans without further mishap and 'Lofty' called the factory. Although it was closed, he managed to contact someone in the export department and asked him to arrange for Alan Currie to telephone.

"The call came through. 'Alan, you will find a C-type in the Experimental Department, minus engine. Get one of the seven-ton trucks, put the bloody car on the back of it and get on the Dunkirk ferry tonight. You will be met by the Belgian lorry which will bring the car to Le Mans. Thank you very much.' The car should have arrived before midday on the Thursday. Come midday, no lorry. Eventually it arrived at 6.00pm, having run a big end or something on the way.

"Then Ted Brookes and Les Bottrill overnight rebuilt this bloody car – everything on it was different because this was an old C-type and the crashed car was a new one. I'd got a dispensation from the organisers after diplomatic dealings: 4.00pm on the Friday afternoon was the deadline for special scrutineering, and I got there with five minutes to spare!" The works-prepared engine and various other parts had been removed from the yellow Belgian car, XKC 047, and fitted to the green XKC 012, which was given a yellow stripe, all that time allowed.

NEAR MISS AT 1954 LE MANS

Of the new D-types, number 12 (XKC 403, registered OKV 2) was for Stirling Moss and Peter Walker, number 14 (XKC 402, registered OKV 1) was for Tony Rolt and Duncan Hamilton, and number 15 (XKC 404, registered OKV 3) was for Peter Whitehead and Ken Wharton. Apart from Wharton, who had replaced Ian Stewart following the Scot's decision to take up a business career after pressure from his father, the driver line-up was unchanged from the previous year.

Practice was relatively uneventful for the works Jaguars apart from the fact that the scavenge pump bush seized on the shaft on number 12. Walker set the best time in practice, but the Ferraris were not far adrift and lapping at over 118mph. Ferrari fielded three 4.9-litre cars led by Gonzalez and Trintignant. Regular Ferrari drivers Hawthorn and Farina were both unavailable (Farina was injured and Hawthorn had to rush back to England because his father had been fatally injured in a car accident), so other drivers were drafted in.

Rolt continued to be generally impressed with the new Jaguar: "In horse-handling terms, the D-type had a very light mouth; it had to be driven with your finger tips, not with armfuls of effort. It was a stable car which understeered slightly, and at Le Mans you could balance this with the throttle – you could steer with the rear wheels.

"But the car was exhausting to drive. There was bad wind-buffeting on our necks and right shoulders – we used to wear towels to deal with this – but the 1955 wrap-around screen solved that. I couldn't get comfortable really, because the cockpit was cramped – I think it was shaped round Norman Dewis, or Stirling! But you could see over that screen without the rain getting through. There was never any tendency for the car to lift at high speed, but without the fin it wasn't directionally stable – you had continually to make minor corrections. The fin worked beautifully.

"The engine was terribly good, very reliable, very flexible, but you couldn't over-rev it – 5800-6000rpm was about the limit. But the cars were driven from Coventry to Le Mans, on the road, and pottering about the paddock was no problem. The gearboxes, of course, were pretty awful, with weak synchromesh and that high first gear which made getting away from the Le Mans pits, uphill, a nightmare. We had clutch trouble at first as a result. So the engines just had to be flexible!"

'Lofty' England disagrees with Rolt's comments: "The gearboxes did *not* have weak synchromesh and there was no trouble starting away from the pits. We never had clutch trouble."

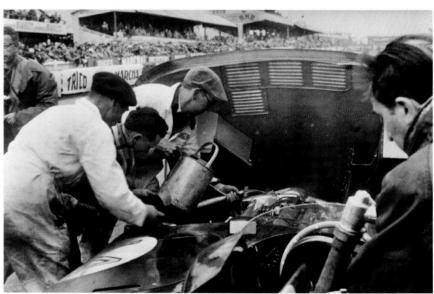

Despite rain being forecast, the crowd was said to be the largest yet and the atmosphere, as ever at Le Mans, was wonderful. The famous Le Mans village began to be created that year and there was a strong contingent from Britain. No fewer than 64 aircraft landed at the adjoining airfield.

For once Moss did not make the best Le Mans start and the order as the field went under the Dunlop bridge was Manzon (Ferrari), Cunningham (Cunningham), Marzotto (Ferrari) and Gonzalez (Ferrari). The first lap at Le Mans always seems to last an eternity and as all necks were craned to spot the first cars, the shout of "Ferrari" went up. Three of the red machines led – Gonzalez, Marzotto and Manzon – and then came the Jaguars of Moss, Rolt and Wharton, the latter with evidence on his car's nearside front wing of the jockeying for position at the start.

As it began to rain Moss moved up to third behind Marzotto and Gonzalez, with Rolt fifth but closing. Then Moss took Gonzalez for second

TOP **For the first hour or two at Le Mans in 1954 Stirling Moss, who was still leading the Jaguar team, diced with the Ferrari works entries, in particular Froilan Gonzalez in the big 4.9-litre 375 'Plus'.** ABOVE **During the third hour Moss handed XKC 403 over to Peter Walker, who was soon back in the pits with misfiring that seriously delayed Jaguar's fastest car.**

place, the pace remaining very rapid despite the weather, with speeds reaching 180mph, and Rolt overhauled Manzon for fourth place. After 1hr 40min of racing and with the rain now torrential, Moss briefly took the lead on lap 22, but Gonzalez soon regained it.

After 31 laps Rolt pitted for fuel and Hamilton took over. He did two laps and came in again with misfiring problems. The plugs were changed and, after 3min 18sec, he was off again. Meanwhile Moss had come in on lap 32 and handed over to Walker, who was also troubled now by misfiring. After six laps he came in again for the fuel filter to be removed and rejoined after a stop of 2min 58sec. He did just one more lap and returned for the plugs to be changed and for further investigation, which took nearly 15min. Walker then did a lap of 33min because he had to stop on the circuit, almost certainly to remove the filter again. During all this drama Hamilton came in again after only

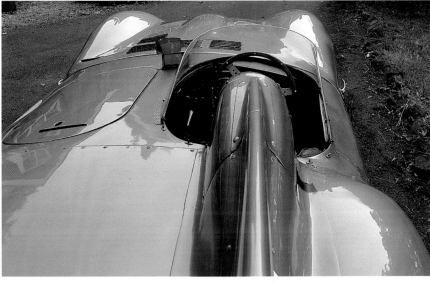

11 laps for *his* fuel filter to be removed, a stop which took a precious 8min 47sec.

These Jaguar delays meant that the three Ferraris had a commanding lead after four hours, with the steady Whitehead/Wharton combination fourth. This improved to third by the sixth hour and then became second when the Marzotto/Maglioli Ferrari retired with gearbox trouble. A few minutes before midnight Moss had an alarming moment when his brakes failed approaching the Mulsanne Corner at 160mph – luckily he was able to take to the escape road and slow down with the gears. Hamilton remembers this as a harrowing experience for Moss, and a terrifying one for the two gendarmes enjoying a quiet smoke in the middle of the road! Moss got back to the pits but nothing could be done and the car was out.

With ten hours gone the Rolt/Hamilton car had worked its way back up to third position, one place ahead of the Whitehead/Wharton car, which was also now experiencing fuel starvation problems – it finally retired at 3.25am after three long stops. Meanwhile the Ecurie Francorchamps C-type was running like clockwork in seventh place. Then at 6.35am, with the rain still pouring down, the Rosier/Manzon Ferrari succumbed to gearbox trouble, so the order was now Ferrari, Jaguar, Cunningham, Jaguar, Cunningham. The surviving Ferrari had a two-lap lead, but the Jaguar, with Hamilton at the wheel, was lapping faster.

Conditions were changing all the time, with the Gonzalez/Trintignant Ferrari, able to use its immense power, benefiting as the course dried, the Rolt/Hamilton Jaguar regaining ground when the heavens opened. At 8.23am another heavy shower fell and Trintignant very nearly lost the big Ferrari going under the Dunlop Bridge. By hard driving and faster pit stops the Jaguar was closing in, but then came near disaster. A Talbot got in Rolt's way,

ABOVE & RIGHT **The fourth D-type to be completed, OKV 3 (XKC 404), was driven at Le Mans by Peter Whitehead and Ken Wharton, who retired in the early hours of Sunday morning. The third of the OKV trio, this car has been owned for many years by Martin Morris, who has used it for long-distance continental touring and campaigned it in historic racing probably more regularly than any other D-type.**

and in avoiding this mobile chicane he hit the sandbank at Arnage. As a result he had to pit and spent over 2min knocking out the damage. It would prove crucial.

Gonzalez and Hamilton were matching their times pretty evenly around midday on the Sunday, but when Trintignant took over Rolt was able to gain valuable seconds every lap. Then more high drama. At 2.22pm the Ferrari came in for a final routine fuel stop and driver change – and would not re-start. A horde of mechanics worked on the car and soft plugs had to be fitted to one bank before the engine would fire, one of the mechanics holding the throttle open as Gonzalez got in. There were three infringements of the rules during this pit-stop: more than the permitted number of people worked on the car, it was worked on with the engine running, and the starter was not used to re-start before leaving the pits.

"The Ferrari should have been disqualified," says 'Lofty' England. "They had four people working on the car and the regulations said the car could only be re-started by the driver sitting in the driver's seat with no outside assistance. They had two mechanics working under the bonnet. They got the engine going while another mechanic was sitting in the driver's seat, before changing over with Gonzalez. I thought we ought to protest, but the Old Man didn't want to."

The Ferrari lost 6min in the pits. Then at 2.55pm Rolt, unable to see in torrential rain, came in to swop his goggles for a visor. 'Lofty' England immediately sent him on his way: "It was the last hour and everyone's jammed in the pits – you can't move. Rolt comes in and shouts 'visor'. There's no hope of getting him a visor – it would take half an hour. 'Do another lap,' I say, and I ask old Duncan to get dressed up. When Rolt comes back in again, I say 'Out' and I put Duncan in."

Rolt was not amused, but 'Lofty' explained that it was the quickest solution in the circumstances. Then James Tilling, the commentator, said, "The Jaguar team have stopped Monsieur Rolt and replaced him with Duncan Hamilton, who is known to be the outstanding driver in the wet." Rolt was even less amused...

"Gonzalez," Duncan told me in 1994, "reckoned that I, rather than him, was the fastest driver in the world in the wet. I was getting wheelspin in top gear at 170mph though..."

According to Malcolm Sayer's records, Hamilton's average for the last 12 laps was 4sec a lap quicker than Rolt had been managing, but the conditions kept varying. The tension was incredible as Hamilton attacked and Gonzalez responded, both driving in masterly fashion in treacherous weather. At one point Duncan reduced the gap to 1min 32sec, and as the last laps were reeled off the margin fluctuated: –25.4sec, –22.2, –24.9, –24.1, –10.4, +5.3, +6.7, +1.5, +1.5, +.0.04, –19.7.

The final margin was 1min 45sec – just 2½ miles

– after 24 hours of gruelling battle and virtuoso performances from Rolt, Hamilton and, above all, Froilan Gonzalez. The fates had favoured Ferrari on this occasion, but that is motor racing. All were covered in glory and the D-type had acquitted itself brilliantly on this most challenging debut. Top speeds down the Mulsanne Straight were given as 160.1mph for the Italian machine and 172.8mph for Britain's best, so the value of Sayer's aerodynamic work was there for all to see. Meanwhile the Belgian C-type had finished fourth thanks to good speed and complete reliability.

As for the fuel problems which lost Jaguar the race, can 'Lofty' England throw any light on their cause? "We can only assume. In those days you used to have one fuel tank for three pits. These were only cleaned out once a year. After we refuelled the first time, the trouble started. It was our fault, frankly, because we had had this filter problem with Moss in '53. The D-type had the same size filter as the C-type, but it was very inaccessible. After 1954 these small tanks in the pits were replaced by one big tank that supplied everyone."

'Lofty' has a lovely story about an experience on the Monday after the race: "The organisers had

ABOVE **The Hamilton/ Rolt car (XKC 402) suffered the same misfiring problem as Moss/Walker, but removing a blocked fuel filter cured it and the D-type then went perfectly. Hamilton/Rolt began a heroic drive in appalling conditions as they chased the leading Ferrari of Gonzalez/ Trintignant.** LEFT **With an hour to go and the second-placed D-type closing on the leading Ferrari, the rain became torrential and Rolt, unable to see through the goggles he is holding up, was forced to call at the pits for a visor.**

the cars which had finished first, second and third setting off to go to Paris. There was Gonzalez with the Ferrari, while Bob Berry and I took the D-type because Rolt and Hamilton had gone home. Old Gonzalez asked if he could try the D-type. I said, 'Of course, pleasure'. He said, 'It's fantastic, like driving a touring car – this bloody Ferrari just shakes your arse'. He took me for a ride in it. It was pretty difficult to imagine trying to drive for 24 hours with the thing on the shake. Gonzalez really was a he-man! You had to stand up with both feet to put the brakes on!"

On 17 June Malcolm Sayer sent Bill Heynes a report entitled 'Points of Interest at Le Mans'. Discussing Ferrari, he noted that fuel consumption worked out at 7.1mpg and that, 'They were refuelling to the nearest lap, ie, if driven hard they would not have enough fuel for one more lap before refuelling'. The dry weight was approximately 23cwt and the front brakes on the winning car were one-third used at the end of the race.

'They all suffered from front-end lift and instability at maximum speed, especially numbers 3 and 5 (which had a sharper nose above the radiator intake). They did not appear to know that this was the cause of much of the lift, so were not enlightened. They were slower than Jaguar on maximum speed but attained their maximum sooner. They consider the Jaguar has far better cornering abilities. They were braking at the same point as Jaguars before Mulsanne. They were aware of the inefficiency of their body shape, but cannot afford to hire the only wind-tunnel in Italy which is state-owned. At present they consider that they can win on sheer power, despite their body, on most of the European circuits. They were surprised to observe the amount of steering lock we provide, especially on such a short wheel base, and said they had, "far, far less".'

As for the Cunninghams, Sayer reported that their chassis frame had, 'no effective diagonal bracing. It therefore twists so much that the door cannot work if one rear wheel is jacked'. He commented that the bodies were designed by eye, 'with no theoretical basis'. The Ferrari-engined Cunningham broke a rocker arm in practice, he reported, and 'ran on 11 cylinders during the race'.

Under the heading of 'Jaguar Body Items' Sayer advised that, 'The passenger's seat lid needs stiffening to stop the inward panting at high speeds which photographs confirm. This was reported by Dewis during testing but disbelieved due to the force required to do this. The same lid needs a single quick-action fastening for easy access to the tools. The spare bulbs were in cardboard boxes which came to pieces in the wet. A socketted and labelled board is indicated. A windscreen which swept round to meet a differently shaped head-fairing, and which included the driving mirror, would probably decrease both drag and driver discomfort. This would need a wind-tunnel check first.'

A day later Heynes issued his own report on the work to be done to the cars in preparation for Reims, the next race. It was fairly minor stuff: starter removal was to be made easier, the rear torsion bar anchorage was to be improved, and a modification was needed to prevent the axle fouling on the fuel tank. Car number 14, the Rolt/Hamilton car, had been stripped and assessed: 'Preliminary examination shows that the engine is in quite good condition generally'.

Under the heading 'Petrol System', we learn more about the misfiring problems. 'The petrol system has been thoroughly checked and further tests taken with the car jacked up at 35 degrees to give the effect of maximum acceleration in second gear, and the pumps run continuously for three hours. Checks have been taken without a filter, with a clean filter, and with one of the dirty filters that was causing trouble in the race. A full report is being issued by Mr Emerson, but briefly the results are that the flow is satisfactory under these conditions without a filter in position, or with a clean filter fitted; with a dirty filter, however, the flow is definitely below requirements and the longer the car is running the worse the flow conditions become. It is believed that this is due to the folds of the filter, which is impregnated paper, collapsing and gradually reducing the effective area of surface. The dirt which was in the filter, of course, had a restricting influence by itself but was not wholly responsible, as with the clean system we were operating the restriction tended to increase by an easily measurable amount on every gallon pumped. The Prolator filter is being abandoned completely and a consideration is being given to a much larger filter with a more reliable type of filtering medium.'

OTHER RACES IN 1954

William Lyons was very particular about which events Jaguar entered, but Reims on 3/4 July was next on the agenda. Apart from the fact that this

BELOW **At Reims the D-type gained its revenge over the Ferraris. Wharton/Whitehead in OKV 3 inherited the lead after Rolt/Hamilton had been slowed towards the end. Peter Whitehead drove in the debut victories of both the 'C' and the 'D'.**

fast circuit was expected to suit the D-types, Jaguar felt obliged to support the event after the co-operation it had received with tyre testing earlier in the year. The three Le Mans cars were entered with the same driver pairings, and the 12-hour race started at midnight in a light drizzle. 'Thousands of gallons of champagne had been consumed by spectators,' reported *Autosport*, 'who, curiously enough, came in droves to watch the start at this ridiculous hour.'

Moss led and set a cracking pace, only Maglioli's 3-litre Ferrari posing any sort of threat in the early stages. Wharton and Rolt were well-placed until the latter was suddenly shunted down the escape road at Thillois, as 'Lofty' recalls with great amusement: "Rolt arrived in the pits yelling blue murder. 'Kill him! Kill him! Bloody fool!' Behra had hit him straight up the back, a fairly hard bump. So I had a quick look at the car, decided what parts were wanted and told Tony to do another lap while we got ourselves ready. While he was gone Behra arrived in his pit, and he clearly wasn't going to do any more motor racing with his Gordini for a long time. So by the time Tony got back, I was able to say, 'You needn't bother, you don't have to kill Behra'."

While the D-type was being repaired (it really only needed new rear lights), the opportunity was taken to refuel the car, but without Rolt realising it. Meanwhile Moss's pace was too much for the Maglioli Ferrari, which retired with a broken gearbox. Wharton was now second, the Walters/Fitch Cunningham third and the Gregory/Biondetti 4½-litre Ferrari fourth. Moss then had to make a 6min stop as one plug had lost its electrode. This dropped Moss to fourth, but soon after Walker took over the car retired with a sheared propshaft weld – something that 'Lofty' thought highly improbable.

The Wharton/Whitehead D-type now led, but Rolt, in third place, was becoming a worried man because he feared he must be due to run out of fuel at any time. When Whitehead pitted for a visor the big Cunningham took the lead, followed by the Rolt/Hamilton car – but the Jaguars had a stop in hand and took over the two leading positions when the American car refuelled. Rolt and Wharton traded lap records but gradually Rolt opened up a one-lap lead. The second works Jaguar was followed by the Belgian C-type, which was nine laps in arrears.

With just 30min to go, Hamilton heard unpleasant sounds from the rear axle and pitted. A damaged subframe member, deranged when Behra had used the D-type to help him slow down, had made a hole in the diff casing and the gears were running without oil. It was patched up to enable the car to hobble to the finish, but Hamilton's ill fortune was Whitehead's good luck. He and Wharton headed home a fine Jaguar 1-2-3, the game Belgians in third place.

Jaguar's next event was to have been the Nürburgring 1000Kms on 29 August. Mercedes-Benz had re-entered GP racing in 1954 and was concentrating its efforts on the single-seaters, but a team of 300SLR sports cars was entered. Once again there were rumours of a larger-engined version, and once again Mercedes then announced its withdrawal. As a result the organisers cancelled the event...

On 13 July Bill Heynes had issued a confidential report detailing preparations for the Nürburgring, and then going on to discuss developments for 1955. The intention had been to take three race cars and a practice car to Germany, so Jaguar was obviously taking the long-awaited showdown with Mercedes seriously. Rather than quote the report in full, I have extracted sections of special interest (the comments under 'Rear Axle' are particularly interesting):

XK.120D

Whilst the performance of the cars in this year's Le Mans race and the race at Rheims was satisfactory, there are still a number of improvements which ought to be embodied in the cars before the 1955 racing season, and it is important that these points are given immediate consideration so that work can go forward without the need for a last minute rush before Le Mans next year. Certain of the items will need very considerable development time, and quite a number will need design time to be spent on them.

Mr Jones is to be generally responsible for following all these jobs up, and it is important, therefore, that he is given facilities for completing any work which is deemed necessary.

The notes are made to include all desirable features, but this does not mean to say that all this work can be started on immediately.

1) Revised 4-speed synchromesh gearbox to incorporate oil feed to the bearings and a more robust drive to the Plessey pump.
2) A progressive bump stop, preferably rubber, as used by Ferrari is to be investigated with an object of keeping the soft suspension at normal loads and increasing rate as deflection takes place.
3) Lightened prop shaft, if possible, incorporating some shock absorbing medium to prevent 'snatch' and so relieve the shock loading on the universal joints and transmission generally.
4) Rear Axle. A real effort must be made to introduce either de Dion or a fully independent rear axle, preferably with inboard brakes.
6) Frame. There is no question the frame can be modified using smaller section tubes in certain places, and the method of putting the frame together must be considerably modified in order to avoid the distortion which has taken place in every frame so far built. The frame front crossmember requires to be built as a complete unit, and the same applies to the frame rear crossmember...One further point which must be given consideration is the quality of the tubes. On the original light alloy frame these tubes were specially bought to drawing and were absolutely free from blemish. The quality of

LEFT **Despite the familiar registration, this is XKD 406 taking part in the 1954 TT at Dundrod. Piloted by Moss/Walker, the car was fitted with a 2½-litre engine to take advantage of the handicapping system, but dropped down the order after a piston failure in the last hour.**

the tubes supplied for the cars we are now racing is distinctly poor.

7) Brakes. Since the inclusion of the scoops on the brakes the performance of this item has been entirely satisfactory, the wear figures being well within the safety margin even for a 24-hour race. The weight of the front brakes, however, are a cause for considerable concern in the handling of the vehicle as the speeds become higher, and it is felt possible that the two-pad brake might be adequate and save quite a bit of unsprung weight, providing a saving in overall weight of the car can be achieved. This matter is to be discussed with Messrs Dunlop at an early date.

8) Brake Operation. While the operation of the brake is satisfactory where normal road surface is encountered there is, it is believed, serious trouble with shake-off which results in the driver being left with rear brakes only until considerable pumping has taken place. I would like consideration given to an all-servo system, that is, with the servo motor working on all four wheels. By this means a short pedal travel could be accomplished, and our experience has shown that the servo part of the brakes is completely reliable...My reasons for taking this view of the brake control are as follows:

a) With the present system, when the pump is lost the drivers are still under the impression that they have no brakes owing to the very high difference in foot pressure between the one condition and the other.

b) The lack of confidence which has been the main reason for adopting this dual system could be dispelled, I believe, by the fitment of a far more efficient handbrake. It does appear that the present handbrake, suitably operated, could be satisfactory for one emergency stop, which is, of course, all it should be asked to do.

c) By this means it ought to be possible to eliminate any talk of variable pedal position, which whilst to the extent we have it at present is not serious, it does affect driver morale and confidence to a very serious extent.

d) There is no doubt that by the adoption of this principle we could simplify the whole of the operating mechanism.

9) Carburation. The present system of three dual Weber carburettors will persist for the immediate future, but urgency must be placed on the development of both the SU and the Lucas system of fuel injection. Tests which have so far been carried out indicate that this system can be far more economical with equal power than the normal carburettor, which is going to prove a very valuable asset in relation to a number of pit stops and the fuel tank capacity. This work is being carried out by Mr Wilkinson under Mr Emerson's jurisdiction, and it is important that it is given the highest priority.

10) Cylinder Head. The 35/40 head development is to be completed and tests are to be carried out on the 3½-litre engine to try and increase the speed range to make it safe to operate these engines at 6000rpm with a ceiling of 6500. This may mean certain modifications at the bottom end as well, but tests must be carried out with this development in mind.

11) Body. In the main the body design and structure seem to be satisfactory. A reduction in weight could be made in the bonnet by rather more intelligent planning of the duct, diaphragm and hinges. The back end of the body could also be considerably improved constructionally, not only with a view to saving weight but with a view to cutting out the amount of welding and riveting employed and the number of pieces.

12) Jacking. The various jacking systems which we have produced – mostly at the last moment – were all completely unsatisfactory. The latest scheme with a turn-over lock looks most promising but needs a little practical development, firstly to make sure that it will operate under all conditions, i.e. with a flat tyre, and secondly, to considerably reduce the weight for ease of handling and yet leave it robust enough to do the job.

The new D-types had not yet been seen in anger in the British Isles, but on 29 August Ken Wharton demonstrated a car at Shelsley Walsh. Despite the car still having a Le Mans axle ratio, his time of 40.70sec showed this was no gentle demonstration. At the Brighton Speed Trials a week later Norman Dewis gave a demonstration *and* competed in a D-type. On a day when a young man called Ivor Bueb – a significant Jaguar name of the future – demolished the record for 500cc racing cars, Dewis was quicker on the demonstration run and unofficially broke the sports car record.

The next event for the D-types was to be the TT, once again at Dundrod and still run on a handicap system that penalised larger-engined cars. For this reason the factory built a 2482cc version of the XK engine. Three cars were entered for the usual drivers with Moss/Walker (XKD 406) and Whitehead/Wharton (XKC 403) in 2½-litre cars, and Rolt/Hamilton (XKC 402) in a regular 3½-litre car. Initially the intention had been to enter a fourth car, a C-type to be driven by Norman Dewis and Bob Berry. The use of a C-type would have been interesting in view of Stirling Moss's memories of the event:

"The 2½-litre engine was actually quite good except that it was a bit heavy. Dundrod was a difficult circuit and a C-type would probably have been better there, but once the D-type existed Jaguar couldn't really put it away just because it didn't suit a particular circuit. That would have been a mistake commercially."

"Traction was the problem at Dundrod," says Tony Rolt, "particularly out of slow corners, where we always lost time with wheelspin. This didn't matter so much at Le Mans, but Dundrod was a different story – the car really bounced from crag to crag. We all used to nag for a proper de Dion rear end."

The entry for the TT was an imposing one with 3.8-litre and 3.3-litre Lancias, 3-litre Ferraris, 2½-litre Astons and a host of smaller-engined cars. The circuit was notoriously dangerous and even the great Gonzalez suffered a nasty accident during practice. It so upset him that he told Hawthorn, who visited him in hospital, that he would never race again, and he rarely did thereafter. The handicapping system required the larger-engined cars like the 3½-litre D-type to do 90 laps, the smaller-engined D-types 88 laps, and so on all the way down to the tiddlers which had to crawl round just 67 laps.

The rather odd outcome was that one of these tiddlers, a 745cc DB Panhard, actually won! The 3½-litre D-type retired with loss of oil pressure at about one-third distance, and Moss, who had been going well in his 2½-litre car, had a piston fail an hour before the finish. He waited for the flag and crawled across the line to take fourth in class. The Whitehead/Wharton car fared best of the Jaguars, finishing fifth on handicap and second in class despite being delayed by a puncture.

Peter Walker took OKV 3 to Prescott in mid-September but the twisty course and wet conditions did not suit the D-type – the car was never designed as an all-rounder.

Work on the 2½-litre engine had not been abandoned and on 24 September Heynes issued a list of instructions to Messrs Emerson and Wilkinson. This included testing an aluminium block, checking the crankshaft for torsional vibration up to

7500rpm, and testing SU and Lucas fuel injection with both the XK120C and 35/40 heads. As an aside, the work list also included the instruction to build up a sample production 2-litre four-cylinder engine, 'and develop to a suitable state for use in saloon car'. This was the old XK100 engine rearing its head again.

In late October Jaguar bravely took OKV 3 to the Guild of Motoring Writers Test Day at Goodwood. Maxwell Boyd did three laps and wrote about the experience for *Autosport*. He raved about the positive steering, the gearchange and the power but, above all, 'the D-type's servo-assisted disc brakes have a stopping power with the lightest of pedal pressures that simply defies description or comparison'. However, he did comment that, 'a racing driver might well have a case in pleading for some sort of independent rear suspension...'

INTO 1955

There were to be four driver changes for 1955. Stirling Moss was initially expected to continue with Jaguar after agreeing a GP drive with Maserati, but then he accepted an offer to drive F1 cars and sports cars for Mercedes-Benz, so the number one spot in the Jaguar team fell vacant. By happy coincidence Britain's other world-class driver, Mike Hawthorn, decided to leave Ferrari for the fledgling Vanwall F1 team, and on hearing this news 'Lofty' England quickly signed him up.

In November Peter Walker had joined several new drivers for a test session with XKC 404 and XKD 406 at Silverstone, where the conditions started wet and did not fully dry out during the day. By the time the track was described as 'semi-dry', Bob Berry had recorded a best of 1-54.5, with Walker on 1-57, Jimmy Stewart on 1-58 and Ninian Sanderson on 2-01. Later test sessions were held with Ivor Bueb, Geoff Duke and Don Beauman, but Walker did not take kindly to being tested further and was not retained for 1955.

"My view was that you can't go on forever with the same drivers just because you like them," states 'Lofty'. "You're silly to miss out on the youngsters. Jimmy Stewart was easily the smoothest and actually the best driver of the lot, so we signed him. I tried Don Beauman at the request of Mike Hawthorn. He was no better than the others but Mike said he would like to see him in the team [they had been at school together at Ardingly], so we had him. Geoff Duke had raced with Aston Martin but didn't get on there, and the other drivers weren't very pleasant to him – motorcycle bloke, you know! I didn't take him on but I reckon he could have become a super driver."

Wharton was dropped because, 'Lofty' says, "he drove for Daimler without asking permission and the Old Man went hopping mad". It has been stated that 'Lofty' approached Ascari (who owned a Mark VII and had a son working at Jaguar) and Villoresi, but he denies it. When 'Lofty' visited Ulster in December to talk to the Ulster Automobile Club, suggesting to them that they drop handicapping for the TT, he also took the opportunity while he was there to acquire Desmond Titterington's signature on a contract.

The final line-up for 1955 was Mike Hawthorn, Tony Rolt, Duncan Hamilton, Jimmy Stewart, Desmond Titterington and Don Beauman.

During 1954 considerable testing had been done with the 'light alloy car' fitted with SU and Lucas fuel injection systems. Back-to-back tests were carried out with carburettors and Lucas PI with the result that fuel consumption was found to be 25 per cent better with injection, 'with a general overall improvement in the performance characteristics'. Work was also done on slide throttles. 'An outstanding feature,' reported Bill Wilkinson, 'is the general smoothness of the engine when fitted with petrol injection, which must reflect in a reduction of the mechanical stresses to which such a high speed engine is subjected.'

As a valued consultant to Jaguar, the occasionally fractious Harry Weslake was also involved, and he had heated correspondence early in 1955 with Lucas's Bernard Scott, causing Heynes to try to pour oil on troubled waters.

On 29 January Weslake wrote to Scott: 'I understand from Mr Heynes of Jaguar Cars that you have carried out extensive work on port injection of fuel and as I am responsible for the design of the Jaguar combustion heads I would like to be kept informed of the work. I have carried out comparative tests between port and head injection, and there is no doubt that a considerable gain in HP can be obtained by the use of direct injection as against port, and as I am developing a Grand Prix engine, which is showing comparable figures to those of foreign competitors by the use of port injection, I know that I can get a considerable gain by the use of direct injection. Will you please help in this matter? It is obvious that the Germans are getting a great advantage from the use of direct injection, and I can see no reason why we should not do the same.'

Scott replied that they were, 'well aware of the valuable work that you have been doing on your contract with Jaguar Cars Limited. Our position at the moment is one of some difficulty. The resources on this particular development are strictly limited and for many good reasons we have placed them all at the disposal of Messrs Jaguar with the object of establishing once and for all the merits of this type of system. Until this end is achieved, you will understand I am sure, that it is impossible for us to work with others or on other projects. We have in fact already refused many other approaches.'

Weslake was not impressed and replied as follows: 'No doubt this was a most difficult letter to write as obviously you had received instructions not to give any information on the results you had obtained when using port injection on the Jaguar engine. The following facts will throw a different light on this subject. Firstly, I am responsible solely to the Chairman and Managing Director, Mr Lyons, who relies on me to keep improving the power output and efficiency of the Jaguar range of engines, and I am quite certain that he would not agree to the with-holding of any information which I might require. Secondly, I own the patents which are incorporated in the Jaguar cylinder heads and therefore have a right and a say in the use of these patents.'

He went on to say that he wanted comparative figures on using port injection against carburettors. 'The Le Mans race is of great importance to the Jaguar Company and the fitting of various accessories and instruments has to be considered with very great care. Take, for instance, the fitting of the petrol filter which was too small and the trouble it caused in last year's Le Mans. The one object that Mr Lyons and myself have got is to win at Le Mans and as I am responsible for getting the necessary HP, I will not stand any interference or with-holding of information which may retard me in achieving the best results. I have not taken up this matter yet with Mr Lyons, but shall do so if I do not receive a satisfactory answer.'

Scott sent Heynes a copy of this letter and said in his accompanying note, 'Frankly I don't understand half his remarks which appear in any event to be contradictory. His whole letter appears to read as if he and Mr Lyons are doing the development work and yourself and Jaguar Engineering don't come into the picture!'

As the saga continued, Weslake wrote to Heynes. 'I received a very cagey letter from Scott of Lucas, and I have replied in no uncertain terms. Our main object is to win Le Mans and this with-holding of information just makes me mad. I am not interested in their inner secrets, and for your information, I used a flat slide as a throttle in WEX carburettors back in 1923. Work is progressing fast on the 2in inlet valve 35/40 head, and it should be with you by mid-week.'

Finally, Heynes wrote to Weslake assuring him that Lucas was not withholding information and that, 'they cannot afford to get involved in other work and supplying other sets of equipment at the same time as these experiments are going on, so don't go off the handle without good cause as, you may jeopardise co-operation with the technical people, which you will, of course, have to have in the course of this development. I was very pleased to hear that the 2in inlet valve head will be with us by mid-week. Everyone here is very keyed up awaiting the results...'

That the factory was taking no chances with blocked filters again is confirmed by the fact that on 4 February Dewis tested the Lucas PI on the 'light alloy car' with, 'very fine powder supplied by the MIRA lab added to petrol tank, also a handful of fine sand. Car run at high speed for 250 miles approx. No trouble experienced'.

The factory was working on a batch of new cars for Le Mans and the fact that 12 engines were to be built up shows how seriously it was taking the preparations. Meanwhile XKD 406 had been shipped to the US where Briggs Cunningham and his drivers, Phil Walters, Bill Spear and Bill Lloyd, had all found the car quicker than the team's Ferrari. As a result Cunningham decided to run a D-type for the 1955 season. XKD 406 was then taken to the Daytona Speed Trials, where it set a new record and was the fastest at 164.136mph over a measured mile, beating several 4.5-litre and 4.9-litre Ferraris.

The Cunningham D-type was then entered in the Sebring 12 Hours for Mike Hawthorn and Phil Walters. Apart from the odd lap the D-type led from a host of Ferraris, Taruffi's being the main challenger for the first few hours. Hill/Shelby then took up the Ferrari challenge to the leading Jaguar, and began closing in when the D-type encountered problems. The last hour was marred by confusion and contemporary reports vary. Some have it that the D-type had oil pump problems, others that its plugs were fouling. An announcement over the public address suggested the Ferrari was leading and indeed it was given the chequered flag. However, half an hour later Hawthorn and Walters were declared provisional winners, and eight days later this was made official – but the confusion prevented Jaguar obtaining maximum publicity from this important victory.

A strong D-type presence was a feature of the *Daily Express* International Trophy meeting in May. Hawthorn (XKC 404), Rolt (XKC 403) and Hamilton (XKD 406) were driving factory cars, while Ecurie Ecosse had two brand new D-types for Stewart (XKD 501) and Titterington (XKD 502). Stewart had the misfortune to aquaplane off in practice and caused considerable damage to his car. In the race Hawthorn was slow away from pole but within a few laps he had taken the lead, with Rolt in second place followed by the Astons

(now fitted with Girling disc brakes) of Parnell and Salvadori. Then Parnell passed Rolt but Hawthorn responded with a new lap record, which Salvadori then equalled as he too passed Rolt. Four laps from the end, however, Hawthorn was showered with water in the cockpit when a top hose blew. The Astons profited from this misfortune and scored a 1-2 with Jaguars finishing 3-4-5-6, the final order being Parnell, Salvadori, Rolt, Hawthorn, Hamilton and Titterington.

The 1955 D-types differed from the '54 cars in several ways. The front framework was now of steel tubing and for reasons of practicality was bolted to the monocoque tub. A separate frame to carry the radiator and oil cooler was also now attached by bolts rather than being integral. The engines were fitted with the wide angle 35/40 cylinder heads with 2in inlet valves and 1¹¹⁄₁₆in exhaust valves. Weber carburettors were retained and power output for the works cars was now around 270bhp.

The first two 1955 cars (XKD 501/2) were the Ecurie Ecosse pair, the third was for Ecurie Belge (XKD 503) and the next five (XKD 504/5/6/7/8) were what have come to be known as 'long-nose' cars. These differed from the others most noticeably in having a 7½in longer bonnet for better air penetration, but there were other changes. The bonnet had two brake cooling ducts, the third lamp was deleted, and the two headlamps were uprated to 100 watts. The exhaust pipes were traditionally routed to the rear of the car instead of terminating below the sill area.

"We realised that we had to have still more power if we were going to be successful for another year," stated Heynes. "To get more power without going to exaggerated timing, which would make a loss at the bottom end, it was necessary to increase the valve size still further. This entailed a redesign of the cylinder head which included altering the inclination of the exhaust valves from 35 to 40 to keep them clear of the larger inlet valves."

ABOVE **At the Daytona Speed Trials Phil Walters in XKD 406 achieved some good publicity when he 'smashed the NASCAR sports car record for the measured mile on the beach, Walters averaging a blistering 164.136mph for the two runs'.**

ABOVE **Sayer designed a longer nose to improve penetration for the new batch of works cars built for the 1955 season. Like all his designs this was given the wool tuft treatment to check the airflow pattern.**

The long-nose shape had been developed by Malcolm Sayer using facilities at the Royal Aircraft Establishment at Farnborough. The only improvements that could be suggested by RAE staff were air-tight riveting and wax-filling of the body joints before an event. They also pointed out that a conventional racing roundel cost 4mph at 160mph, but that they had developed a special low-drag paint for aircraft use.

The first long-nose car was completed in mid-May and Norman Dewis spent three days testing it at Lindley. The second was completed a few days later and he tried that on 18 May, and four days after this he tested both cars at Gaydon with 2.69:1 axles and Dunlop Stabilia tyres. Next day he assessed the merits of ¹⁵⁄₃₂in and ⁷⁄₁₆in lift camshafts (the latter would be used), and a day later he sampled XKC 401 with a ZF diff. The following day he drove the first new Le Mans car at night to check the lights, and the day after he reported, 'still hopeless to get away from standstill or below 2000rpm. More investigation on carbs'.

TRIUMPH AND TRAGEDY AT LE MANS

Six D-types, five of them long-nose cars, were taken to Le Mans. Number 6 (XKD 505) was for Hawthorn and Ivor Bueb, who was drafted in at short notice following Ian Stewart's decison to

retire (see page 90), number 7 (XKD 506) was for the usual pairing of Rolt and Hamilton, and number 8 (XKD 508) was to be driven by Beauman and, since Titterington was unfit, reserve driver Dewis. Number 9 (XKD 507) was the Cunningham-entered car for Spear and Walters. The factory took one spare car (XKD 504), and Bob Berry was the second reserve driver. The sixth D-type, the Belgian entry, was a short-nose car to be driven by Jacques Swaters and Johnny Claes.

The event began tragically when John Lyons, William's son, crashed fatally on the way to Le Mans. The lack of an heir would deeply affect the course of Jaguar's history in years to come.

The entry was a strong one once again. Ferrari entered three new 360bhp 4.4-litre cars, said to be the fastest ever to compete at Le Mans, but their driver line-up was not the strongest. The Aston Martins had a strong driver line-up but lacked ultimate power, while the Maseratis were considered dark horses. And then there was the German threat. Mercedes-Benz chose to pair Fangio and Moss, the Englishman fresh from his remarkable Mille Miglia victory, in its lead car – this was surely the strongest partnership ever seen in motor racing. The 300SLRs were basically two-seater versions of the all-conquering W196 GP cars, and indeed the mechanics referred to the sports car as the W196S. They had the advantage of indepen-

dent suspension and 302bhp, but the disadvantage of drum brakes. To combat this the team had developed a very clever air-brake which was worked by raising a rear-mounted panel into the airstream. It caused some controversy in practice.

"The brakes on the Jag were far better but the Merc was more powerful," Moss told me. "On the straight, if we were behind a Jaguar, we could keep up with it. If we were alongside, we probably weren't quite as fast – but there wasn't much difference. But then we had the air-brake. 'Lofty' England was the first to leap up and down and say, 'You can't allow that'. 'Why not?' he was asked. 'Because if my drivers are following they can't see when this thing goes up'. So the next day we had windows cut in it, which I thought was very funny. But I could see his point.

"We didn't realise at the time that the air-brake was better than ordinary disc brakes because obviously you weren't loading the tyres *and* you were getting downforce – there was a double advantage. We could actually go through corners more quickly with it, and it didn't make the front end go light. You really could feel it pulling you up tremendously effectively. I remember once going onto the straight, putting my foot down and hearing the sound of the engine completely change. I thought I'd broken the engine. I looked in the mirror to see if I could pull over, and I'd forgotten to put the brake down – it was that efficient. It really worked even at, I suppose, 80mph, and obviously at 180mph it was far better."

'Lofty' England, however, flatly denies complaining about the device: "The scrutineers made them put windows in. How could a Mercedes driver see behind in his mirror with this thing sticking up?" Did the air-brakes create any problems for the Jaguar drivers, because it has been stated that they caused turbulence and restricted vision? "I asked Mike Hawthorn about visibility and he said, 'No, I just have a look round the outside'."

Hawthorn and Hamilton became good mates, often had a few glasses of beer together, and talked a great deal about their driving. "We were very frank and honest with each other," Hamilton

TOP **The drivers have just sprinted across the track for the Le Mans start in 1955. Mike Hawthorn is already aboard number 6 as Tony Rolt, a big man, squeezes into number 7.** ABOVE **The three 1955 Le Mans works cars were fitted with long-nose bodywork.**

TOP **Hawthorn and Fangio thrilled the Le Mans crowds with a masterful display of high-speed racing.**
ABOVE **Rolt had some difficulty getting his recalcitrant D-type to start and set off in mid-field, followed here by the Belgian D-type of Jacques Swaters.**

remembered when I interviewed him. "Take the straight at Le Mans, where the long-nose D-type felt very light. Mike asked me how I went through the kink, even though my pace was a bit slower than his. 'Well,' I said, 'quite frankly I'm lifting. I get a hell of a drift on which is taking me right out to the trees on the edge. I don't want to collect one'. He asked how much I was lifting. 'I move my foot back on the throttle about half an inch. It doesn't make the car go slower, but it makes the old heart feel at peace'. I asked what he was doing and he replied, 'The same as you!' He was very fast in a D-type, and amazing at Le Mans that year.

"The long-nose was a very good car and greatly improved on the earlier D-types. You could stick it on a postage stamp at any speed – and at 180mph you could stick it on sideways! You never backed off in a 'D' – just put full throttle on."

Tony Rolt can add further thoughts about the D-type: "It was very good on long, fast corners, like the Dunlop Curve and Indianapolis. But that axle was heavy, and traction was always a problem. Even changing up to top gear on the Mulsanne Straight could provoke wheelspin if it was very wet! That huge petrol tank, when it was full, didn't affect the handling much, but of course we noticed a lack of acceleration at first, until the load began to lighten. In fact the weight helped traction more than it harmed the handling balance. There's no doubt that the car was at its peak – and it will live in my memory forever – in single-seater form in 1955. It was so much faster than anything I'd driven before that at first I was convinced third gear was good enough. Then you stuck it in top and it just went on and on. Marvellous!"

Unlike previous years, Jaguar flew the cars out to Le Mans to avoid problems on the way. Once practice began Hawthorn's car suffered a persistent misfire that could not be cured, as 'Lofty' England explains: "We changed everything, but to no avail. So the night before the race, I said, 'Change the engine'. It was lucky we did because when we took the gearbox off we found a tooth had broken off one of the gears – so we changed the gearbox as well. The only running the car had done before the event was when I drove it about 40kms down the road and back, and up to the circuit.

"Before the race I told Hawthorn to take it steadily for the first few laps. Fangio made a bad start so he was behind Hawthorn, but when Fangio closed up the dice started. It was fabulous – the best Grand Prix I'd seen in a long time..."

Before a record crowd estimated at 400,000, Castellotti in a 4.4-litre Ferrari led away, followed by Hawthorn, Maglioli's Ferrari, Walters' Cunningham, Beauman, Swaters, Levegh's 300SLR and Salvadori in the first of the Astons. Rolt had had trouble starting his D-type and was working his way through the field, as was Fangio, who within a few laps moved from 14th to fourth. The reason Fangio had made a poor start was that the gear lever disappeared up his trouser leg when he jumped into his Mercedes! By the sixth lap the order was Ferrari, Jaguar, Ferrari, Mercedes, Jaguar, Mercedes, Jaguar, Mercedes, Aston Martin, Maserati. Hawthorn was closing on Castellotti and Fangio, soon up to third, was homing in on the Englishman.

For the first 16 laps the red, green and silver cars circulated within seconds of each other, thrilling the crowd. Then both Hawthorn and Fangio overtook Castellotti, who struggled to maintain the pace as it hotted up, the lap record falling repeatedly. On the 28th lap Hawthorn lowered it to 4min 6.6sec, which was to be the fastest of the race. Hawthorn, by his own admission driven on by his anti-German prejudice, was driving flat out with nothing in reserve. Fangio told Hawthorn afterwards that he, too, was on the absolute limit. Side by side much of the time, they sometimes even grinned at each other in enjoyment and mutual admiration.

Then, very abruptly, this absorbing dice was brought to a sudden, sad and sobering conclusion when the worst disaster in motor racing history occurred. According to Malcolm Sayer's post-race report, the accident happened at 6.27pm when Hawthorn's number 6 D-type was completing its 35th lap.

Much has been written, at the time and subsequently, about the awful sequence that lasted for just a few seconds and left 85 people dead and many more injured. Some of the words have been sensationalist for the sake of it, having little regard for all the facts. In studying the causes of the accident, one enters the realms of recollection, theory, statements made in the heat of the moment, misreporting, possibly partisan contemporary comment, argument, counter-argument and supposition. All three of the drivers involved – Mike Hawthorn, Pierre Levegh and Lance Macklin – have been blamed, and one recent account has continued to point the finger at Hawthorn as well as ridiculing many of 'Lofty' England's comments. What actually happened?

Shortly before the accident Hawthorn had lapped Levegh's Mercedes and had a slight lead over Fangio, who was behind Levegh and about to lap him. Leaving White House, the fast corner before the pits straight, Hawthorn overtook Macklin's Austin-Healey before preparing for a planned pit-stop. He moved well over to the right-hand side of the road and began to slow down, with Macklin behind him. To avoid hitting Hawthorn's Jaguar as it slowed, Macklin swung left to a position in the centre of the road, 16ft from the right-hand edge of the track. Levegh, closing fast, did not deviate from his line and struck the Healey as it moved into his path. With the Healey's unusually long tail acting as a launching pad, the Mercedes took off and crashed into a concrete parapet on the left-hand side of the track, throwing Levegh out. He was killed instantly and the car exploded. As it did so, components such as the engine and front suspension scythed through the crowd. Meanwhile the Healey careered into the pit wall, skidded across the track and came to rest on the left-hand side. Fangio managed to pass unscathed between Macklin's Healey and Hawthorn's D-type, which stopped just beyond its pit. Hawthorn jumped out and ran through to the back of the pits, his immediate reaction to blame himself for the accident.

Many of the verbal and written accusations have been against Hawthorn, even though he was cleared by the official French enquiry. To counter the anti-Hawthorn slant of some accounts, Paul Frère, who stated that he was good friend of Hawthorn's, wrote of his own theories, backed up by a photo sequence which did not become available for some months after the accident due to the amateur photographer being one of those injured. Frère is a highly respected, intelligent, multi-lingual Belgian engineer, racing driver and journalist who finished second in that year's Le Mans, won the race in 1960, and drove for Ferrari, Jaguar and Aston Martin. At the time of the accident he was standing in the Aston pit, waiting to take over the DB3S he was sharing with Peter Collins.

Frère stated that White House corner was 765 yards (700 metres) from the first pits. The photographs he studied showed the D-type being followed by the Healey at a distance Frère stated to be 650 yards (600 metres) from the Jaguar pits. This refutes suggestions that the cars were only 200 yards from the pits when Hawthorn, supposedly, suddenly swerved across the Healey's bows. But would a driver of Hawthorn's experience, even though he was racing Fangio, pull in front of a slower car and immediately brake, thereby risking being shunted from behind and put out of the race? The implausibility of this suggestion is emphasised by his knowledge that Levegh and Fangio were in close proximity, that he was the one driver in the situation able to concentrate more on his rear than on his path (because he alone had a clear road ahead of him), and that his

Many factors combined in a split-second to cause a dreadful disaster that can never be fully explained.

claim to have signalled his intentions was confirmed in *Autosport* Editor Gregor Grant's eye-witness account.

What about Macklin's actions in moving across the track into Levegh's path? If, as may have happened, he was looking in his mirror at the crucial moment when Hawthorn started braking or increased his rate of braking, he would have had less time to react and he would have perceived Hawthorn braking more sharply than was actually the case. Macklin swung to the left to avoid the D-type and the Healey skidded, but he skilfully held the slide and brought the car under control again – all in a split-second. Levegh had an ideal view of proceedings from behind and should have seen the Healey suddenly closing on the D-type, the gentle swerve, the fighting for control. If Macklin had time to do all that, why did Levegh not move even a little from his course up the centre of the road?

Levegh had Fangio right behind him, about to overtake. Was he concerned about moving over into Fangio's path, either because he might risk an accident or baulk his team leader? Imagine the pressure of having the great Fangio coming up behind you – Levegh was only having a one-off guest drive but Fangio was disputing the lead. Fangio himself stated that Levegh raised his hand to

indicate danger. Was he signalling that he wanted to go to the left but, by this time, it was too late? Was he, at the crucial moment when he needed to react, looking in his mirror? It would have been a natural thing to do and good driving to monitor Fangio's position. Does this explain his lack of reaction? It has been suggested that at the age of 50 he was too old to be handling such a powerful machine: his lap times were very respectable, but his reactions could not have been as sharp as a younger man's.

'Lofty' England can add further impressions from his perspective in the pits. The start of the accident occurred out of his sight, but it unfolded in front of him. "Macklin flew across the road and I could see what was going to happen. Fortunately I stopped our mechanics getting down to the pit-lane, otherwise they'd have had their chips. The Healey hit two blokes in the pit next to us, and then went back across the road again. Macklin walked across and said to Hawthorn, 'That was your bloody fault' or something similar – but that's the sort of thing someone says in the heat of the moment. Mike was obviously disturbed by this.

"Hawthorn over-ran our pit for the simple reason that there was no-one down there to stop him. He rolled past, stopped outside the Cunningham pit, and jumped out. I was expecting a massive accident with 20 cars in a great pile, and I think he thought the same thing – so he naturally got out of the car, went through the pits and disappeared out the back. I got hold of him and said, 'Come on Mike, get back in, you must do another lap'. We couldn't change drivers where the car was because this had to happen in front of our own three pits, and you weren't allowed to push the car back. So I got him back in the car again, made him do another lap and then get out."

Fangio is said to have made statements blaming Hawthorn at the time and does so in his ghosted autobiography. However, on 1 July *Autosport* carried this report under the heading 'FANGIO BLAMES NOBODY': 'Despite earlier, and highly misleading, versions of statements alleged to have been made by Juan Manuel Fangio after the Le Mans disaster, the World Champion stated at an enquiry at Le Mans last Monday, that, in his opinion, no person could be blamed for the accident. Fangio said he was about 600 metres behind Levegh, when the French driver signalled that he was about to overtake another car (Macklin's Austin-Healey). He (Fangio) immediately lifted his foot, and, although he recalled seeing the Austin-Healey spinning across the track, was not clear in his mind exactly what caused the crash, as he was too occupied in making sure of avoiding the British car. He maintained, however, that Levegh's signal saved him from being involved in an accident, as he was able to brake his car in time to avoid hitting the gyrating Austin-Healey.'

I recently asked Stirling Moss, who was in the pits waiting to take over from Fangio, and had experience of both the D-type and the 300SLR, for his opinion. "My own feeling is that it was one of those dreadful racing accidents that happen. Various ingredients were put there and caused the accident. I think if it had been Fangio and not Levegh in the car, it might have been avoided – but it happened so quickly."

The organisers allowed the race to continue, reasoning that to stop it would hamper the emergency services. Bueb took over from Hawthorn and Moss relieved Fangio. While Bueb did a fine job considering his unfamiliarity with the car and the race, he could not keep up with Moss, who built up a healthy cushion. The race order then was Fangio/Moss, Hawthorn/Bueb, Castellotti/Marzotto, Rolt/Hamilton and Beauman/Dewis. At quarter-distance it was Mercedes, Jaguar, Jaguar, Jaguar, Mercedes. The Cunningham D-type retired soon after with engine problems.

Unaware of the scale of the tragedy, Salvadori and Collins were having fun in their Astons. Past the pits they obeyed team orders about who should lead, but around the rest of the circuit they diced furiously lap after lap. When Salvadori spun, Collins, laughing heartily, waited for him so they could continue their game and remain in the cor-

rect order next time they passed the pits – what a different era!

At midnight the Moss 300SLR led the Hawthorn D-type by two laps, but then one of the D-types had a misfortune which 'Lofty' recalls with amusement: "Beauman went into the sand at Arnage. He'd just about dug out the car, after working for about an hour, when somebody [Colin Chapman's Lotus] hit him and pushed him back again! He arrived back at the pits with sand everywhere – in his eyes, ears, mouth, all his clothes, choc-a-bloc with sand, poor sod!"

The two remaining 300SLRs were withdrawn at 1.45am on orders from Stuttgart and, with the Ferraris all out, the Hawthorn/Bueb Jaguar motored on without serious opposition. At 6.50am the Rolt/Hamilton D-type retired with major gearbox problems, but the remaining factory car continued to run reliably through foul weather to take the chequered flag, with the Collins/Frère DB3S Aston second and the Belgian D-type an excellent third. The winning car had achieved a record distance of 2569.6 miles, averaged 107.067mph, spent 23min 6sec in the pits, used fuel at the rate of 11.1mpg, changed two rear tyres at half-distance, and swopped all four for 'cut treads' three hours later.

"Had it not been for this accident the race would probably have been one of the most interesting in the history of Le Mans," reckoned Bill Heynes. "Fangio and Hawthorn were perfectly matched in the first three hours. It is doubtful whether Ivor Bueb, who was driving for the first time for Jaguar, could have held Stirling Moss...but it was almost certain that, despite the assistance of air brakes, the trouble which Mercedes were having with their drum brakes would have influenced the end of the race."

"I think the great thing about '55," states Eng-

BELOW **In the aftermath of the Le Mans tragedy, Mike Hawthorn and Ivor Bueb, who was competing in a 24-hour race for the first time, drove well in appalling conditions to take a hollow victory.**

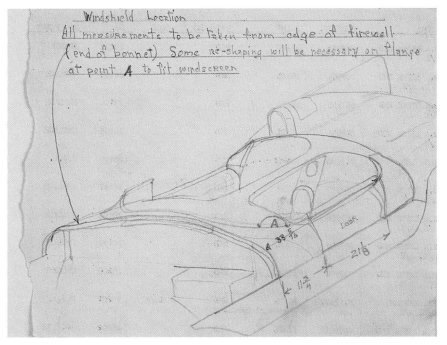

In the sketch: *Windshield Location. All measurements to be taken from edge of firewall (end of bonnet) Some re-shaping will be necessary on flange at point A to fit windscreen*

ABOVE **Following the awful accident in 1955 new regulations were introduced, one of the aims being to slow down the cars. Bob Blake drew this sketch when working on body alterations.**

land, "was that in spite of the accident, which might have set Hawthorn back a lot, he still drove in a magnificent manner in bloody awful conditions, and Ivor Bueb, who had never driven in a long-distance race, or in a race at night, did a perfect job of driving with him. The two of them did a wonderful job."

OTHER RACES IN 1955

The immediate reaction to the accident in France was a complete government ban on all organised motor sport in that country, so the Reims 12 Hours was cancelled. The next event for a factory D-type, therefore, was the sports car race at Aintree accompanying the British GP (in which Moss scored his first GP victory). Two D-types (XKD 505 and XKD 506) were taken to Aintree for Hawthorn to try in practice, and he raced XKD 506. The circuit suited the Astons far better and, after leading for a lap, Mike was relegated to fifth, as England ruefully recalls: "He was seen off by the Aston Martin team who all boxed him in – really carved him up."

According to Roy Salvadori, who was driving one of the four Astons, team manager John Wyer told the drivers, "If you get in front of Mike, I don't want any inter-team fighting – whoever is leading should hold the lead and the rest of you should hold your positions". As a result they were so busy jockeying for position among themselves off the line that they allowed Hawthorn to rocket into the lead. According to one biographer, Mike was not in good form that day because he had had a huge row with his girlfriend the night before, got very drunk and had a bad hangover. 'Lofty': "Hawthorn didn't have a hangover, but he had been stuck in the Birkenhead tunnel, with all its exhaust gases".

In an interview with Salvadori, I asked how the Jaguars compared with the Astons, and why the Astons were so much quicker through corners. "They had to be because they never really had the power. I think they were developed very well, right to the limit until there was nothing left. With the Jaguars, though, I would say that they had further development potential. Jaguars had this wonderful shape, but Astons had much better brakes. It was really hard work racing against D-types because you had to nail them. They would leave you on the straight, but we had the advantage on braking and cornering. If you were close enough, you could always overtake a 'D' going into a corner – but it had to be the right corner.

"At Aintree, for instance, it was no good passing a 'D' on the corner before the straight, or two corners before the straight, because the Jaguar would just muscle past again with its extra speed. So it was best to overtake at the end of the pit area, or the next corner. Then you'd work like mad on the infield to scrape enough of an advantage before you got back to the straight, where you'd see the Jaguar come tearing up in your mirror. As long as you were ahead at Melling you had a chance of staying there.

"We were on a par with each other's times on British circuits, so it was always very close. Aston drivers got a bad name on short circuits because we had to play some tricks to get in front of the D-types. You had to shut the door, or get them on the loose stuff so they couldn't use their power. The favourite trick after you overtook a D-type was not to take a corner flat out, but to go through at its speed and edge it over towards the grass! This could give you half a second if you got the D-type off-balance so that the driver couldn't put his foot down early enough."

Salvadori also provides fascinating insights into the style of the Jaguar drivers: "Duncan was always rough, but you could be rough with him – you had to adapt your style of driving to those around you. Moss was extremely good and very fair, and so was Rolt. So you would drive one way against one driver, and a different way against another. If I knew somebody was likely to chop me, I'd take the greatest delight in giving him the same treatment!"

Ex-works and Ecurie Ecosse D-types were clocking up a good selection of successes during the 1955 season, but the fourth, and final, event for the factory cars was the Dundrod TT, celebrating its Golden Jubilee and this time run without a handicapping system. Shortly before the event, de Dion rear suspension, which had proved so effective on the Astons, was fitted experimentally to XKC 401 and tested at Silverstone. 'Lofty' England: "Bill Heynes was always against having sliding joints on drive shafts because they could lock up. So when we did the de Dion system, he put doughnuts in. We went to Silverstone only about a week before the TT, and within 10 laps the dough-nuts were split. No good."

Despite this failure, the decision was taken to race XKD 505 with the new suspension trans-planted from XKC 401. 'Lofty' again: "Metalastik made new doughnuts but we didn't have time to test anything. I couldn't see the de Dion car lasting very long, so I took the ex-Aintree car [XKD 506], to which we'd done nothing apart from changing the shock absorber settings. We did five laps in practice with the de Dion car – nobody noticed it by the way – and again the doughnuts started split-ting up, so I decided to put it away and continue with the other car. It went very well except that for some reason it used gallons of oil.

"We calculated that we could do two-thirds of the 80-lap race without refuelling and the whole race on one set of tyres, because by this time we had Stabilia tyres and their wear was practically nil. Due to the oil consumption, however, the car would need oil earlier than petrol. The night before the race we checked everything, but there was no obvious oil leak. We even cut a hole in the bonnet so we could save time by pouring oil in without opening it – we were expecting to put in two gallons of oil!

"So we started the race and Hawthorn made an early pit-stop. All we had to do was fill it up with fuel and put Titterington in. It didn't need much oil – perhaps a pint or thereabouts. We were in the lead, but then it started to rain – the Stabilia tyres weren't very good in the wet. This was where Moss closed up a bit, but then Mercedes put out a sign for Moss to come in. The next thing I see, somebody rushes out, grabs the bloke with the sign and pulls him away. So Moss goes past, and on the next lap it's announced he's hit a bank and is coming round slowly. He arrives and half the bodywork is missing from the back – he'd worn through a tyre and it had exploded.

"So then we had a big Mercedes pit-stop – the biggest chaos you've ever seen. They had about seven people working on it, not permitted of course, and cut half the bodywork off so that the car no longer complied with the regulations. Moss takes over from Neubauer, the team manager, and tells the mechanics what to do. Then he gets in the car and goes like bloody hell – and of course he went on to win. Then Fangio and Hawthorn had a big dice. Mike was seeing off Fangio but the crank broke on the D-type engine with about two laps to go, and that was that.

"But the laugh was this tyre business. Mercedes were supposed to be so efficient – supposed to be. I knew Rudi Uhlenhaut quite well: nice guy, part-British, his mother came from Finchley, like Wally Hassan and me. At the '55 Motor Show we dis-played the 2.4 saloon and Uhlenhaut came along and asked for a ride in it. While we were out with the car I asked him how Mercedes came to make a mistake with its tyre wear calculations in the TT.

'We didn't,' he said. 'Our calculations were right, but when you came in we saw your tyres were vir-tually untouched. So we thought we had made a mistake and waved Moss on!' That tickled me."

It has been stated that Jaguar protested the lead-ing Mercedes. 'Lofty': "No, I supported a protest put in by John Wyer. It looked so obvious that old father Moss said, 'That's it, the boy's out'. Ray-mond Baxter was commentating and said, 'Unfor-tunately Moss is obviously going to be disquali-fied, because you can't have seven people working on the car, and you can't drive with no rear wing on it'. But the stewards hadn't the guts to chuck out the Mercedes. They claimed there was nothing in the regulations to say the car had to comply dur-ing the race, only at scrutineering. I'd never heard such rubbish in all my life."

Both Hawthorn and local man Titterington ("he kept the expenses down," quips 'Lofty') had driven superbly and Lyons sent them both a bonus cheque. Moss is full of praise for Hawthorn's per-formance: "Mike did a fantastic job with the D-type because it certainly was not comparable with the SLR at Dundrod, or at Le Mans". Hawthorn won a special place in the hearts of everyone at Jaguar, none more so than with England, who found him co-operative and undemanding: "He wanted so little – just the four-spoke steering wheel that he liked. If Hamilton was 5sec a lap slower he'd complain that his car wasn't going well, so I'd get him to swap cars with Hawthorn. Mike would go even faster in Duncan's car than in his own, but Duncan's times would be no better. On his day Hawthorn was unbeatable. But he wasn't always fit: he had kidney trouble and some-times he looked really awful."

TOWARDS 1956

In late 1955 the Engine Development section of the Experimental Department carried out further bench tests with an XK120D engine equipped with petrol injection, continued work on a 2.4-litre engine with an aluminium block, and conducted flow tests and a dimensional check on a 3-litre Fer-rari engine. Flow tests on the Ferrari engine were compared with a twin-plug '55 XK engine with the 35/40 head and a single-plug '54 XK engine with the wide-angle head. In mid-November Jack Emer-son was able to report that the petrol injection (PI) engine could produce as much power as one fitted with carburettors. In late December E.W. Downing, who did much of the PI research at Lucas, arranged to discuss progress with Bill Heynes over lunch – at a pub called 'The Engine'!

The Le Mans accident led to regulation changes for 1956, including the requirement for a full-width screen. On 1 December 1955 Phil Weaver sent Heynes a fascinating memo. The references to 'Production' are a little confusing since Weaver was actually referring to the factory cars.

ABOVE **In 1956 William Lyons was knighted and Her Majesty The Queen visited the Coventry factory. She was shown the 1955 Le Mans winning D-type.**

RIGHT **When Mercedes-Benz pulled out of racing at the end of 1955, 'Lofty' England tried to engage Stirling Moss to join Mike Hawthorn in the Jaguar team. It would have been a formidable pairing...**

Models for Le Mans
3½-litre Production D-type
Preliminary tests have been carried out, first with an extended screen with the existing tonneau cover, and secondly with the extended screen with the tonneau cover taken from the top of the screen, and thirdly with a hard top which is actually wider and taller than the minimum.

The first condition with the wider screen only shows a probable loss in maximum speed of 10.7mph. The second condition shows a loss of 6.3mph and the hard top body shows a loss of 3.9mph. It is thought that this latter figure could probably be reduced, but there would be a serious difficulty in making the D-type body as it is produced at the moment sufficiently airtight to ensure that the drivers were not gassed, although no doubt this difficulty could be overcome if new bodies were individually built from scratch, which we are proposing to do in any case so that lighter gauge material may be used and to bring the body up to the full width as specified in the regulations.

The second part of this memo is momentous as it refers, for the first time, to what would become the E-type: it is quoted on page 129.

The first of a series of meetings was held on 5 December to discuss the specification of the 1956 cars. Petrol injection was being seriously considered now, and various changes also had to be made to meet the new regulations. A smaller petrol tank of 28.6 gallons (instead of 36.5 gallons) was to be fitted for Le Mans and there would be a new propshaft tunnel to allow for larger seats. Doors were to be fitted on both sides and lengthened to give an opening of 19.7in. The new windscreen (with consequent modifications to the top skin) and separate stop lights were discussed. It was proposed to reduce the bonnet skin and all valances and ducts to 20swg, and to reduce the centre section, inner and outer side members, front cross beam and diaphragm to 18swg. It was planned to have

lighter rear bulb holders and reflectors, and to recess these behind a Perspex panel. The minutes of the meeting state: 'All panels to be properly recess rivetted where necessary and also panels to be properly caulked with chromate-impregnated jointing compound before rivetting'. As for rear suspension, 'For the five Le Mans cars this will be standard with the addition of roll bar and ZF differential. The other five cars may be de Dion or independent'.

At a meeting on 30 January 1956, the specification for individual cars and the races they were to contest was detailed. There is also mention of a '2½-litre engine in D-type car. Mr Weaver to fit 2½-litre engine in frame to check for clearances'. Alongside this Bob Blake pencilled, 'New body wheelbase is 6in longer. 200bhp for 180mph. 7500rpm. Aluminium block. Use lighter brakes and wheels'. This would be the first reference to the construction of the new E-type. Following another meeting on 20 February, it was stated about the same project, 'layout to be done using as many existing chassis components as possible'. Reference was also made to a five-speed gearbox for the D-types: 'Design to be completed. Stampings to be ordered'. Under 'Independent Rear Suspension' was the comment, 'Basic design now cleared for 1st prototype in the process of being detailed for manufacture of one set for try-out'.

In fact a new batch of six long-nose D-types would be built for the 1956 season, and the first to be completed (XKD 601) was fitted with Lucas PI. These cars differed from the '55 versions in many detailed ways apart from those already described, although not all of the initial thoughts were incorporated. By redesigning the bracketry and using lighter gauge materials, weight was reduced by around 50lb.

With Mercedes-Benz withdrawing from motor racing for 1956, Jaguar saw an opportunity to bring Moss back into the fold. The idea of a Moss/Hawthorn 'dream ticket' was irresistible to 'Lofty' England, so he arranged a meeting with Moss's father and Ken Gregory, his manager, at White Cloud Farm, the Moss family home. "They

said they wouldn't want Moss driving a different car from Hawthorn, so that restricted it to Moss driving *with* Hawthorn. I agreed to that and said, 'I will pay him £1000 a time'. We had Le Mans, Reims, Sebring and the Nürburgring – four races. We only paid Hawthorn £2000 a year so I was being rather generous, especially as I obviously expected to pay Hawthorn the same as Moss. Then I asked them to understand that Hawthorn would be the number one driver, but they couldn't accept that. In the end Stirling decided to sign for Aston Martin in sports car racing."

For the Sebring 12 Hours no fewer than four cars, all painted in the traditional American livery of white with blue stripes, were prepared for a joint effort by the works and the Cunningham team. The new car (XKD 601) was sent out for Hawthorn/Titterington, while the other driver pairings were Johnston/Spear (XKD 504), Hamil-ton/Bueb (XKD 508) and Cunningham/Benett (XKD 507). The Hawthorn and Hamilton cars both retired with brake seizure brought on by high ambient temperatures, as England recalls.

"The brake temperatures were quite incredible – something like 1200 degrees C. We were still using round-pad brakes and when a car stopped in practice the brake hoses almost caught fire, so we had to bind them with asbestos. And of course the higher the temperature, the quicker the rate of wear. In the race Hawthorn led but simply ran out of brakes. Then my dear friend Duncan arrived in

the pit with the wheels locked, causing the pad to weld to the disc. Ivor got in and about five yards later half the pad came off."

Since the Johnston/Spear car retired with engine trouble, the only D-type finisher was the Cunning-ham/Benett car, in 12th place after an early delay. 'Lofty': "The car stopped out on the circuit. Briggs Cunningham, the most charming bloke, managed to push it three miles back to the pits in this heat, and he was no boy as he was over 50 by then. He was laid out behind his pit and his crew didn't dare tell him the problem. The car had run out of fuel – they hadn't filled it properly when they refuelled. So they told him both petrol pumps had failed..."

The next event for the works was a domestic one – the *Daily Express* meeting at Silverstone. Three cars were entered for Hawthorn (XKD 603), Titterington (XKD 604, with de Dion rear) and Jack Fairman (XKD 504), who had rejoined the team for '56. Moss, now with Aston, led ini-tially but team-mate Salvadori displaced him at Stowe, followed by the D-types. Salvadori was cer-tain he had Hawthorn on his tail and considered him a hard driver who would not give an inch. It was vital for Salvadori that he led through the next left-hander, Club, otherwise the Jaguar would power away on the fastest section of the course. He moved to the right to force the D-type, if it was going to have a go, to pass him on the outside. However, the D-type driver was Titterington, who tried to pass on the inside and spun. Moss and

ABOVE **A new batch of six long-nose cars was built for the 1956 season and this one, XKD 606, was the last D-type made. Look closely and it can be spotted that the '56 cars had a passenger door. In the colours of Ecurie Ecosse, this illustrious machine would take the Scottish team's second Le Mans win in '57.**

ABOVE **The most obvious distinguishing feature of the 1956 cars is the use of a full-width windscreen, required by new regulations.** RIGHT **This shot of Les Bottrill testing at MIRA shows Malcolm Sayer's clever use of a flexible tonneau cover over the passenger area – an effort to reduce the aerodynamic damage done to his design by the 1956 regulations.**

Hawthorn squeezed through the mêlée, but Collins hit the 'D', Parnell went off, and Sanderson's Ecurie Ecosse 'D' went up a bank. Hawthorn pressed on in second place and broke the lap record before retiring with steering maladies, while Fairman went well but dropped out when a drive shaft snapped.

Two cars were taken to the Nürburgring for Hawthorn/Titterington (XKD 601, still with PI) and Hamilton/Frère (XKD 603). Frère rolled his car in practice. "He claimed that he had done a slow roll in the air and landed on the wheels about 50 feet down the road," recalls 'Lofty'. A replacement car (XKD 504) was driven out from Coventry by Norman Dewis, but in the race it lasted only six laps before its gearbox broke. Hawthorn held third place but was black-flagged twice ("a bit of anti-Jaguar feeling on the part of the officials," says 'Lofty') for allegedly passing slower cars on the wrong side and then ramming another that cut across him. He was also suffering from petrol fumes as the PI auxiliary tank, situated in the passenger seat, had split. He pitted, the leak was sealed and Titterington took over. Sadly a half-shaft broke on the last lap.

An interesting memo prepared in May 1956 notes some fascinating developments in progress or being considered. Discussing the 2½-litre engine, the notes mentioned, 'triple valve springs ¹⁵⁄₃₂in lift, piston shape, wet sump layout at 45 degrees to be tested, titanium con rods'. With the five-speed gearbox we learn, 'Design now cleared. Manufacture in process'. As for independent rear suspension, the report states, 'In the process of manufacture. Car required'. By June further progress had been made in several of these areas. XKD 505 had been fitted with independent rear suspension and it was hoped to have the five-speed gearbox completed by the end of the month, although there was a question mark over its eligibility for Le Mans.

Since Le Mans had been postponed by six weeks for track widening in the pit area to be completed, Reims was the next fixture. Not being a championship round, it attracted only a weak entry, but Jaguar had its reasons for attending, as England explains: "It was an exercise to make sure we could win Le Mans because this was the first year that fuel consumption was restricted. It was limited by tank capacity: originally it was to have been 120 litres, but I persuaded them it ought to be 130 with each refuelling limited to 120, so that you never ran out completely. I considered it dangerous for a car suddenly to cut out going round a long curve – the bloke behind could hit you up the back."

The line-up for Reims was Hawthorn/Frère (XKD 601, now on Webers), Titterington/Fairman (XKD 603) and Hamilton/Bueb (XKD 605, on PI). Hawthorn had been asked to drive for Vanwall in the GP that followed, so 'Lofty' suggested he should do an extra pit stop and have some rest. The race was a walkover for the Jaguars which, with the Ecurie Ecosse entry, held the first four places, Hawthorn/Frère in the lead followed by Hamilton/Bueb.

"When Ivor came in for the last stop," recalls 'Lofty' ruefully, "I said to Duncan, whom I could see was up to something, 'No nonsense, Duncan, you will win this race anyway, Frère's got to make another stop'. So Hamilton gets in, goes like a lunatic and completely ignores all pit signals. He came in at the end and said, 'Suppose I'm in trouble?'. I said, 'Not really. There won't be any trouble because you're not going to drive for us again'.

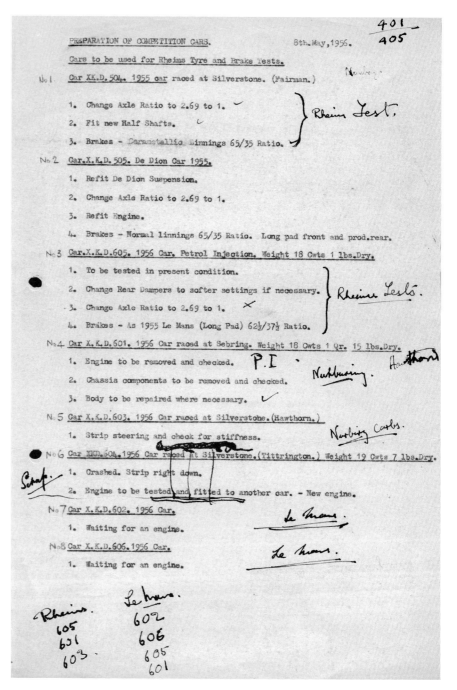

And he never did – but we remained friends." Hamilton, having overtaken Frère, went on to win the race, breaking the lap record in the process.

"That Christmas Duncan sent me a card and a parcel," adds 'Lofty' as a postscript. "The parcel contained a mortar board and cane. Anyway, some months later he was due at the factory to collect a D-type that he'd bought, so I told the gate police to tell me immediately he arrived. I knew he would come straight up to my office and I would have about half a minute's warning. I got the call to say he had arrived, put the mortar board on, took the cane in my hand and sat down menacingly at my desk. There was a knock on the door. At my summons it opened – and a commissionaire walked in. He seemed to find the situation amusing and started to buckle at the knees. 'What's so funny,

ABOVE **This fascinating document concerning the 1956 works cars has been annotated by Bill Heynes. It details the events they were to be used for and includes the fateful word 'Scrap' by XKD 604.**

ABOVE **Night start for the Reims 12 Hours. This race was a happy hunting ground for predatory Jaguars and 1956 was no exception. With the three works cars supplemented by an Ecurie Ecosse entry, D-types took the first four places – but the order was not quite as 'Lofty' England wished it to be.** RIGHT **Malcolm Sayer (left), who played such a major role throughout the period covered by this book, and Bob Blake, the brilliant American artist in metal, survey the Hawthorn/Bueb car at Le Mans scrutineering in 1956.**

RIGHT **A magnificent line-up of D-types at Le Mans in 1956, with the Belgian entry (nearest camera), the Ecurie Ecosse car and the four works machines (including a spare car). The difference between the short-nose and long-nose cars is clearly seen.**

man? Go and fetch Mr Hamilton'. When he returned with Duncan, a number of heads were craning to try and see in through the door..."

WORKS DISARRAY AT LE MANS

The next event was the big one – Le Mans. It was to be the factory's swansong. The new regulations decreed full-width windscreens, a proper passenger seat with leg-room, a minimum fuel consumption of 10.8mpg, a maximum of 52 starters, and a 2½-litre maximum for prototype cars as opposed to so-called production cars. Malcolm Sayer cleverly devised a flexible Vybak tonneau cover to run from the screen top over the passenger compartment to lessen the aerodynamic disadvantage of having to remove the solid cover previously fitted over the aperture. Other changes included quick-change disc brake pads and modified combustion chambers.

With Hamilton sacked, Ken Wharton was drafted into the team again, as number two to Fairman (XKD 602, with PI). Hawthorn was again teamed with Bueb (XKD 605, with PI) and Frère was paired with Titterington (XKD 603, on Webers). A spare car (XKD 606) was also taken. During practice Titterington damaged his car and the spare was substituted. Hawthorn's car had engine problems and a spare engine was fitted.

"Before the race started," says England, "I learned that a memorial to the people who had been killed was going to be unveiled opposite the pits, just before the race started. I feared that relatives of the dead might start an anti-Hawthorn or anti-Jaguar demonstration, and decided that we wouldn't start the race if this happened. So I briefed my drivers. 'Any demonstration on the other side of the road and I raise my hand. You stand exactly where you are at attention. When everyone else has gone, we push our cars away and that's the last time we ever come here'. But nothing happened – not a sign."

With everything set fair, Jaguar had reason to

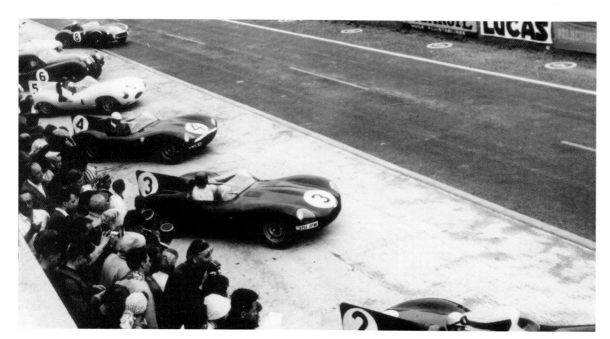

LEFT **Start of the 1956 Le Mans. In the background Moss in the Aston once again shows his prowess at Le Mans starts, with Frère (just visible in the foreground), Fairman (3), Flockhart (4), Swaters (5) and the Bolton/Walshaw XK140 FHC yet to join the fray.**

ABOVE **With about 23hr 50min of the race still to go, Paul Frère had the misfortune to lose his D-type in the Esses and hit the wall. Jack Fairman arrived, spun on the greasy surface to avoid hitting Frère's car, and was struck by the spinning Ferrari of de Portago. Two-thirds of the Jaguar team pottered round to the pits to retire...**

LEFT **Hawthorn had a healthy lead in the one remaining D-type (XKD 605) when his car suddenly suffered a misfire. The several stops it took to solve the problem effectively put him out of the hunt.**

RIGHT **In spite of their lowly position and with no hope of success, Hawthorn and Bueb gave it their all. From a deficit of 26 laps, they worked their way up to sixth place by the conclusion.**

feel confident. But on the second lap the confidence evaporated. After fresh rain, the surface was especially greasy and Frère lost his car coming into the Esses, damaging the tail irreparably against the bank. Fairman spun to avoid Frère, briefly escaping unscathed until de Portago's spinning Ferrari collected him. Two Jaguars were out within minutes and soon Hawthorn was in trouble as well, losing the lead with a series of stops due to a misfiring engine.

"We should have walked it," claims 'Lofty'. "No-one else dared run an engine bigger than 3 litres, because of the fuel consumption, but we could do it perfectly all right. There was an official who checked we didn't put too much fuel in, so I said to him, 'It is entirely your responsibility to make sure we don't put in more than 120 litres. Now are you quite sure? Say these words after me...' Then we had injection pipe trouble with Mike's car, and after we refuelled it I asked the official how much it had taken – 125 litres. I told this bloke he'd made a great mistake, and that he'd better see the Course Director and say, 'I have made a mistake, but Mr England's being very kind and says the next time they stop, they will put in five litres less'.

"The injector pipe had split longways out of

sight. By the time we'd traced this and fixed it, we were 26 laps behind – hardly worth restarting. So I said to Mike and Ivor, 'Look, I reckon if you have a bloody go, you can finish eighth'. 'We're on,' they said, 'we'll have a bloody go.' They finished sixth and do you know how much the prize money was? £30 between them. But they couldn't have cared less because they'd enjoyed themselves so much. During the race one would come in and say, 'What's it like, Mike?' 'Wet!' Then next time, 'What's it like, Ivor?' 'Still wet!' Great chaps – super. Our mechanics loved Hawthorn most of all – great bloke."

The story of the winning Ecurie Ecosse D-type is told in the next chapter (see page 119). As for the factory team, Jaguar decided to retire at the end of the season. 'Lofty': "We reckoned our cars weren't good enough to win the next year, so we pulled out for one year with the intention of returning the following year. The idea was to use the car that eventually became the E-type.

"Then we had the great fire at the factory in February 1957. It was more important to keep the works going than go motor racing. In fact we got so much publicity from the fire that we didn't need to go motor racing – much cheaper to burn the works down!"

RIGHT **The Jaguar and Aston Martin teams took part in a televised challenge on the BBC programme Sportsview – wheels and plugs had to be changed. Norman Dewis once told me that they cheated like mad, Phil Weaver having turned down the plugs and spinners so that hardly any thread was left. One blow with the hammer and off came the wheels. One twist of the plug spanner and out came the plugs. Jaguar won easily!** FAR RIGHT **With the factory fire of 12 February 1957 Jaguar found a cheaper alternative to motor racing in attracting publicity! As far as is known, this D-type has not yet been rebuilt...**

CHAPTER NINE

PRODUCTION D-TYPES & XKSS

The C-types had continued to be raced with great success, both in Europe and the US in 1954, but many C-type owners naturally wished to update to the new D-type when it appeared. Among the private teams still campaigning the C-type during 1954, the Scottish Ecurie Ecosse outfit must have been the most active, best organised and most successful. Not only had Ecurie Ecosse graduated from XK120s to C-types, but in 1953 one of its drivers, Ian Stewart, had raced for the works, as would another, Jimmy Stewart, in 1955.

'There has never been,' stated David Murray, the Ecurie Ecosse patron, in private correspondence, 'any official liaison between Ecurie Ecosse and Jaguar Cars Limited. Ecurie Ecosse has simply been a customer who has been given the first opportunity of purchasing the previous year's competition cars from the factory'. However, cars were offered to the team at very attractive prices, and Jaguar did a good deal to help the Scottish team because it was an excellent and valued adjunct to the works efforts. 'In cases,' Murray continued, 'Ecurie Ecosse has been able to point out to Jaguars certain suggested improvements but on the other hand Jaguar developments and improvements passed on to Ecurie Ecosse greatly out-number the former'.

The first three D-types to be built in 1955 – XKD 501, 502 and 503 – can be described as 'production' cars, in the sense that they were not works

cars. The first two were supplied to the Scots and the third to the Belgians. Murray explained in his book, *Ecurie Ecosse*, that there were delivery setbacks and the team's cars were not finally ready for collection from the factory until the afternoon of practice for the international meeting at Silverstone, where they were to make their debut.

However, the first private owner of a D-type was Duncan Hamilton, who had also enjoyed the same distinction with the C-type. He acquired OKV 1 (XKC 402) in early '55 and drove it home in the snow! 'I know of many sports racing cars,' he wrote in his hilarious autobiography, *Touch Wood*, 'that would be undriveable under such conditions. No one ever had to take a Jaguar to a race on a transporter. 'Lofty' always says that if you cannot drive a car on the road it will never be reliable in a race. I completely agree with that view'. Hamilton once even drove his GP Talbot Lago on the road when his transporter broke down 200 miles from Albi. "Never sent the D-type in a truck," Hamilton told me. "Drove it to all the meetings. I would always stay at Claridges in Paris in the Champs Elysée and leave it outside. People used to come from miles around to see the thing. The D-type made a super road car, but everybody used to think I was a bit odd!"

The first event for Hamilton's D-type was a regular fixture for him – the Morocco Grand Prix at Agadir. He drove in convoy from Casablanca with Dan Margulies, who had acquired his old C-type,

ABOVE **Like a good proportion of the total, this production D-type, XKD 527, was exported to the US and raced in California. It has been owned for more than 20 years by Nigel Dawes since its return to Britain.**

and Margulies' mechanic, one Graham Hill. The circuit was a tortuous course, undulating and with many bends. Hamilton had fitted a very low 4.09:1 axle before leaving England and the result was that he left black tyre marks all over the course. And during practice he had a typical Hamilton adventure.

"My gearbox locked up going up round the back of the houses and there was a bloody great drop onto rocks on my right. As the gearbox locked solid, I spun all the way up the hill and stopped with the rear wheels over the edge. Graham Whitehead – very nice chap, we always used to go toddling round together – saw the skid marks going up the hill, over the brow and knew it must be me. He eased off and crept over the hill, and I was just bouncing in the D-type. He came and sat on the bonnet while they got me out of it – another lucky one!" Most of Duncan's stories were slightly embellished, but he was a wonderful raconteur.

In the race he retired after 12 laps with a locking back brake. 'The race for the *grosses cylindrées*,' stated *Autosport*'s reporter, 'proved disappointing in British eyes, for Duncan Hamilton's Le Mans D-type Jaguar – a star attraction – went out shortly after quarter distance, gearbox trouble being given as the reason for retirement'. This intrepid reporter was that chap Graham Hill! From Agadir the entourage travelled to Dakar, an extremely fast circuit. A 2.75:1 axle was fitted and, according to Dunlop's internal report on the

event, the D-type was reaching 183mph on the straight, although Hamilton claimed to be touching 200! He reported that the D-type felt entirely stable at maximum speed but he was concerned about his tyres. Deciding to play safe during the race, he came in for a quick stop to have them checked and this cost him his second place.

Returning to Britain, Hamilton took part in the Empire Trophy race at Oulton Park, but could only finish seventh owing to a combination of a tired D-type (after its African adventure), a wet track and a handicap which favoured the small cars in these conditions. At the Easter Monday meeting at Goodwood the following weekend, Hamilton's 'D' and Mike Sparken's Ferrari occupied the front row. Duncan reckoned they were so busy watching each other, instead of the starter, that when the Ferrari jumped the start he went as well. The starter, the Duke of Richmond and Gordon, told him it was the only time he had seen two cars in top gear before the flag fell! Both were penalised 15sec, which handed the race to Salvadori's Aston, the D-type finishing third.

A few days later Hamilton travelled to France to compete once again for the Coupe de Paris at Montlhéry. He was confident of victory but the organisers felt a French win would be more to their liking and placed André Pilette in a GP Gordini on the front row alongside Hamilton, even though the Frenchman had not practised the car. The D-type was as fast as the Gordini and led initially, but it could not hold the lighter car on acceleration. Hamilton averaged 99.5mph to the winner's 100.05mph, so it was close.

On 5 April Norman Dewis noted in his log, 'Testing first production XK120D. Steel tube frame. 2nd gear jumps out of engagement on over-run. Clutch spin 1st & reverse. Steering tightened on rack. Check rear end for fouling wheel or prop shaft. Fit heel rest. Set carbs. Acc pedal very heavy. Driving door difficult to close!' He continued to test the car over the next few days in an attempt to cure the gearbox problems, and on 7 April he noted, 'Testing Hamilton's D-type solid drive axle. No improvement on cornering in the wet'.

ECURIE ECOSSE

The *Daily Express* International meeting at Silverstone saw the debut of Ecurie Ecosse's two new D-types (XKD 501 and 502). Jimmy Stewart aquaplaned off the course in practice and the damaged car could not be repaired for the race, while Desmond Titterington had brake trouble and could finish no higher than sixth. A day later Michael Head took Hamilton's car to victory at Djurgard Park, Helsinki, and a week later Titterington scored the first Ecurie Ecosse D-type win in the Ulster Trophy race at Dundrod in XKD 502.

The Scottish team had a disastrous trip to the Nürburgring with both cars crashing badly in practice when the brakes failed. As a result, Jimmy Stewart decided to retire from racing, as 'Lofty' England recalls: "Jimmy went upside-down due to a problem with the front hub adjustments, as did Mr Titterington. Both had too much play in the front hubs, the brakes knocked-off, and the pedal went down to the boards. Jimmy was upside-down with the petrol pumps going for about 10min which, having had a shunt the previous year at Le Mans with an Aston Martin, he didn't like very much. Later on his father, Bob, rang me – he was obviously in tears – and said, 'Jimmy's decided he doesn't want to race anymore, it's really upset him'. He was a very good driver, and I'd got him down to drive with Hawthorn at Le Mans."

At the end of May Hamilton took OKV 1 to Goodwood, where he won his heat and the final of the sports car race. In second place was Bob Berry in OKV 2 (XKD 403), which had been acquired by Jack Broadhead. Two more new cars were delivered in time for the fateful Le Mans in 1955 – the familiar Belgian team's XKD 503 and Briggs Cunningham's XKD 507. The latter retired after five hours, but the Belgians took a superb third place. From Le Mans Hamilton travelled to Portugal for the Oporto GP, where, as he said in his autobiography, 'after five years of trying I eventually survived the race without personal injury or mechanical trouble'. He finished third behind Behra and Gregory, with Berry fifth. In early July the dreadful 1955 season claimed another victim when

works driver Don Beauman was killed in a GP Connaught at Wicklow, where Titterington won his race in XKD 501 to improve Ecurie Ecosse morale after a bad run.

At the British GP meeting at Aintree, a course which did not suit the D-types, Ninian Sanderson and Berry finished in sixth and seventh places. Hamilton's next event with his car was the Lisbon GP, where he experienced brake trouble and then a complete failure. He took to the escape road, ducked under a wire and, unable to stop, ended up, so he claimed, going down the main street amid trams and taxis!

Duncan had also acquired XKD 406 and lent it on several occasions to Michael Head, who finished sixth at Kristianstad in the Swedish GP. Head teamed up with Peter Whitehead in another Hamilton car (Duncan also purchased XKD 510 at about this time) to tackle the Goodwood Nine Hours, but the pair retired at half distance when the engine seized. Titterington and Sanderson, however, finished an excellent second for Ecurie Ecosse, while Berry and Dewis came fifth, regretting that they had set a modest target speed.

Hamilton was inclined to lend his cars to friends, and included among them was Peter Blond. On one occasion at Silverstone Blond complained to Hamilton during practice that the D-type was down on power, and suggested, "...a blockage in the air intake. 'Nonsense,' roared Duncan. 'Not driving it properly. These cars are immaculately prepared by my staff'. I opened the bonnet and out fell a dead hare. For a moment I thought I had triumphed! But Duncan, quick on his feet, hoisted the offending animal in the air and pronounced, 'Look, it could only just have happened. It's still warm'.

"Couldn't win! We dined at 'The Green Man' and returned home not over-refreshed to Clare Court. It was a typical June night – ink black, steady drizzle. I was following the great man at a respectful distance up a long straight hill. Suddenly I became aware of his car spinning ahead of me. I braked my immaculately-prepared car which

ABOVE **Ecurie Ecosse acquired the first two new cars to be built in 1955, and Desmond Titterington won the Ulster Trophy on home ground at Dundrod with XKD 502.**

RIGHT **Following his acquisition of OKV 1, Duncan Hamilton added a second D-type to his stable when he purchased XKD 406. Here he is seen in typical fashion, hurling the car around Goodwood in 1955.**
BELOW **Apart from the three works cars, the D-type force at Le Mans in 1955 was strengthened by entries from Cunningham (Spear/ Walters, XKD 507, number 9) and Ecurie Francorchamps (Claes/Swaters, XKD 503, number 10). Note the Mercedes, which had made a bad start, using their air brakes into Mulsanne Corner.**
BELOW RIGHT **The Belgian car of Claes/Swaters put in a fine run to finish third at Le Mans in 1955.**

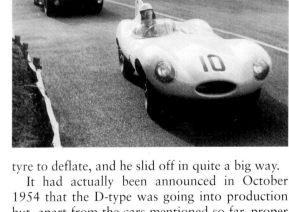

lurched violently to the left. And then there were two of us, spinning like a pair of expensive catherine wheels up the road – up one bank, down the other. I came right out of the cockpit! Seemed to go on forever. Finally, it all went quiet and I saw Duncan in the gloom, calmly pulling the bodywork away from the wheel of his now short-nosed, finless 'D'. He eyed me coldly and said, 'Something the matter with the brakes as well?'!"

Another trip to Aintree was a worthwhile one for Ecurie Ecosse as the cars finished first and second in the sports car race, ahead of Salvadori in a DB3S and Harry Schell in a Ferrari. For the TT Berry shared the Broadhead car with Sanderson, but early on he touched a bank, which caused a

tyre to deflate, and he slid off in quite a big way.

It had actually been announced in October 1954 that the D-type was going into production but, apart from the cars mentioned so far, proper organised manufacture did not begin until mid-1955. A small production line was laid down in the main assembly shop at Browns Lane and testing of these cars began in July, with the first car delivered in August. An initial price less than twice that of the XK140 had been publicised, but the final figure was fixed at £3878 (including purchase tax). A run of 100 cars was laid down, but not all would be built – in August the target was reduced to 67. However, only 42 were completed and despatched as follows: USA, 18; Britain, 10; Aus-

tralia, three; France, two; and Belgium, Canada, Cuba, East Africa, Finland, Mexico, New Zealand, San Salvador and Spain one each.

Les Bottrill, who started with the Service Department in 1950, transferred to the Competition Department in 1954, and now runs a Jaguar workshop in the US, track-tested every single production D-type. "We did most of the test work at MIRA but drove them there on the road. We used to put 300-400 miles on each car, generally running them in. Depending on the gearing, a stock 'D' would run about 145mph on the long straight at MIRA, whereas the works cars, which were geared for high-speed circuits, would do 170mph.

"I hit crows occasionally: one punched a big dent in the front while I was going at about 140mph and sent quite a shock through the car. On another occasion it was frosty and one part of the track had a little ice on it. I pulled in and then Ken Richardson, the chief tester for Triumph, went out in a TR3. I saw him barrelling round, and started to worry that he might come off on this icy bit, the north bank that was in total shade. So I set off to chase him round and try to flag him down. He thought I was racing him, so I had to pull in front of him and slow him down. We hit the ice, but luckily we were going slow enough by then."

INTO 1956

The following year, 1956, started well for Jaguar with a win in the Monte Carlo Rally and a knighthood for William Lyons. Hamilton's season opened with a visit with two of his D-types to the GP of Dakar. He drove the older one, fitted with a 2.53:1 axle and 17in wheels, and lent his newer one (XKD 510) to Graham Whitehead. The two of them, and initially Perdisa in a Ferrari and later

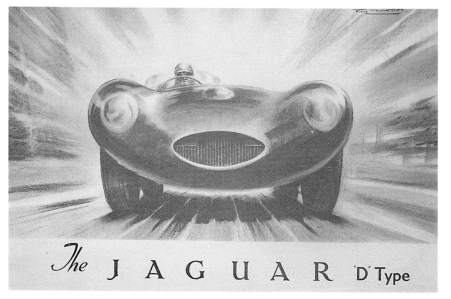

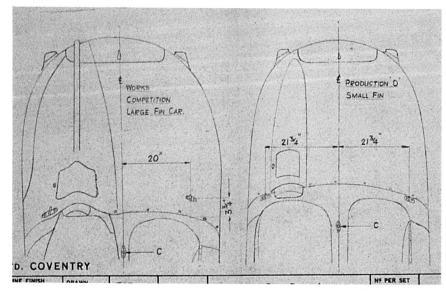

ABOVE **There are few more thrilling places to sit than a D-type cockpit. Not only does it feel very different from the C-type, but you drive a D-type more with the wrists than the arms.** ABOVE RIGHT **A proper assembly line was laid down in the main shop at Browns Lane to build the production D-types. The bodies were made by Abbey Panels.** RIGHT, TOP **Sayer always paid great attention to detail and any excrescence that would create drag. The fuel filler sits neatly in the head fairing.** RIGHT, MIDDLE **Like the works D-types, the production cars had double wishbone front suspension, disc brakes and Weber carburettors.** RIGHT, BOTTOM **Production D-types left the factory with a neat wraparound screen for the driver. For the unprotected passenger goggles are essential, and towards the end of a longish journey it is often necessary to hold one's head on!**

Behra in a Maserati, duelled for third spot until Hamilton had the engine blow up in spectacular fashion three laps from the end. Whitehead was classified fifth.

For the Sebring 12 Hours the factory ran four cars in conjunction with the Cunningham equipe (see pages 107-108), and their efforts were supplemented by a couple of private D-types. Jack Ensley and Bob Sweikert finished an excellent third in the former's car (XKD 538), while Alfonso Gomez Mena and Santiago Gonzales (XKD 521) were eighth. In the US several private owners were active throughout the season, as was the Cunningham team. In Australia, meanwhile, two of the three D-types shipped there enjoyed particularly active competition careers.

The Hamilton, Broadhead/Berry and Ecurie Ecosse teams continued to clock up appearances and successes during 1956. The Scottish brigade acquired a third car (XKD 561) at the beginning of the season and their driver line-up was supplemented by the arrival of Ron Flockhart and Alan Brown. Notable successes included a win for Sanderson at Spa and fourth place for Flockhart/ Sanderson at Reims behind the works D-types.

In 1956 Ecurie Ecosse took on its most ambitious challenge yet when it entered Le Mans with a single car (XKD 501) for Flockhart and Sanderson. In fact, according to David Murray, a significant motive for attending was the fact that there was to be a gold cup for victory in the 25th anniversary race the following year, and 1956 would be good experience for a serious attempt at that. As described in the previous chapter (see page 111), Jaguar lost two works cars on the second lap and the third was badly delayed with a fuel injection problem.

"I told the drivers," recalls chief mechanic

'Wilkie' Wilkinson, "to do 15 laps to learn the circuit, which was really pretty easy to remember, and then to do five more laps well within themselves, without over-revving. We timed these laps, took an average and told them to maintain this in the race. We would hang out plus or minus signs depending on whether their times were faster or slower than this average."

With the works effort blunted and other opposition falling by the wayside, the race developed into a titanic tussle between the Flockhart/Sanderson Jaguar and the Moss/Collins Aston Martin. Each led for periods in what was a wet race until 8.00am on the Sunday, but then on a drying track the Jaguar gradually pulled away and built up a two-lap advantage by 10.00am. 'Wilkie': "Moss, who was a better driver than our two, was certainly catching up on the bends in the Aston Martin, but on the straights our car was faster."

It was a truly great moment for Ecurie Ecosse when they took the flag, saving Jaguar's bacon that day. Murray claimed that the D-type was running strictly to orders and had power in hand: 'We could have gone faster, but the old shoestring Ecosse had to think of the next race date, had to make sure that the car finished in good condition'.

The splendid Belgian privateers backed up the Scottish victory with a fine fourth place in XKD 573. Another gallant entry was a private XK140 Fixed-Head Coupé driven by Bolton and Walshaw. This virtually standard car with 25,000 miles on the clock circulated reliably in 12th place until, with several hours to go, it was called in by the officials and disqualified for refuelling a lap earlier than allowed, some hours previously. I discovered several years ago, talking to the then owner of the car, that this was a mistake and the French apologised profusely, giving Bolton and Walshaw a free entry for the following year's event. The car they probably should have disqualified? None other than the winning D-type!

THE XKSS

In October 1956 Jaguar announced its temporary retirement from motor racing. By that time 42 production D-types had been delivered but demand had dried up, so 25 of the original batch total of 67 remained unsold. From today's perspective, with the D-type so revered and highly desirable, this seems extraordinary. Jaguar's answer to this problem was to create a proper road-going version – the XKSS. The 'SS' is believed to have stood for 'Super Sports'.

A variety of erroneous claims have been made over the years as to who had the idea and the reasons for the XKSS's evolution. For example, it has been stated that the unsold D-types were lying around going rusty, even though aluminium does not rust! 'Lofty' England gives the definitive statement: "One of the important things in America, especially to Briggs Cunningham, was the Sports Car Club of America [SCCA], which ran production sports car races. They should have accepted the D-type because it was used as a road car, but they didn't. So we decided to make the D-type acceptable to the SCCA, and had to build 50 examples of this revised car. That's the reason."

Furthermore 'Lofty' states that the motivation was not even to use up the remaining D-types: "It so happened we used them for that reason, but we were planning to make more cars because we didn't have 50 D-types lying around. Plans to convert to the XKSS were discussed by Sir William with Bill Heynes, and in turn with Phil Weaver, who got a D-type over to the Competition shop. There Bob Blake carried out the prototype work as instructed, but using some initiative. Sir William naturally went to the Comp shop to see and approve the prototype job."

To create the XKSS, the basic D-types were altered in several ways, although none was of major structural importance. The central division between the driver and passenger was cut out, the head fairing removed and a second door fitted for the riding companion. The doors could be fitted with side screens and a folding hood was provided. A full-width, framed windscreen with wraparound styling and two wipers was fitted. A luggage rack was mounted on the tail, and the additional headlamp trims and delicate bumpers were a foretaste of the items to appear later on the E-type.

Bob Blake, who built the prototype XKSS, was a brilliant American panelbeater who had joined Jaguar from Cunningham. "Malcolm Sayer just drew a flat-plane, single-radius glass for the windscreen, and I made all the frames and the bits and pieces, including all the little wooden tools to make everything from. I made the first set of bumpers by cutting down the big old wide bumper, using the top radius and the bottom radius, cutting the flute out and welding the two pieces together. The back bumper went into production as a plain aluminium casting, quite thick but hollow in the back with bosses so that it could be bolted on – all made from my original. When it was finished the original car went to New York for the motor show and we never saw it again – but by the end of the show the 25 cars were over-sold."

'Lofty' England's statement that the XKSS was created for SCCA racing seems to be supported by this passage in *Road & Track* magazine in April 1957: 'The new car fully meets the rules and regulations of the Sports Car Club of America as to the definition of a "production-sports" model, and is in fact an excellent example of a genuine dual-purpose machine – in marked contrast to a trend (in some areas) towards effeminate, super-luxurious

BELOW **Prince Philip finds out what it is like to be a passenger in the new XKSS. To his left is Sir William Lyons, and Bill Heynes (clasping his hands together) was also present.** BELOW RIGHT **The Duke of Kent has long been a Jaguar enthusiast and favoured customer, and here he tries the XKSS at MIRA with Norman Dewis as passenger.**

ABOVE **The XKSS was one of the ultimate road cars of its era. This is XKSS 707, one of the original 16 factory-built cars, now owned by Allen Lloyd.** LEFT **The XKSS is positively plush in comparison with the D-type.** BELOW LEFT **The D-type's open exhaust was protected to avoid the risk of a passenger finding the XKSS just a little too hot!** BELOW MIDDLE **Subtle headlamp trims on the XKSS were a foretaste of E-type styling.** BELOW RIGHT **It seems remarkable that Jaguar should have had so many unique XKSS parts made, but at least 50 cars were to be built.**

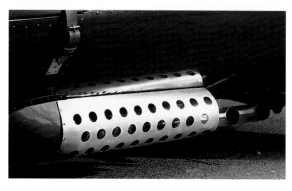

ABOVE **It is amazing how different the XKSS looked without a head fairing and with a proper windscreen – but opinion is divided on the success of the styling.** RIGHT **The hood is a snug fit but vision is rather restricted.** FAR RIGHT **The windscreen was clearly a compromised addition in styling terms, but it made the car considerably more civilised and usable.** BELOW RIGHT **A new dashboard complete with cubby hole was constructed for the XKSS. Note the rod-mounted mirror, a feature that would be seen on the E-type.**

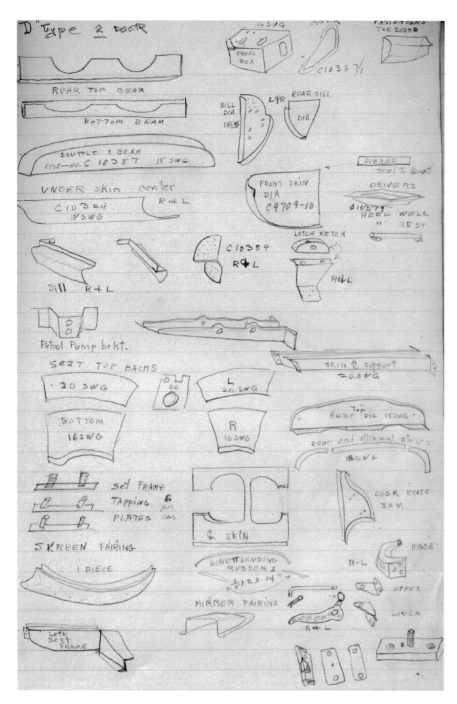

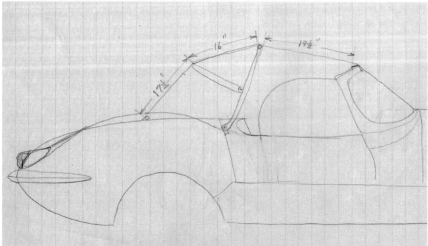

two-seaters.' The respected US magazine continued: 'Nevertheless, the interior comfort features of the SS are truly typical of past and present XK Jaguars, and the top and side-curtains are carefully executed to complement the "daily-driving" side of its dual nature. As for the competition side of the picture, a power to weight ratio of under 9lb/hp (with driver) takes care of that and one can only hope that other manufacturers will now be encouraged if not forced into offering something competitive.' Top speed was given as 146mph, 0-60mph as 5.5sec and 0-100mph as 13.5sec.

Some 16 cars had been completed, or semi-completed, when the factory fire broke out during the evening of 12 February 1957 and destroyed the remaining nine. Of these 16, 12 went to the US, two to Canada, one to Hong Kong and one remained in Britain. As the fire destroyed jigs and tooling, XKSS production was concluded. Two D-types (XKD 533 and 540) would later be converted by the works to XKSS specification.

INTO 1957

In the US the Cunningham team, now strengthened by the services of that fine driver Walt Hansgen after he beat Briggs's cars in XKD 529, con-

LEFT **In translating the ideas for the XKSS into reality, the brilliant craftsman Bob Blake made sketches in a large exercise book. Here are many of the extra components needed to turn the D-type into a more practical road car.**

BELOW **Bob Blake designed and fabricated a rudimentary hood for the new XKSS.** BELOW LEFT **In an effort to turn the D-type into a touring car, a small luggage rack was to be added to the tail. The bumper style would be copied for the E-type.**

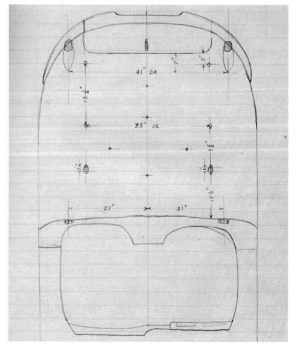

RIGHT **Aiming to repeat its Le Mans success, Ecurie Ecosse entered two cars in 1957. Number 15 (XKD 603) was driven by John Lawrence and Ninian Sanderson into second place.** BELOW RIGHT **Duncan Hamilton, prolific buyer of racing Jaguars, acquired an ex-works long-nose car (XKD 601) and asked Masten Gregory to partner him at Le Mans in 1957. They finished sixth after various delays.**

BELOW **The second Ecurie Ecosse entry (XKD 606), with Ivor Bueb and Ron Flockhart at the wheel, led the Jaguar domination which resulted in D-types finishing 1-2-3-4-6.**

tinued to amass a good haul of wins and placings with its D-types, as did several private owners. For 1957 Jaguar loaned XKD 605 to Cunningham and Hansgen clocked up several successes with this fuel-injected car, including victory in the Watkins Glen GP for the third time.

XKD 605, in fact, had been flown out in time for Sebring at the beginning of 1957, and Hawthorn and Bueb were on hand to pilot it. They ran strongly but were delayed by brake problems and could do no better than finish third. This car had been fitted with the first works 3.8-litre engine, a configuration Alfred Momo had been developing for some time for Cunningham. In correspondence in February 1957 about the first factory versions, Heynes wrote to Briggs: 'We are also running one 89mm bore engine on the bench which comes out just under 4 litres'. On 3 March Norman Dewis was testing this car when, 'Brake pipe broke on rear caliper at 150mph!!' A few days later he ran old OVC 501 (XKC 401): 'D-type transmission brake: Complete failure'.

Back in Europe, Ecurie Ecosse acquired three ex-works D-types (XKD 504, 603 and 606) following Jaguar's temporary withdrawal from motor racing at what team patron David Murray described as, 'financial arrangements which were, to put it mildly, generous'.

Ecurie Ecosse started the season with a second trip to Buenos Aires, where Flockhart badly damaged XKD 606 in practice when, in Murray's words, he 'demolished a lamp-standard made of highly unbendable concrete'. During the race Sanderson survived an unpleasant experience when a bird smashed the windscreen and one lens of his goggles, but together with Robert Mieres he finished fourth.

Two events clashed on 12 May and Ecurie Ecosse sent a single car to each. At Spa Sanderson and John Lawrence were completely outclassed by Tony Brooks, who was quite brilliant, and Roy Salvadori in the new 3-litre Aston Martin DBR1s. Although Henry Taylor and 'Freddy' Rousselle held second and third places in their D-types while it was wet, the Astons finished in the top two positions with the Scots well down the field. Hamilton was fourth. On the same day Flockhart tackled the legendary Mille Miglia in a solo effort. At Pescara he lay seventh behind five works Ferraris, but then retired when rough roads caused the rear bodywork and rubber fuel tank to break away. Flockhart tried a roadside repair with barbed wire from a farm fence, but to no avail.

Three Ecurie Ecosse cars were entered at the Nürburgring and again finished well down. However, Flockhart and Lawrence took the first two places in the St Etienne GP, with Hamilton third. A month earlier Captain Ian Baillie had taken his car (XKD 511) to Monza for record-breaking. He reported to England and Heynes that, despite heavy wind and rain resulting in bad visibility, he had, 'attempted and obtained all International Class C records up to 200 miles'.

No fewer than five D-types were entered for Le Mans in 1957. Ecurie Ecosse took two for Bueb/Flockhart (XKD 606, with a works-prepared 3.8-litre PI engine producing 297bhp at 5500rpm) and Lawrence/Sanderson (XKD 603). The French team Los Amigos entered a car (XKD 513) for Jean Lucas and Jean-Marie Brussin, and the Belgian team had another (XKD 573) for Frère/Rousselle. The quintet was completed by Hamilton (XKD 601, also with a 3.8 works engine but on Webers and producing 282bhp at 5500rpm), who had invited Masten Gregory to join him. From the factory 'Lofty' England, Malcolm Sayer and Len Hayden went along to assist.

Initially Hawthorn's Ferrari and Moss's Maserati disputed the lead, followed by a further selection of the Italian cars and the Aston team. However, within a couple of hours or so the opposition had shot their bolt and Bueb/Flockhart had their car firmly in the lead. As the Astons fell by the wayside, the Jaguars took a stranglehold by occupying the first four places. Hamilton/Gregory were delayed by electrical maladies and the exhaust system breaking up, which resulted in flames appearing in the cockpit (Duncan said the shoulder of his sweater was singed), but the pair then charged hard and made progress through the field. The result was spectacular Jaguar domination, with D-types placed 1-2-3-4-6 in the order Bueb/Flockhart, Lawrence/Sanderson, Lucas/Brussin, Frère/Rousselle and Hamilton/Gregory.

In private correspondence in 1961 Ron Flockhart gave some fascinating insights into driving at Le Mans. 'The impression I have of the D-type Jaguar, which is probably unique, is that its handling characteristics are similar to those of the D-type ERA. I found at Le Mans, particularly with

TOP **In the US Briggs Cunningham and his team campaigned D-types actively and successfully. They had first used XKD 507, a new 1955 long-nose car, at Le Mans.** ABOVE & LEFT **The French Los Amigos team's D-type (XKD 513) was prepared by the factory and tested at MIRA by Norman Dewis before the 1957 race. Driven by Jean Lucas and Jean-Marie Brussin, this ageing car – very much a production version – achieved a remarkable third place.**

ABOVE **Ecurie Ecosse and XKD 502 have even featured, and triumphed, in American fictional adventures set in 2007 AD.** RIGHT **Not a Ferrari in sight! This Italian movie poster for Cornel Wilde's** *The Devil's Hairpin* **shows a couple of D-types escaping the mayhem behind them.**

the tail fin, that the faster it went the more stable the car became. It was my practice to relax completely down the Mulsanne Straight (race traffic permitting!) and flex my fingers and arms, the car steering itself at around 170mph.

'A good personal test of chicken or hero driver was to take the slight right-hand kink at the end of the Mulsanne Straight absolutely flat – no secret cheating by easing off a couple of hundred rpm, but an honest 5800rpm on the 1957 3.8-litre. It could be done, but only just. If the track were damp, then this game was for chicken drivers only. Both Ivor Bueb and I discovered this in our own fashion – something the spectators missed! However, in conditions of crosswind this was not possible and I recall once at Goodwood one blustery day at practice where the Jaguar with tail fin was a handful through Fordwater and past the pits.

'The 3.4-litre Jaguar engine (and the later 3.8-litre) in my opinion come under the same category as the Gypsy Major and Rolls-Royce Merlin aero engines – it feels as if it would go on forever. However the 3-litre version was never as successful. I don't think the design lent itself to continued operation above 6000rpm. There was no marked difference in performance between the Lucas fuel injection 3.8-litre Jaguar and the normal carburettor D-type. The only noticeable difference was that the Lucas injection gave smoother acceleration with no spitting back and hesitation round a slow corner on part throttle. I still consider the 3.8-litre Jaguar engine to be capable of winning Le Mans at a higher speed than our 113mph of 1957, if mounted in a suitable chassis – the E-type?'

In July an interesting report was put together by Heynes which reveals certain developments taking shape. These include a straight-port three-carburettor engine, Holset Schwitzer supercharger and 3.4 aluminium cylinder blocks, of which 'six blocks will be obtained as soon as possible'.

D-TYPE TWILIGHT

Later in 1957 the Scots were invited to take part in a curious contest at Monza called the 'Race of Two Worlds', a 500-mile race between American Indianapolis cars and European racing cars. The event was boycotted, however, by the newly-formed International Professional Drivers Union and the only Europeans to take part were Ecurie Ecosse, which had no intention of foregoing a slice of the £30,000 prize fund. The full Monza circuit was not used because it did not suit the Indianapolis cars, so the D-types stood little chance of success running anti-clockwise on a banked bowl against eight cars designed precisely for this form of track.

'The Monza cars,' wrote Murray, 'ran virtually standard in 1957. A dash from Le Mans to Monza was followed by a quick decoke and the transferring of scoops which were used at Le Mans to cool the brakes, to act on the tyres'. The D-types were restricted to a maximum of 160mph by problems with tyre temperatures after Jack Fairman had an exciting moment during an investigative visit to the track. "Just as I was approaching the banking at about 165mph, the entire right-hand back tread came off with a noise like a six-inch shell".

Because of the bumpy nature of the track, the race was run in three 166-mile heats with an hour's break between each. The Indianapolis cars had only two gears, so Fairman, using his four-speed 'box to full advantage, led first time round – he once told me that he laughed so much he nearly went off the course! The American cars gradually

fell apart until only three were left, but the D-types ran like clockwork in their wake and finished a creditable 4-5-6, driven respectively by Fairman (who acquired the nickname 'Fearless' from this event), Lawrence and Sanderson.

During these years private D-types were being raced all around the world. Several distinguished drivers cut their teeth on them, none more famous than Jimmy Clark in the car registered TKF 9. Le Mans, however, was not to yield any more success. Not only was the 'D' becoming venerable, but a 3-litre capacity limit was imposed for 1958 and the XK engine was not reliable at this size. Time and again these 3-litre engines let the side down, although 'Lofty' England maintains that, "the first engines made with 3.4 blocks, short-stroke crank and tall pistons gave *no* trouble". While Jaguar built its 3-litre by reducing the capacity of the 3.4-litre engine, the game Scots cleverly achieved the same size by increasing the bore and stroke of the 2.4-litre unit.

Duncan Hamilton remained faithful to his D-types longer than most. He raced XKD 601 with Ivor Bueb at Le Mans in 1958 and on this occasion the 3-litre engine did not fail. They were in serious contention for outright victory when one of the 'creepers' (as Roy Salvadori once graphically described the little French cars to me) literally stopped in the middle of the track during a cloudburst. Hamilton somehow missed it but put a wheel on the grass and somersaulted, his car coming to rest upside-down over a water-filled ditch. But for immediate assistance from a couple of spectators sheltering nearby, he reckoned he would have drowned. Jean-Marie Brussin (XKD 513) was not so fortunate and crashed fatally during the race. The two Scottish cars retired very early on with piston trouble and Maurice Charles crashed his car (XKD 502).

Ecurie Ecosse entered a single D-type (XKD 603) for Masten Gregory and Innes Ireland in 1959, but its engine gave up the fight as usual. The same car was entered for Ron Flockhart and Bruce Halford in 1960, but the crankshaft broke after the car had been running as high as fourth place.

If Jaguar was to try to regain the glory of its halcyon days, it needed a new car...

LEFT **It seems impossible to believe that the production D-types were difficult to sell, but here is the evidence.**

LIGHTWEIGHT E-TYPE
DESIGN & DEVELOPMENT

ABOVE **E2A, the new competition car built in 1960, very obviously had evolved from the D-type, but radical differences below the skin included full monocoque construction from the front bulkhead back and, at last, independent rear suspension.**

The beginnings of the E-type and its competition derivatives go back to 1955. Strangely, the dreadful accident at Le Mans that year had a direct influence on the conception of the E-type. Following the tragedy, the regulations were revised and the salient changes were detailed in the 16 November issue of *The Motor*. 'Of first importance,' the article stated, 'is the ban on prototypes of more than 2½-litre capacity and the appointing of a special committee to examine them'. Apparently the D-type qualified as 'standard production cars, unlimited capacity', which was further defined as, 'at least 100 replicas must have been built or provided for'. Jaguar had not actually constructed this many D-types, but had every intention of honouring the spirit of the regulations. This 100-car stipulation, however, was to have major significance in the planning of the D-type's successor.

On 1 December 1955, Phil Weaver sent William Heynes an intriguing memo. The first part of it was quoted in Chapter 8 (see page 107), and the second part ran as follows:

2½-litre Prototype

Two courses are open to us on this car – one is to design a prototype as small and light as practicably possible and run it purely for one season as a prototype only.

On the other hand, it is likely that next year we shall be faced with a proposition which permits only cars of 2½-litre capacity in all categories. This would mean we could possibly run the 2½-litre car as a prototype, as I feel we would not want to put through another 100 cars, with such limited use, as the present D-type in production to make the car valid for the production car race, in which case it might be advisable to consider making the prototype car in such a manner that it would have at least limited demand in a better equipped version, such as the Porsche, for purposes other than racing. In this case the closed type body would seem to be the most satisfactory answer.

Digressing for a moment from the E-type story, some of these comments are interesting in the context of the production D-types and the XKSS. We have confirmation that the production 'D' was proving difficult to sell and the reference to, 'a bet-

LEFT **As thoughts turned to a D-type successor, design was influenced by new, but at this stage unknown, regulations expected in the wake of the Le Mans tragedy. The new 2½-litre sports car was to be both a racing car and a road car. There are hints of the XKSS in this early E-type model.**
RIGHT **Bill Heynes and 'Lofty' England favoured a return to racing as soon as possible, but Sir William Lyons was rather more cautious. This memo prompted a series of exchanges over the following months.**

ter equipped version' might be a most apt description of the subsequent XKSS.

It is pretty clear that this was the beginning of the E-type story and that, with the requirement to build a smaller 2½-litre car for racing, this could be combined with a roadgoing version with some commercial potential. Since a Le Mans winner could be used on the road in that era, it is certainly not too far fetched to imagine a detuned version being sold in limited quantities.

THE E1A PROTOTYPE

Naturally it was Malcolm Sayer who created the shape of the new car, and he liaised with Bob Knight under the overall direction of Bill Heynes. Other people who played a significant role included Tom Jones and Cyril Crouch. Knight has said that "design at Jaguar was invariably development led", and Crouch confirms this by referring to the design of the C-type, D-type and prototype E-type as "fag packet jobs", in that they were built first and drawn afterwards.

Phil Weaver was the Superintendent in the Competition shop: "When we finished racing in 1956 the firm decided to call us the Prototype shop and we continued with the E-type, which is what they thought was going to succeed the D-type. The first car we built was done more or less by word of mouth between Sayer and Knight in the Drawing Office, and that was E1A. It was a lovely little car, about a two-thirds scale model of the eventual E-type with a 2.4-litre engine." By now Bob Blake, the brilliant craftsman and artist in sheet metal who had joined Jaguar when Briggs Cunningham gave up racing, had become heavily involved too: "Malcolm had me up in his office and he said, 'We're going to do an E-type – it'll be much like the D-type but we'll do it as a production car as well'."

LEFT **Malcolm Sayer's E-type design evolved into a sleeker shape, perhaps with the competition version more in mind. The fact that he compared it with the D-type also shows that racing was intended.**

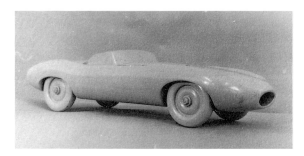

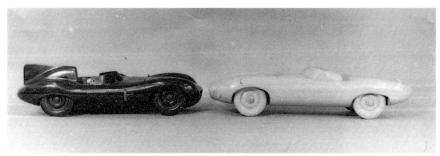

As for the car's name, the first layouts termed it a '2.4 2-seater', but early on the logical E-type name was adopted and indeed Sayer, in his early paperwork, referred to the 'E-type Prototype'. It was probably Phil Weaver who christened the first car E1A, the 'A' standing for aluminium.

"Malcolm Sayer and I discussed it back and forth," continues Bob Blake. "First he showed me the rough shape, then he worked out the precise

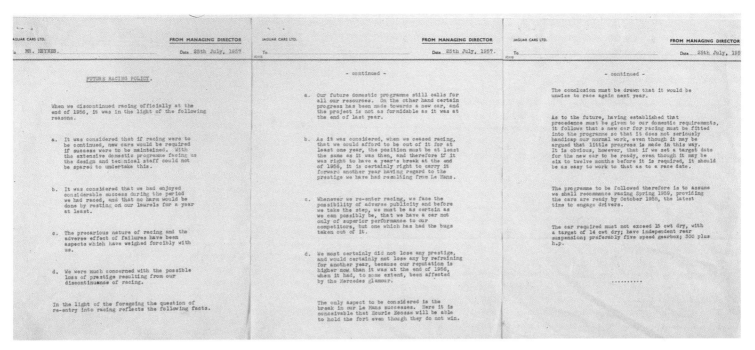

JAGUAR CARS LTD.   FROM MANAGING DIRECTOR

To MR. HEYNES.   Date 25th July, 1957.

FUTURE RACING POLICY.

When we discontinued racing officially at the end of 1956, it was in the light of the following reasons.

a. It was considered that if racing were to be continued, new cars would be required if success were to be maintained. With the extensive domestic programme facing us the design and technical staff could not be spared to undertake this.

b. It was considered that we had enjoyed considerable success during the period we had raced, and that no harm would be done by resting on our laurels for a year at least.

c. The precarious nature of racing and the adverse effect of failures have been aspects which have weighed forcibly with us.

d. We were much concerned with the possible loss of prestige resulting from our discontinuance of racing.

In the light of the foregoing the question of re-entry into racing reflects the following facts.

JAGUAR CARS LTD.   FROM MANAGING DIRECTOR

To   Date 25th July, 1957.

- continued -

a. Our future domestic programme still calls for all our resources. On the other hand certain progress has been made towards a new car, and the project is not as formidable as it was at the end of last year.

b. As it was considered, when we ceased racing, that we could afford to be out of it for at least one year, the position must be at least the same as it was then, and therefore if it was right to have a year's break at the end of 1956, it is certainly right to carry it forward another year having regard to the prestige we have had resulting from Le Mans.

c. Whenever we re-enter racing, we face the possibility of adverse publicity and before we take the step, we must be as certain as we can possibly be, that we have a car not only of superior performance to our competitors, but one which has had the bugs taken out of it.

d. We most certainly did not lose any prestige, and would certainly not lose any by refraining for another year, because our reputation is higher now than it was at the end of 1956, when it had, to some extent, been affected by the Mercedes glamour.

The only aspect to be considered is the break in our Le Mans successes. Here it is conceivable that Ecurie Ecosse will be able to hold the fort even though they do not win.

JAGUAR CARS LTD.   FROM MANAGING DIRECTOR

To   Date 25th July, 195

- continued -

The conclusion must be drawn that it would be unwise to race again next year.

As to the future, having established that precedence must be given to our domestic requirements, it follows that a new car for racing must be fitted into the programme so that it does not seriously handicap our normal work, even though it may be argued that little progress is made in this way. It is obvious, however, that if we set a target date for the new car to be ready, even though it may be six to twelve months before it is required, it should be as easy to work to that as to a race date.

The programme to be followed therefore is to assume we shall recommence racing Spring 1959, providing the cars are ready by October 1958, the latest time to engage drivers.

The car required must not exceed 15 cwt dry, with a target of 14 cwt dry; have independent rear suspension; preferably five speed gearbox; 300 plus h.p.

....

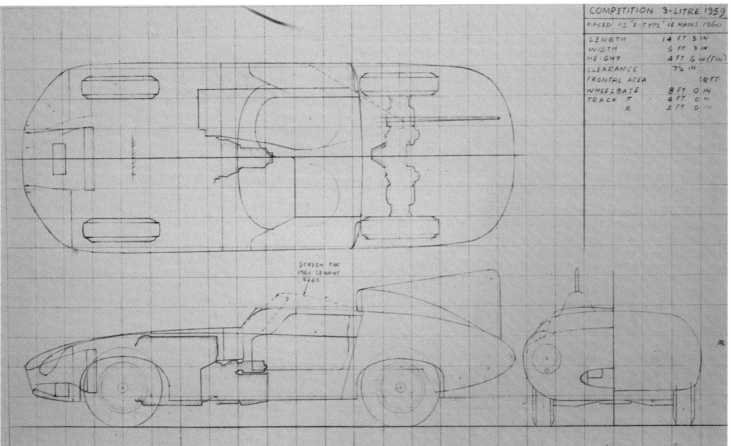

COMPETITION 3-LITRE 1959	
RACED AS 'E-TYPE' LE MANS 1960	
LENGTH	14 FT 3 IN
WIDTH	5 FT 3 IN
HEIGHT	4 FT 6 IN (FIN)
CLEARANCE	7½ IN
FRONTAL AREA	SQ FT
WHEELBASE	8 FT 0 IN
TRACK F	4 FT 0 IN
R	4 FT 0 IN

SCREEN FOR 1960 LE MANS REGS

ABOVE **The car Heynes had wanted to build for 1958 was finally created in 1960. Below his heading, 'Competition 3-litre 1959', Sayer later added 'Raced E-type Le Mans 1960'.**

shape and we got together on the internal construction of it. We sat down and had a good natter about the best way to produce the shape and how to do the internal construction, the doors and things like that. I said we'd rivet everything and not weld anything, so we did a great deal of 'spin-dimpling' and flush-riveting.

"I really liked to work with Malcolm because he was so precise in his measurements. He'd give me a set of figures for a body shape and I'd make the formers, and I think only three times in all the years that I worked with him did I find any error in his mathematics. At any point, you could put your finger, or a drawing pin, on the skin of a car and he could give the dimension to within a thousandth of an inch. Mr Heynes was really in charge of the whole damn thing, and experience had taught him that Malcolm was so good that the team to make the car had to be built round him."

In general terms the construction of E1A followed D-type practice at the front, having a multi-tubular subframe attached to the bulkhead. However, rearwards from here the construction was a genuine monocoque, without the D-type's additional A-frame tubular structure running to the rear through the transmission tunnel. The car, which measured 14ft 2in in length and 5ft 3in in width, had no bonnet bulge because the 2.4-litre engine did not require one.

The late Bill Heynes described to me the car's first run on 15 May 1957: "We took it down to the test track with Sir William, 'Lofty' and the drivers, and I said to Dewis, 'Come on and drive it'. But he said he wouldn't. Nobody would drive it! So I did, and went over 100mph in it. After that they all wanted to try it. It was a good little car." Over the following months E1A would be extensively tested by Norman Dewis in between rather more important development work on the saloons.

A report sent by Sayer to Heynes in July 1957 confirms that the project was still considered to have a dual role, and there is mention for the first time of a larger engine: 'For production cars, we could save the cost and weight of undershields and louvres and let radiator air out under the car; this is provided the single louvre at the back of the 'bulge' for 3.4 engines can prevent overheating when stationary. There is a need for fins or their equivalent for racing.'

Meanwhile a debate was raging between Lyons and Heynes about the pros and cons of returning to racing with a 3.8-litre racing version of the E-type with independent rear suspension. Eventually it was decided to abandon any thoughts of the factory re-entering racing in 1958 and concentrate on developing the car for a full '59 season.

On 10 June 1958 Heynes sent a fascinating memo to Sir William in which he proposed building 10 or 12 competition E-types for the 1959 season. Three were to be sold to Ecurie Ecosse, three to Cunningham and three retained for a factory team, with possibly a couple of spares and one more spare 'for disposal in whatever way you thought fit'. These cars were to have fuel injection, titanium front and rear suspension parts, self-locking diffs, and five-speed gearboxes. A 3-litre engine then being bench-tested, and predicted to give 280bhp, was to be fitted with a view to Mike Hawthorn testing the car at Silverstone in July.

'After completion of tests at Silverstone,' continued Heynes' memo, 'and providing that these are successful, ie, that the car in the condition in which it is being presented to Mr Hawthorne [sic] can equal or better the lap record, we should take the decision to re-enter racing for next year, this would allow Mr England to make the necessary arrangements to sign up the drivers we require before the competition have picked over them, which I think you will agree is essential.'

What is even more intriguing about this document is that Heynes goes on to talk about a new mid-engined car, the G-type: 'There is no suggestion that we should abandon development of the G-type with the centrally mounted engine, but if the proposals are accepted we would not show our hand with this model until Le Mans and then we could have the choice of entering one of the new cars or three of the new cars as we thought fit, without having first displayed the car to all and sundry at small meetings such as Silverstone, Argentine, etc...work is still proceeding on this [the G-type] and will not be affected at this stage by the present project [the E-type], and I would still make sure that we had three cars, if required, ready and fully tested in time for Le Mans. It will also mean that if the E-type shows itself superior, as I believe it will do, over the Aston and the Lister, we should be able to have a further year's development if we thought it necessary.'

So it sounds as though Heynes was suggesting a full factory team of E-types to contest all major 1959 events, supported by full teams of brand new cars for Ecurie Ecosse and Cunningham (as opposed to hand-me-downs, as with the Ecosse 'C's and 'D's), together with a team of mid-engined G-types for Le Mans. It was an ambitious plan, but sadly it was not to come to fruition – and the G-type project would fizzle out.

On 10 July Hawthorn duly tested E1A at Silverstone and 'Lofty' England filed a rather pessimistic report. His recollection today of that test and another with Ivor Bueb is that, "they were not very quick". Progress continued slowly on both the road and racing E-type projects for some time to come. "There was no great urgency to push along with the 'E'," says Dewis. "We knew we wanted a sports car, but we were a small team and we had so many other things going on that it was a matter of fitting the 'E' in."

ABOVE **With Sayer's designs for a new prototype completed, Bob Blake and colleagues began constructing the car that would become known as E1A.**

ABOVE **Apart from extensive testing by Norman Dewis, the new small sports car was lent to Christopher Jennings, Editor of The Motor. Under conditions of great secrecy he took it to his weekend home in Wales. As a result of his eulogistic private report, the E-type project was given the go-ahead.**

In July 1959 Sayer issued a report on the 'Drag Effects on New Regulation Windscreens'. From this we learn that the 'rear-engined competition 2-str' and the 'competition E-type' had both been wind tunnel tested – presumably in model form. Under existing regulations and fitted with 300bhp engines, maximum speeds were projected to be 208mph for the G-type and 203mph for the E-type – both sensational figures.

It would have been towards the end of 1959 when the decision was taken to start building a true competition version of the E-type. Several production prototypes had been built by this stage, and here the project was to divide into two distinct cars. Steel had superseded aluminium for the production prototypes, as Heynes explained: "Initially it was intended to use aluminium for the body structure, but the greater ease with which steel can be fabricated, and also repaired in the case of an accident, as compared with aluminium, led us to sacrifice the weight which we would otherwise liked to have saved".

THE E2A PROTOTYPE

The competition E-type was designated E2A and the Competition Shop notes state that, 'the car commenced building properly Jan 1st 1960. Car finished build Feb 27th 1960. First test run around works Sunday morning Feb 28th. Mr Heynes drove it up by-pass Feb 28th. First Lindley test Feb 29th'.

E2A was initially intended solely for testing, but the story goes that Briggs Cunningham was over at the factory, spotted it being built, and persuaded Sir William to have it ready for Le Mans. Indeed there was even talk of two cars, but only one was completed. Its first public appearance was at the Le Mans test weekend in April, but within an hour one of the drivers experienced an engine failure

that was probably caused, according to 'Lofty' England, by missing a gear. This confirmed the low opinion he and Dewis had formed of this driver, whose name was Ed Crawford.

Dan Gurney was retained for the race as partner to Cunningham's number one driver, Walt Hansgen, who was considerably quicker than his teammate and set the best time of practice, which seemed to bode well. However, in the race things did not go smoothly after a good start. By the second lap Hansgen was lying third behind Masten Gregory, whose Camoradi 'Birdcage' Maserati had overtaken no fewer than 18 cars on the Mulsanne Straight, and Olivier Gendebien in a Ferrari. Unfortunately on the third lap he came into the pits with injection problems, and replacing an injection pipe took over 8min, costing him two laps at this early stage.

After two hours Hansgen was up to 16th place. As he handed over to Gurney the heavens opened, but E2A continued to make good progress and reached sixth place when Hansgen took over again after three and a half hours. During the sixth hour, however, he had to pit for 15min for another injection pipe to be changed. Further stops were necessary and finally the car retired when its 3-litre engine suffered a burned out piston while lying in 34th position.

After its disappointing Le Mans foray, E2A was fitted with a 3.8-litre carburettor engine and shipped to the US, where Cunningham's team ran it with mixed success. Hansgen took a win against weak opposition at Bridgehampton and a good second at Elkhart Lake. World Champion Jack Brabham drove at Riverside, but in the qualifying race he was unable to get through for the main 200-mile event. However, he was allowed to compete in a consolation race in which it was decreed he could qualify if he finished in the top three. He came second – Cunningham believes with the collusion of other drivers – and thereby reached the main event, in which he finished a lowly 10th.

"They'd already paid Jack," Cunningham told me. "I think they'd sent him a cheque for $5000 for his expenses. He wanted to drive the car, but it was very upsetting for him because he was the World Champion. Somehow the organisers had to get him in the main race, so I guess they fixed it with the other guys to make sure he did OK in the second qualifying race. Poor Jack was obliged to put on a good show and the car just wasn't up to it". The car's short career petered out when Bruce McLaren failed to qualify at Laguna Seca.

Meanwhile during 1960 work continued on developing the production E-type, and prototypes 4 (850001) and 5 (850002), respectively blue and red roadsters, were run extensively. Prototypes 6 (885001) and 7 (885002) were the first Fixed Heads, the latter surviving today as the earliest prototype in existence, registered 9600 HP.

A new GT World Championship was planned

for 1961. With the 3.8-litre engine allowed and the new E-type almost ready for launch, this must have appealed strongly to Jaguar. Indeed there were plans to build 100 'GT E-Types', and Malcolm Sayer sent a memo to Bill Heynes on this subject on 9 December 1960: 'The estimated weight is 21cwt which is 1.7cwt less than the standard open car. This is unpleasantly high, and more extensive changes may be needed to make it a successful competition car'.

The main alterations from standard specification for the '100-off' cars were detailed by Sayer as, 'Bonnet, doors and boot lid in high quality, expoxide fibre-glass (material cost approx same as polyester type because less of it is used, and labour cost similar); production type detachable hard-top instead of hood because this saves about 25lb; dry sump engine with oil cooler; minimum of trim; no heater; no radio; perspex windows (but glass screen); lightened seats and bumper; and 30-gallon fuel tank'.

There was also mention of 'racing team cars' and the variations between these and the '100-off' cars were listed as, 'Reshaped fibre-glass top; larger brakes, with alloy calipers; perhaps even less trim and no bumpers. The difference in weight between racing and 100-off cars will be negligible'. Under the heading 'Possible Further Changes' Sayer suggested, 'Lightened rear axle support structure, alloy axle casing, alloy block, lightened scuttle and dash structure, lighter wheels'.

In proposing a reshaped roof, Sayer makes the first reference to an idea that would see light of day much later and be termed the 'low drag coupé'. Exciting though these plans sounded, once again they came to nothing. It is probable that at this stage, in December 1960, the small design and development team was just too stretched to cope with anything beyond the production E-type.

The E-type was still not ready for launch, nor would it be ready for production when it finally was launched in March 1961. The large Mark X saloon, codenamed 'Zenith', was also taking priority with a launch scheduled for October 1961. Indeed during late '60 and early '61, the blue and red roadsters and 9600 HP were very intensively tested and modified as pressure grew to complete the cars for launch. Matters were not helped by snow, ice and fog interrupting all road testing in mid-December. The maximum speed was one area giving concern and 9600 HP was repeatedly run up and down the new M1 and at MIRA in an attempt to achieve the magic 150mph.

Designated as the Press Car and lent to various magazines during early '61, 9600 HP was then readied for its March launch at the Geneva Show. In the usual panic of these things, it was driven flat-out by Bob Berry from the factory to Geneva, where Sir William was waiting. It made the press launch with 20min to spare...

That the E-type caused a sensation is very well

ABOVE **Although it set fastest time in practice at Le Mans in 1960, E2A had a disappointing race with fuel injection problems hampering the progress of drivers Walt Hansgen and Dan Gurney. It finally retired with a burned out piston.**

known. With its clear Le Mans lineage illustrated by its remarkable performance, with its sophisticated ride and handling provided by Bob Knight's new independent rear suspension, with its modest price and, above all, with its body of pure, simple, sensual beauty, the E-type took the world by storm. It was to become a cult car and very much a symbol of the Swinging Sixties.

"The body shape on the E-type car," claimed Heynes proudly, "breaks away considerably from traditional styling. The outer lines of the body have been evolved from the purely functional shape that was employed for the D-type car for sports car racing where the importance of low drag for such races as Le Mans was the overruling factor. The basic outline of the car was developed from experience gained with the various bodies constructed for the Le Mans race and such features as the wide overhanging wings, the small air intake and the carefully streamlined nose of the car are all the results of this experience. The body, or main structure of the E-type car, consists of a stressed shell fuselage with a nacelle, or subframe, on the front made of high-tensile steel tubes, which contains the engine and front suspension."

LEFT **The production E-type was launched at Geneva in March 1961 to universal acclaim. Much was made by Jaguar of the car's ancestry and its close relationship to the D-types. This prototype, registered 9600 HP, became the press car.**

THE E-TYPE GOES RACING

Due mainly to production problems, very few E-types escaped from the factory over the next few months and those that did, and remained in the UK, were either dealer demonstrators or intended for competition use. Some, like Robin Sturgess's roadster (850012), were both. On 16 March, the day the Geneva Show opened, Claude Baily issued a Project Specification to the Production Department with instructions for 'variations required to build seven competition E-type cars'.

The modifications related entirely to the power unit, clutch and transmission. The blocks were to have 10 thou machined off the top face, the heads were to be flowed with 25 thou machined off the face and shorter valve guides fitted, 9:1 compression ratio pistons were to be fitted two grades lower than bore grinding, and the inlet manifolds were to be flowed by the Experimental Department. Further modifications included a Nimonic head gasket, lightened flywheel, Metalastik competition crank damper, close-ratio gearbox, polished and crack-detected con rods, different valve springs and the adoption of carburettor trumpets.

Of these seven cars, two each went to John Coombs, Tommy Sopwith (Equipe Endeavour) and Peter Berry, and a single car was supplied to Sir Gawaine Baillie. The first two to be completed, and the most serious competition cars, were 850005 (registered ECD 400) for Sopwith and 850006 (registered BUY 1) for Coombs. These two cars made the E-type's racing debut at Oulton Park in April and scored a remarkable victory against strong Ferrari and Aston Martin opposition. Roy Salvadori led initially in the Coombs car before dropping back to third with brake problems, but Graham Hill kept Innes Ireland's Aston

DB4GT at bay to take a fine win with the Equipe Endeavour car.

"I had quite a dice with Graham," recalls Salvadori, "and I was ahead of him for about two-thirds of the race, but then the brakes went completely. I just had no brakes: I was pumping, but I think the old discs had torn up the pads and worn them out. Apart from the brakes, the car was very good to drive, very comfortable and safe. It was very neutral with no understeer or oversteer, just pleasant. I think the car was still fairly standard at that stage – amazing really."

Bob Berry told me that the feeling at the factory, "was that it was some fairly inspired driving by the pilots rather than anything else". When I put this to Salvadori his reply was typically modest: "They were new cars and they did everything we wanted them to do – they were very easy to drive. I just felt very privileged to be in at the start."

Sopwith remembers the event well: "Before the off, three of the entrants, Ronnie Hoare [the Ferrari importer], 'Noddy' Coombs and I all expected Jack Sears in the Ferrari to win. Not only did it surprise us, but I think there was a moment when Ronnie Hoare thought I'd fixed it – which I most certainly hadn't."

The E-type made its international debut at Spa on 13 May. For this the factory prepared a more highly modified engine, Bill Wilkinson building up a power unit with Iskederian XM3 cams and altered valve timing. Power at 5750rpm was improved from 243.5bhp to 276bhp, and torque from 222.1lb ft to 252lb ft. Mike Parkes ("arguably the best long-distance sports car racer of all," says Sopwith) took ECD 400 to a fine second place sandwiched by the Ferraris of winner Willy Mairesse and third-placed Graham Whitehead. Mike MacDowel was there representing the

RIGHT **The E-type had a fairytale racing debut at Oulton Park in April 1961. Against a field that included 250GT Ferraris and DB4GT Astons, Roy Salvadori led in BUY 1 until he experienced brake problems, but Graham Hill took over in ECD 400 to give the E-type victory in its first race – just like the XK120 and C-type!**

factory and recalls a problem in practice: "We fitted a big fuel tank for this race and it leaked. The only fix we could think of was chewing gum, literally, but it held for the race!"

Later that month Sears and Salvadori were entered in the Sopwith and Coombs cars respectively at Crystal Palace. This was the famous occasion when Salvadori could not be beaten and won no fewer than four races in a day. Showing his remarkable versatility, he climbed from single-seater to saloon to sports racer, and then into the E-type. The opposition included Parkes and Whitehead in Ferraris, but Sears led initially until Salvadori soon asserted his ascendancy, Sears following him home for a fine Jaguar 1-2.

"I raced ECD 400 on several occasions that season," recalls Jack Sears. "It was a splendid car, so smooth and incredibly refined for a competition car, but of course it wasn't a competition car. It was a road car, but a jolly quick one. Compared with the DB4GT Aston that I'd raced for Tommy Sopwith the year before, the Jaguar was much more refined, with a smoother engine. The roadholding was very good and much more manageable than the 3.8 Mark IIs."

At Brands Hatch Ferrari took some revenge during the 10-lap GT race. Salvadori led for eight laps before his engine went off song, leaving Parkes to win in the Ferrari. Hill's challenge faded when a rear brake locked, causing him to lose valuable time, and he could only finish third. Despite his engine running on only five cylinders, Salvadori pushed Parkes hard right to the end, but in fairness the Ferrari driver set a new lap record and earned high praise in the magazine *Motor Racing* for 'taking on the world's best'.

The British Empire Trophy meeting at Silverstone in May was also not so successful for the E-types, but there was a good reason – Stirling Moss was competing in Rob Walker's Ferrari 250GT Berlinetta. In a class of his own, he led from start to finish. Behind him, Salvadori, Hill and Bruce McLaren held the next positions for a while until Hill retired with overheating and Salvadori had problems, allowing McLaren in the new Peter Berry Racing E-type to take second place.

Phil Weaver then drew up a long memo that he sent to Bill Heynes and 'Lofty' England. Entitled 'Preparation of Standard E-type for Racing', it detailed a long list of minor modifications to the engine, gearbox, rear suspension, final drive unit, brakes, clutch, instruments, bonnet, exhaust, body, radiator, engine mountings, wheels, tyres, upholstery and trim.

At the supporting race to the British GP at Aintree, Sears drove the Coombs E-type after his Ferrari had been damaged when the trailer on which it was travelling became detached. Parkes was in the Sopwith E-type and Dennis Taylor in the Berry car. This time there were no Ferraris but two Astons, with Lex Davison in a Zagato-bodied ver-

sion and Sir John Whitmore in a regular DB4GT. The race began badly for Parkes when the gear lever came away in his hand as he left the line. Sears then led until he was slowed by overheating and a lack of brakes with just two laps to go. Davison won with the E-types in the next two places.

The principal E-types continued to have a reasonable season and during July such people as Robin Sturgess (850012), Jack Lambert (850016), Bruce McLaren (850015) and Peter Sargent (850009) also obtained their examples. The first Fixed Head (860001), which was to be Henlys' London demonstrator, was delivered in August and followed shortly by the fourth, which was to be campaigned by Dick Protheroe.

McLaren, like fellow GP drivers Innes Ireland (860009) and John Surtees, acquired his example purely for road use, but he had had some experience on the track during the year with the Berry car. Writing at the end of the season in the magazine *Motor Racing*, he extolled the virtues of the E-type on road and track.

'I have thoroughly enjoyed my racing with the Peter Berry stable, especially since Peter took delivery of his first E-type Jaguar. I'm really sold on this car and I also count myself pretty fortunate in being one of the first private owners of an E-type. It's fabulous value for money, and as an exhilarating road car, it must have few if any equals, regardless of price.

'On the track, too, it is proving quite a power, although the racing E-types are not so very far removed from the normal production job. The pale green Peter Berry car which I drive, for example, has a cleaned up cylinder head, harder brake pads, a more open exhaust and, of course, everything is put together pretty carefully.' McLaren went on to mention that he had proved this point by trying his own car at Silverstone and finding that 'it handled exactly like the racing version'.

ABOVE **Tommy Sopwith's Equipe Endeavour E-type (850005) was campaigned extensively in 1961. Following its debut win in Graham Hill's hands at Oulton Park, it was also raced by Mike Parkes and Jack Sears.**

ABOVE **E-types were rare in 1961, especially in Britain, and most of the early ones to escape the factory were raced. Robin Sturgess in 2 BBC, later registered 848 CRY (850012), leads Jack Lambert in RL 26 (850016).**

'The car can be oversteered or understeered at will, although inherently there is a small amount of understeer through the corners. Take Copse Corner as an example. I brake and change down to third then turn well into the bend before I put my right foot back on the accelerator. This sets the tail out to the left and by applying opposite lock and putting the power on hard, I can hold the car in an oversteering drift round the bend...

'It's obvious the E-type is destined to be with us a long time and no doubt it will win a lot of races, and carry on the fine tradition of the C- and D-types. I can see a great potential in this motor car, and I am sure it can go considerably faster than at present. So far I've had two E-type drives for Peter Berry, and on both occasions I've finished second after seeing Stirling Moss disappear into the distance with the Walker/Wilkins Ferrari Berlinetta. The Italian car has a tremendous amount of steam in a straight line, but I think the Jag is faster through the twisty bits...and as I've said, there's more to come!'

Towards the end of 1961 plans were revived to build several GT racing versions of the E-type and to give these cars full factory support during 1962. On 2 January Tom Jones and Derrick White, the South African engineer who was to be very involved in future developments, put together a proposal for Bill Heynes. It has variously been stated that the intention was to build three, four or even six of these cars. With saving weight as a priority, all panels were reduced in thickness by 2swg but remained steel. It seems that four shells were built, and these were constructed with a revised roofline to improve the shape aerodynamically. Sayer termed this style the Low Drag Coupé. Further modifications included fitting a steel box section above the axle line to take a 30-gallon bag-type petrol tank, aluminium bonnet and doors, Perspex windows and a roll-over bar. Assembly of

one car began, and this had an aluminium diff casing, lightened front and rear suspension components, and revised front suspension pick-up points.

Just to confuse matters further, it seems that another Project Specification was issued in January 1962 and authorisation was given to build, '6 E-Type open bodies in aluminium. Jaguar to purchase 6 sets of body panels in aluminium (less outer skin panels) material equivalent to production steel components. Details to be despatched to Messrs Abbey Panels for assembly into complete bodies, including external skin panels. Production of skin panels to be arranged between Abbey Panels and Mr Silver [John Silver, the Jaguar Production Director]'.

Again, sadly, it seems that policy changed and the team of Low Drag Coupés was not to be. The single car that had been started continued to come together slowly and was fitted with a 3.8-litre full-race engine with an aluminium block and wide-angle head. But the car would not see light of day for some time and it was decided to throw the factory's support behind the Coombs roadster. Although it was widely believed that the 1962 World Championship of Makes, or at least Le Mans (which was of more importance to Jaguar), would once again be contested by GT cars rather than sports prototypes, this decision was probably influenced by the fact that Jaguar knew this expectation to be wrong. In February the Coombs car, now registered 4 WPD, was sent to the factory for preparation for the new season.

It was totally stripped and rebuilt with an aluminium bonnet, doors and boot lid. Other modifications included a 35/40 wide-angle head, three 45 DCOE Weber twin-choke carburettors, $\frac{7}{16}$in lift cams, uprated torsion bars and springs, a servo, front calipers and discs from the Mark IX saloon, harder rear subframe mounting rubbers, a new master cylinder, Perspex side windows, a competition seat and a 26-gallon fuel tank. Offset 15in wire wheels were fitted with Dunlop R5 green spot tyres, and the rear suspension radius arm mounting bushes were turned through 90 degrees to improve stiffness.

In this form 4 WPD appeared at Oulton Park for a 25-lap race with Graham Hill at the wheel. "Graham left Tommy Sopwith's team," says Coombs, "because I offered him a £1000 retainer, which was double what he asked for. But my stipulation was that he remained 100 per cent with me on anything he did apart from Formula 1. He subsequently told me it was the first time he realised that he was of any value financially. It was also the first time anybody had doubled what he had asked for!" Hill and the other five E-type drivers in the race could do nothing about Parkes' Berlinetta Ferrari, which romped to victory, but Hill would henceforth play a very important part in the creation of the Lightweight E-types.

Although the Lightweight was still some way

off, Enzo Ferrari had taken the E-type threat sufficiently seriously to instruct his engineers to design a new car. The initial work was done by Giotto Bizzarrini, who is quoted as saying that Ferrari "requested a light, lower slung car...more competitive than those that we had at that time, but especially in comparison with the E-type Jaguar and Aston Martin". When Bizzarrini and other members of the staff walked out, the project was taken over by Mauro Forghieri. The result, of course, was the legendary 250GTO. Surprisingly traditional in concept, it had a typical twin-tube Ferrari chassis and retained a solid rear axle. But it had the heart of any classic Ferrari, a very powerful V12 engine, placed as low and far back as possible. Designed from the outset for competition use, the car was light and very rigid.

Two E-types appeared at the Le Mans practice weekend. Cunningham brought the roadster he had been racing in the US while Peter Sargent and Peter Lumsden arrived with their car, now heavily modified with its own version of what Sargent describes as "a coupé-style roof in aluminium". They had also fitted an aluminium bonnet that had had to be specially made, since Jaguar refused to sell them one of a very large batch that had been mistakenly made by Abbey Panels. On the Mulsanne Straight the British E-type was third fastest at 155.34mph and the American car fifth fastest at 144.78mph – but a GTO managed 164.66mph.

The Easter Goodwood meeting will always be remembered for Stirling Moss's awful accident which prematurely ended his career, but in the sports car race Salvadori was behind the wheel of the Coombs E-type and had a big shunt at Madgwick on the second lap. The car was subsequently rebuilt with one of the lighter-gauge steel shells that had been prepared for the embryonic team of Low Drag Coupés. The engine, gearbox and back axle were retained, but otherwise the car was rebuilt with fresh components, although to the same specification as before. The car's soft-top was replaced by an aluminium hard-top in the style of the production glass-fibre item.

A strong field lined up for the GT race at the International Trophy meeting at Silverstone. Parkes and Masten Gregory were in GTOs, Jimmy Clark and Mike Salmon were in Zagato Astons, and Hill in the Coombs entry headed the E-type challenge. Parkes took another win, while Hill initially held second but could not resist Gregory and had to be content with third. Hill, however, was much encouraged by the rebuilt E-type and felt it had the potential to be a winner.

In June Hill and Dewis carried out extensive testing of the Coombs E-type, trying a variety of combinations of suspension settings, tyre pressures and wider wheels. Following the Silverstone race Hill had complained of excessive understeer, and suggested more negative camber on the front and toe-in instead of toe-out at the rear. The car was

then fitted with a ZF limited slip differential, and shortly after with 6 × 15in light alloy disc wheels at the front and 6½ × 15in cast magnesium BRM wheels at the rear, both with 650 × 15in Dunlop R5 D9 tyres. Grahan Hill, of course, was by now a BRM driver and on the way to his first World Championship.

At a further test Hill complained that "the car felt more like a touring car than a racing car, too softly sprung", so the rear wheels were set up with negative camber of 1½ degrees and the tyre pressures gradually increased. Stiffer torsion bars and uprated rear springs were tried and in this state the car was taken to Mallory Park for its next event. In the heat and in the final Parkes once again was unbeatable in a GTO, but Hill did well to hold off another GTO driven by Surtees, who broke the lap record trying to catch the Jaguar.

Hill was now happier that the E-type felt more like a racing car but, according to a report by Derrick White, Hill stated that, 'the car still required much stiffer springs, anti-roll bars and dampers (the car appeared to roll more than the Ferraris)'. It was noted that he had out-accelerated Parkes off the line in both the heat and the final at Mallory Park, but that he had been out-braked into the first corner. Indeed the brakes came in for repeated criticism, as did the seat, which failed to hold his shoulders laterally during cornering so that he had to push hard on the steering wheel to hold himself in position. The centre of gravity was calculated and found to compare unfavourably with the GTO at 0.38:1 against 0.30:1. Indeed John Coombs told me, "The great thing about the Ferrari was that the V12 engine was so low in comparison with the E-type".

In his next report White suggested altering the front suspension pick-up points to give anti-dive characteristics and compared the E-type with the contemporary GP Lotus. He suggested that a 58in

ABOVE **Robin Sturgess replaced his roadster with a Fixed Head E-type for 1962 and transferred his 2 BBC registration. Here he is winning at Snetterton in March.** OPPOSITE TOP **Peter Lumsden and Peter Sargent considerably modified their early E-type (850009) by fitting a coupé-style aluminium roof and in 1962 competed at Le Mans.** MIDDLE **Briggs Cunningham shared his works-prepared E-type with Salvadori at Le Mans in 1962 and a fine fourth place was the result.** BOTTOM **Pictured during the 1980s, the Briggs Cunningham with the same E-type, which he kept for many years at his museum in California.**

track, rather than the standard 50in, would help considerably to reduce weight transfer and body roll angle during cornering. 'In order to corner at the same speed as the GP cars it would seem necessary to have the same proportion of weight transfer, and proportionately larger tyres – say 900 or 950 × 15in section – if Dunlops could be persuaded to make them'. How interesting that White was suggesting not only an 8in wider car, but also tyres of considerably greater width than GP cars! With what we now know of tyre development over the following few years, the E-types would surely have stolen a march on the Ferraris had he been allowed to pursue his ideas.

Three E-types were entered for Le Mans in 1962. Lumsden and Sargent had their familiar modified early car, Maurice Charles had a specially-prepared car that he would share with John Coundley, and the factory built up a new Fixed Head for Briggs Cunningham to share with Salvadori. The factory-prepared engines for the Lumsden/Sargent and Cunningham cars were found to be producing 299.5bhp and 296bhp respectively. The Cunningham car was based on a standard steel shell and incorporated some of the modifications developed on the Coombs car, together with certain elements of the Low Drag Coupé. A Monza filler cap fed the 30-gallon bag-type fuel tank and the engine, which was to 4 WPD specification, additionally was dry-sumped. Alloy wheels and a rear axle oil cooler were fitted.

"I was supposed to drive a big Maserati for Cunningham," says Salvadori, "but when I got to Le Mans I found I couldn't get in it – I think they were all made for Stirling! So Briggs asked me if I'd partner him in the works Jaguar he had coming over, and within a couple of hours it arrived with the works mechanics. I said I'd love to, and told him I already knew E-types – it was the only car I ever felt really comfortable in with my long legs. In fact, this one was the most comfortable competition car I ever drove and I had my best Le Mans ever with it."

The Charles/Coundley car retired after nearly three hours with engine maladies, but the other two E-types circulated like clockwork, the British-entered car the faster of the two and looking good for third place until disaster struck late in the day. The gearbox, which had been rebuilt at Jaguar, the job done by an apprentice, gave trouble with an hour to go. "Coming out of Arnage," recalls Lumsden, "the car suddenly started to rattle and shake, and smoke came out of the gearbox". He handed over to Sargent, who remembers "the gearbox screaming louder and louder, so I went round the circuit for the last hour in top gear only and even down the straight it wasn't possible to squirt it". The ailing car finished fifth, the Cunningham car passing it for fourth place in the last half hour. The race was won by a Ferrari prototype followed by a couple of GTOs, the Cunningham

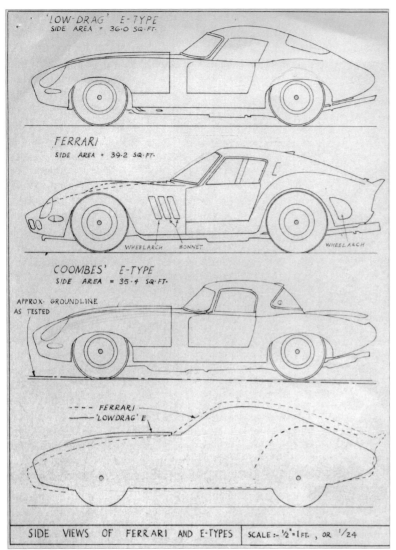

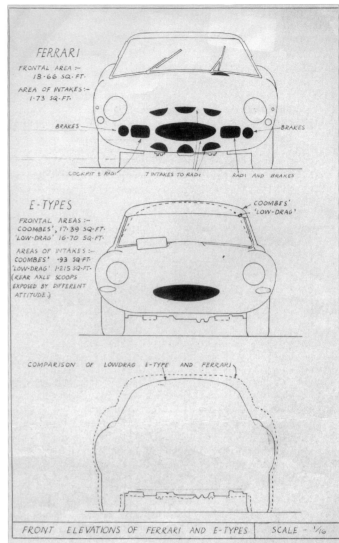

E-type therefore coming third in the GT class.

In preparation for the August Bank Holiday Brands Hatch meeting, further work was carried out on 4 WPD, which was stiffened up, fitted with larger rear wishbones and given a seat with better lateral support. The car was tested at Silverstone, where Hill reported rear-end steering, weaving under braking (the cause turned out to be a loose hub nut) and excessive wheelspin under acceleration out of corners. There was a considerable improvement after the $^{13}/_{16}$in rear anti-roll bar was changed for one of ¾in. The brakes, however, still required pumping after a few laps, and continued to cause concern during mid-week practice at Brands. Hill had to contend with no fewer than six GTOs, including Salvadori in a Coombs-entered one, but managed to qualify fourth.

Graham was one of several drivers entered at Brands who took part in the German GP the same weekend. After winning it, he returned for Monday's race in good form. Having requested a lower axle ratio to improve his chances off the line, he was confident that he could hold the Ferraris if only he could get to the first corner in the lead. In torrential rain he initially out-accelerated Parkes's

GTO until he had to change gear, and at that moment Parkes hit the E-type's offside rear wing and pushed the car wide at Paddock Bend. This incident, together with a misfiring engine, allowed five Ferraris to slip past, but Hill re-took David Piper's GTO and finished fifth behind Parkes, Salvadori, Ireland and Surtees.

The Coombs GTO ("a wonderful car, so progressive, and the only Ferrari I really liked," says Salvadori) was to play a significant role in the Lightweight E-type story. In an interview with Coombs, I expressed surprise that he, as a Jaguar dealer, ran a Ferrari.

"We wanted certain things modified on the E-type, but I think Jaguar resented Graham doing design work on its cars and, secondly, me agreeing to this. It was suggested by Mr England in a letter that maybe it would be a good idea if I managed the team, if I was capable of it, of which he had doubts, and that Mr Hill continued his driving and stopped trying to re-design cars, which he obviously wasn't very good at. Since we weren't getting anywhere with the E-type, I thought I'd buy a GTO. Mr England's attitude changed after that...

"If he produced an all-aluminium, lightweight

ABOVE LEFT **Towards the end of 1962 Jaguar borrowed John Coombs' Ferrari 250GTO and gave it a thorough examination. Malcolm Sayer, who was not impressed with all the Ferrari's louvres and vents, prepared comparative drawings of the GTO, Coombs E-type and his Low Drag design.** ABOVE **Both E-type shapes had a smaller frontal area and fewer drag-inducing intakes than the Ferrari 250GTO. The embryonic Low Drag car was clearly the better E-type option, which only emphasises the opportunity Jaguar missed in not pursuing this theme in 1961-62.**

E-type, he said, would I enter that in place of the Ferrari? I said I would, provided the car was competitive, because all we were trying to do in motor racing was win races. That's what Jaguars subsequently did, but that's why we bought the Ferrari."

The Coombs E-type returned to the factory as usual to be prepared for the TT at Goodwood a fortnight later, but apparently little work was carried out owing to lack of time. Stiffer rear dampers were fitted, 'obtained from Girling to cure the bounding and consequent sliding of the rear', stated the factory report. A 26-gallon fuel tank replaced the normal 14-gallon one, 'with the spare wheel positioned above it, and filler cap accessible through lid in offside of bootlid'. Two holes were cut into each side window, the lower hole on the driver's side having a duct to direct fresh air into the cockpit.

Ireland was fastest in practice followed by Surtees, Parkes and Hill, all in GTOs, and then Salvadori in the E-type followed by Piper's GTO and Clark's Zagato Aston. In the race Surtees led until Clark's spinning Aston took him out, and Salvadori finished fourth. Roy remarked at the time that he "was faster on the Lavant Straight but due to the inferior power/weight ratio, lost out on acceleration out of corners". Obviously a lighter and more powerful car was urgently required.

Derrick White put together some suggestions about how this could be achieved, pushing for lighter components, a five-speed gearbox, suspension changes and wider wheels. Phil Weaver also committed his thoughts to paper in July: 'By using titanium extensively in the construction of chassis components and body, an all round reduction in weight could be achieved, but only at great expense. It would seem therefore that to build a car in the genuine 15/17cwt range necessitates reducing the overall scale, the end product being a smaller, compact vehicle, using a multi-cylinder engine of 3 litres capacity weighing around 400/450lb, preferably designed with a low C of G, so that the final C of G of the car would also be low. This coupled with an adequate width of track should produce a successful car, particularly if such important details as weight distribution and adequate size of tyre are settled at the design stage.'

During September the Experimental Department managed to borrow the Coombs GTO and examined it thoroughly. Malcolm Sayer gave it the wool tuft treatment and tested it in the MIRA wind tunnel together with the Low Drag Coupé and 4 WPD: 'Drag on the Ferrari was 10½% worse than the low drag 'E' and 7½% better than Coombs' car'. Of the Ferrari he had this to say: 'It had a very good shape, particularly its front half, but drag had been greatly increased by the many holes and leaks in the body, many of which were useless and could be eliminated by careful development. Front end...an excellent shape, the low height of the 'V' engine and of the headlamps (4in below legal minimum) permitted a much better profile than we can achieve'.

On Bill Heynes' instructions the GTO's engine was removed and bench-tested, which did not amuse John Coombs when he happened to call in. George Buck reported to Heynes that it produced 288bhp. The engine was then refitted (with some difficulty as someone tidying up at the weekend had inadvertently disposed of all the nuts and bolts, most of which were metric) and the car was taken to MIRA for testing. With Dewis driving and White as passenger, plus half a tank of fuel, the GTO recorded a standing quarter-mile of 13.5sec, slightly quicker than the E-type's 13.7sec. The Ferrari was fitted with a 4.6:1 axle and the E-type with a 3.77:1 one. The GTO was found to have a maximum speed of 147mph whereas the E-type could manage only 132mph, but the British car's acceleration was slightly quicker up to 100mph. 'Roll angles' and 'drift angles' were found to be similar, but the Italian car understeered considerably on the steering pad. However, the GTO benefited from a more rapid and precise gearchange, better visibility due to the lower bonnet, and a superior pedal layout.

An extensive report put together by Derrick White and Tom Jones concluded, 'it is obvious...that the superior engine power of the E-type must be more than offset by the lighter weight, better aerodynamics, superior gearbox and better handling of the 250GTO Ferrari'.

On 16 November 1962 White and Jones sent the Competitions Department instructions detailing a new car that was to built. It was described as 'E-type – 1963 Competition – 1st Aluminium Body'. The familiar Coombs car, 4 WPD, was to be entirely rebuilt around a new aluminium shell, and a further 11 new cars were to be built to similar specification. They would become known as the Lightweight E-types.

BELOW **Peter Lumsden and Peter Sargent were heading for third place at Le Mans in 1962, but gearbox problems in the final hour dropped them back to fifth.**

CHAPTER ELEVEN

LIGHTWEIGHT E-TYPE IN DETAIL

The instructions Derrick White and Tom Jones put together and issued to the Competitions Department on 16 November 1962 detailed the work to be carried out in creating a new aluminium-bodied E-type for John Coombs. This specification would largely be followed in the construction of a further 11 examples through 1963 and into early 1964.

THE FIRST LIGHTWEIGHT

The most radical changes, of course, were in the body material specification and construction. The new Lightweight E-type had an aluminium monocoque based on the original 96in wheelbase production E-type Open Two-Seater. It was produced off production tooling, but was strengthened in areas of high stress. The instructions from White and Jones ran, 'weld and gusset aluminium body where necessary, strengthen rear engine mounting, strengthen mid engine mounting, strengthen kick-

up/floor joint, provide mountings for bucket seat, fit diagonal safety belt from Coombs' 'E', fit production 'E' windscreen, fit hardtop from Coombs' 'E'; and fit 14-gallon light alloy fuel tank'. Items that would be taken from the old car were the sliding Perspex side windows, complete aluminium bonnet, windscreen wipers and washer, and seats (but with extra lateral support for the back of the driver's seat).

From the instructions we learn that a new 3.8-litre engine with an aluminium crankcase – the most significant mechanical novelty – would be built up with a 35/40 head, petrol injection and dry sump. This engine was, 'to be supplied by Mr Wilkinson, with parts from Coombs's E-type engine where necessary'. The throttle mechanism would be revised, both Graham Hill and Roy Salvadori having felt that a smoother, more progressive set-up was necessary. A new header tank to suit the petrol injection would be designed and a high-pressure fuel pump would be fitted at the rear

ABOVE **Although the 1962 E-type had more power than the Ferrari 250GTO, it was considerably heavier. Jaguar's answer was to create the Competition E-type, now better known as the Lightweight.**

ABOVE **This stunning Lightweight is number 11, the ex-Dick Wilkins car (S850668) that had never been raced until the present owner, Nigel Corner, began campaigning it in recent years in historic racing.**
RIGHT **The lighter weight was achieved by using aluminium alloy for the monocoque and engine block, saving 250lb over the steel-bodied E-type and 100lb over the GTO.**

of the car. The wiper motor and battery would be re-positioned, an oval oil tank and mounting would be made up, a Coventry Radiator oil cooler would be obtained, and a production E-type water radiator, without a fan, would be fitted.

The gearbox from 4 WPD would be reconditioned and mated to this engine, and the propeller shaft would be retained. The rear axle would have a light alloy casing and an oil cooling system employing an SU pump, together with a radiator 'positioned by Mr Sayer'. The ZF differential would be retained and a 3.54:1 ratio was selected. Lightened half shafts with spacers would be used.

As for the suspension, at the rear the hub carriers, hubs, 6L × 15in wheels, 700 × 15in Dunlop R5 D9 tyres, wishbones, radius rods, $^{11}/_{16}$in anti-roll car, 25 per cent stiffer 'vee' mountings, radius rod front bushes, cross-beam and coil springs would all be carried over from the old 4 WPD. Additionally, new Girling adjustable dampers, spring pads and light alloy inner fulcrums would be fitted, and the camber angle set at –2 degrees. For the front end, the suspension and steering components to be retained from the old Coombs car were the vertical links, hubs, 6L × 15in light alloy wheels, 650 × 15in R5 D9 tyres, torsion bars and $^7/_8$in anti-roll bar. As with the rear, Girling adjustable dampers would be fitted at the front. Other new items to be made up or modified included lightened production upper and lower wishbones, upper and lower fulcrum shafts, front and rear upper and lower fulcrum mountings, and front fulcrum upper frame mountings. The upper fulcrum mountings would be fitted $1^9/_{16}$in lower on the frame and crossmember to provide more camber change.

A rack and pinion steering assembly with a different rack, rack housing and mounting rubbers would be used, together with altered tie rod levers. The steering column and wheel would be taken from 4 WPD, but a new aluminium upper mounting was to be employed for the steering column. The camber angle would be set at –2 degrees and castor at +3 degrees. The instructions added, 'Steering geometry to be checked in position on the car, by preventing one vertical link from steering, and lifting this link through its normal travel with the torsion bar, damper and wheel removed. If the steering geometry is incorrect the steering wheel will turn while the vertical link is being lifted or lowered. This should be corrected by raising or lowering the rack ball joint'.

The existing brakes would be retained: $11^1/_2$in discs front and rear, $2^1/_2$in light alloy front calipers from the Mark IX saloon, and $1^1/_8$in cast iron rear calipers from the production E-type. The production E-type pedal gear with '2 × $^5/_8$in master cylinders and balance bar system, modified pad angles and no servo' were further instructions for the Competitions shop, which was also told to leave off the old car's front disc air scoops but to transfer the rear ones.

THE 'PRODUCTION LIGHTWEIGHTS'

The other 11 cars, which might loosely be termed the 'Production Lightweights', were built to a similar specification as the pioneering Coombs version, although each had special features. From the individual Specification Sheets for each car we learn of more modifications (which had already been carried out on the 1962 Coombs car and automatically transferred to the 1963 Lightweight) and the standard specification for the Production Lightweights.

The body shape remained the same on the standard Lightweights but the aluminium hardtop and bootlid had rearward facing vents for heat extraction. Neither bumpers nor headlamp trims were fitted. Rather than the usual filler flap and hidden cap, a large exposed fuel filler cap was positioned in the offside rear tonneau area. The bonnet motif bar and chrome bonnet trims were also deleted. Standard front and rear combined sidelights and flasher units were retained. External bonnet locks, similar to those on the D-type, were used and supplemented by small bonnet straps mounted just ahead of the catches. The front subframe, which carried the engine, front suspension and radiator, remained in steel and was attached to the aluminium bulkhead in the usual E-type way.

The interior was very much more stark than on production road cars and no trim was used at all. The side windows, which were Perspex, slid up and down rather than winding in the more usual way. The driver's seat had a light alloy frame and safety harness fittings were provided, but no belts were supplied.

The most notable change to the engine, as on the Coombs car, was the use of an LM8 WP aluminium alloy cylinder block. The capacity was unchanged at 3781cc and to this was fitted the 35/40 wide-angle cylinder head with $1^{11}/_{16}$in exhaust valves and $2^3/_{32}$in inlet valves. Camshafts with profile XK1237 and $^7/_{32}$in lift were used ini-

ABOVE **Light alloy wheels, similar in appearance to those introduced on the D-type, were used on the 12 Lightweights. The clean appearance of the cars was helped by the lack of external trim such as bumpers and headlamp cowl surrounds.**

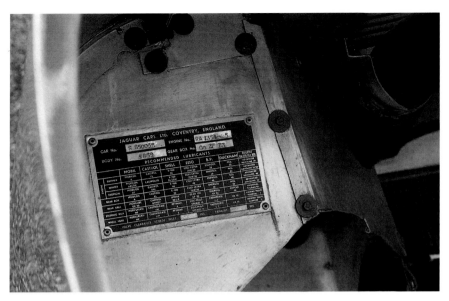

ABOVE **Only 10 of the 12 cars constructed are known to survive, with one written-off and another missing. The chassis plate is mounted under the nearside front wheelarch.**

tially, but later replaced by camshafts with even higher lift of 15⁄32in. A 15 thou Nimonic head gasket was used.

A Lucas mechanical petrol injection system was employed with six separate butterfly throttles and 6¼in trumpets. A Lucas 100lb psi electric fuel pump was fitted and Super Shell 100-octane petrol was specified. The fuel tank was a 14-gallon production item modified for petrol injection. A modified oil filter was fitted and oil pressure stated as 50lb psi at 5500rpm at 100°C. This engine featured dry-sump lubrication and used a special combined scavenge and pressure pump driven from the crank, and a second pump driven by a shaft from the front of the power unit and located adjacent to the number four main bearing. Oil tank capacity was 2½ gallons and the sump was cast in aluminium.

A modified and Nitrided crankshaft was used and the connecting rods were stamped from EN16 material. Main and big end bearings were lead indium VP2, and X-rayed Brico squish-crown pistons were used on most cars. A competition crank damper was fitted, Bimetal and steel thrust washers were specified, and there was a lightened flywheel. Laycock Hauserman cover plates and driven plates were used for the clutch.

The cooling system consisted of a standard radiator and header tank with an aluminium-bodied CI rotor water pump and ran at a pressure of 7lb psi. No fan was fitted and temperature was stated to run at 65/70°C. In standard Lightweight form power was given as 297bhp at 5500rpm and torque as 300lb ft at 4500rpm for most cars, but the Bob Jane car (number 10) was rated at 293bhp at 5750rpm. Fuel consumption for all cars was given as 0.517 pints/bhp per hour at 5500rpm and the compression ratio was 9.5:1.

A Jaguar-made E-type close-ratio gearbox was used initially and had ratios as follows: first 2.98:1, second 1.75:1, third 1.21:1, fourth 1.00:1 and reverse 2.98:1. Later Lightweights used a ZF

five-speed gearbox, and some earlier cars were updated. Negating the benefit of the extra gear, the ZF unit was considerably heavier, which compounded the stress problems experienced with the aluminium blocks, and it absorbed more than twice as much power – 55bhp against 25bhp. The ratios were first 2.73:1, second 1.76:1, third 1.23:1, fourth 1.00:1 and fifth 0.83:1 (reverse was not quoted).

The propshaft was from the production E-type and the 4HU Salisbury axle was fitted at the factory with a 3.54:1 ratio (but this could obviously be changed to suit different race circuits). A Thornton Tork-Lok differential was used and Motorex 314 axle oil suggested. It has been stated that the diff housings were aluminium: although the factory had these made, it seems they were never used. Certainly this is corroborated by the factory specification sheets, which state that the axle was 'cast iron'. Dunlop R5 D9 tyre sizes were 650 × 15in front and rear. Light alloy disc wheels with peg drive were employed and initially the size was 6L × 15in, but on some cars rim widths gradually increased during development.

The front suspension was similar in principle to its production cousin, with identical upper and lower wishbones, which were polished and cadmium-plated. However, subtle changes were made to the other related components, including lightened spindles and alterations to vertical links, tie rod levers, upper fulcrums, upper front fulcrum housings, upper rear fulcrum housings, lower fulcrums, and lower front and rear fulcrum housings. Uprated torsion bars were adopted with a setting bar length of 15¹³⁄₁₆in. The telescopic shock absorbers were uprated, had less travel and integral bump stops. A ⅞in anti-roll bar was fitted at the factory, but this could be changed to suit racing requirements. Castor angle was set at 4½ degrees positive with 1⁄16in toe-in.

The rear suspension again remained very similar to the production E-type but was lightened and used certain components from the Mark X saloon, including the lower crossmember bracing plate. The cross-beam was standard production E-type and the hub carriers, lower wishbones and lower fulcrums were modified Mark X parts. The track was increased slightly by adding a ½in block to the drive shafts and using a modified Mark X lower arm. The hub carriers were standard apart from having a large lightening hole drilled through the web. The standard E-type ¹¹⁄₁₆in rear anti-roll bar was used but the suspension mounting rubbers were 25 per cent stiffer than those used on production road cars. The radius rod bushes were turned so that the holes were at right angles to the car's centreline. The camber angle was set at −2 degrees with 0-¹⁄₁₆in toe-out.

As for the brakes, the upright brake carriers were special forgings and Mark IX saloon calipers were utilised with alloy piston blocks and special

LEFT **Although of unchanged capacity, the engine was very highly modified with a wide-angle head, Lucas petrol injection, higher-lift cams, improved exhaust manifolding and dry sumping. Still with its petrol injection, this is the engine in the famous Lindner/Nöcker Lightweight (the Corner car, like others used actively in historic racing, has been converted to Weber carburettors).**

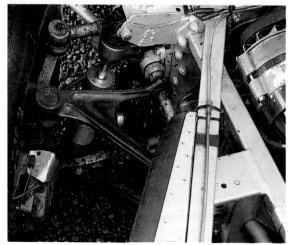

FAR LEFT **Visually similar to standard E-type suspension, but improvements were made to the Lightweights by modifying bracketry and altering mounting points. The header tank and its mounting were different, and the wide-angle head can be recognised by the extra splay of its cam covers.**
LEFT **Stiffer torsion bars (which also transform a standard E-type), uprated dampers with integral bump stops and a ⅞in anti-roll bar helped to turn the Lightweight into a competition car, and calipers from the old Mark IX saloon improved braking.**

hubs. The discs were of 11¼in diameter at the front and 10¾in at the rear, all having a thickness of ½in, and for the rear brakes air scoops were fitted underneath to provide cooling. The pedal gear, front master cylinders, handbrake pads and pedal box were production items. A Kelsey Hayes brake booster from the production E-type was fitted to earlier Lightweights, such as the Qvale and Cunningham cars, but not to the later Atkins, Lindner and Jane cars. The pedal load for cars with the booster was not given, but for cars without it was 150lb for a 0.9g stop. The front/rear braking distribution was 64.5/35.5.

The steering rack was lowered. This is con-

firmed by the fact that the E-type 'picture frame' (the cross member at the front of the main sub-frames to which the rack is bolted) has two sets of holes drilled in it, one set for the standard cars and the other for the competition version.

The new cars achieved their principal aim of being lighter, weighing some 250lb less than a steel monocoque E-type and, more importantly, 100lb less than a Ferrari 250GTO. However, total dry weight (without driver or fuel, but with oil and water) seemed to vary from car to car, and was given as 2240lb for the Atkins and Jane cars, 2072lb for the Cunningham (5115 WK) and Qvale cars, and 2220lb for the Wilkins car. Mid-laden

RIGHT **Although the Lightweight makes a thrilling road car, it reveals its competition purpose by being extremely noisy, with a continuous cacophony from the fuel injection, myriad rattles and a lack of sound-deadening.**

RIGHT **The aluminium construction can clearly be seen in the boot area. This car left the factory weighing 2220lb.** FAR RIGHT **The remote oil tank for the dry-sump lubrication system holds 2½ gallons.**

weight (with half a tank of fuel and a driver) was given as 2272lb for the Cunningham and Qvale cars. The centre of gravity in this condition was calculated to be 19in from the ground.

The cars were built over a period of 10 months from March 1963 to January 1964, not in one batch, and were delivered as follows: two in March, one in April, two in May, two in June, and one each in July, October, December and January. Initially it was intended to build 18 aluminium-bodied cars with special chassis numbers, but this decision was rescinded and the Lightweights were given ordinary production chassis numbers with an 'S' prefix, possibly for homologation reasons.

The whole matter of homologation was most curious. In order to homologate a car for international GT racing, it was necessary to build 100 examples in one year. However, it seems that body shape was free, enabling Ferrari to claim that the 250GTO was merely a re-bodied version of the 250GT. Jaguar had no wish to build 100 aluminium-bodied E-types, so it seems that on the homologation papers the company stated that the standard cars were the Lightweights and the steel-bodied ones were the specials. For example, the wheels were listed as 'light alloy disc *or* wire spokes', the valves as '53.2mm *or* 44.4mm' and the body as 'aluminium *or* steel'...

CHAPTER TWELVE

LIGHTWEIGHT E-TYPES IN COMPETITION

The first two examples of what the specification sheets called GT E-types were completed hurriedly to enable them to compete in the Sebring 12 Hours in March 1963. They were shipped to Briggs Cunningham and Kjell Qvale, the latter the owner of a large garage business in San Francisco who probably imported more British sports cars into the US in the 1950s and 1960s than anyone else.

For Sebring Cunningham entered two other E-types besides his new Lightweight, which was to be driven by Walt Hansgen and Bruce McLaren. One was his Le Mans Fixed Head and the other the roadster he had been racing in the US for a while. The Qvale car was to be shared by Ed Leslie and Frank Morrill, with preparation by Joe Huffaker. After three hours the Cunningham Light-

weight lay sixth, headed in the GT class only by Dan Gurney's new AC Cobra and one of a host of GTOs, while the Qvale car was eighth. Brake problems then dropped Hansgen/McLaren to eighth at the finish, the Qvale Lightweight taking seventh place overall and winning the over 3-litre GT class.

The Qvale organisation also ran a highly modified Fixed Head at this time in the US, and Huffaker was able to compare it with the Lightweight: "The new car was lighter and had more torque, but the coupe was a slippery car and I doubt if the Lightweight was as aerodynamic. It had a 35/40 head and PI, so it was quicker than the coupe – although that would do 170mph at Daytona. The Lightweight pretty much fell apart at Sebring: we beat it to death and it wasn't too neat a car. We

ABOVE **An intense aura has built up around the legendary Ferrari 250GTO, but Lightweight E-types beat GTOs surprisingly often. One such occasion in 1963 was the thrilling Daily Express meeting where Graham Hill led Mike Parkes and Roy Salvadori.**

ABOVE **During the winter of 1962-63 the John Coombs E-type, which was virtually a works car, metamorphosed once again, this time into the prototype Lightweight which Graham Hill took to victory on its debut at Snetterton.**

and Innes Ireland and obtained their autographs! Coombs still had his GTO, and Hill practised both this and the Lightweight E-type. He decided to drive the British car, which had just been homologated as a GT car under Appendix J regulations. Hill dominated and led Mike Parkes in a GTO from start to finish, setting the fastest lap in the process and finishing 1.4sec ahead. Salvadori was third in the Atkins E-type.

Later in April Mike MacDowel took 4 WPD to Loton Park, the hillclimb near Shrewsbury, and beat Jaguar stalwart Phil Scragg's ordinary E-type, which must have made Scragg feel he could do with a Lightweight. On 3 May the fifth Lightweight was registered by Jaguar and delivered a fortnight later to Peter Lindner, the German Jaguar importer. Around the same time the other Peters, Lumsden and Sargent, took delivery of the sixth Lightweight.

The next major meeting was the *Daily Express* Silverstone event. In the presence of HRH Princess Margaret, Lord Snowdon and 100,000 other spectators, the programme got under way with a thrilling GT race that had everyone present on the edge of their seats.

'Bang on the stroke of 10.15,' reported *Autosport*, 'all the Grand Touring cars were unleashed – to the delight of all, into the lead went the E-type Jaguars of Graham Hill and Roy Salvadori, chased by Parkes in the 250GTO Ferrari, Protheroe's E-type and Peter Jopp's AC Cobra V8. It was a fabulous battle in front; Parkes slipped past Salvadori, to tack the Maranello car onto the tail of Hill's Jaguar. For three laps, Graham held grimly onto his lead but, with the stands roaring excitement, Parkes took the E-type at Woodcote, and Salvadori was also trying hard to overtake Hill. Protheroe sat firmly in fourth place...

'Try as they might, neither Hill nor Salvadori could get ahead of the Ferrari. Parkes, Hill and Salvadori were giving the crowd their money's worth – their progress through Woodcote being somewhat frightening. Four laps to go, and Parkes still held the E-type. Then, next time round, Mike unaccountably lost it at Becketts, and abruptly left the tarmac for the countryside. This left Hill in the lead, but Mr Salvadori thereupon decided to change the picture. On the last lap but one, he came up alongside Hill at Stowe; Graham conceded Club Corner, but they tore up Abbey Curve and through Woodcote literally nose-to-tail. Through Copse and Salvadori kept in front. His previous lap was a new GT record at 102.9mph. At Maggotts the cars were almost side-by-side, then just as Parkes had done a few minutes earlier, Roy completely lost it – and the race. Hill steamed on to take the chequered flag, and a chastened Salvadori extricated himself, and took a safe second. Protheroe, although doubled by the newer E-types, was third, having averaged over 96mph.'

Salvadori has not forgotten that race: "That

were going to race it again at Laguna Seca but somebody dumped it pretty good in practice, so we only ever raced it at Sebring. There wasn't a lot you could do with it in the US and I don't know why we bought it. It just sat in the showroom, but I suppose it brought people in. We rebuilt it after Laguna Seca and sold it."

There was much controversy concerning what constituted a GT car. *Autosport* felt that it was difficult to differentiate the prototype Ferraris, Cobras and Chaparrals from 'out-and-out sports-racing machinery'. Bruce McLaren expressed the view in his column for *Motor Racing* magazine that he thought the Sebring race had been solely for Grand Touring cars: 'I must admit that I'm a little confused as to when a car is a GT and when it is a sports car. It seems to me that an E-type coupé or a GTO is a GT. The E-type with a hard-top is – just. The Cobras without hardtops look like sports cars to me and the open Ferraris and Chaparrals are definitely sports racers'. At least some 200 Cobras had already been built and, of course, many more would be produced, which is more than can be said for Ferrari, which produced only 39 GTOs.

At Snetterton at the end of March Graham Hill raced the reincarnated Coombs Lightweight for the first time. In dreadful conditions he took a fine win despite strong competition which included Roy Salvadori in a Cooper-Monaco and Innes Ireland in a Lotus 19, as well as a plethora of more nimble Lotus 23s.

In April the fourth Lightweight was delivered to Tommy Atkins for Salvadori to race. It was painted metallic green and registered 86 PJ. "All the preparation work," remembers Salvadori, "was done in rented garages that were later taken over by Brabham. Although they were only lock-up garages, the standard of preparation by Gordon Whitehead and another mechanic was to a very high standard."

The first major British race meeting of the year was the Easter Monday event at Goodwood. It was also the day that, aged 12, I met Graham Hill

stands out as a race I should have won. For no reason whatsoever, Parkes lost it going into Becketts and wrapped the Ferrari up into the bank – I still can't understand how it happened. Then Graham and I went at it, and I managed to pass him on the inside of Club with just two laps to go. Going into the last lap Graham tried to pass me into Woodcote, a very quick corner, rather messed it up, nearly got past, but then got into a bit of trouble and lost time. We came out and I thought, 'this is a piece of cake, I've got him'.

"Then going into Becketts I did exactly the same thing as Parkes. I don't know what was wrong. I never ever thought you could get into trouble there. The car just turned back-to-front and I went off the road. Fortunately I didn't bend it and got back on the road, but that was that. You might get the E-type sideways, but it didn't snap like that and neither did the GTO. There was something peculiar about Becketts that day."

All the Peters – Lindner and Nöcker, Lumsden and Sargent – congregated for the Nürburgring 1000Kms with their two Lightweights. The large, high-quality entry included Ferrari 250P prototypes for Surtees/Mairesse and Parkes/Scarfiotti, and a good selection of GTOs. In practice Lindner was 1sec slower than the fastest GTO and 2sec up on the British E-type privateers. The start of the race was sensational...

Everywhere you will read that Lindner made a brilliant start and not only led away but remained in front at the end of the first tortuous lap of the old 14-mile 'Ring. Not so! It was Lumsden: "I made a good start and led past the post after the first lap". Unfortunately he then heard "an awful banging noise" and decided to call at the pits. Nothing was discovered and he continued, pressing on to claw back the places he had lost.

"We were doing well and lying fourth. It was raining, but the car was going well, the rain was stopping, and I thought I was only about 20sec behind the chap who was third. So I kept up the pressure. I came over one hill to find that it had been hailing and raining on the other side, and a little voice said, 'you are now going to leave the circuit'. And I did". The accident occurred at *Flugplatz*, and as he rolled end-over-end Lumsden demolished 150 yards of fencing. The car was taken back to the factory and rebuilt around a new aluminium monocoque. Lindner, meanwhile, had been well placed but was forced to retire with lack of oil pressure.

E-TYPE DRAMAS AT LE MANS

Le Mans in 1963 was significant for several reasons. It saw the appearance as an 'unofficial entry' of the unique Rover-BRM gas turbine car, driven by Graham Hill and Richie Ginther, and the new Lola GTs, which directly led to the birth of the Ford GT and the Ferrari 250LM. The field of just

ABOVE **British privateers Peter Lumsden and Peter Sargent took their new Lightweight to the Nürburgring 1000Kms. Amazingly Lumsden led the entire field, which included Ferrari prototypes, on the first lap, but later he crashed very heavily.**

48 cars was also the smallest entry since the war. Aston Martin entered three cars (two Project 214 machines and the new Project 215), there were no fewer than 11 Ferraris (including four GT cars), a couple of AC Cobras (fitted with fastback hardtops) were making their Le Mans debut, and Lumsden/Sargent entered their Lister-Jaguar coupé (which rated as a prototype).

Briggs Cunningham entered three Lightweight E-types, one the car that had debuted at Sebring, the others the seventh and eighth to be completed. It has been stated that all three were fitted with ZF five-speed gearboxes, but 'Lofty' England maintains that they had, "early examples of the all-synchro close-ratio Jaguar-made gearboxes". There is also some confusion about who exactly drove the individual cars, which were numbered 14, 15 and 16 to coincide with their registration numbers of 5114 WK, 5115 WK and 5116 WK. It seems that 14 had Walt Hansgen and Augie Pabst at the controls, while 15 was piloted by Bob Grossman and Briggs Cunningham, leaving 16 in the hands of Roy Salvadori and Jim Richards.

"I definitely drove with Richards in practice and in the race," remembers Salvadori, "although I actually drove all three in practice. I think I made a very good time and the suspicion was that my car might be better, so I was asked to try the other two. In fact, I went quicker in them, particularly in Hansgen's – but Hansgen himself was a terribly quick driver.

"Actually I didn't tell the team the full story about my really quick lap – I got a tow from Sears in one of the big 4-litre Ferraris. I should have been honest about that! But by then I had got the message about how to play Le Mans that year. Briggs asked me to start the race, but I feared there was going to be a big old dust-up between Hansgen and myself. So I asked whether it wouldn't be better to have Richards start the race. I wasn't absolutely sure I could trust myself not to get involved in an inter-team dice, which would have been stupid. Although the cars had gone pretty well in practice, in the race we all had gearbox trouble with the lower gears seizing up."

RIGHT **Briggs Cunningham entered three Lightweights for Le Mans in 1963. The first retired with gearbox failure, the second crashed at 170mph on another car's oil, and the third lost eighth place with loss of brakes at Mulsanne Corner, forcing its driver, Bob Grossman, to use the straw bales to slow down...**

ABOVE **Having eventually struggled back to the pits, the damaged Cunningham car was rebuilt using the front half of the bonnet from the car that had retired with gearbox problems. Hence the black tape running across the join in this 'cut-and-shut' bonnet.** RIGHT **Passing the burned out wreck of the Surtees/Mairesse Ferrari, which had caught fire at 10.45am while heading for almost certain victory, the surviving Cunningham car, driven by Grossman and the team owner, gamely kept going to finish ninth.**

The gearbox problems did not take long to surface. The Hansgen/Pabst car went out in the first hour, and during the third the Salvadori/Richards car spent 20min in the pits having its gearbox worked on. It had circulated in 15th place for the first hour, moved up a place during the second, and then, as a result of the stop, rejoined in 34th place. It dropped further places in the next couple of hours, and then disaster...

At 8.20pm Bruce McLaren was travelling down the Mulsanne Straight at three miles a minute in his Aston Martin when the engine blew up and dropped 25 litres of oil on the fastest part of the course. There was supposed to be a system of lights to warn the drivers of just such an occurrence, but they did not operate. Grossman was lucky and threaded his way through a mêlée involving six cars, only one of which, the Cobra of Bolton/Sanderson, was able to continue. Roy Salvadori was less fortunate.

"Having had our problem with the gearbox, we weren't really in the hunt but at least we were still going. I couldn't get the seat belt done up properly and had a loose lap strap, but I didn't bother about it – which says something about the way I was driving by that stage. I was doing about 170mph and I could see something glistening on the road. I thought, 'No, it can't be. That's oil. Oh, no'. I didn't lift off immediately I hit it, because that would have been disastrous. So I came back very much on the throttle and the car went sideways. I remember thinking, 'Salvadori, you really are the cat's whiskers, you've held it', and I nearly did, but then I just touched the grass and the car suddenly went back to front.

"I thought that was the end. I tucked down as far as I could because I didn't want the roof coming in on me – it was only a hardtop. The car hit the bank, and I must have been thrown up into the hardtop and out of the back window, which is a Perspex piece with the rubber around it. I was thrown onto the tarmac and soaked in petrol because the tank had split. The car did another spin in the road, went into the bank again and caught fire. Another car on the other side of the road was also on fire."

The firefighters attended to both cars, the other one an Alpine-Renault in which Bino Heinz was sadly burned to death. The burned-out E-type was a total write-off and would not be rebuilt.

"Jean-Pierre Manzon, Robert's son, had also shunted and was lying right next to me in the road. I thought we were going to be clobbered because everyone was going to come off on this oil. But I could barely move – I could move my arms but otherwise I felt paralysed. I managed to get my fingernails into the edge of the grass and hauled myself up to a bank, but I was worried about the trail of fuel behind me because I was covered in it. The Jaguar was well alight – and I remember its horn was blowing the whole bloody time."

Mercifully Salvadori's injuries were confined to extensive bruising, although he feels he suffered more from that accident than any other. He was unable to move for two weeks: "It's impossible to imagine how much you can suffer with bruising". He adds that at that stage he never wanted to return to Le Mans because the organisers claimed that the warning lights had operated and blamed the drivers. He is adamant that there were no lights in operation.

Meanwhile the Cunningham/Grossman car was circulating in 18th place and in the succeeding hours it benefited from retirements to move up to seventh place (headed by two Ferrari prototypes, three GTOs and one Porsche prototype), but later slipping back to eighth. It remained there for the next four hours until it overtook the Porsche during the 16th hour, but then its progress was halted.

"Grossman arrived at the end of the straight," explains 'Lofty' England, "put the brakes on and found there weren't any [a pin in the linkage had snapped]. He went straight on, through the straw bales and down the escape road. He finished up with a very flat-fronted E-type. He got on the telephone link between the Mulsanne signalling post and the pits, and I told old Briggs – a wonderful sportsman who always wanted to finish at all costs – that he should tell him to try to get it back.

"This be-draggled E-type arrived maybe half an hour later with a smashed front and both front tyres flat. Within limitations you were allowed to change bits and we had a spare pedal box, radiator and subframe. So I got hold of Rainbow and said, 'Get down to the town like a flash, Frank, and get the bonnet off the other car'. We were going to take this crumpled thing behind the pits, take everything off and then, by some miracle, reappear with a repaired car.

"Briggs, being an honest gentleman, knew what we were up to. 'You can't do that,' he said. 'We'll have to ask permission, we daren't risk it.' So he goes to ask permission, and of course they loved old Briggs. 'Well, Mr Cunningham, unfortunately the regulations don't allow you to change anything as big as a complete bonnet. The only thing we suggest you do is cut the front off the damaged one, do the same thing with the good one, and bolt the two together'. Do that to two lovely £250 aluminium bonnets! Frankly it was like sawing a woman in half..."

Reports vary as to how long this rescue act took, some stating 1hr 50min, another 1hr 14min. After raw egg had been stuffed in the radiator to help seal it, the car motored on to finish ninth behind six Ferraris (including two 250P prototypes and three GTOs), the surviving Cobra and the Porsche prototype. John Bolster, *Autosport*'s respected Technical Editor, made a telling comment in the magazine a week later: 'To compete against 12 cylinders you need 12 cylinders. It's as simple as that'.

OTHER RACES IN 1963

Around this time Dick Protheroe managed to acquire the Low Drag Coupé from the factory. His former mechanic, Cornelius Vickers, remembers that Protheroe was very friendly with Sir William and "managed to scrounge this car out of him". He took it straight from the factory to Reims, where the French GP was supported by a race for sports and GT prototypes. Outright victory went to a 3-litre Ferrari prototype, but Protheroe took a magnificent second overall and won the GT class against what *Autosport* described as a, 'strong GTO challenge...the three GTOs of Bianchi, Noblet and Dumay, who, despite desperate measures, could not get near the tantalising E-type Jaguar'. From Protheroe's private log, we learn that he was 74sec behind the winner, and beat Bianchi by 1.5sec and Noblet by 3.1sec. It was a superb result and makes one feel that if only the factory had put some real development effort behind the Lightweight E-types...

LEFT **Malcolm Sayer first considered a reshaped E-type for GT racing at the beginning of the decade. One such car, which he described as the Low Drag E-type and which had a heavily revised tail, was slowly constructed and finally sold to Dick Protheroe.**

At the end of June Peter Nöcker, driving Lindner's Lightweight, defeated a GTO after a long tussle at the high-speed Avus circuit in Berlin, averaging 132mph and setting a fastest lap of 137mph.

The Grovewood Trophy race at Mallory Park in July saw the first appearance of the ninth Lightweight, which had been bought by Peter Sutcliffe. In practice Hill tried both the Coombs cars – GTO and E-type – and found he was quicker in the Jaguar by 0.1sec. In setting a time of 54.4sec, he also equalled Surtees' lap record, set in a GTO. On this occasion the GTO opposition was provided by Jack Sears in the Maranello example, Mike Salmon in the Coombs car and David Piper in his own car, with Hill, Salvadori and Sutcliffe in Lightweight E-types.

"I had a rare duel with Graham that day," remembers Sears. "I led for the first half of the race with Graham snapping at my heels. Then he drew alongside me coming into the hairpin, which is a very slow one. I was on the inside line and we braked together, we went round the bend together and we came out together, but then he just about

out-dragged me into the downhill left-hander before the startline. Now, of course, he was on the inside for the left-hander, and although the difference between the inside and outside lines was only a yard or two in distance, he still just managed to out-drag me. I suppose he got three-quarters of his car in front of me. There certainly wasn't room for two of us to go round side by side, so I had to drop in behind him. I slipstreamed him down to Gerard's and stuck on his tail, but I just couldn't get by again. We crossed the finish line literally one behind the other.

"The cars were very evenly matched. The E-type had more torque but couldn't rev so high. The GTO engine really worked from 5000rpm to 7500rpm – that's when it was producing all its 300bhp – whereas the E-type would pull better at lower revs. As a result the E-type was better on slower circuits. At Goodwood neither Salvadori nor myself in Lightweights could look at the GTOs, especially through the very fast sweeping bends from Madgwick onwards, through Fordwater and down to St Mary's. The GTO could be taken immensely quickly through these demanding corners, and gave a greater sense of stability than the E-type."

Another who had experience of the GTO was John Surtees: "The GTO was only a codge-up of the previous short-wheelbase 250GT. It did nothing extremely well, but it did everything quite well. It was a very sympathetic old car to drive: you could hang it out, or have it sideways, or make it understeer. This made it more competitive than the E-type, which I think was much more critical to set up. The E-type was better in some ways, but the GTO was a good all-round car. Like saloon car racing at that time, there was a lot of cut and thrust in GT racing and probably the GTO was just a bit more driveable, more forgiving."

Sutcliffe clocked up his first win in his new car the same weekend at the Archie Scott Brown Memorial meeting at Snetterton. In the Sports and GT race supporting the British GP, the real stars, like Salvadori and Parkes, drove prototypes, so lap times were well down as Sears and Piper in GTOs led Protheroe home.

During practice for the Guards Trophy meeting at Brands Hatch, John Coombs was told by the scrutineers that his E-type could not run with alloy wheels. He argued in vain that Lightweights had raced at Le Mans with these wheels and was told that the car would not be allowed to start. He decided that there was little point in practising the E-type and Hill took over his GTO. Towards the end of practice, however, he received a note from the scrutineers saying he could run the E-type after all. Coombs felt it was too late for them to change their minds, but he was still fined £500 by the RAC for wrongfully withdrawing a car – this sum was later reduced to £15 by Lord Shawcross at appeal. The race turned out to be a disappoint-ment for the E-types which did participate. Sutcliffe went off at Paddock Bend, Sargent had ignition problems and Protheroe retired with fuel vaporisation. Hill also retired the Coombs GTO and Sears took the class in another GTO.

A tremendous grid lined up for the TT at Goodwood. The front row comprised Hill (GTO), Parkes (GTO) and Ireland (DB4GT), the second row McLaren (DB4GT) and Salvadori (Atkins E-type), and the third row Roger Penske (GTO), Sears (Coombs E-type) and Piper (GTO). Protheroe shared the fourth row with yet another GTO and Lumsden was on the fifth row. With the police swarming around Goodwood looking for Great Train Robbery getaway driver Roy James, who had practised for the Formula Junior race, the largest grid ever to assemble at the Sussex circuit left the line. Salvadori was initially sixth but soon moved up to fourth, gaining a further place when Ireland spun three times! In fact Ireland had several more spins due, no doubt, to the fact that the scrutineers had disallowed the 7in wheels on the Project 212 Astons and insisted on narrower ones. The race ended with Hill and Parkes taking the first two places in their GTOs, followed by two of the Coventry cars.

There were no Lightweights at the Coppa Inter Europa three-hour race before the Italian GP, but Salvadori in a Project 212 Aston took a good win against Parkes in the GTO on Ferrari territory. Apparently the crowd cheered Roy on with gusto because they thought they were watching an Italian driver in a British car beating a British driver in an Italian car! Totally irrelevant to the Lightweight E-type story but a nice tale...

At more minor events, Sargent won at Brands, Sutcliffe at Mallory and Nöcker at Montlhéry – a good run for the various Peters. In October the tenth Lightweight was delivered to Australia for Bob Jane to campaign, and two months later he won the Australian GT Championships at Calder. The same month the eleventh car was supplied by Mike MacDowel at Coombs of Guildford to Richard Wilkins. This car, which has been photographed for this book, was not used for racing but kept for occasional road use, and therefore remains extremely original. The final car to be completed by the factory was delivered to Phil Scragg in January 1964 and would be hillclimbed.

INTO 1964

The Lumsden/Sargent Lightweight underwent considerable development following its major accident at the 'Ring in 1963. Samir (pronounced 'Sammy') Klat was then doing research at Imperial College, London, and joined the Lumsden/Sargent team at Le Mans running the Costin-bodied Lister-Jaguar that year. Klat proceeded to exert strong influence on many areas of the E-type.

Together with a fellow research student, Klat

built up an alternative engine with a twin-plug head and asymmetric pistons. The body came in for considerable revision as Klat developed his own Low Drag roofline, with a more raked and flush-fitting windscreen. The nose was extended, becoming reminiscent of Frank Costin's Vanwall, Klat having learned a good deal from the distinguished aerodynamicist. Following modifications to the rear, Klat and his student colleague discovered a phenomenon which they did not fully understand, but which would later be termed 'ground effects' when it changed the face of Formula 1 15 years later...

In February Graham Hill tested the Coombs car at Silverstone with Derrick White. Hill telephoned 'Lofty' England with his views and 'Lofty' passed these on to Bill Heynes. He considered the car to be improved on the 7in wheels that had been tried. The car was still too soft, although it was better on the Koni dampers previously fitted by Coombs. Through corners the car hit its bump rubbers on the outer side, causing the inner rear wheel to lift and spin. Hill was critical of the brakes and experienced excessive understeer through Abbey Curve. He suggested mounting the steering rack solidly and also complained of lateral movement in the rear suspension assembly, leading 'Lofty' to suggest mounting that solidly as well. The engine was good and approaching Stowe he saw 6100rpm, which equated to 148mph, but the better shape of the Ferrari GTO is illustrated by the fact that Parkes had achieved 177mph in one at the same point...

During March and early April the Lindner car was prepared at the factory for the Le Mans test weekend in mid-April. The most radical alteration to it was the fitting of Sayer's Low Drag Coupé hardtop – not before time. Engine work included stripping and rebuilding with $^{15}/_{32}$in lift cams, slide throttle, a larger oil tank and new exhaust pipes. A ZF five-speed gearbox and new Powr-Lok differential were also to be fitted, together with 7in front and 7½in rear cast magnesium wheels with, respectively, 650L and 725L tyres. A 1in front anti-roll bar was specified, plus provision for solidly mounting the steering rack, as had by now been done on 4 WPD.

The test weekend, which was also attended by the Lumsden/Sargent Lightweight, went smoothly, although the Saturday was wet and the Sunday began wet and later improved. The Lindner car's engine was now quoted as developing 322bhp at 6000rpm and at this engine speed in fifth gear the car's velocity was calculated at 169mph. Both E-types recorded identical times of 4min 7.3sec, and were beaten only by six Ferrari prototypes and one Cobra; this was quicker than the fastest GTO (4min 12.7sec) and the best of the new Ford GTs (4min 21.8sec). Sargent's top speed on the straight was given as equal fifth fastest (with Salvadori's Ford GT) at 168mph, behind three Ferraris and

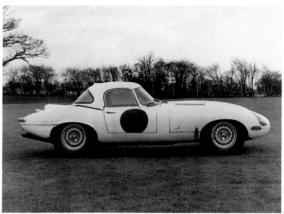

another Ford GT, while Lindner was ninth fastest on 154mph.

The next race meeting of significance was the *Daily Express* International at Silverstone in early May. Graham Hill chose to pilot the Coombs GTO and Jack Brabham was drafted in to handle the E-type. 'Lofty' England: "I'd been going on at Coombs, saying 'why the hell don't you give this Jackie Stewart bloke a drive', because he was doing very, very well in Formula 3. 'Oh, I don't want one of those lunatics from Formula 3,' said Coombs. Old Jack unbelievably did 30 laps of

ABOVE & RIGHT **The famous Lightweight in which Peter Lindner, the German Jaguar importer, was tragically killed at Montlhéry in 1964. The car in its current form, now on display at the Rosso Bianco Collection in Germany, was built by Lynx using a spare monocoque obtained from the factory, but most of the mechanical components and some repaired body parts were retained from the original car. The car was modified to Malcolm Sayer's Low Drag Coupé form at the factory in preparation for Le Mans in 1964.**

unofficial practice a few days before and couldn't get anywhere near Salvadori's time [Salvadori's record was 1min 42.4sec and Brabham's best was 1min 45.4sec]. Brabham did another load of laps in official practice and still couldn't get down to it [his best was 1min 45.2sec], so they put Dan Gurney in. He did about 10 laps and actually got down to the same sort of time as Salvadori. Then it rained on race day and Gurney said, 'I ain't gonna bust my ass in that thing', and didn't try. I could have gone faster."

"Gurney drove the car in the race," says Coombs, "because Jack thought it would be better and Gurney was quicker. It was raining for the race and I remember Gurney saying on the grid, 'I won't be trying and I may come in on the second lap'. Whereupon Michael MacDowel was livid. Gurney was saying the brakes were bad, the car didn't handle and this, that and the other."

After the first wet lap the order was Hill and Piper in GTOs leading Protheroe, Salvadori and Sutcliffe in E-types. The final order after 25 laps was Hill, Salmon (Aston Martin), Sears (Cobra), Piper, Salvadori and Protheroe. Gurney finished eighth and, according to *Autosport*, 'never looked happy in the E-type'.

'Lofty' was displeased: "I said to Coombs, 'I've had enough of this nonsense – we have an interest in this project and we're going to invite Jackie Stewart down'."

Meanwhile in mid-May Protheroe and Sutcliffe entered a 500km event at Spa. The strong field included GTOs and Cobras, but Protheroe did well to qualify fourth. For the first eight laps of the race he disputed second place until he lost all but one of his gears in the ZF 'box. He finished 12th, a couple of places behind Sutcliffe, who took a good victory at Montlhéry a week later.

The Nürburgring 1000Kms was not a happy event. Practice was a tragic affair with two drivers killed, and Protheroe badly damaged his Low Drag Coupé. In the race Sutcliffe found a spinning Cobra in his path and flipped his E-type right over and back onto its wheels. The Lindner car had its gearbox seize and Lumsden/Sargent had the clutch centre fall out.

'Lofty' England's faith in this young Scot called Stewart was put to the test at Silverstone on 3 June, as Jackie himself remembers: "Coombs was not at all keen for me to get into the car. I think 'Lofty' insisted on it. John's a great character and he's always had famous people drive for him. I think he was sceptical about Dan and Jack, but Graham and Roy were established people and they were fine. But for John Coombs to have any young, inexperienced driver in his car was certainly not on. We were all frightened of him."

"It was 'Lofty's idea to have Jackie down," confirms Coombs, "after the business at the May Silverstone meeting. I was against it because Jackie hadn't really started by then and I was very much

against amateurs. Anyway he arrived in his Mini – very polite in those days and with short hair!"

'Lofty' put together a report on the day which was sent not only to Heynes, White and Weaver, as usual, but also, unusually, to Sir William. The conditions were humid with a slight wind, and the track was 'mainly dry but with wet patches and water on the road at entrance and exit of Club Corner'. The car was in the same condition as when run in May. The test started at 10.07am, and Stewart sensibly ran carefully for the first couple of laps. Then he started to motor. It should be recalled that Brabham had managed 1-45.4 and Salvadori's record stood at 1-42.4. On his seventh lap Jackie recorded a remarkable 1-43.6 and Coombs was not pleased.

"I called him in because I thought he was going to stuff it. He was asked if everything was all right. 'Och, fantastic car. Fantastic'. What are the brakes like? 'Fantastic'. How does it handle? 'Fantastic'. Everything was fantastic. 'Shall I go out again?' I told him I thought he was going a bit quick and that he should get out of the car. 'Noo, noo, I'm not trying yet. I won't bend it'."

TOP **The Lumsden/ Sargent Lightweight was the subject of fascinating research at the cutting edge of technology. It was visually modified with Dr Samir Klat's version of the low-drag treatment (this was rather flatter than Sayer's), and tested with wool tufts in the time-honoured way.**
ABOVE **The Lindner/ Nöcker Lightweight's first race with Sayer's low drag body was the Nürburgring 1000Kms. The stoved-in door shows that the car escaped a tangle with another competitor, but it retired with gearbox seizure.**

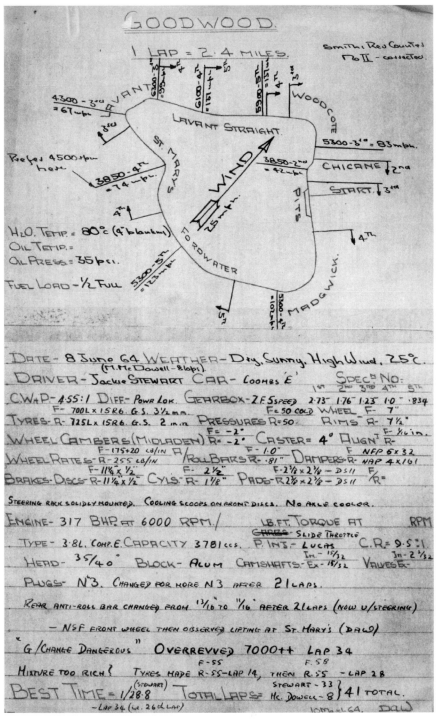

ABOVE A young, virtually unknown, wee chappie from Scotland was given a test drive in the Coombs E-type by 'Lofty' England. Within a few laps Jackie Stewart posted better times than the established stars. A few days later he tested at Goodwood and Derrick White produced this report.

'Lofty' England also had a word with Jackie: "I asked him what he thought of it. 'Och,' he said, 'I'll go a bit faster when I get used to it'. So I said, 'Well, go back and go a bit faster then'."

The brakes were bled and the rev limit increased by 200rpm to a reading of 6500rpm, although the actual figure was 6300rpm. Stewart's second lap was 1-44.2, his third equalled Salvadori's record of 1-42.4 and his fourth was better still at 1-41.9...

England's faith had not been misplaced and the conclusion to his report summed it up well: 'It was interesting to note that this driver, who had not previously driven a lightweight E-type, put up a better time on a not completely dry track than that

achieved by anyone else with this type of car'.

"It was a big deal for me to get a drive for John Coombs," recalls Jackie. "Before I started to race seriously and before I got a chance to drive for Ken Tyrrell, I suppose my ideal would have been to drive for Coombs, or Equipe Endeavour, in a touring car or a sports car. I always thought that was the epitome of the finest way to go motor racing, because I never really thought I'd be a single-seater driver, and I never really thought I'd go very far."

One suspects that Coombs still had his doubts, for Stewart was entered at a relatively minor Jaguar Drivers Club meeting at Silverstone a few days later. But he was invincible against Roger Mac in the ex-Atkins/Salvadori Lightweight and Frank Gardner in a Willment Cobra. *Autosport* commented that he drove 'brilliantly'.

The Lumsden/Sargent and Lindner/Nöcker cars were entered for Le Mans and factory engine development engineer George Buck had designed a new tuned exhaust for the Lindner car. "This engine," states Buck, "gave the highest power ever achieved from a 3.8, namely 344bhp, and this was a sustained reading, not a flash one." For the first two hours Lindner held 19th place with Lumsden just behind. During the third hour the British car moved ahead and by the end of the fourth hour it was up to 14th, but the German car was now back in 21st place. After five hours Lumsden/Sargent were 12th overall and fifth in the GT class, but sadly their run ended when the gearbox failed. Meanwhile the other E-type dropped back still further, and then came in for a three-hour stop for the head to be changed due to overheating. Its retirement at 7.20am was the sad finale to the E-type's exploits at Le Mans.

Meanwhile the factory delivered two more interesting cars during July. Both were given the 'S' prefix that also preceded the Lightweight chassis numbers, and they appeared on Derrick White's list of '63 competition cars as numbers 13 and 14. One, built as a road car for Sir Hugh Ropner, had a steel monocoque with some aluminium panels, an iron block engine, wet sump, triple Webers and a wide-angle head. The other was a Fixed Head with a steel monocoque but with an aluminium block engine, and was completed for Pierre Bardinon, a wealthy French businessman and later a renowned Ferrari collector.

Protheroe took his Low Drag Coupé to the 12-hour race at Reims, the scene of earlier triumphs, and once again won his class. Back in Britain Bob Jane had brought his Lightweight over from Australia and entered it for the GT race supporting the Grand Prix at Brands Hatch. Stewart was having a second outing in the Coombs E-type and Salvadori was in Atkins' brand new, unpainted Cobra. Stewart took the lead, which he held for 15 of the 20 laps. However, this was the infamous 'black-flag' race, when Jack Sears was called into the pits by the officials to be told he had started from the

157

wrong grid position, due to his team-mate non-starting. There was no stopping Sears that day and he was inspired. In his anger he hurled his massive Cobra round Brands in a brilliant display which took him right through the field to victory.

By this stage the AC Cobras had become the main threat to the E-type. Wearing their Daytona coupé coachwork, they had won the GT class at Le Mans, and five of these monsters were entered for the TT. In practice they underlined their supremacy by beating the four GTOs, a lone Aston and four E-types, although Nöcker's car non-started. The GT class was again a Cobra benefit

LEFT **Jackie Stewart raced the John Coombs Lightweight, enhancing his growing reputation with several wins and a fine second place behind Jack Sears' Cobra at the British GP meeting.**

and Dan Gurney, whose car Carroll Shelby claimed was producing 385bhp, took the class honours, with Lumsden fifth.

This disappointing season for the E-types took a tragic turn when Peter Lindner was killed in his Lightweight at Montlhéry in the Paris 1000Kms. Protheroe and John Coundley finished seventh overall and took a class win. Peter Sutcliffe then took his Lightweight out to South Africa where he enjoyed some success. In spite of a cracked block, he finished third in the Kyalami Nine Hours behind Piper in a 250LM and Sears in a Cobra. In other races he went on to enjoy several seconds and thirds, and one win.

In club racing, meanwhile, production E-types were clocking up a prodigious number of victories, as they would continue to do for many years. Some of the Lightweights would also continue to race, but in lesser arenas. The Coombs car, for example, was sold to Red Rose Racing and brought Brian Redman many of his early successes, establishing him on a long and highly successful career.

The Lightweight E-type has often been dismissed as a half-hearted attempt that never enjoyed the fruits of a concerted factory effort. With all his experience of running one, John Coombs can judge whether this verdict is fair: "If you look through the results of the E-type against the GTO, you will find they are very good. One was built as a production two-seater sports car, the other as a racing car. I consider the Jaguar did a fabulous job in beating them at any time."

POSTSCRIPT

As we saw earlier in this story, thoughts at Jaguar turned at various times to a mid-engined sports racing car. These thoughts started with the still-born G-type (see page 132) and surfaced again in the early 1960s. When the Lightweights were being proposed, a memo was put together which suggested the building of a, 'New GT Prototype for 1963 or 1964'. Bill Heynes was keen for Jaguar to re-enter international motor racing. Equally Malcolm Sayer had his ideas on the subject, as did Derrick White.

For several years thought had also been given to building a V12 engine. Ferrari had proved the effectiveness of this configuration, both in terms of power output and low height, and a V12 would also have potential for the road cars. Previously the V12 engine had been confined to relatively low production, highly specialised motor cars. Like the XK twin overhead camshaft unit of the late 1940s, a production V12 would be both a technical achievement for the company and a most prestigious boost to its image.

Bob Knight recalls that Bill Heynes was keen to build the V12 engine and the mid-engined racing car in the early 1960s, and that Sir William Lyons wanted to produce a large limousine. A meeting

ABOVE **Life is full of 'if onlys'. With a stronger sense of urgency and commitment, the mid-engined XJ13 prototype, first mooted as the G-type back in the late 1950s, could surely have been a star.**

took place between the two in the middle of the Experimental Shop and it was agreed that Heynes could have his racing car if Lyons could have his limousine!

The outcome was that Knight issued a 'Project Specification for project number ZX 558/04/01' on 3 June 1965. The first paragraph of seven pages of instructions ran, 'Build one prototype competition car for development purposes to specifications set out below, including mock-ups of sections of the car as required'. This sensational car would be known as the XJ13.

Fully monocoque in construction, the XJ13 was clothed with a body that was Sayer's final, and ultimate, masterpiece. Mid-engined in configuration, it was powered by a new twin overhead camshaft V12 engine of 5 litres which had been designed by Heynes and Baily. Unfortunately the project would not be pursued and the XJ13 was still-born in the sense that it was never raced. One example was eventually completed in late 1966 but it was not run for some time. By this time Jaguar had joined forces with BMC to form British Motor Holdings, and within two years the company would become part of the appalling British Leyland saga.

For a variety of reasons Jaguar did not want the press to know that it had a possible Le Mans challenger, and Sir William gave orders for the car not to be circuit-tested. This eventually became too

much for Norman Dewis, who discussed his frustration with 'Lofty' England. 'Lofty' in turn said that if Dewis wanted to take it quietly to MIRA one Sunday he knew nothing about it! This Dewis did and several days later he was summoned to Sir William's office. According to Norman, the conversation went something like this: Sir William: "I thought I gave orders that the XJ13 was not to be tested." Norman: "Yes you did, sir." Sir William: "And yet you took it to MIRA?" Norman: "Yes I did, sir." Sir William: "When I give an order I expect it to be obeyed. Don't ever disobey me again." Norman: "Yessir." Sir William: "Well man, how did it go?"

The car would subsequently be tested by ex-apprentices David Hobbs and Dickie Attwood, and at MIRA Hobbs would record the highest lap speed ever achieved on an enclosed circuit in Britain, namely 161.6mph. Both Attwood and Hobbs have told me they felt that the car had potential if only it could have been produced and developed sooner. Jackie Stewart was asked to test the car and suggested taking it to Kyalami in South Africa to avoid the British winter, but Jaguar budgets did not quite run to that sort of approach.

The XJ13 could have enjoyed a great career against cars like the Ford GT40s, Ferrari 275LMs, Ferrari P4s, Chaparrals and Porsche 907s. It could have recreated the great days of the 1950s, but it was not to be.

The 1950s, however, were great days for Jaguar.

The C-types and D-types undoubtedly accelerated engineering development, created a good atmosphere at the factory and stimulated a loyal workforce. They immeasurably enhanced both the company's name and British prestige. Above all they obtained the publicity that advertised the company's superb production cars, and this, without question, established Jaguar as one of the great names in automotive history. It was no small achievement!

ABOVE & BELOW **With its four-cam 5-litre V12 engine making its presence known just behind your ears, the XJ13 is an exciting and emotive car to drive in. It was quite simply Malcolm Sayer's ultimate creation.**

CHASSIS HISTORIES

This subject is a minefield and it is necessary to make certain qualifying statements. Wherever possible this information has been checked and double-checked, but it should be regarded as opinion only. Owners, vendors and buyers should establish factual information for themselves. No responsibility under any circumstances can be accepted or assumed. The vast majority of the information is correct, but I fear that I may inadvertently be perpetuating one or two myths. Equally exclusion from this listing of a particular car laying claim to a chassis number does not constitute proof that that car is not genuine – omission may be an error.

The C-types, having a distinct chassis and body, are more straight-forward to identify. However, it should be remembered that during rebuilds of original cars an old body has on occasions been substituted by a new body simply, and innocently, to improve the condition of the car. Subsequently an old body may have turned up with a spurious chassis, leaving such a car's claim to authenticity strengthened by the fact that its body is undoubtedly an original factory item.

D-type identities are rather more complicated to unravel because there has long been debate about which is the more important component in proving a car's validity: the frame (sometimes known as the front frame or subframe) *or* the monocoque tub (otherwise known as the body). Instances where these have been split have led to two claimants to an original number. If the engine is added to the equation, it can be seen that there could be three claimants to a single car's identity – and such cases have occurred. It can further be added that certain people in recent years have fabricated complete cars which may, or may not, contain just a few minor original components. Greatly inflated values and, on occasion, dishonest practice have led to muddied waters and false claims.

The exhaustive data which follows is a distillation from many sources over many years, and from the research of many individuals. Experts around the world have checked facts and/or contributed information. I would like to acknowledge the considerable and invaluable input from Chris Keith-Lucas, the late Andrew Whyte, *Jaguar World* magazine, Paul Skilleter, Lynx, John Pearson, Terry Larson (USA), Adrian Hamilton, Terry McGrath (Australia), Ole Sommer (Denmark), Tom Groskritz (USA), Aubrey Finburgh, Les Hughes (Australia), *Jaguar Driver* magazine, John May, Martin Morris, Nick Mason, Paul Vestey, Willie Tuckett, Bryan Corser, Mike Barker and a large number of other owners past and present.

The supplier was, in most cases, the Jaguar importer or distributor. The cars were driven at the events recorded by the owner at that time, unless otherwise stated. Registration numbers given are not necessarily the original numbers.

With the benefit of a Second Edition, this listing has been further revised due to additional and/or altered information now being available. A surprisingly high proportion of cars have also changed hands since the First Edition was published.

C - T Y P E S

XKC 001
Engine number E1004-8 (later E1051) **Body number** n/a **Registration number** n/a **Despatch date** n/a **Colour** BRG **History** First works car to be built; 1951 Le Mans, driven by Johnson/Biondetti, ret'd; 1951 TT, Johnson/Rolt, 4th & lap record; early 1952, disc brake testing; *Daily Express* Silverstone, Rolt, ret'd; 1953 development work including disc brakes; last known to exist 22/6/53; company paperwork dated 31/8/53 states, 'dismantled and parts passed to Service Department'.

XKC 002
Engine number E1002-8 **Body number** n/a **Registration number** n/a **Despatch date** n/a **Colour** BRG **History** Second works car; 1951 Le Mans, Moss/Fairman, ret'd; 1951 TT, Moss, 1st; 1952 *Daily Express* Silverstone, Moss, 1st; Le Mans, long nose body, ret'd; Goodwood 9 Hours, Whitehead/Stewart, crashed; last known to exist August 1952; dismantled.

XKC 003
Engine number E1003 **Body number** n/a **Registration number** n/a **Despatch date** n/a **Colour** BRG **History** Third works car; 1951 Le Mans, Walker/Whitehead, 1st; 1951 TT, Walker, 2nd; early 1952, fitted with disc brakes; Easter Goodwood first race with disc brakes, Moss, 4th & fastest lap; Mille Miglia, international disc brake debut, Moss/Dewis, ret'd; Monaco GP, Moss, disqualified; dismantled.

XKC 004
Engine number E1006 **Body number** K1006 **Registration number** MDU 214 **Despatch date** 23/5/52 **Colour** Pastel Green **History** First production car; sold to Duncan Hamilton, UK; 1952 Isle of Man, ret'd; Oporto GP, ret'd; Boreham, 2nd; Turnberry, 2nd; Wakefield Trophy, The Curragh, crashed; 1953 Oporto GP, crashed; repaired; sold to Jack Howey and kept by him until c1961; he fitted perspex section to bonnet to enable engine to be viewed; later owned by John Undery (Devon, UK), Guy Williams (Sussex, UK), Stuart Cranfield (Sussex, UK), rebuilt by Lynx, C. Brierly (Yorkshire, UK), George Stauffer (Wisconsin, USA); sold, via Adrian Hamilton, to Casper McDonald Hall (Hampshire, UK).

XKC 005
Engine number E1007 **Body number** K1007 **Registration number** MDU 212 **Despatch date** 26/5/52 **Colour** Pastel Green **History** Sold to Bill Cannell & Tommy Wisdom, UK; 1952 Monaco GP, Wisdom, finisher; Reims GP, run as factory car & with disc brakes, Moss, 1st (first win by a disc-braked car); Boreham, Moss, 1st; Turnberry, Moss, 1st; Goodwood, Moss, 2nd; 1953 Mille Miglia, run as factory car (with engine number E1005-8, cylinder head number RJ29, 3.31:1 axle, race number 638), Rolt/Hayden, ret'd; 1953 sold to Brigadier Michael Head, with drum brakes; then painted white; 1953/4 various minor successes in UK and Scandinavia; 1955 sold to Rosemary Vickers (Scotland); re-registered FST 777; driven on occasions by John Barber; crashed at Brands Hatch; later owned by David Lewis, Tony Wood (now registered AWW 3 & dark green); displayed at Donington Collection; 1984 sold to Humphrey Avon (Sussex, UK).

XKC 006
Engine number E1008 **Body number** K1008 **Registration number** JWS 353 **Despatch date** 4/7/52 **Colour** Dark Green **History** Sold to Ian Stewart, UK, and run under Ecurie Ecosse; 1952 Jersey Road Race, 1st; Charterhall, 1st x 2; Boreham, spun off; Crimond, 1st; Turnberry, 1st in heat, 3rd in final; Wakefield Trophy, The Curragh, 1st; Goodwood, 1st; Castle Combe, 1st; Charterhall, 1st; 1953 repainted in Ecurie Ecosse metallic blue; Easter Handicap, Goodwood, Sanderson, 6th; Charterhall, 1st; Ibsley, 1st; Silverstone, 1st; Charterhall, 4th; Thruxton, 2nd; Snetterton, 1st; Isle of Man, ret'd; Snetterton, 1st x 2; Leinster Trophy, Wicklow, Scott-Douglas, 2nd; Silverstone, 5th; Charterhall, Sanderson, 6th; sold to Hans Davids (Holland); 1954 Spa, 1st; Zandvoort, 1st; Amiens, 2nd; sold to Bryan Corser (Shrewsbury, UK), square boot lid fitted to tail; 1955/6 sprinted; sold to Anthony Barrett-Greene, (Staffs, UK); sold & shipped to USA; owners included Robert Allen; 1974 re-imported; 1974/75 rebuilt by Lynx for the late Bill Lake (Sussex, UK).

XKC 007
Engine number E1009 **Body number** K1009 **Registration number** n/a **Despatch date** 1/8/52 **Colour** Dark Green **History** Supplied to Hornburg, USA; first C-type exported to USA; 1952 Elkhart Lake, Phil Hill, 1st; Torrey Pines, California, 1st; sold to Carlyle Blackwell (Hollywood); sold to Robert Lane (California); sold to Jack Ratteree (Arizona); sold to Rich Johnson (Arizona); sold to Terry Larson, who restored car; sold to Jeffrey Pattinson (London, UK); sold to Gerald Nell (Wisconsin, USA), used as concours car, 1994 Jaguar Club of North America National Champion.

XKC 008
Engine number E1011 **Body number** K1012 **Registration number** MHP 825 **Despatch date** 26/8/52 **Colour** Cream **History** Sold to Leslie Johnson, UK; 1953 Mille Miglia, with overdrive fitted, ret'd; later owners included John Hogg, John Bekaert (3rd in 1957 *Autosport* Championship), Jackie Epstein (mid-1960s); Ian Barclay Wilson (UK); 1996 sold to David Wenman (UK).

ABOVE **Apprentices, like policeman, seem to get younger! This car is almost certainly XKC 011 – note the louvres in the door.**

XKC 009

Engine number E1010 **Body number** K1010 **Registration number** n/a **Despatch date** 1/8/52 **Colour** Gunmetal **History** Supplied to Hoffman, USA; 1952 Elkhart Lake, George Weaver; Seneca Cup, Watkins Glen, John Fitch, 1st; sold to Dr M.R.J. Wyllie; 1954 Seneca Cup, 1st; late '50s David Darrin (New Jersey); campaigned extensively at Watkins Glen, Limerock & Bahamas; 1983 ownership passed, on his death, to sons; campaigned at VSSCA & SCCA events; 1994, JCNA Mahway, 3rd; 1992 body restored by Bill Bassett, Rhode Island; David Darrin Jr. & Drake Darrin (New York, USA).

XKC 010

Engine number E1012 **Body number** K1013 **Registration number** n/a **Despatch date** 2/10/52 **Colour** Silver **History** Supplied to Hornburg, USA; sold to Art Feuerbacher (St Louis); Madera, California, Sherwood Johnson, 3rd; 1953 Sebring 12 Hours, Johnston & Wilder, 3rd; later owned for 27 years by Arthur Seyler (Cleveland) and used in over 80 races; 1991 sold to Fred Simione (Philadelphia, USA).

XKC 011

Engine number E1005 **Body number** n/a **Registration number** n/a **Despatch date** n/a **Colour** BRG **History** Works car; 1952 Le Mans, long-nose body, ret'd; 1952 Goodwood 9 Hours, Moss/Walker, 5th; 1952 Shelsley Walsh, Walker, record; 1952 Prescott, Walker, record; 1952 Goodwood, Panhard rod fitted, Rolt, 1st; 1953 Mille Miglia (with engine number E1007-8, cylinder head number N.355, 3.31:1 axle, race number 542), Moss/Morris-Goodall, ret'd; 1953 Targa Florio, lent to Wisdom, 17th; 1953 Isle of Man British Empire Trophy, Moss (cylinder head number RJ 29, SU carbs, 3.54:1 axle, race number 52), 2nd in heat, 4th in final; evaluating oil cooler; Jan 1954 assessing Avon & Pirelli tyres, Moss favoured Avons; then on loan to Dunlop for testing (painted battleship grey and registered POV 114); Jan 1957 sold by Jaguar to Michael Salmon (then working in Service Dept), repainted

metallic blue; 1957/58 extensively campaigned; 1959 sold to Gordon Lee; sold to Robin Sturgess, Len Newman & N.W. Moore; 1963 sold to Guy Griffiths (Chipping Camden, UK); repainted dark green; Penny Woodley (Stratford-upon-Avon, UK).

XKC 012

Engine number E1001 (& E1054 & E1052) **Body number** n/a **Registration number** n/a **Despatch date** n/a **Colour** BRG **History** Works car; 1952 Le Mans, long-nose body, ret'd; 1952 Goodwood 9 Hours, Rolt/Hamilton, crashed after breakage; 1952 tested by *The Motor* and timed at Jabbeke at 143.75mph; 1953 Jabbeke (cylinder head number W.262, 3.31:1 axle), 148.435mph; testing with Weber carbs; 1953 *Daily Express* Silverstone, Rolt (cylinder head number N.352, 4.09:1 axle, Lockheed 2 L-S brakes, race number 36), unplaced; 1953 Le Mans reserve car driven in practice by Dewis; 1953 Reims 12 Hours, borrowed by Peter Whitehead for himself and Moss (cylinder head number RJ 78, Weber carbs, 3.31:1 axle, Dunlop disc brakes from XKC 001, new triple-plate clutch, race number 4), 1st; 1953 Goodwood 9 Hours, Moss/Walker (engine number E1054, 9:1 compression, 3.92:1 axle, race number 1), ret'd (number 1 con rod broken); 1953 TT, Whitehead/Stewart (engine number E1052, 9:1 compression, 3.54:1 axle), ret'd (g/box); March 1954, engine changed to E1005-8; taken to Le Mans as substitute for XKC 047 which had crashed en route, rebuilt with parts from 047 and became new 047; owned by Tom Groskritz (California), who feels this hybrid car is more correctly referred to as XKC 012.

XKC 013

Engine number E1013 **Body number** E1011 **Registration number** n/a **Despatch date** 9/10/52 **Colour** Silver **History** Supplied to Hoffman, USA; sold to Robert Blackwood; 1952, Albany, Georgia, broke clutch; later owned by James Lazor (Cleveland), 1980 J.B. Lazorus (USA), Anthony Mayman (UK); now registered VSU 669; sold to Hon Alan Clark (Saltwood, Kent, UK).

XKC 014

Engine number E1014 **Body number** K1014 **Registration number** n/a

Despatch date 7/10/52 **Colour** Cream **History** Supplied to Hoffman, USA; sold to Commander John Rutherford; 1953 Daytona Beach, NASCAR Speed Week, achieved 134.07mph; owned in late-1960s by Ralph Steiger (Ohio); sold to David Burtner (USA); raced with slant-six Valiant engine and Borg Warner T10 gearbox; 1988 restored by Peter Jay/RS Panels; Berkhard von Schenk (Germany).

XKC 015

Engine number E1015 **Body number** K1015 **Registration number** n/a **Despatch date** 14/10/52 **Colour** Cream **History** Supplied to Hornburg, USA; sold to J. Hall (not Chaparral man); raced once by owner; sold to Masten Gregory; 1953 Golden Gate Park, California, 1st; April, Bergstrom Air Force Base, 3rd; July, Offutt Field Nationals, Omaha, 1st; August, Lockbourne Air Force Base, Ohio, 2nd; August, Thompson International, Connecticut, 1st; road tested by *Road & Track*; Floyd Bennett races, New York, burned out; wreck sold to Tage Hansen; rebuilt; 1954 Mount Washington, competed as chassis, Sherwood Johnston, 1st & broke course record; used by owner on road for some years; sold to Merril C. Wells (Maine); December 1960 sold to John Howe (Massachusetts); August 1964 sold to Mark Daniels (Milwaukee), who carried out extensive restoration, later sold to Campbell McLaren (Scotland); now registered TKV 500; sold via John Harper, who restored car, to Tom Candlish (UK).

XKC 016

Engine number E1016 **Body number** K1016 **Registration number** n/a **Despatch date** 16/10/52 **Colour** Blue **History** Supplied to Delacroix, Paris, France; sold to Henri Peignaux, Lyons; driven on occasions by Luc Descollanges; 1953 Soleil-Cannes Rally, fastest at Montlhéry, but then crashed; Mille Miglia, Descollanges, crashed; 1950s-1990s history not researched by us; now non-original body; Philippe Renault (France).

XKC 017

Engine number E1017 **Body number** K1017 **Registration number** n/a **Despatch date** 7/10/52 **Colour** Birch Grey **History** Supplied to Hornburg, USA; sold

to Sterling Edwards (San Francisco); 1952 Torrey Pines, California, 3rd; also raced by Irv Robbins, including Palm Springs; Pebble Beach, crashed by mechanic (hit straw bale); late-1953 sold to Louis Brero; 1954 March Field, Riverside, California, 5th; Torrey Pines, Six Hour Race, 1st; various successes in other races & hillclimbs; 1955 sold to Ray Seher (Nevada); raced 14 times including Santa Rosa, California, 3rd; Sacramento races, 1st in class x 2; 2nd overall x 2, 1st overall; Stockton, 1st; Santa Rosa, 1st; Stockton, 1st; Kotati Air Field, 2nd; 1956 Salinas, 1st (on same day that James Dean was killed on Highway 101 on way to this race); Santa Rosa, 1st; Kotati Air Field, 2nd; Walnut Grove; Stockton; Laguna Seca, 3rd; sold to Leon Mandell (publisher of *Autoweek* magazine); raced about six times for owner by several local drivers including Bob Bryan; 1961 Golden Gate Park, Bob Potter, 2nd; sold, at this race meeting, to Chuck Davies; restored, painted black, used for concours & occasional daily use; 1966 Pebble Beach, 1st; January 1967 featured in *Road & Track*; 1969 sold to Orin Palmer (California); 1970 raced at Laguna Seca; car then stored; 1987 sold to Terry Larson (Arizona) and used in many vintage races and events.

XKC 018

Engine number E1018 **Body number** K1018 **Registration number** n/a **Despatch date** 27/10/52 **Colour** Bronze **History** Supplied to Belgian Motor Co, Brussels; sold to Juan Manuel Fangio; sold shortly after to Jose Millet, Buenos Aires (Jaguar distributor); 1953 Mendoza, 3rd; sold to Snr Magnasco; sold to Ernesto Tornqvist; c1983 sold to Bill Tracy (Florida, USA); 1997 sold to Georgio Acutis (Anguilla, West Indies).

XKC 019

Engine number E1019 **Body number** K1019 **Registration number** n/a **Despatch date** 24/10/52 **Colour** Silver **History** Supplied to Belgian Motor Co, Brussels; sold to Hermann Roosdorp (Antwerp); 1953 Spa 24 Hours, with Ulmen, 3rd; Nürburgring 1000Kms,

BELOW **Ray Seher in XKC 017 at Salinas, California, in 1957.**

crashed by Ulmen; Jabbeke, achieved 234kph; sold to J.L. van Dieten (The Hague, Holland); 1954 Zandvoort, 5th; later owned by Mr Maasland, K. de Groot (Amsterdam), Preston Smith (Pennsylvania, USA); August 1991 included in Coys Nürburgring sale; sold to Hugh Taylor (UK); 1995/6 sold to Hugh Palmer (UK); 1998 sold, via Coys, to Clinton Burke (Leicestershire, UK).

XKC 020

Engine number E1020 **Body number** K1020 **Registration number** n/a **Despatch date** 9/10/52 **Colour** Silver **History** Supplied to Hoffman, USA; sold to Imported Car Co, Hoopeston, Illinois; sold to Frank Larson (Decatur); 1953 Offutt AFB, Nebraska, 3rd; Wilmot Hills, Wisconsin, Fred Wacker, 1st; Fort Worth, Texas, Carroll Shelby, 1st x 2; 1955 sold to W.L. Petrie (Houston); sold to Gustav O'Keiff who fitted Chevrolet V8 engine, Dunlop disc brakes and Halibrand disc knock-off wheels; July 1957 Galveston, Texas, Mason O'Kieff, 5th; November 1958 Hammond Harvest Races, Louisiana, Mason O'Kieff, 3rd; sold to Herb Stetler (Louisiana); April 1960 Riverside, A.J. Foyt practised but did not race; sold to Tom Dreyfus (New Orleans); 1970 stolen from Dreyfus's driveway and not found.

XKC 021

Engine number E10210-8 **Body number** K1021 **Registration number** PUG 676 **Despatch date** 23/9/52 **Colour** Suede Green **History** Supplied to Appleyards, Leeds, UK; may have been used for short time by Ian Appleyard; November 1952 sold to Bill Holt or Mrs Mary Holt (Bramham, Yorks); used by Bill Holt for club racing without any great success; February 1953 sold to Mrs Mary Holt; February 1954 work done at factory when mileage was 4624; fitted with ex-HWM engine; May 1954 sold to Mike Connell (Norfolk); possibly raced by Roy Salvadori; car damaged, possibly at Silverstone, and further work done at factory in November, mileage on 8164; March 1955 sold to David S. Boston (Liverpool); prepared and raced by Dick Protheroe; May, Goodwood, 3rd; April 1956 sold to Maberly Parker (Wales); March 1960 sold to Michael Richardson; lent to Bill MacKay for 1960 Scottish Speed Championship; July, sold to Hillhead Auto Co, Glasgow; January 1961 sold to Kenneth More, assumed to be the actor (Middlesex); advertised in *Autosport* with Hayes, Middlesex, address; August sold to John Buncombe (Burnham-on-Sea); by September 1962 owned by Ronald Bateman (Inverness); re-registered ARB 3; April 1965 sold to John Hallihan, shipped by him to Sydney, Australia, for restoration; re-registered TST 225; 1983/84 sold to Bill Marshall; restoration continued, later returned to UK; now registered YSV 242, owned by David Lomas (UK).

XKC 022

Engine number E1022 **Body number** K1022 **Registration number** n/a

Despatch date 28/10/52 **Colour** Red **History** Supplied to Hoffman, USA; 1953 sold to H.W. Wessels III; Floyd Bennett Field, Long Island; bought by Masten Gregory when XKC 015 caught fire in practice and used in race, leading for some laps before retiring; Thompson, Connecticut, 1st; 1954 Argentine 1000Kms, with Dale Duncan (race number 18), 14th after overheating caused by malfunctioning water pump; Gregory sold car shortly after; 1956 sold to William Wilson (New Orleans), achieved two overall wins and a class win from four events; c1966 sold to David Rubin (New York), still owned by him, reported as being in good unrestored condition.

XKC 023

Engine number E1023 **Body number** K1023 **Registration number** n/a **Despatch date** 18/11/52 **Colour** Red **History** Supplied to Hornburg, USA; sold to Joe Henderson (Seattle & Tacoma); driven by Jack Douglas & Bill Pollack; 1953 Seattle Seafair 100-mile race, Pollack, 2nd; 1955 Road America, Elkhart Lake, Jack Douglas, 11th; Torrey Pines, rolled by Douglas; body repaired; sold to Ces Critchlow (Huntington Beach, California); 1956 Palm Springs, ret'd; Torrey Pines, rolled again; acquired by Horvath Motors, Costa Mesa, damaged body replaced with a Devin fibreglass body; 1961 traded by Horvath Motors in return for having their building repainted; 1962 acquired by Frank Schierenbeck, who owned a Jaguar service garage in Costa Mesa, in return for rebuilding an engine; 1963 Schierenbeck clocked at 165mph at Orange County Airport; registered and retained by Schierenbeck until 1997; discovered and purchased by Terry Larson; sold to Christian Jenny (Switzerland).

XKC 024

Engine number E1024 **Body number** K1024 **Registration number** 878 FUF (now) **Despatch date** 25/11/52 **Colour** Dark Green **History** Supplied to Hornburg, USA; sold to Alec Thomson (Denver); 1953 Bergstrom AFB, Austin, Texas, Lone Star 200-mile race, Phil Hill, 2nd; sold to James Harrison (Colorado Springs, Nevada); March Field, Riverside, California, East v West meeting, crashed; several later owners in California; sold to Bob Reid (Geneva); 1988/89 restored by John Pearson/RS Panels; sold to the late Jim Wallis (Otford, UK); car sold by Coys of Kensington to Dalle Carbonare (Italy); 1997 sold, via Terry Larson, to Fred Bohlander (California, USA).

XKC 025

Engine number E1025 **Body number** K1025 **Registration number** n/a **Despatch date** 19/1/53 **Colour** Dark Green **History** Supplied to Moto Maroc, Casablanca, Morocco; sold to Armand Roboly; 1953 Hyères 12 Hour race, France, with John Simone, 2nd; Tour de France, ret'd; later in USA; 1962 reported to have been seen at Stuckers Auto Parts, Stanton

Island, New York, for sale for $300; 1976 advertised in Hemmings by Al Lendzion for $800 'or swop for 1941 Buick Coupe' – picture shows full rolling chassis but no body, engine or gearbox; 1990/91 restored by Hall & Fowler, UK; registered XSV 894; Hubertus Graf Donhoff (Germany); sold, via Adrian Hamilton, to Paul Burdell (UK); sold to David Cohen (Canada); 1997? sold to purchaser in Japan.

XKC 026

Engine number E1026 **Body number** K1026 **Registration number** n/a **Despatch date** 24/11/52 **Colour** Cream **History** Supplied by Hornburg, USA; sold to Kjell Qvale; sold to fiction writer Al Coppel; 1953 featured on front cover of *Road & Track*; sold to Sterling Edwards whose C-type (XKC 017) had been crashed; Madera, California, 2nd; sold to Julio Mariscal (Mexico City), triple Webers fitted; 1974 returned to USA; restored by Hill & Vaughan (Phil Hill); same owner until 1987; later owned by George Gillette (Denver, USA); 1991 failed to sell at Christie's Pebble Beach; later sold to John Coombs (UK); 1996 sold, via Adrian Hamilton, to Jack Croul (USA).

XKC 027

Engine number E1027 **Body number** K1027 **Registration number** GE 11413 **Despatch date** 15/1/53 **Colour** Cream **History** Supplied to Marcel Fleury, Geneva; February 1953 sold to John Simone, a former USAF colonel who had received Legion d'Honneur for his French resistance efforts; Agadir GP, 3rd; Marrakesh GP, 2nd; October 1953 sold to Jacques Jonneret (Geneva); 1954 Nimes GP, France, 1st; Bern GP, Switzerland, 4th; Barcelona GP, Spain, 4th; Montlhéry GP, France, 2nd; also 4 firsts, 2 seconds and 1 third in hillclimbs in France, Italy and Switzerland; Geneva Rally, crashed; December 1954 sold to Paul R. Vogel (Geneva); 1955 various hillclimbs in Switzerland, 3 seconds and 2 thirds; GP des Frontières, Chimay, Belgium, ret'd while lying 3rd; 1962 sold back to Marcel Fleury; 1975 sold to Ole Sommer (Naerum, Denmark).

XKC 028

Engine number E1028 **Body number** K1028 **Registration number** n/a

ABOVE **The mysterious XKC 020 was stolen in New Orleans in 1970 and has not reappeared.**

Despatch date 24/11/52 **Colour** Silver **History** Supplied to Hornburg, USA; sold to Charles Hughes and Kurt Kircher (Colorado); some club racing history; later owners included William Franz (Ohio); sold to Pat Black (Ohio); 1981 sold to Joe Eagle; raced extensively until 1988, including Road America & Monterey; in 1985 driven on parade lap of Kansas City Follies GP by Phil Hill & Masten Gregory; sold to Bob Baker (Nebraska); used for Colorado Grand & raced at Laguna Seca & Sears Point; reported to be in good, unrestored condition; 1995 sold, via Terry Larson, to Philippe Reyns (Arizona, USA).

XKC 029

Engine number E1029 **Body number** K1029 **Registration number** n/a **Despatch date** 24/11/52 **Colour** Pastel Green **History** Supplied to Hornburg, USA; sold to Mexico; 1953 Carrera Panamericana, Paca Ibarra (whose entry was sponsored by Mexican Govt), ret'd; 1954 sold to Javier Velazquez; later owned by William Frey (Massachusetts, USA); sold to Brian Classic (UK); sold to C. Brierley; registered JSV 258; sold to Allan Dunkerley (UK).

XKC 030

Engine number E1030 **Body number** K1030 **Registration number** n/a **Despatch date** 17/12/52 **Colour** Black **History** Supplied to Hoffman, USA; sold to David Hirsch; 1953 Sebring 12 Hours, Harry Gray/Bob Gegen, 4th; Bridgehampton, rolled by Gray; later owned by Jake Kaplan, Herb Hoefler Jnr & others (New England); 1958 sold to Gordon MacKenzie (Millbrook, New York); raced in 1960s and modified to 3.8-litre, together with E-type IRS and D-type style head fairing, entered in over 100 races in '50s and '60s; sold in same area in 1970s; now owned by Edward Sutherland (Sudbury, Massachusetts, USA).

XKC 031

Engine number E1031 **Body number** K1031 **Registration number** n/a **Despatch date** 12/1/53 **Colour** Silver **History** Supplied to Hornburg, USA; supplied to International Motors,

Hollywood; sold to Donald Parkinson; 1953 Pebble Beach, California, car damaged; sold to Jack Rataree (Arizona); sold to Rich Johnson (Arizona); sold to Richard Mellen (Illinois, USA).

XKC 032

Engine number E1032 **Body number** K1032 **Registration number** n/a **Despatch date** 2/1/53 **Colour** Birch Grey **History** Supplied to Belgian Motor Co; 1953 displayed at Brussels Show; sold to 1950 World Champion, Giuseppe Farina; lent to Ferrari for evaluation; Panhard rod fitted in place of 'A' bracket; 1953/54 to Ernie Erickson (USA); fitted with triple Webers; 1954 Abraham Lincoln Trophy, Washington DC, 2nd or 3rd; Chanute, Illinois, 2nd; 1955 sold to Doc Wyllie, who sold XKC 009; Seneca Cup, Watkins Glen, 1st (for third year); November, Fairchild Airport, Maryland, 2nd in class; September 1957 sold to J.P. Jefferson Scott, fitted with SU carbs once again; owned and used by him until 1980; during ownership, fitted with Ford 4.7 V8 and Borg Warner all-synchro 'box; Jaguar units refitted; passed through Dan Margulies (London); 1983 sold to Pat Burke (Sydney, Australia); August 1984 driven by Stirling Moss & Warwick Brown at Amaroo Park, Sydney; substantial restoration by John Pearson; owned by Kerry Manolas; 1990 auctioned by Brooks at Monaco & reported sold for £868,000 to Boris Messmer (Germany); 1994 car auctioned by Brooks but withdrawn; sold to Amailia Palmaz (USA).

XKC 033

Engine number E1033 **Body number** K1033 **Registration number** n/a **Despatch date** 19/1/53 **Colour** Dark Green **History** Supplied to Hornburg, USA; sold to Mr McManus; sold to Ridelle Gregory (Masten's brother) shortly after; Novice Race, March Field, Riverside, California, 1st; March 1954, Lone Star races, Austin, Texas, 2nd; Del Monte Trophy, Pebble Beach, 3rd; fitted new head and Webers; various later owners, mainly in same state; reported to have been fitted with bonnet from XKC 024; 1956 Palm Springs, Tom Groskritz, ret'd; later owned by George Boyd; car badly damaged when building collapsed due to tornado; 1970s sold to Walter C. Hill (Florida, USA), restored to XKC 003 specification.

XKC 034

Engine number E1036-8 **Body number** K1034 **Registration number** n/a **Despatch date** 23/1/53 **Colour** Dark Green **History** Supplied to Hoffman, USA; sold to Jack Shepherd (Tampa, Florida); 1953 Sebring 12 Hours, believed car driven by George Huntoon/Phil Stiles; 1954 sold to Lorin McMullen (Fort Worth, Texas); Fort Worth race meeting, 3rd x 2; later sold in heavily damaged state and fitted with V8 power unit; early 1960s remains sold to Mark Daniels (Milwaukee); sold to Jim Grief (Wisconsin); sold to Ali Lugo; some parts may have been fitted to XKC 015; original chassis frame believed

to be with Jaycox brothers (Long Island, USA).

XKC 035

Engine number E1037 **Body number** K1035 **Registration number** n/a **Despatch date** 15/1/53 **Colour** Birch Grey **History** Supplied to Delacroix, Paris, France; sold to Henri Peignaux (Lyons); sold to Jean Heurtaux; 1953 Soleil-Cannes Rally; Mille Miglia, accompanied by Madame Heurtaux as co-driver (Capt Crespin failed to arrive in time), completed course but unplaced; Planfoy Hillclimb, St Etienne, broke record but Heurtaux crashed fatally after finish; many years later remains found in France and returned to UK; owned at some stage by John Harper; owned & rebuilt by Phil Bennett; intervening history not researched by us; now registered WWK 4; now owned by Allen Lloyd (UK).

XKC 036

Engine number E1034 **Body number** K1036 **Registration number** n/a **Despatch date** 12/1/53 **Colour** Cream **History** Supplied to Moto Maroc, Morocco; sold to Guy Berthomier (Casablanca); Dakar GP, 1st over 2-litre class; Marrakesh GP, 4th; Portuguese GP meeting, Oporto, crashed; August 1953 factory quoted £53 for new chassis and £315 for new body; owned by C. Bavery (France) for many years; sold to Philippe Renault; sold, via Adrain Hamilton, to Matt Spitzley (Oxfordshire, UK); 1993 auctioned by Coys at Silverstone but failed to reach reserve; 1997 sold, via Terry Larson, to Bill Marriott (USA).

XKC 037

Engine number E1038-8 **Body number** K1037 **Registration number** NDU 970 **Despatch date** 1/9/53 **Colour** BRG **History** Works car; built as production car; completed 20 April 1953; reserve Le Mans car & used by Experimental Dept; *Daily Express* Silverstone, Moss, rolled car in practice, rebuilt (at cost of £272 15s 0d) overnight at factory (cylinder head number W.266, gearbox number JH.13310, 4.09:1 axle, Lockheed 2 L-S brakes, Champion NA10 plugs, race number 35), 7th; July, car prepared for sale; September, sold as a home delivery export car, via Lewis and Hodgkiss, Kenya, to John Manussis of Kenya; painted Birch Grey with blue wheels, Kenyan emblem on both flanks; TT, Dundrod, crashed; rebuilt at factory again, reportedly with new body and chassis; owner wanted car prepared for 1954 Le Mans but problems with insurance company over repair (cost £772 12 9d); 1954 raced by Gerry Dunham Jnr and owner; Webers fitted; Goodwood, Dunham, 3rd; Reims 12 Hours, Manussis/Dunham, ret'd; exported (legal requirement within year of purchase) to Australia; August sold, via Peter Whitehead, to Dr John L. Boorman (Cessnock, New South Wales); used as road and race car, mixture of successes and accidents; two large accidents, after second one written-off by insurance

company, wreck sold to young Frank Gardner; engine, steering and exhaust fitted, for a time, to Gardner's racing XK120 (660162); car rebuilt possibly with glass-fibre bonnet but more likely fabricated from 18g alloy, chassis fabricated by Gardner & XK120 parts fitted; bonnet shape altered, fitted first with XK120 grille, then Allard J2 grille; March 1957, Mt Druitt, 1st; NSW TT, 1st; several further successes, remaining unbeaten in sports car scratch races at Mt Druitt & Bathurst in 1957, almost winning the ARDC Championship; October, Bathurst 100 Handicap, 2nd; October 1958, sold to Frank Matich of Leaton Motors; raced by Matich, recorded 146.34mph at Bathurst; early 1959 may have been sold to Barry Graber (Sydney); shortly after sold to Ross Dalton; June 1959 raced at Orange & Lowood; 1960 raced at Orange, Huntley Colliery & Hume Weir; 1961 restored to more original appearance, XK150 disc brakes fitted; early 1962 advertised and possibly sold to T. Watts, who raced car at Towac, NSW, in November 1963; March 1964 sold to John Kinsella (Sydney) with blown block, which was replaced by 3.8 E-type block; 1966 sold to Peter Lonergan (Queensland); 1969 sold to Ian Cummins for £2500; 1970 commenced five-year restoration; 1976 crashed at Silverdale hillclimb, rebuilt again; 1977 sold to George Parlby (Sydney) for $40,000; c1985 sold by Toyshop, NSW, to USA for a reported $102,000; sold to Eric Trabor (Switzerland); 1994 sold to Greg Johnson; 1995 being restored and prepared for historic racing by Terry Larson; still owned by Greg Johnson (California, USA).

XKC 038

Engine number E1039 (later E1052) **Body number** K1038 **Registration number** OVC 915 **Despatch date** n/a **Colour** BRG **History** Works car; 1953 prepared for Mexican Road Race but plan abandoned; 1953, *Daily Express* Silverstone, Walker (cylinder head number W.264, 4.09:1 axle, race number 34), 5th; 1954 displayed at Geneva Motor Show; sold to Duncan Hamilton; British Empire Trophy, Oulton Park, 1st in heat, 4th in handicap final & 1st on road; Members' Goodwood, 2nd; Aintree, 1st; Montlhéry, 1st; sold to Dan Margulies; raced extensively UK and overseas by owner and once by his mechanic, Graham Hill; 1955 Castle Combe, 1st; Sardinia, 3rd; 1956 Targa Florio, with David Piper, 16th (delayed by crash); sold to Gillie Tyrer; 1957 sold to Peter Mould; 1958 sold to Peter Sargent; later owners included Tom Gibson, Frank Sowden, Rupert Glydon, Michael Hall & Sir Anthony Bamford; Ralph Stross, Cheshire; 1995 restoration by John Pearson, owned by Sir Anthony Bamford (Uttoxeter, UK).

XKC 039

Engine number E1040 **Body number** K1039 **Registration number** RKX 991 **Despatch date** 21/4/53 **Colour** Dark Green **History** Supplied to Henlys,

London, though effectively direct sale to Peter Whitehead; Goodwood, Graham Whitehead, 1st; Silverstone International, Graham Whitehead, 6th; Hyères 12 Hours, driven by owner with Tom Cole, 1st; Lisbon, 6th; Pescara, with Hamilton, ret'd; January 1954 Mt Druitt 24 Hours, NSW, Australia, with Tony Gaze & Alf Barrett, ret'd after leading; taken by owner to New Zealand; sold to Jack Tutton, New Zealand, President of Canterbury Car Club; C.W.F. Hamilton Trophy, Christchurch, 5th (provisional as Tutton protested that he was baulked by fourth-placed 498cc Cooper Norton); 1957 sold to Des Wilde; soon sold to David Young; known to have been raced from November 1958 to January 1961; 1962 sold to Garth Forsythe; 1966 sold to Ian and Ray Archibald, South Island Jaguar distributors; raced in historic events; sold to Peter Agg (UK); sold to Francesco Scianna (Italy); 1997 sold to Staffan Svenby (Sweden).

XKC 040

Engine number E1035 **Body number** K1040 **Registration number** SEH 721 **Despatch date** 10/3/53 **Colour** Dark Green **History** Supplied to Byatts, Stoke-on-Trent, UK; sold to Jim Swift (director of Byatts); club raced with some success; various later UK owners; 1960 sold by Chequered Flag, London, to Bill Dunn (Jacksonville, Florida, USA); sold to Walter Hill around 1980 and restoration begun; still owned by Walter Hill (Florida, USA).

XKC 041

Engine number E1041 **Body number** K1041 **Registration number** KSF 181 **Despatch date** 24/3/53 **Colour** Metallic Blue **History** Supplied to Rossleigh, Edinburgh; sold to Merchiston Motors, the Ecurie Ecosse base; 1953 driven by Jimmy Stewart, unless otherwise stated; Charterhall, 2nd; Ibsley, 3rd; Castle Combe; Silverstone, 12th; Charterhall, 3rd; Thruxton, 1st × 2; Snetterton, 2 × 3rd; Empire Trophy, Isle of Man, 5th in heat, 6th in final; Snetterton, crashed; Silverstone GP meeting, 6th; Thruxton, 1st; Charterhall, Ian Stewart, 2nd; Goodwood Nine Hours, Bob Dickson, 4th; Nürburgring 1000Kms, Ian Stewart/Roy Salvadori, 2nd; July 1954 sold to Sir James Walker (Berkshire), who retained car for several years; 1956 new gearbox fitted by works; several later owners in north of England; 1963 owned by M.N. Slater of Golden Fleece Enterprises, Yorkshire; 1969 offered for sale by Chris Renwick; 1970 offered for sale by Brian Classic; 1971 sold to Gavin Sandford-Morgan (Australia) and displayed in Birdwood Motor Museum from late 1972; December 1976 sold to John Blanden (Adelaide) and still owned by him; occasionally raced by owner's son, Richard; February 1982 driven at Sandown 'Tribute to the Champions' meeting by Stirling Moss & Alan Jones.

XKC 042

Engine number E1042 **Body number** K1042 **Registration number** KSF 182

Despatch date 2/4/53 Colour Metallic Blue History Originally intended for export to Carlos Lostalo, Argentina, but allegedly cancelled due to customs difficulties; supplied to Rossleigh, Edinburgh; sold to Ecurie Ecosse; Charterhall, Sanderson 4th & Lawrence, unplaced; Ibsley, Scott-Douglas, 4th; Charterhall, Sanderson, 2nd; Thruxton, Scott-Douglas; Snetterton, Lawrence, unplaced; Empire Trophy, Isle of Man, Sanderson, 4th in heat, 5th in final; Snetterton, Lawrence, 2nd & 3rd; Silverstone GP meeting, Sanderson, 11th; Thruxton, Lawrence, 3rd; Charterhall, Jimmy Stewart, 3rd; Goodwood, Sanderson/Dixon; Goodwood Nine Hours, Lawrence/Curtis, 5th; Nürburgring 1000Kms, Jimmy Stewart/Lawrence, 6th; 1954 sold to John Keeling & raced with some success; Paris Cup, Montlhéry, crashed; later owners included a Mr Elkins & Nigel Dawes (Tewkesbury, UK) from early 1970s; car driven and impressions published by Philip Porter and Paul Skilleter during Dawes's ownership; late 1983 sold to Peter Alpar (Victoria, Australia); sold, via Adrian Hamilton, to Campbell McLaren (Scotland); sold to Dick Skipworth (Thame, UK), joining the rest of his Ecurie Ecosse collection.

XKC 043
Engine number E1044 Body number K1043 Registration number n/a Despatch date 4/6/53 Colour Dark Green History Supplied to J.W. Lagerwij, The Hague, Holland; sold to R.E.L.M. Tielens (Meerssen, near Maastricht); raced, but not successfully; 1959/60 sold to Hans van der Ham (Heerlerheide, near Maastricht); raced more extensively, including many appearances at Zandvoort, many midfield finishes; in early 1960s made last appearance at hillclimb near Vaals; disappeared from scene; at some stage sold to Oscar Chiararia; 1968 found by Pieter Zwakman's partner while looking for an XK in south of Holland; car was spotted in a meadow without engine, gearbox and wheels, used by owner's children to play on; most missing parts found stored at owner's garage, including manifold with triple Webers; sold to Zwakman and partner; 1970 sold to XK specialist Aubrey Finburgh; totally restored from very poor condition at Finburgh's Classic Autos company, completed in 1991; still owned by Aubrey Finburgh (Totteridge, UK).

XKC 044
Engine number E1043 Body number K1044 Registration number n/a Despatch date 1/9/53 Colour Black History Supplied to Fredlunds, Sweden; sold to Oscar Swahn; some local successes; sold to Arne Fredlund (son of importer); 1954 Skarpnack, Stockholm, 2nd; sold to Curt Lincoln; 1955 Djurgard, Helsinki, 1st & 2nd; Kingsland Trophy, Brands Hatch, 3rd; late 1950s owners included Folke Strid, Hagersten & Tore Bjurstrom (Orebro); sold to Fredland again; being restored until Fredland Snr died; sold to Eric Magnus Alvan (Bromma); later

1960s imported to UK by Nigel Moores; sold to Roberts Harrison (Pennsylvania, USA); sold to Kiichi Harvyyama; sold to Yoshiyuki Hayashi (Japan); 1991 restored by John Pearson (Towcester, UK); sold to Samuel Mann (USA); 1996 sold, via Terry Larson, to John Pentis (Australia).

XKC 045
Engine number E1046 Body number K1045 Registration number n/a Despatch date 10/4/53 Colour Red History Supplied to Compagnia Generale Auto, Milan; sold to Mario Tadini; 1953 Mille Miglia, with Franco Cortese, ret'd; returned to factory for work; sold to Ivo Badaracco (Lugano, Switzerland); 1954 Swiss GP meeting, 3rd in over 1.6-litre sports car class; sold to Silvio Moser (Switzerland); used mainly for hillclimbs; sold to Hans Maag; used mainly in hillclimbs in 1960s; sold to Anthony Bamford; sold to Richard L. Hubbard; sold to W.T. Aken & Co. (Nigel Bradshaw, St Annes, Lancs, UK); sold to Bob Roberts, former owner of Midland Motor Museum (Bridgnorth, UK); raced occasionally for Roberts by Mike Barker; sold to Jaguar Daimler Heritage Trust (Coventry, UK).

XKC 046
Engine number E1048 Body number K1046 Registration number MVC 630 Despatch date 9/4/53 Colour Metallic Blue History Supplied to Delacroix, Paris, France; sold to Sir James Scott-Douglas Bt and used as Ecurie Ecosse team car; Castle Combe, 1st; Reims 12 Hours, with Sanderson, 4th; Spa 24 Hours, with Gale, 2nd; Nürburgring 1000Kms, crashed in practice; rebuilt and sold to Berwyn Baxter; 1954/55 used successfully in club racing; 1955 sold to Max Trimble and successfully club raced; sold to Lord Ebury; 1957 fatal accident at Prescott hillclimb; later owners included John Houghton, who used it on the road; sold to Tom May who took around 15 years to restore car; late 1970s sold to Tony Hildebrand; early 1980s sold to Lord Anthony Rufus-Izaacs; mid-1980s sold, via Adrian Hamilton, to Tony Wang (Long Island, USA).

XKC 047
Engine number E1047-8 Body number K1047 Registration number n/a Despatch date ?/5/53 Colour Yellow History First intended for Ian Appleyard to rally in 1953; supplied to Belgian Motor Company, Brussels, Belgium; sold to Roger Laurent (Vilvorde, Belgium); prepared by factory for Le Mans as Ecurie Francorchamps entry; Le Mans, with de Tournaco, 9th; Spa 24 Hours (with cylinder head number 1047, 3.31:1 axle), ret'd; Nürburgring, with Olivier Gendebien, ret'd; 1954 crashed by Frank Rainbow and John Lea en route to Le Mans; XKC 012 sent out to Le Mans and fitted with engine and other parts from 047; completed car became known as 047; Le Mans, with Swaters, 4th; Reims 12 Hours, with Swaters, 3rd; Zandvoort, 3rd; Dundrod TT, with Swaters, 16th on handicap, but 7th on road; sold to

Walter Arnold (Germany); Barcelona Cup, 7th; early 1956 Wolfgang von Trips considered purchasing car but decided against; car exported to USA; later owners included Lt Col James Gallagher (Texas); now owned by Tom Groskritz (Costa Mesa, California, USA), but see XKC 012.

XKC 048
Engine number E1045 Body number K1048 Registration number OHP 43 Despatch date 14/10/53 Colour French Blue History Supplied to Henlys, London, UK; sold to Colonel Ronnie Hoare; used as road car abroad and in UK; 1956 sold to Michael Crowley-Milling, who painted car dark green, fitted different windscreen, all-weather equipment and used also as road car; later displayed for a while at former Stratford Motor Museum; sold to Stanislaus Count Donhoff (Germany).

XKC 049
Engine number E1050 Body number K1049 Registration number RAU 450 Despatch date 16/7/53 Colour Dark Green History Supplied to C.H. Truman & Co, Nottingham, UK; used in club racing by Don Truman; 1955 sold to Gillie Tyrer who fitted XK120 Roadster windscreen & hood; sold to Louis Manduca; unlimited sports car race, Brands Hatch, Archie Scott-Brown, 1st; Boxing Day Brands, Scott-Brown, 2nd; later owned by John Woolfe & Gordon Lee who raced with success; mid-1970 raced by David Duffy, advertised for sale by Rod Leach; later owned by Peter Hall (Maldon, Essex); 1994 auctioned by Brooks, sold to Mr Kogan (Canada).

XKC 050
Engine number E1049 Body number K1050 Registration number ZU 2357 Despatch date 16/8/53 Colour Dark Green History Last production car; supplied to Frank Cavey & Sons, Dublin; sold to Joe Kelly; Dundrod TT, with Jack Fairman, 2nd in class, 7th on road; Wakefield Trophy, The Curragh, 2nd; 1954 Dundrod TT, lent to Joe Flynn & Torrie Large, 5th in class, 13th on road; 1955 Empire Trophy, Oulton Park, crashed; wreck sold; later owners included Paul Emery, C. Unsworth, K. Jeans, David Harvey (1965, Surrey), Jeremy Broad (Midlands), Bryan Corser (Shrewsbury, condition when purchased described as 'frightening', registered SVM 737, two-year rebuild, painted Tyrolean Green, owned until 1980), & Tony Swan (c1985); sold to Steve Earle (California, USA).

XKC 051
Engine number E1053-8 Body number n/a Registration number LSF 420 Despatch date n/a Colour BRG History Works lightweight, 1953 Le Mans, Rolt/Hamilton (Dunlop disc brakes, Webers, cylinder head number RJ 65, 2.93:1 axle, race number 18), 1st; 1953 TT, Rolt/Hamilton (9:1 compression, 3.54:1 axle, race number 6), ret'd; 1953 Prescott, Walker (4.27:1 axle), fastest sports car of the day; 1954 sold to Ecurie Ecosse,

painted metallic blue; it has been claimed that this car took part in Argentine 1000Kms, but David Murray states that cars were shipped on 14/12/53, yet Dewis tested 051 on 17/3/54, having already tested 052 & 053 in preparation for Ecurie Ecosse on 2/12/53 and 26/11/53 respectively; also Murray states that team's older car was allocated to local drivers, this corroborated by 'Aeneas' in Autosport 15/1/54, suggesting one 1953 Ecurie Ecosse car was sent to Argentina, but not 051; also car bearing number 18 put on show at Ford Motor Co's '40 Years of Sports Cars' exhibition at Detroit museum in January/February 1954; British Empire Trophy, Oulton Park, Rolt 3rd in heat, Sanderson 5th in handicap final & 2nd on road; First Easter Handicap, Goodwood, Rolt, 2nd; Race Two, Members' Goodwood, Sanderson, 3rd after spinning when in 2nd place; Race Four, Sanderson, crashed; Daily Express international sports car race, Silverstone, Peter Walker, 3rd and Team Prize; Aintree, Scott-Douglas, 6th; Snetterton, Scott-Douglas, 4th, 8th & ret'd; Goodwood, Scott-Douglas, 12th & 13th; Oulton Park, Titterington 1st & Scott-Douglas 8th; Charterhall, Lawrence, 1st; Silverstone GP meeting, Titterington, 6th; Zandvoort, Scott-Douglas, 2nd; 1955 British Empire Trophy, Oulton Park, Sanderson, 6th in class & 16th on handicap; Easter Goodwood, Rolt, 4th; car sold to Bill Smith (Lincoln), colour changed to red; Ulster Trophy, Dundrod, 1st; Eastern Counties 100, Snetterton, 3rd; sold to Geoffrey Allison (York); 1956 colour changed to white and used for successful club racing season; Mallory Park, 1st; sold to Miles Brubacher (California) and used as road car in 1957; chassis restored; 1968 sold to Briggs Cunningham and displayed at Costa Mesa museum, California; car sold to Adrian Hamilton (Duncan's son); rebuilt with aid of David Cottingham & rebodied by RS Panels in 14swg; original 18swg body retained by Hamilton but not used due to poor condition & impracticality; still owned by Adrian Hamilton (Hampshire, UK).

XKC 052
Engine number E1054 (& E1055-9 & E1058-8 & E1052-9) Body number n/a Registration number LFS 672 Despatch date n/a Colour BRG History Works lightweight, 1953 Le Mans, Whitehead/ Stewart (Dunlop disc brakes, Webers, cylinder head number RJ 78, 3.31:1 axle, race number 19), 4th; Silverstone, Rolt (with engine number E1058-8, cylinder head number RJ 47, 4.09:1 axle), ret'd; Goodwood Nine Hours, Rolt/Hamilton (with engine number E1052-9, 3.92:1 axle, race number 2), ret'd; 2/12/53 tested by Dewis in preparation for Ecurie Ecosse; sold to Ecurie Ecosse (with engine number E1055-9, 3.31:1 axle), painted metallic blue; 1954 Argentine 1000Kms, Ian Stewart/Jimmy Stewart, crashed; rebuilt at factory; henceforth Jimmy Stewart during 1954 unless stated otherwise; British Empire Trophy, Oulton Park, 4th in heat, 6th in final; Easter Handicap, Goodwood,

1st; Race Two, Members' Goodwood, 1st; Race Four, 1st; Ibsley, 2nd to Flockhart in Mark II BRM; Race Seven, 1st; *Daily Express* international sports car race, Silverstone, 4th and Team Prize; Aintree, 3rd; Snetterton, Roy Salvadori, 1st x 2 & 3rd; Whit Goodwood, 1st & 7th; Oulton Park, Sanderson, 2nd & 3rd; Charterhall, Sanderson, 2nd & 3rd; Silverstone GP meeting, Rolt, 10th; Zandvoort, Hans Davids, 7th in heat & unplaced in final; Charterhall, Salvadori, 1st; Goodwood, Titterington, 4th; Barcelona Cup, Salvadori, 2nd; sold to Peter Blond; 1955 used for club racing in UK; Spa, lent to Hans Davids, 4th; Six Hour handicap race, Silverstone, Maurice Charles; later owners included Alan Ensoll and Tom Candlish (1957/8); c1971 sold to Martin Morris (Exeter, UK).

XKC 053

Engine number E1051 (& E1055-8 & E1054) **Body number** LM3 **Registration number** LFS 671 **Despatch date** n/a **Colour** BRG **History** Works lightweight, 1953 Le Mans, Moss/Walker (Dunlop disc brakes, Webers, cylinder head number RJ 35, 2.93:1 axle, race number 17), 2nd; Lisbon GP, Moss (with engine number 1055-8, 3.31:1 axle), 2nd; Goodwood Nine Hours, Whitehead/Stewart (with engine number E1055-8, 3.92:1 axle, race number 3), 3rd; TT, Moss/Walker (with engine number 1054-9, 3.54:1 axle, race number 7), ret'd but lap record to Walker; 25/11/53 tested by Dewis in preparation for Ecurie Ecosse; sold to Ecurie Ecosse (with engine number E1051-9, 3.31:1 axle), painted metallic blue; Argentine 1000Kms, Sanderson/ Scott-Douglas (race number 22), 4th; Castle Combe, Jimmy Stewart, 2nd; British Empire Trophy, Oulton Park, Sanderson, 2nd in heat, not used in final due to damaged oil cooler; Ibsley, Sanderson, 2nd & 3rd; Silverstone, Sanderson, team prize; Aintree, Sanderson, 5th; Snetterton, Titterington, 3rd & 4th x 2; Goodwood, Sanderson, 2nd & 8th; Oulton Park, Sanderson, broke valve in practice; Silverstone GP meeting, Sanderson, 8th; Zandvoort, Sanderson, 2nd in heat & 1st in final; The Curragh, Titterington, ret'd; Charterhall, Sanderson, 2nd; Barcelona Cup, Sanderson, 3rd; sold to J.K. Hunter; 1955 John Lawrence; 1956 sold to Gillie Tyrer, re-registered WKA 9 and used for club racing; owned for many years by Tom Gibson (Cropton, Yorkshire); restored by owner and David Hodgson; early 1960s raced by Keith Schellenberg; converted by Dick Protheroe to 3.8 litres; Church Fenton, covered standing quarter mile in 12.6sec; 1988 sold, via Adrian Hamilton, to Alan Lawson (Ripley, Surrey, UK); 1992 sold to Bob Baker (USA); 1995 mechanically rebuilt & prepared for historic racing by Terry Larson; 1996 sold to Kerry Manolas (Australia); 1998 sold, via Adrian Hamilton, to Rob Walton (USA).

XKC 201

Engine number E1002-8 (& various others) **Body number** n/a **Registration number** n/a **Despatch date** Not sold

Colour BRG **History** Prototype known as the 'light alloy car', built during 1953 to works order number WCR 1148; first monocoque construction car, effectively prototype D-type; 1953/54 used for extensive testing to prove alloy structure, 1954 tested at Reims; taken to Le Mans private test session; 1954/55 used for extensive testing of PI; company paperwork stated, 'reduced to produce'.

XKC 301

Engine number n/a **Registration number** n/a **Colour** BRG **History** Named unofficially as the 'Brontosaurus'; all-enveloping body; built during 1953 to works order number WCR 1148; designed by Lyons with possibility of record-breaking in mind; run a few times in late '53; company paperwork stated, 'being reduced to produce by Service Department'.

D - T Y P E S

XKC 401

Engine number E2001-9 **Registration number** OVC 501 **Colour** BRG **History** Prototype D-type and first to be completed; first tested on 13/4/54 at Lindley, frequent testing at Lindley, Silverstone on 3/5/54; Le Mans tests on 8/5/54, set unofficial lap record; frequent testing at Gayden & Lindley; 25/5/54 evening test at Gaydon with Moss; 27/5/54 filmed for television with Rolt driving; development testing continued in late 1954; 3/2/55 taken to Silverstone for driver tests; 14/2/54 used at MIRA for BBC recording; tyre testing; ZF diff evaluated; mid-1955 de Dion rear suspension fitted to car and later removed; car never raced; retained by Jaguar & lent for many years to National Motor Museum (Beaulieu, Hampshire, UK); displayed by Jaguar at 1958 & 1966 Geneva Shows; displayed in reception/ showroom at Browns Lane in recent years; some work done on car in 1980s by John Pearson; owned by Jaguar Daimler Heritage Trust (Coventry, UK).

XKC 402

Engine number E2004-9 **Registration number** OKV 1 **Colour** BRG **History** First works car to be completed; 4/5/54 registered for road; Le Mans, Hamilton/Rolt (race number 14), 2nd; Reims 12 Hours, Hamilton/Rolt, 2nd; TT, Dundrod, Hamilton/Rolt, ret'd; displayed at Paris Salon; January 1955 sold to Duncan Hamilton; road-tested by John Bolster for *Autosport*; Morocco GP, Agadir GP, Morocco (4.09:1 axle), ret'd; Dakar GP (2.75:1 axle, 17in wheels), 3rd; British Empire Trophy, Oulton Park, 7th; Easter Goodwood, 3rd; Coupe de Paris, Montlhéry, 2nd; Djurgard Park, Helsinki, Michael Head, 1st; Johnson Trophy, Goodwood, 1st; Oporto GP, 3rd; Lisbon GP, ret'd; as XKC 402 is stamped over the number XKC 405 it would appear that following one of this car's many accidents XKC 405 may have been dismantled and certain parts incorporated in XKC 402; 1956 sold to 'Jumbo' Goddard and

converted to quasi-XKSS by Hamilton, before factory created this model; screen frame made & central member between cockpits removed by Parvis Bridge Eng, Byfleet; Hamilton claimed car was inspiration for XKSS but denied by factory; believed registered 3 APB for a while, then back to OKV 1 (which had been retained by Hamilton); used as road car for many years; rolled following accident with lorry, but not badly damaged; Mont Ventoux hillclimb, France; 1965/66 taken by Goddard to Australia, continued to be used as a road car; October 1968, Oxley hillclimb, Tamworth, NSW; October 1984, auctioned & sold to Robin Davidson (London, UK).

XKC 403

Engine number E2005-9 **Registration number** OKV 2 **Colour** BRG **History** Second 1954 works car; Le Mans, Moss/Walker (race number 12), ret'd (achieved new record speed on Mulsanne Straight, 172.97mph); Reims 12 Hours, Moss/Walker, ret'd; TT, Dundrod, fitted with 2 1/2-litre engine, Whitehead/Wharton, 5th; refitted with 3.4 engine (E2004-9 which had been fitted, at least temporarily, back in April); 1955 *Daily Express* Silverstone, Rolt, 3rd; sold to Jack Broadhead for Bob Berry to race; Goodwood, 2nd; Oporto GP, 5th; Goodwood Nine Hours, with Dewis, 5th; TT, Dundrod, crashed; rebuilt, according to Berry, "with a similar integral body subframe assembly which was originally built by the factory as a prototype"; 1956 painted lighter green; Silverstone, 3rd; Goodwood, 1st; heavily crashed at same Goodwood meeting (cartwheeled at St Mary's); car virtually written-off; rebuilt, according to Berry, "with spare steel frame and production monocoque. To the best of my recollection all the running gear, ie, front and rear suspension (upon which we did quite an amount of work of our own), brakes (which were the full power system), steering, plus the engine/gearbox assembly, were all transferred from the older car"; 1956-58 continued to be raced by variety of drivers including Jack Fairman, Ron Flockhart, Peter Blond & cyclist Reg Harris; 1958 engine changed at works from E2004-9 to E2065-9; soon sold to Gerry Crozier; 1960 sold, via Chequered Flag, to David Jaycox (Canada); later owners included George Gordon, James Mace & James Catto between early 1960s & 1980; during this time one driver was killed & car was crashed, around 1964, by A. Smith at Mosport Park; 1980 sold in damaged state to Geoffrey Miller (Canada); soon sold to Lynx; car re-imported was to late D-type production spec with steel frame; early 1980s rebuilt & sold to James Wallis (Sevenoaks, UK); 1995 sold to Robert Cooper (Gloucestershire, UK).

XKC 404

Engine number E2006-9 **Registration number** OKV 3 **Colour** BRG **History** Third 1954 works car; Le Mans, Whitehead/Wharton (race number 15),

ret'd; Reims 12 Hours, Whitehead/ Wharton, 1st; Brighton Speed Trials, Dewis; Prescott Hillclimb, Walker; used for Guild of Motoring Writers test day, Goodwood; displayed at Brussels Motor Show; 1955 Silverstone, Hawthorn, ret'd, but set new lap record; Goodwood Nine Hours, car lent to Hamilton/Rolt, ret'd; February 1957 sold to John Coombs (his great friend John Young states that he owned OKV 3, bought it for about £3000, "you couldn't sell them!"); 1959 sold to Dickens & Cartwright; sold to Chipstead Motors; sold to John Love (South Africa); Luanda GP, Rhodesia, 1st; 1960 South African GP (Libre race), 7th (2nd sports car); sold to Neville Austin; Bulawayo, two races, 1st & 2nd; Salisbury, 6th; 1961 Border 100, East London, 6th; Laurenco Marques, 1st; Kyalami Nine Hours, crashed; December 1961 sold to Rondalia Touring Club, who began restoration; 1966 sold to Paul Hawkins, who shipped car to UK; rebuild completed by Temple Panels, London; 1967 sold to John Melville-Smith (Malvern, UK); crashed at Prescott & rebuilt at works; completed May 1968; 1969-70 raced for owner by Martin Morris; 1971 crashed at Snetterton; crashed car sold to Morris & rebuilt; then raced extensively and very successfully during 1970s & 1980s; also used for touring in Europe, America & New Zealand; raced in 1990s by David Morris; still owned by Martin Morris (Exeter, UK).

XKC 405

Engine number n/a **Registration number** n/a **Colour** n/a **History** Never completed; frame could have been used for rebuilds of either XKC 402 or XKC 403; if the latter car, then frame would have been destroyed when car had its second (or first?) major accident.

XKD 406

Engine number E2003-9 **Registration number** RRW 21 (later 3 CPF) **Colour** BRG **History** Works 1954 car; TT, Dundrod, fitted with 2 1/2-litre engine, Moss/Walker, 18th; 3.4 engine fitted; used for display purposes and driver tests; early 1955 shipped out to USA, loaned to Briggs Cunningham; tested by Spear, Walters, Lloyd & Cunningham; Daytona Beach, Walters, achieved 164mph; Sebring 12 Hours, Hawthorn/Walters, 1st; shipped back to UK; *Daily Express* Silverstone, Hamilton, 5th; sold to Hamilton; lent to drivers such as Abecassis, Peter Whitehead & Michael Head; Swedish GP, Kristianstad, Head, 6th; winter 1956/57 sold to J. Forbes Clark (Wolverhampton); used for hillclimbs & sprints; later owners included Peter Skidmore (1970), British hillclimb champion Sir Nick Williamson Bt (hillclimbed at Shelsley Walsh), John Beasley (1980), Martin Hilton; sold to Alan Lawson (Ripley, Surrey, UK); 1997 sold to Nicolaus Springer (UK); 1998 sold to Lukas Huni (Switzerland

XKD 501

Engine number E2008-9 **Registration number** MWS 301 **Colour** Metallic Blue

History Supplied to Ecurie Ecosse, May 1955; *Daily Express* Silverstone, Jimmy Stewart, crashed in practice; rebuilt by works; Nürburgring, Jimmy Stewart, crashed; Wicklow, fastest finisher; Charterhall, Titterington, 1st & 2nd; Snetterton, Titterington, 1st × 2; August, Goodwood Nine Hours, Titterington/Sanderson, 2nd; Crimond, Sanderson, 1st × 2nd; Aintree, Titterington, 2nd; March 1956, Snetterton, rolled in practice by 'Wilkie' Wilkinson; rebuilt; Aintree, Sanderson, 2nd; Charterhall, Lawrence, 3rd × 2; Silverstone, Sanderson, spun; Goodwood, Flockhart, 2nd & 1st; Reims, Flockhart/Sanderson, 4th; Le Mans, Flockhart/Sanderson, 1st; Kristianstad, Flockhart, Sanderson, Lawrence; Goodwood, Flockhart, Sanderson, 3rd; 1957 Mille Miglia, Flockhart, ret'd; Nürburgring, Fairman/Lawrence; 1960, Charterhall, Turnbull, spun; Goodwood, Mackay; Charterhall, Mackay, 3rd & 6th; retired from racing & retained by Ecurie Ecosse backer, Major Thomson (Peebles, Scotland); October 1970 auctioned and sold to Sir Michael Nairn (Scotland).

XKD 502

Engine number E2020-9 **Registration number** MWS 302 **Colour** Metallic Blue **History** Supplied to Ecurie Ecosse May 1955; *Daily Express* Silverstone, Titterington, 6th; Ulster Trophy, Titterington, 1st; Dundrod, Titterington, 2nd on handicap; Nürburgring, Titterington crashed; rebuilt by works; Charterhall, Sanderson, 5th & 4th; Snetterton, Sanderson, 2nd; Crimond, Smith, 3rd × 2; September, Aintree, Sanderson, 1st; 1956, Snetterton, Brown, 3rd, Sanderson 4th; Goodwood, Brown, 2nd; Oulton Park, Sanderson, 4th; Aintree, Flockhart, 3rd; Charterhall, Sanderson, 1st, Flockhart, 1st; Silverstone, Brown, 2nd in class; Spa, Sanderson, 1st; Goodwood, Titterington, 1st & 3rd; Aintree, Titterington, 2nd; Reims, Flockhart/Sanderson, 4th; Silverstone, Titterington, 1st in class; Kristianstad, Titterington/Flockhart, ret'd; Goodwood, Sanderson, 5th; late 1956 sold to Maurice Charles (Cardiff, UK); c1958 crashed and rebuilt, possibly using body from XKD 508; early 1960s fitted with IRS, but later removed; later owners included Jack Alderslade, Michael McGrath, Hexagon of Highgate, David Clifford, Robert Cooper, Vic Norman (who had car rebuilt at Lynx mid-1980s), Hon Patrick Lindsay & Albert Obrist; sold to Yoshiyuki Hayashi (Japan); 1995 sold to Peter Rae (UK); 1996 sold to Robert Sarrailh (France).

XKD 503

Engine number E2011-9 **Registration number** Le Mans trade plate 070 DU **Colour** Yellow **History** Supplied to Belgian Motor Co (possibly on loan only); works prepared for 1955 Le Mans, Claes/Swaters (race number 10), 3rd; returned to works for testing; shipped back to Belgium; sold to Ernest Erickson (Chicago, USA); September inaugural Road America meeting, Elkhart Lake, Wisconsin, 3rd;

March 1956, Walterboro, 5th; June, Lawrenceville, 1st Class C Modified; July, Beverly, 4th; sold to Alfonso Gomez Mena; 1957 Havana GP, 6th; Sebring, ret'd; car then disappeared and further history appears to be unknown; it is possible that car may have acquired identity of XKD 521, also owned by Mena (see XKD 521).

XKD 504

Engine number E3001-9 **Registration number** Le Mans trade plate 164 WK, later RSF 302 **Colour** BRG (later Metallic Blue) **History** Works 1955 long-nose car; Le Mans, spare car; used by works for testing PI; Silverstone (with carburettor engine number E3002-9), Fairman, ret'd; October, fitted with engine number E4001-9; Nürburgring 1000Kms, Frère/Hamilton, ret'd; used for testing at Reims, Frère/ Bueb; March 1957, fitted with engine number E3002-9; 1957 sold to Ecurie Ecosse; Spa, Lawrence; Nürburgring, Bueb/ Lawrence; St Etienne, Lawrence, 2nd; 'Monzanapolis', Sanderson, 6th; Spa, Sanderson; 1958, Sebring, Sanderson/ Bueb, ret'd; Silverstone, Fairman; Nürburgring, Sanderson/Bueb; Le Mans, Fairman/Gregory, ret'd; Goodwood, TT, Gregory/Ireland, 4th; 1958 sold to Mike Salmon; repainted BRG; raced often & successfully; 1961 Snetterton Three Hours, 1st; 1962 sold to Peter Sutcliffe (Huddersfield, UK); again raced often & successfully; 1963 Snetterton, crashed heavily; car sent to works for repair & received frame from XKD 505 purchased from Maurice Charles; 1965 sold to Neil Corner; raced successfully in early Griffiths Formula historic racing & used as road car; 1981 sold to Paul Vestey; rebuilt by Lynx with new frame, XKD 505 frame removed and sold by Lynx to Bill Lake; used for Mille Miglia twice with Adrian Hamilton as co-driver; 1991 Spa, Nigel Corner; Magny Cours, Gary Pearson, crashed; 1994 original frame purchased from Peter Sutcliffe & refitted; Paul Vestey (Alresford, Hampshire, UK); 1995 sold to Harry Leventis (UK); 1998 sold, via Adrian Hamilton, back to Paul Vestey (Hampshire, UK) and being repainted in Ecurie Ecosse Blue.

XKD 505

Engine number E3002-9 **Registration number** Le Mans trade plate 774 RW **Colour** BRG **History** Works 1955 long-nose car; Le Mans, Hawthorn/Bueb (race number 6), 1st; prepared for British GP meeting, Aintree, where Hawthorn was to drive this car but withdrawn during practice and XKD 506 substituted; overhauled at works & fitted with de Dion rear suspension; TT, Dundrod, withdrawn during practice; used by works for testing; fitted with engine number E3003-9 with PI; prepared for 1956 Easter Goodwood meeting but not raced; fitted with rear axle oil sump with 6 pints capacity; April, tested extensively by Hawthorn & Fairman, the latter crashing car at Silverstone; 14/9/56 tested at Silverstone by Hawthorn & Bueb with independent rear suspension; 17/11/56 Dewis tested IRS; 26/6/57 ditto,

from Dewis's log, 'this has 3 degrees neg camber. The understeer is just as bad as with a normal axle. The diff unit now has a sump holding 1 gal of oil approx. with an electric pump for circulating. Highest temp was 120 degrees C. Cooling duct fitted from the passenger lid to the rear disc brakes'; car continued to be used for testing until June 1958; history then vague; it has been stated that parts of this car were used in a rebuild of XKD 601 and that there is no record of XKD 505 having been sold; however the list of Experimental cars states, 'XKD 505 BRG, sold'; early 1980s frame stamped XKD 505 removed from XKD 504 during rebuild by Lynx and sold to the late Bill Lake, who had an authentic car built up around this frame with a real monocoque; sold to David Lomas (UK).

XKD 506

Engine number E3003-9 **Registration number** Le Mans trade plate 032 RW **Colour** BRG **History** Works 1955 long-nose car; Le Mans, Hamilton/Rolt (race number 7), ret'd; fitted with number E3007-9; British GP meeting, Aintree, Hawthorn, 5th; TT, Dundrod, Hawthorn/Titterington, ret'd; fitted with engine number E3005-9; tested late 1955 at Silverstone; fitted with engine number E3001-9; 1956 shipped to USA; painted white with blue stripes; Sebring 12 Hours, Johnston/Spear, ret'd; remained with Cunningham for '56 & '57; returned to works & scrapped.

XKD 507

Engine number E3004-9 **Registration number** Le Mans trade plate 210 RW **Colour** White with blue stripes **History** Le Mans, Spear/Walters (race number 9), ret'd; application form completed by Cunningham in 1964 to register car in California states, 'This vehicle was given to me by the Jaguar Automobile Co, Coventry, England, in 1955, and shipped to Conn. Est. price $9,500'; September, Road America inaugural meeting, Johnston, 2nd; Watkins Glen GP, Johnston, 1st; Hagerstown, Maryland, Johnston, 1st (this win gave Johnston the 1955 SCCA National Championship for class C modified sports cars); 1956 Sebring, Benett/Cunningham, 12th; raced by Cunningham team during 1956, '57 & '58; special fin fitted by Momo at some stage; on display at Cunningham's museum for many years; c1987 sold to Collier Museum (Florida, USA).

XKD 508

Engine number E3005-9 **Registration number** Le Mans trade plate 194 WK **Colour** BRG (later White with blue stripes) **History** Works 1955 long-nose car; Le Mans, Beauman/Dewis (race number 8), ret'd; shipped to USA to Briggs Cunningham; fitted with engine number E3006-9 & painted in Cunningham colours; 1956 Sebring 12 Hours, Hamilton/Bueb, ret'd; remained with Cunningham & modified by Momo; returned to works and scrapped.

XKD 509

Engine number E2015-9 **Registration number** n/a **Colour** BRG with white wings and stripes **History** First production line car; supplied to Hornburg, USA; 1955 sold to Albert R. Browne (Menlo Park, California); 1956 Sebring 12 Hours, Brero/Weiss, ret'd; June, Texas National Championship races, Fort Worth, Brero, 3rd & 7th; June, Road America, Brero, 2nd; July, Beverly, Brero, ret'd; Elkhart Lake, Brero, 2nd; Nassau, Brero, 3rd; March 1957, Stockton, Brero, 1st; later owner believed to be Brian Classic; sold to Nigel Moores; James Moores (UK).

XKD 510

Engine number E2017-9 **Registration number** YPC 614 **Colour** BRG **History** Supplied to Henlys, London; despatched 24/9/55; registered 26/9/55; sold, via Coombs, to Richard Wilkins (Bishops Stortford); sold to Duncan Hamilton (believed early 1956) with 250 miles recorded; 1956 Dakar GP, Graham Whitehead, 5th; Easter Meeting, Goodwood, Tony Dennis, crashed fatally; sold in damaged state to Gerald Ashmore (West Bromwich, Birmingham); rebuilt using new monocoque (damaged tub stored on roof of Ashmore's garage, later sold to Nigel Moores and built up with damaged subframes from XKD 606); raced by Ashmore for several seasons; 1959 sold to Neville Taylor (Sheffield) and part-converted to XKSS; crashed at Shelsley Walsh hillclimb; presumably rebuilt; sold to Cycle & Carriage Co, Singapore; September 1963, Johore GP, Yong Nam Kee, crashed fatally breaking car in two with front half going over a cliff to the beach below; damaged items put into store; 1967 sold to John Hallihan, who shipped car, valued for insurance purposes at £299, to Australia; 1974 sold to Ian Cummins (Australia); rebuilt using new tub together with XKD 526 as pattern by Classic Autocraft, and three replica D-types created; 1981 rebuild completed; 1982 auctioned and sold to Bib Stillwell (first owner of XKD 520), by now based in USA; raced in historic events in USA; damaged at events at Laguna Seca & Detroit; sold to Bob Baker (Nebraska); sold to Victor Gauntlett/Peter Livanos (UK); sold again to Ian Cummins (Australia); 1997 sold to Warren Daley (NSW, Australia).

XKD 511

Engine number E2019-9 **Registration number** TNG 959 **Colour** BRG **History** Supplied to Mann Egerton (Norwich, UK); Sept 1955 sold to Capt Ian B. Baillie; 1957 took various International Class C speed records; raced without success; sold to M.V. Mackie; sold to James Boothby; mid-1960s sold to Guy Griffiths; car now white; raced by daughter Penny; still in her ownership, now as Penny Woodley (Stratford-upon-Avon, UK).

XKD 512

Engine number E2014-9 **Registration number** J 26 **Colour** BRG **History**

Supplied to St Helier Garages, Jersey; sold to Lord Louth; Chimay, Belgium, 5th; raced in South Africa; Johannesburg race meeting, 2nd x 2; raced by John Love; 1957 sold; later owners included a Mr Watson (car raced by Malcolm Gardner), Jimmy de Villiers, Ian Brown (Rhodesia); 3.8 engine fitted & raced by Bruce Huntley & G. Pfaff but without success; 1961 Kyalami, ret'd; 1962 sold to Russ Taylor (UK); registered 516 EYR; 1964 sold to Jackie Epstein; 1965 sold to Nigel Moores; 1988 possibly sold to Yoshiyuki Hayashi (Japan); 1989 sold to European collector; auctioned by Brooks and sold to REX Collection (Sweden) for £1.2m; 1992 auctioned by Brooks and sold to David Cohen (Canada) for a lesser amount; raced by Robert Brooks at Laguna Seca; sold, via Adrian Hamilton, to Paul Burdell (UK) and still owned by him; 1994 raced at Laguna Seca & rolled without great damage.

XKD 513

Engine number E2022-9 **Registration number** 6478 AT69 **Colour** French Blue **History** Supplied to Delecroix, Paris; sold, via H. Peignaux, Lyons, to Jean-Marie Brussin; 1957 Le Mans, with Jean Lucas, as Los Amigos team, works prepared, 3rd; 1958 Le Mans, with Guelfi, 3-litre engine (EE1208-10 with 35/40 head) fitted by works, Brussin crashed fatally; bonnet and tail section torn off in accident & scrapped at Le Mans; car sat in storage until sold, in 1960, to Michelotti; damaged body panels cut away leaving rear bulkhead crossmembers and footbox area intact; 1963 car displayed at Geneva motor show with very stylish GT body; late 1960s car imported into USA by Richard F. Carter (Georgia); used only for display purposes to generate money for a church; 1973 sold to Andrew Gortway (UK); shipped to Lynx where upper bodyshell removed and separated from the original tub panels left from XKD 513; XKD 513 then sold for £14,000 to Laurence Bristow & restored by Lynx to its original configuration using the original chassis and the rest of the car's original components together with a complete works original tail section (originally fitted to XKD 511), new bonnet and rebuilt tub using whatever possible of the original; the only panels not used in the restoration of XKD 513 were those damaged in the Le Mans accident; (Bill Lake purchased what was left of the Michelotti bodyshell and had Lynx build it up as a road going car, using a written-off 4.2 E-type, registration 20 KOG, as donor car. This coupé was later sold to Roland Urban, France); restored XKD 513 sold to Peter Giddings (USA); raced extensively in California; sold to Bob Baker (Nebraska); January 1986 on front cover of *Road & Track* road tested by Phil Hill & the late Innes Ireland; sold to Bill Chizar (California); sold to Terry Larson (Arizona, USA), used regularly for historic events including Monterey, Colorado Grand & Copperstate 1000 & Swiss Tour, plus Factory D-type cavalcade to Le Mans.

XKD 514

Engine number E2018-9 **Registration number** PWX 2 **Colour** Battleship Grey **History** First production line car to be delivered; August 1956 supplied to Glovers, Ripon; sold to Sir Robert Ropner (Bedale, Yorks); used as road car for many years; 1959 factory fitted 3.8 engine; hillclimbed by owner and raced once by son, Bruce; maintained by factory and 'Wilkie' Wilkinson; 1974 sold to Adrian Hamilton on behalf of Robert Danny; sold to Ole Sommer (Naerum, Denmark).

XKD 515

Engine number E2023-9 **Registration number** RRU 1 **Colour** Special Blue **History** Supplied to Henlys, London; sold to Col. Ronnie Hoare; used as road car; 1959 sold to John Coundley; sold back to Hoare; 1961 sold to Nigel Moores; 1972 mentioned by Michael Bowler in Jaguar 50th anniversary supplement in *Motor* as having only 14,000 miles on the clock; 1988 sold to Yoshiyuki Hayashi (Japan); 1989 sold to Brooks/Louwman stable.

XKD 516

Engine number E2020-9 **Registration number** n/a **Colour** Cream **History** Supplied to Hoffman, USA; sold to Cdr. John Rutherford (Palm Beach, Florida); raced at Nassau; 1956 Daytona Beach, achieved 161mph; 1974 sold to Hon Alan Clark (later UK Govt Defence Minister); registered WPG 4; sold to Tony Charnock; used as road car; 1976 sold to Nick Mason (of Pink Floyd); "having an exceptionally low mileage, the car required virtually no restoration other than cleaning and repainting"; now registered XKD 1 and Dark Blue; used by owner for Pomeroy Trophy; 1977 Retrospective GP, Montreux, raced by owner; featured in article by Mel Nichols in *Car*, 1992 featured in series of Shell advertisements; mileage stated as '19,492 and correct'; 1992 Ulster Trophy, Dundrod Restrospective, John Watson, 1st; Nick Mason (London, UK).

XKD 517

Engine number E2026-9 **Registration number** TKF 9 **Colour** Pastel Green **History** Supplied to Henlys, Manchester, UK; sold to Gillie Tyrer; 1956 Queensferry Sprint Trials, organised by Chester Motor Club, achieved 131.58mph over flying 1/4-mile; sold (according to log book) to Futura Rubber Co (Alex McMillan); raced quite successfully by McMillan in club events; Silverstone final 1955 meeting, 1st x 3 and best lap of the day; 1956 sold to Murkett Bros (Huntingdon); painted white and raced by Henry Taylor; Snetterton, 1st; 1957 Spa, 3rd; 1958 sold to Jock McBain & raced for Border Reivers team by Jim Clark; competed in 20 events with no retirements & achieved 12 wins; Team manager Ian Scott-Watson mentioned in correspondence with 'Lofty' England that they had a driver of 'extreme promise'; Clark achieved first 100mph lap on an unbanked track in the UK; also raced for Border Reivers by Jimmy & John Somervail

& Jock McBain; winter 1958/59 sold to Alan Ensoll who tried to convert car into an XKSS; sold to Robert J. Duncan (Crumlin, Northern Ireland) and raced there; 1964 sold to Bryan Corser (Shrewsbury, UK); rebuilt as D-type & painted BRG; sold to Walter Hill; 1979 sold to Willie Tuckett; regularly used in historic racing; crashed in early-1980s and rebuilt by Martin Morris; driven by author during preparation of this book; William Tuckett (Devon, UK).

XKD 518

Engine number E2028-9 **Registration number** KDB 100 **Colour** Red **History** Supplied to Henlys, Manchester, UK; sold to Peter Blond; 1956 club raced; sold to Jonathan Sieff; sold to Monty Mostyn of Speedwell Garage; sold to J. Houghton; sold to Jean Bloxham; sold to John Coombs/Richard Wilkins; sold to Clive Lacey; attended first International E-type Day at Donington Park in 1974; sold by Adrian Hamilton to Peter Golant, Led Zeppelin manager, (Sussex); 1982 sold, via Adrian Hamilton, to George Stauffer (Wisconsin, USA) and kept in his office; 1997 sold to Chris Cox (N. California, USA); 1998 reported sold at Monterey Classic Car auction to Roger Williamson (Texas, USA).

XKD 519

Engine number E2009-9 **Registration number** n/a **Colour** Pastel Green **History** Supplied to Hornburg, USA; sold to A.R. Krause (Bellflower, California); modified by owner and raced quite successfully by son Bill; 3.8 engine fitted; 1958 Sports Car GP, Riverside, Bill Krause, 3rd; Chevrolet engine fitted later; 1960 Riverside, with V8, ret'd; sold to Jim La Guardia; 1974 sold to John Bailey; work done by Lynx, including fitting original-spec engine and painting in pale yellow; John Bailey (Birmingham, UK).

XKD 520

Engine number E2021-9 **Registration number** 444 **Colour** BRG **History** Supplied to Brysons, Australia; sold to Bib Stillwell (Melbourne); March 1956, Moomba TT, Albert Park, 2nd; Argus Cup, Albert Park, 1st; Bathurst 500, NSW, 3rd and fastest sports car; Rob Roy Hillclimb, broke sports

ABOVE **XKD 516 recorded 161mph at Daytona Beach in 1956 and is owned today by Pink Floyd drummer Nick Mason.**

car record; South Australia Trophy, Port Wakefield, 1st; car prepared for Land Speed Record (presumably Australian) attempt, 2.93:1 axle fitted, project then abandoned; Bathurst Road Racing Championship for Sports Cars, 1st; Queensland TT, Lowood, 2nd; Australian TT, Albert Park, 5th; Australian GP meeting, Albert Park; early 1957 sold, via Sydney dealer John Crouch, to Ampol for Sydney TV & radio personality Jack Davey for £5250; painted red & screen fitted on passenger's side; 30/6/57 crashed by friend Bill Murray into articulated lorry; mid-1957 wreckage sold to Frank Gardner; rebuilt by owner at his Whale Beach service station, with body repairs by Alan Standfield, in just 3 months and painted white; Bathurst Road Racing Championship, 2nd; Mt Druitt, 1st; Racing Car Scratch Races, Orange, 3rd x 2, on both occasions behind F1 cars; over 1500cc race, Schofields, 1st; November 1958 sold to Peter (or David) Finch (Turramurra) when Gardner moved to England; bored to 3.8 and painted green; raced in NSW & Queensland for 3 years; late 1960 3.8 block obtained from works; September 1961 crashed at Warwick Farm and replica long-nose bonnet fitted; May 1962 sold to Ash Marshall; restored, painted red, registered ASH 222 & used for drag events; later owned by Peter Bradley (Sydney); June 1965 sold to Rick Parkinson; 1966 Paul Hawkins heard from Gardner that car was

BELOW **Bib Stillwell in XKD 520 at Albert Park, Melbourne, in 1956.**

for sale, considered buying it but as he already had several, mentioned it to friend Richard Attwood; early 1967 sold to Attwood (Wolverhampton, UK), who later became an F1 driver and Le Mans winner; displayed at his Mercedes-Benz garage; 1977 sold to present owner, Mr A. Spencer-Nairn (Jersey), and rebuilt by him.

XKD 521

Engine number E2037-9 **Registration number** n/a **Colour** Cream **History** Supplied to Distribuidora Jaguar SA, Havana, Cuba; sold to Alfonso Gomez Mena; 1956 Sebring 12 Hours, with Santiago Gonzales, 8th; later crashed into house damaging car very extensively; quoted £2000 by Momo to rebuild; decided to purchase XKD 503 rather than have car rebuilt; 1975 car purporting to be XKD 521 advertised in *Autosport* by a 'Mr Herberts' of New York, believed to be Mr Herb Wetson who dealt in a number of D-types in the 1970s and was reported as having spare chassis XKD 523 & XKD 536; it has been suggested that the chassis plate may have been transferred by Mena to XKD 503, and thus that it was this car being advertised; 1991 car bearing this number advertised in Los Angeles; it has also been reported that the chassis plate was affixed to Lynx replica L87/32.

XKD 522

Engine number E2027-9 **Registration number** n/a **Colour** Red **History** 1955 Los Angeles Show car; December, Palm Springs races, car entered by Hornburg, Saturday, driven by Ignacio Lozano, 5th, Sunday replaced by Carroll Shelby, ret'd as uncompetitive; January 1956 Torrey Pines Six Hour endurance race, Johnston, ret'd after damaging car and shared XKD 527; 1957 badly damaged in workshop fire; reported rebuilt by 1959; later owned by Merle Brennan; 1963 sold to Clyde Keeling; fitted at some stage with V8 engine; during 1960s crashed and very badly damaged; 1971 sold to Tom Groskritz; intact chassis frames & remains of bonnet, monocoque & tail section shipped to Lynx who have reconstructed the body, retaining as much as possible of the original; being gradually rebuilt by owner; Tom Groskritz (Costa Mesa, California, USA).

XKD 523

Engine number E2031-9 **Registration number** n/a **Colour** Black **History** Supplied to Jaguar Car New York; sold to Roberts Harrison; sold shortly after to Walter Huggler (Pennsylvania); used for several club events; reputed to be have been driven by George Constantine; V8 Buick engine fitted by Joe Grimaldi & chassis cut to allow engine to be fitted; sold to Jeff Millstein who traced and acquired original engine *or* Lister engine fitted; 1970 sold to Vintage Car Store (Nyack, New York); new frame & tail section purchased from works (may have been bought for XKD 536); car passed to Ali Lugo; sold to Herb Wetson; 1973 advertised by Wetson in *Autosport*; major

components now used in two cars.

One car rebuilt with new Jaguar frame, original tub, bonnet, suspension, rear axle, tail section, rear frame piece & many other original parts; sold to Ron Finger; 1985 sold to Nick Soprano (New York); sold to George Gillette (Nashville); rebuilt by John Pearson; 1995 sold, via Terry Larson, to Bud Lyon (USA).

Wetson sold to Bob Wood (UK) the intact chassis frame together with a tail & the incomplete XKD 560; XKD 523 original frame later passed, via Stephen Curtis, to Lynx; sold to Brian Angliss; sold to Bill Lake; sold, via Lynx, to UK resident; car reconstructed by Lynx around this original frame & other original specification parts; registered VSV 754; owner wishes to remain anonymous.

XKD 524

Engine number E2032-9 **Registration number** n/a **Colour** Black **History** Supplied to Jaguar Cars New York (presumed); sold to Henry Carroll Inc (Binghampton, New York); mid-1956 sold to Paul Pfohl; August, Holland Hillclimb, New York, FTD; June 1957, Lake Erie Race, Dunkirk, New York, Bill Klink, 1st; 1979 supposedly located in California and now painted BRG; 1988 believed to be owned by Pfohl's son and located in California.

XKD 525

Engine number E2033-9 **Registration number** n/a **Colour** BRG **History** Tested for 650 miles in 8 tests before signing off; supplied to Jaguar Cars New York; sold to Briggs Cunningham and painted white with blue stripes; May 1956 Cumberland, C. Gordon Benett, 5th; July, Beverly, Benett, 6th; intended to be Cunningham's own race car but believed to have been reduced to parts to be used on his other cars after all three crashed during one race meeting at Elkhart Lake in 1956. Believed this car no longer exists, but major parts (frame & tub) reported to exist in USA.

XKD 526

Engine number E2042-9 **Registration number** NCN 040 **Colour** BRG **History** Supplied to Andersons Agencies Pty, Brisbane, or Westco Motors, Queensland, Australia (both apparently owned by Cyril and Geordie Anderson); was to have been owned in third shares by Andersons, Bill Pitt and Charles Swinburn, but Swinburn became fatally ill causing him to sell his share to the other two parties; December 1955 car arrived in Australia; 30/1/56, Strathpine, Mrs Anderson, clocked at 120mph over flying quarter, still in 3rd gear!; 19/2/56, Leyburn sprints, Mrs Anderson, clocked 135.2mph over flying quarter, state record; March, Strathpine; Bill Pitt became regular and very successful driver; 1956 race meeting at Lowood; gearbox problems then precluded competition for 5 months; August, Lowood; New South Wales Road Racing Championships, Bathurst, 2nd to Stan Jones (father of Alan) in 250F Maserati;

Lowood TT, 1st; Australian TT, Albert Park Olympic meeting, Melbourne, 4th; Argus Cup, Albert Park, following weekend, Pitt rolled car and thrown out; car badly damaged and trailered back to Brisbane; completely rebuilt; painted bronze, with squared-off mouth and air vents in bonnet; March 1957, Victorian TT, Albert Part, 2nd; later repainted BRG; raced at Lowood & Bathurst; 1958 raced at Orange, Lowood, Bathurst & Albert Park; 1959 raced at Bathurst & Lowood; late 1959 sold to Leaton Motors, New South Wales; repainted yellow with black stripe and driven initially by Frank Matich & later by Doug Chivas; 1961 fitted with aluminium fastback hardtop to enable it to compete in GT racing; June, Catalina Park, Matich; July, Australian GT Championships, Warwick Farm, Matich, 1st; October, NSW Championship, Matich, 1st; November, Warwick Farm, Chivas; December, sold to Barry Topen; 1962 Warwick Farm; March, Sandown Park inaugural meeting, crashed; car remained in damaged state for some time; c1965 sold to Keith Russell (Sydney), who rebuilt car and raced it occasionally during 1966 at Catalina, Warwick Farm, Hume Weir & Oran Park; 1967 sold to Keith Berryman (Riverina, NSW); hardtop removed and stored; car occasionally raced until 1970; c1976 loaned to Ian Cummins to assist with rebuild of XKD 510; car also rebuilt by Cummins/Classic Autocraft, work including re-skinning the monocoque & making a new front frame; 1982 completed; Keith & Sandra Berryman (NSW, Australia).

XKD 527

Engine number E2025-9 **Registration number** YYD 6 **Colour** BRG **History** Supplied to Hornburg, USA; sold to Jerry Austin (Arcadia, California); 1956 Six Hour race, Torrey Pines Road Races, Saturday, with Sherwood Johnston (after Johnston damaged XKD 522), 1st, One Hour race, Sunday, Johnston, 4th; car tested and featured in several US magazines; Palm Springs, crashed damaging bonnet; owner repaired bonnet and ordered new one; 1957 Palm Springs & Santa Barbara, achieved good places; sold to Bill Smith (Salt Lake City) with new bonnet fitted; raced and bonnet damaged; later owned in mid 1960s by Mark Olson (Farmington, Utah), who fitted old bonnet; sold to Dick Merritt (Royal Oak, Michigan) together with new wrecked bonnet (later sold to Walter Hill); sold to Peter van Rossem (Cheltenham, UK), raced occasionally by him; 1975 sold to Nigel Dawes; driven on several occasions for articles by the author, photographed for this book; Nigel Dawes (Tewkesbury, UK); 1995 sold to UK collector (London, UK); 1997/8 for sale with Coys.

XKD 528

Engine number E2039-9 **Registration number** n/a **Colour** Cream **History** Supplied to Hornburg, USA; sold to Continental Motors, Whittier, California; raced by Pearce Woods; January 1956 Torrey Pines Six Hours endurance race;

featured in *Road & Track*; Palm Springs National race, Harold Erb, 3rd; 1958 sold to Carlyle Blackwell Jnr (Hollywood); later fitted with 3.8 engine, 35/40 head and painted yellow & black; Six Hour race, Pomona, California, with Ken Miles, 1st (said to be last big win by a 'D' in US); 1960 Riverside, ret'd; late 1970s restored by Stephen Griswold; 1980/81 owned by Joel Finn & 1982 by Howard Cohen; Laguna Seca, crashed; repaired and raced at 4 events at Sears Point; c1985 sold to Ron Laurie (San Francisco, USA).

XKD 529

Engine number E2038-9 **Registration number** n/a **Colour** BRG **History** Supplied to Hoffman, USA; sold to Tage Hansen, Boston; May 1956, Cumberland, Hansgen, 1st; raced so successfully by Walt Hansgen that he was invited to join the Cunningham team, which he had regularly beaten; November, venue unknown, Harold Erb, 3rd; May 1957, Cumberland, H. Carter, 9th; March 1958 advertised for sale by Auto Engineering, Lexington, 'Walt Hansgen undefeated in this car', $7000; sold to Thomas Rutherford (Massachusetts); 1959 car modified with 3.8 engine, 2.53 axle, disc-type wheels & exhaust exiting at rear; Utah Salt Flats, car achieved speed of 185.47mph, the highest officially recorded by a D-type; 1970s owned by George Boyd; suffered tornado damage to front & rear when building collapsed; sold to Walter Hill; 1980 restoration completed; owner states car to be in good running condition restored to the Bonneville form; Walter Hill (Florida, USA).

XKD 530

Engine number E2044-9 **Registration number** n/a **Colour** BRG **History** Supplied to Suomen Maanviljelijain Kauppa Oy, Tampere, Finland; sold to Curt Lincoln (Helsinki); 1956 over 2-litre race, Djurgard Park, 1st; raced successfully on road, ice and sand; raced by Timo Makinen; 1959/60 overhauled at works; 1961 Formule Libre race, Central Automobile Club of the USSR (believed to be the only time a D-type has ever raced in Russia), H. Hietarinta, 1st; 1966 sold to Nigel Moores collection.

By 1993, two cars claimed the identity of XKD 530.

Original chassis frame bearing XKD 530 number had been fitted with a new monocoque (incorporating some original

BELOW **In modified form XKD 529 achieved 185.47mph (the highest speed recorded for a D-type) at Utah Salt Flats in 1959.**

parts, such as bracketry) and long-nose body manufactured by Williams and Pritchard, engine number E5008 (with wide angle head) and replacement gearbox; 1988 sold by Moores collection to Yoshijuki Hayashi (Japan); March 1989 sold to Mr. Louwman (Holland); April 1989 sold to Hawthorn Classic Cars Limited (Andrew Baber) (Forest of Dean, UK).

Original engine (E2044-9), monocoque (H2030), gearbox (GBD138) and other parts had been acquired from the Moores collection and incorporated into a reconstructed short-nose car; subsequently owned by John Beasley, Robert Brooks & David Clark; at a later date offered for sale in Brooks auction; 1993 sold, via Adrian Hamilton, to Arthur Urciuoli (USA); 1998 sold, via Terry Larson, to Gary Bartlett (USA).

XKD 531

Engine number E2034-9 **Registration number** n/a **Colour** BRG **History**
Supplied to Hornburg, USA (presumed); sold to Jack Douglas (California); painted yellow & raced from early 1956; June, Texas National Championship races, 10th & 11th; June, Great Salt Lake Trophy 100-mile race, 2nd; October 1957, advertised for $7000 by ex-factory mechanic Joe Thrall on behalf of Jack Douglas; winter, sold to Ray Seher (Reno, Nevada); June 1958, Laguna Seca, 8th; February 1959, sold to Tom Groskritz; 1964 used for quarter-mile runs at San Fernando Raceway; new factory D head fitted; used for SCTA Time Trials at Riverside; Tom Groskritz (Costa Mesa, California, USA).

XKD 532

Engine number E2030-9 **Registration number** NKV 617 **Colour** Red **History**
Purchased by Australian Jack Parker direct from the works while visiting England; despatched 12/10/56; shipped to Sydney as deck cargo on a freighter arriving early '57; purchased for famous rally driver 'Gelignite' Jack Murray to race and used as road car by owner; maintained by Murray at his Bondi garage; Murray banned for racing for two years; 1958 Australian GP, Bathurst, ret'd; painted silver during this period; March 1959, Bathurst, 3rd; also Bathurst October 1959, April 1960, October 1960 & April 1961; November 1961 sold to Bob Jane (Melbourne); restored by Jim Shepherd & repainted BRG; used for display purposes at Jane's tyre depots; 1976 car stolen and driven through plate-glass window of Sydney showroom prior to an intended suicide attempt but crashed; repaired & repainted by Shepherd & completed in 1977; 1980 reported to have covered less than 10,000 miles since original purchase; 1980 sold to George Parlby (Sydney) for a reputed $125,000; some further restoration work done; sold to Jeffrey Pattinson, Coys of Kensington, UK; sold to Allen Lloyd (UK).

XKD 533

Engine number E2040-9 **Registration number** 6708AT69 **Colour** French Blue

History Supplied to Delecroix, Paris, with full width screen; sold, via Peignaux, Lyon, to Monnoyeur (of Los Amigos team), Dijon; 1957 Forez Six Hour race, St Etienne; sold to Pierre Chemin (Lyon); 1958 car returned to works for conversion to XKSS & painted BRG; retained by Chemin for long period; later sold to Dr Philippe Renault; 1988 sold, via Rick Cole auction in USA, to David Cottingham (UK); 1989 sold to Kerry Manolas (Sydney, Australia); shortly after sold, via Adrian Hamilton, to Ralph Lauren; 1990 Mille Miglia; reported to be a good original car; Ralph Lauren (New York, USA).

XKD 534

Engine number E2043-9 **Registration number** n/a **Colour** n/a **History** Following display at Attwoods, Wolverhampton, supplied to International Motor Sales, Wellington, New Zealand; despatched 6/9/56; sold to/retained by Jack Shelley; car prepared & raced by Robert Gibbons; January 1957, New Zealand GP meeting, Ardmore, Auckland, sports car race 1st, GP 5th; Lady Wigram Trophy race; 1958 GP meeting, Ken Wharton Memorial Trophy, 1st, GP ret'd; March, Ardmore GP meeting, ret'd; sold to Angus Hyslop; fitted with 3.8 engine & used as tow car; January 1959, Christchurch meeting; January 1960, Ardmore Sports Car Trophy, 2nd; January 1961, Ardmore Sports Car Trophy, 2nd; January, also raced at Levin & Christchurch; 1961 sold to Simon Taylor; January 1962, GP meeting; 1963 sold, via Riley Car Sales, to Gary Bremer; 1964 raced at Renwick, Maunganui, Levin & Pukekohe; 12/5/64, with 21,737 miles recorded, for £1425 NZ, to Noel Foster (Auckland, New Zealand).

XKD 535

Engine number E2048-9 **Registration number** NVC 260 **Colour** Pastel Blue **History** Supplied to C. de Salamanca, Madrid, Spain; sold to Joaquin Palacios; car raced by Rodolfo Bay; 1956 Oporto race meeting (GP?), Portugal, 8th; 1957 Galapagar hillclimb, Spain, broke record; autumn 1957 advertised for sale; around 1959 car put on display in original condition at Le Mans museum with speedometer reading 9800 miles; 1986 sold to Ralph Lauren (New York); sold shortly after to Bob Rubin (New York) and used on 1989 Mille Miglia; 1989 auctioned by Christie's at Monte Carlo and sold for £1,037,383 to Jeremy Agace & Ray Bellm (UK); discovered to have incorrect windscreen, fin, headrest & rivets, with certain interior items also incorrect; complete mechanical overhaul and above items corrected by John Pearson; car painted Green; competed in 1990 Mille Miglia & raced by Bellm; Agace interest purchased by Bellm; 1996 sold, via Brooks, to Peter Teichman (UK). Mileage believed genuine at 15,400.

XKD 536

Engine number E2024-9 **Registration number** n/a **Colour** Black **History**
Supplied to Hornburg, USA; sold to Loyal

Katskee, Omaha; 1955 Nassau Speed Week, damaged car during practice; 1956 Sebring, damaged wheels; June, Texas National Championship races, 7th & 5th; September, Aggie Sports Car race, Oklahoma Airport, 2nd; 1957 sold to Donny Skogmo (Minneapolis, Minnesota); raced by owner and John Barlass; June, Rib Mountain National Hillclimb, Wisconsin, 1st in B Sports class; September, State Fair Races, Milwaukee, 1st; now mustard yellow; c1961 Barlass fitted a 327 Chevrolet V8; 1963 sold to Jerry Dunbar (Wisconsin), car restored, painted red & raced in Mid-West; 1965 sold to Gregory Bergman (Rockford, Illinois); car stripped down & many parts purchased from Jaguar, including new oil reservoir and tail section; 1968 sold to Chuck Sunderman (Rockford, Illinois); Sunderman then moved, with car, to Florida; 1972 sold to Ferrari author Dick Merritt (Florida/Maryland); 1973 sold to Jack Broudy (New York City); sold immediately to Herb Wetanson (Wetson); 1973 sold to David Piper (Surrey, UK); 1973 sold to Tony Charnock; 1976 restored by Lynx & found to have bonnet from XKSS 701 (also owned by Wetson); 1976 sold to John Lees (Ireland); 1984 returned to Lynx for refurbishment; sold to Adrian Hamilton; converted by Lynx to Appendix C spec & painted BRG; 1984 sold to Robert Cooper; 1985 sold, via Adrian Hamilton, to James W. Stollenwerck (San Francisco, USA); 1989 auctioned by Barrett Jackson but failed to sell; at some stage fitted with engine number E2065-9 (this engine was originally fitted in XKD 556, which was dismantled after being virtually destroyed in the factory fire; engine then fitted in 1958 into XKC 403, later removed in Canada and shipped to UK); 1992 sold to Bruce Meyer (California, USA).

XKD 537

Engine number E2047-9 **Registration number** n/a **Colour** Cream **History**
Supplied to Importadora Salvadorena SA, San Salvador; mid-1956 sold to Mauricio Miranda; seriously damaged in accident shortly after; late 1956 returned to works for repair; February 1957 awaiting instructions to proceed when car was completely destroyed in factory fire; car replaced by XKD 549; to assist export documentation, car assumed identity of

XKD 537; raced without success; January 1962 advertised for sale and shipped to USA; 1966 advertised for sale by Thomas Foreman (New Jersey), now red; March 1967 advertised by Herb Wetson as XKD 537; 1977 owned by the late Paul Petty (Connecticut, USA); retained by family; 1997 sold, via Christies, to Frank Pritt (California, USA).

XKD 538

Engine number E2030-9 **Registration number** n/a **Colour** Ivory **History**
Supplied to Jaguar Midwest Distributors Inc, Indianapolis, USA; sold to Jack Ensley (president of company); 1956 Sebring 12 Hours, with Bob Sweikert, 3rd; May, Smartt Field Races, St Louis, Ladies race, Joan Ellis, 5th (last); Sixth race, 2nd; May, Wisconsin GP, 2nd; June, Lawrenceville, 4th Class C Modified; British GP sports car race, crashed; rebuilt at works; Watkins Glen GP, 2nd (to XKD 545); sold to Barney Devlin (Pennsylvania); sold to Harry Heinl (Ohio); sold to Preston Smith (Williamsport, Pennsylvania); early 1980s sold by Vintage Car Store, Nyack, New York; 1984 advertised by Preston Smith in Hemmings Motor News for $175,000; passed to Fred Simeone (Pennsylvania, USA).

XKD 540

Engine number E2029-9 **Registration number** WVM 3 **Colour** BRG **History**
Loaned to Henlys, Manchester; works chassis records state, 'redundant after experiment'; supplied to Coombs of Guildford for £2100; despatched 24/9/57; used for display purposes; late 1957 sold to hillclimber Phil Scragg; winter 1958/59 modified by works to full XKSS spec for owner to use in sports car hillclimb championship; painted, like all Scragg's cars, in light blue; end of 1959 sold to John Browning (Cheltenham); converted at works to 3.8 and hillclimbed; 1962 sold to Betty Haig; re-registered BLH 7; 28/8/62 sold, via Jack Playford or Daniel Hastings, to Laurie O'Neill (Sydney, Australia); re-registered NSW 567; 1964 featured in Sports Car World; owned briefly by Richard Ralph; 1965 sold to Colin Hyams

BELOW **Originally a D-type, XKD 540 was converted into an XKSS by the works in 1959 and enjoyed an active early life as a hillclimb car.**

(Melbourne); 1965 damaged at hillclimb; 1966 & 1967 won Car of the Day at Jaguar Club of Victoria concours d'elegance; 1968 sold to Jaguar dealer Bill Clemens; 1971 offered for sale at $20,000; September 1972, sold to Bryan Corser (Shrewsbury, UK); restored, painted Tyrolean Green and re-registered NT 5000; featured in *Autocar* 20/2/82; 1985 sold to Peter Fowler; registered XK 55; sold to Hermann Graf Hatzfeldt (Germany); used for Mille Miglia and Oldtimer GP, Nürburgring; described by owner as being, 'virtually in its original condition and in perfect running order'.

XKD 541

Engine number E2049-9 **Registration number** n/a **Colour** Pacific Blue **History** Supplied to Hornburg, USA; sold to Harold Fenner (Hobbs, New Mexico); February 1956, Mansfield, set new lap record; May, Mansfield, 1st; sold to Charles Brown Museum (Texas) and owned until 1970; later owned by Roberts Harrison (Pennsylvania); 1985 sold to David McCarthy; raced in historic events by Stephen Griswold; sold to Don Orosco; sold to Bob Baker (Nebraska, USA); 1997 sold to Bob Demaris (USA).

XKD 543

Engine number E2941-9 **Registration number** n/a **Colour** Black **History** Used for display at dealers; February 1957 destroyed in factory fire; engine removed, rebuilt and supplied to Tojeiro; John Pearson states that fire-damaged car was bought by scrap merchants in Wolverhampton & purchased shortly after by present owner; remains in damaged state.

XKD 544

Engine number E2039-9 **Registration number** WKV 340 **Colour** BRG **History** Used for display purposes at dealers; dismantled by factory for spares; chassis thought to be incorporated in experimental glass-fibre XKSS/D-type built at factory (thus car could be first monocoque sports racing car ever built of composites); often claimed car did not exist but noted on list of Experimental cars, though stated 'no chassis number' and 'scrapped'; apparently passed by works to employee called Thompson; car fitted first with Ford Ten engine & later Austin A70 unit; 1959 car advertised in *Autosport* with Austin, or Austin-Healey, engine; 1964 advertised by Michael Hinde, North Wales; sold to Peter Butt; later owners included, John Pearson, David Cottingham, Ron Stern, Guy Black & David Duffy, who had car rebodied by Lynx with an authentic aluminium body; mid-1970s to mid-1980s raced extensively, including Mille Miglia, by Duffy, sold to David Vine; late 1980s sold to Mike Fisher; 1995 Landhurst Leasing, who had acquired car some years earlier, sold to Andrew Pisker (London, UK).

XKD 545

Engine number E2052-9 **Registration number** n/a **Colour** Pastel Blue **History**

Supplied to Hoffman, USA; despatched 16/12/56; sold to George Constantine (Massachusetts); 1956 Watkins Glen GP, 1st; June 1958, Bridgehampton, ret'd; June, Lime Rock, ret'd; sold, as a wreck it is believed, to Bill Sadler (Canada); rebuilt & raced at several events; car fell off trailer; reported rebuilt with use of glass-fibre; 1961 sold to John Cannon (Canada); Mosport, crashed; part-repaired; late-1962 sold to Hugh Dixon, who rebuilt car again, painted it bright red with a blue stripe & raced it at several events; October 1963, Mt Gabriel hillclimb; November 1967 advertised in *Road & Track*; 1968/69 sold to Vintage Car Store, Nyack, New York; July 1969, advertised in *Motor Sport* by 'Vintage Car'; 1969/70 sold to Peter Ashworth (UK); fitted with full width screen & registered XKD 545J; later screen removed and single driver wraparound type screen refitted; November 1980 sold, via Coys, to Peter Briggs and displayed at his York Motor Museum; 1984 restoration commenced by Classic Autocraft and continued by owner; Peter Briggs (Western Australia).

XKD 546

Engine number E2053-9 **Registration number** n/a **Colour** Cream **History** Supplied to Jaguar Cars New York, USA; mid-1957 sold to C.K. Thompson; July, Courtland, Alabama Sports Car Races, Powder Puff Derby, 'Bubba Jets' Thompson, crashed, Moulton Trophy, Powell Thompson (owner's son aged 21), unplaced, The Governor's Cup, 1st; September, Mansfield, Louisiana (car described as D Jaguar Birmingham?), unplaced; October, Gainesville, 3rd; November, Galveston, unplaced; later owned by actor Tim Considine; 1964 reported as being used in a *Perry Mason* TV drama, car filmed being worked on and appeared to be black with no headfairing & a full width screen; 1965 sold to Robert Otten (California); 1972 car sold; 1976 sold to Chris Drake and used in historic events; sold to David Pennell (UK); 1998 for sale with Adrian Hamilton.

XKD 548

Engine number E2055-9 **Registration number** n/a **Colour** BRG **History** Used for display purposes at dealers; January 1957 dismantled for spares, or possibly used to replace/rebuild crashed XKC 403 in 1956.

XKD 549

Engine number E2059-9 **Registration number** n/a **Colour** BRG **History** Used for display purposes at dealers during 1956; intended for conversion to XKSS but used to replace XKD 537 when that car was destroyed in the factory fire; shipped to Mauricio Miranda (El Salvador); see XKD 537.

XKD 551

Engine number E2070-9 **Registration number** ULU 336 **Colour** BRG **History** Used for display purposes at dealers; May 1957 sold to Coombs of Guildford; October 1957 sold to G. Sportoletti Baduel

(London) and used as road car; modified by fitting passenger door, removing central member between seats, fitting full-width windscreen and passenger headrest fairing; retained until at least 1961; 1966 advertised for sale by Paul Hawkins; later owners included Colin Crabbe, David Hoskison & Peter Agg; 1984 sold, via Coys, to Klaus Warner (Germany); 1991 sold to R. Pferdmenges (Germany); sold to Mr Lustenberger (Switzerland).

XKD 552

Engine number E2061-9 **Registration number** n/a **Colour** Battleship Grey **History** Used for display purposes at dealers; supplied to Lowis & Hodgkiss, Nairobi, Kenya; sold to John Manussis; raced locally; sold, within a year, to Nolis John Samaras (Dar-es-Salaam, Tanganyika); 1960 sold, via UK, to C.G. Stuart (Trinidad); 1963-65 owned by Roger Lucas (Montreal, Canada); painted gold; later owned by George Phillips (Toronto); 1989 owned by Eric Traber (Switzerland); shipped to Terry Larson (Arizona) for restoration; sold, via Terry Larson, to Bruce Lustman (Connecticut, USA); used regularly for historic events; 1997 sold, via Terry Larson, to Ned Speiker (California, USA).

XKD 553

Engine number E2046-9 **Registration number** n/a **Colour** White **History** Used for display purposes at dealers; fin fitted at works and allocated to Jack Ensley (Indianapolis, USA); 1957 Sebring 12 Hours, with Pat O'Connor, ret'd after 6 hours; reported as one of four D-types sanctioned by FIA in USA; late 1957 sold to John C. Reuter (though other information suggests second owner was Dr H.E. Rollings, Georgia, who finished 3rd at Courtland, Alabama, July '57); 1958/59 sold to Ed Rahal & raced in SE Region; reputedly won every SCCA race in region 1957-61; 1969 owned by Mike Bradley (UK), who re-imported car & raced in club events; August 1971, sold to Bob Roberts (Bridgnorth, UK); 1972/73 body and running gear overhauled by F.W. Mays; engine now 3.8 (number NC 2872-9), car registered TVD 670G; Brighton Speed Trials, covered standing quarter in 25.09sec; displayed at Roberts' Midland Motor Museum, Bridgnorth; sold to Paul Vestey; sold, via Lynx, to Peter Kaus (Aschaffenburg, Germany) for his Rosso Bianco Collection.

XKD 554

Engine number E2069-9 **Registration number** n/a **Colour** n/a **History** Supplied to Armandora Mexicana SA, Mexico; sold to Julio Mariscal; raced by owner; Puebla race meeting, 1st; Lago del Guadalupe race meeting, 1st; Avandaro GP, Mexico City, 2nd; also occasionally raced in California; later owners included J. Fouch & H. Schlieske (Los Angeles); sold to Gene McManus (Ohio); 1966 sold to George Bullock (Georgia); later re-imported to UK; June 1971 sold to Hon

Patrick Lindsay; car now black and owned today by Patrick's son, Valentine Lindsay (London, UK).

XKD 556

Engine number E2065-9 **Registration number** n/a **Colour** Cream **History** February 1957 tested at MIRA; destroyed in factory fire same day; dismantled for spares; 1958 engine fitted in XKC 403.

XKD 558

Engine number E2064-9 **Registration number** n/a **Colour** Cream **History** Supplied to Oxford Motors, Vancouver, Canada; used for occasional sprint demonstrations at Abbotsford airport; October 1957 sold to James Rattenbury; October 1957, Abbotsford race meeting, 1st; 1958, Abbotsford race meeting, 1st; Shelton race meeting, 2nd; car modified with longer 95in wheelbase, de Dion rear axle, Roots-type blower, Thornton diff, Hillborn fuel injection; 1959, nine race meetings, 1 win; 1960 ditto; April 1961, sold to Starr Calvert (Seattle); Barhdal Trophy, Pacific Raceway, 1st; West Delta Park, crashed; 1964 rebuilt with 7-litre Ford V8, Borg Warner transmission & wide Chevrolet wheels; some success; September 1964, Westwood, British Columbia, crashed, lopping trees 20ft above the ground (according to a local newspaper report), seriously damaging car on landing and suffering a carburettor fire; remains said to be seen spread on hillside many years later; original engine reputed to be owned by Walter Hill (Florida); damaged subframe and other original parts, including monocoque, used by Lynx to build a long-nose car for Philippe Renault (France); this car later owned by Harley Cluxton (USA); sold, via Terry Larson, to Joel Finn USA) and later Chris Mann (UK); short-nose bonnet now fitted; 1994 sold by Landhurst Leasing, via Terry Larson, to Eduardo Baptista (Mexico).

XKD 560

Engine number E2050-9 **Registration number** n/a **Colour** Cream **History** Supplied to Jaguar Cars New York; early history unknown; soon fitted with Chevrolet Corvette V8 engine and sprouted large blister on bonnet; c1958-65 owned by Bob (or Bill) Fuller; reported to be much raced and crashed during its career; November 1958, Hammond Harvest races, unplaced after leading initially; 1973 D-type advertised in *Autosport* by Herb Wetson; purchased by Bob Wood (UK), found to consist of "a completed, assembled but bastardised car", according to later owner Stephen Curtis; it consisted of the XKD 560 frame (cut about to take V8 engine but otherwise original), 'D' steering rack, 'D' wishbones (one bent), torsion bars, uprights, hubs, shock absorbers & anti-roll bar, Chevrolet engine & gearbox, rear subframe & various suspension, but no axle, & the tail and bonnet in poor condition, plus intact XKD 523 frame; most of the monocoque had been replaced with a 'birdcage' type tubular structure; 1978 assorted assembly sold to Stephen Curtis; dismantled by owner and sent to Lynx for rebuilding around a new monocoque; rebuilt with original-type disc brakes, wheels, gearbox, ZF diff & works, wide-angle 3.8 D-type engine from Norman Buckley's record-breaking boat, *Miss Windermere*; sold to USA; 1993 sold, via Terry Larson, to Daryl Harms (USA); sold to Gavin Bain (Christchurch, New Zealand).

XKD 561

Engine number E2036-9 **Registration number** MWS 303 **Colour** Metallic Blue **History** Third short-nose Ecurie Ecosse car; delivered spring 1956; Snetterton, Flockhart, 1st & 2nd; Goodwood, Flockhart, 1st; Oulton Park, Flockhart, 2nd; Aintree, Titterington, 2nd; Charterhall, Hughes, 2nd × 2; Silverstone, Flockhart, 5th; Spa, Titterington, 3rd in class; Goodwood, Lawrence, ret'd; Aintree, Sanderson, crashed; Rouen, Titterington, 7th; Silverstone, Flockhart, 3rd; Charterhall, Lawrence, winter 1956/57 sold to Max Trimble (Walsall, UK); modified at works with full-width screen; April 1957, raced at Oulton Park & Goodwood; May, Spa, crashed very heavily; November, wreck advertised in *Autosport*; sold to Berwyn Baxter (Birmingham); remains sold to Maurice Charles (Cardiff); rebuilt by owner; sold to Clive Unsworth (Lancashire, UK); reported in poor condition in 1980; owned by Clive Unsworth (Lancashire, UK) until his death in 1996; 1997 sold, via Adrian Hamilton, to Amalia Palmaz (Texas, USA).

XKD 565

Engine number E2075-9 **Registration number** n/a **Colour** Unpainted **History** Intended for conversion to XKSS but destroyed in the factory fire.

XKD 570

Engine number E2078-9 **Registration number** n/a **Colour** Unpainted **History** On 18/7/56 Service Dept instructed to remove engine & gearbox, and pass same to Comp Dept (this date coincided with the period when the badly-damaged XKC 403 was in the Comp Dept for repair; this fact, together with the knowledge that Jack Broadhead, owner of XKC 403, was charged the large amount of £1645, and that XKC 403 subsequently was more akin to a production car, led Andrew Whyte to reason that XKD 570 [or XKD 548] may have changed identity to XKC 403.

XKD 571

Engine number E2071-9 **Registration number** n/a **Colour** Unpainted **History** Prior to, or during, the intended conversion to an XKSS, this car was destroyed in the factory fire.

XKD 573

Engine number E2079-9 **Registration number** NKV 479 **Colour** Yellow **History** Supplied to Belgian Motor Co; sold to Ecurie Francorchamps; works prepared for 1956 Le Mans, Swaters/Rouselle, 4th; Montlhéry Autumn Cup, Pilette, 2nd; works

prepared for 1957 Le Mans with new engine using same number, Frère/Rouselle, 4th; Spa, Rouselle, 4th; St Etienne, Bianchi, 5th; Swedish GP, de Changy/Dubois, 6th; winter 1957/58 sold to Baron Janssen de Limpens; used to commute between Brussels and weekend home by sea; 1962 sold to Antwerp Jaguar agent Jacques de Clippel; 1963 sold to Francis Francis Jnr (Paris), arranged by his friend Jabby Crombac after being told of car by Lucien Bianchi; shipped to Japan for inaugural race meeting at Suzuka circuit, 8th; sold soon after to John Coombs; then on long-term loan to Jaguar and displayed for many years in the reception area/showroom at Browns Lane; 1969 advertised in *Autosport* but not sold; now owned by John Coombs (Monaco), car on loan with John Young (Sussex, UK).

XKD 574

Engine number E2085-9 **Registration number** n/a **Colour** Unpainted **History** Being prepared for conversion to XKSS when destroyed in the factory fire.

XKD 601

Engine number E3005-9 **Registration number** 2 CPG **Colour** BRG **History** Long-nose works car; first 1956 car with lightened body; February, tested with PI at Goodwood; Sebring 12 Hours, Hawthorn/ Titterington, ret'd; Nürburgring 1000Kms, Hawthorn/Titterington, ret'd; Reims 12 Hours, with carburettor engine (E4002-9), Hawthorn/Frère, 2nd; late 1956 sold to Duncan Hamilton; works prepared for 1957 Le Mans, with 3.8 carburettor engine (E5006-9), Hamilton/Gregory (race number 4), 6th; works prepared for 1958 Le Mans, with 3-litre engine (EE1201-10 or E1202-10), Hamilton/Bueb, crashed while 2nd; returned to works to be rebuilt; believed parts from XKD 505 used; later owners included Jim Rogers, Peter Sargent, Mrs Patricia Coundley (3/5/64 BDC Antwerp Speed Trials, FTD, 161.278mph in heavy rain to become fastest woman in Europe, rec'd letter of congratulation from Lyons), Anthony Bamford (raced by Peter Brown), Bob Roberts (displayed at Midland Motor Museum), Adrian Hamilton; 1986 sold to Ralph Lauren; restored by David Cottingham; Ralph Lauren (New York, USA).

XKD 602

Engine number E4004-9 **Registration number** Le Mans trade plate 351 RW **Colour** BRG **History** Long-nose 1956 works car; Le Mans, with PI engine, Fairman/Wharton (race number 3), crashed; tub and rear units used in works rebuild of XKD 603.

XKD 603

Engine number Various **Registration number** Le Mans trade plate 774 RW, later RSF 303 **Colour** BRG **History** Long-nose 1956 works car; Silverstone, Hawthorn, ret'd; Nürburgring 1000Kms, with carburettor engine (E4002-9), Frère/Hamilton, crashed; Reims 12 Hours, with carburettor engine (E4003-9),

Fairman/Titterington, 3rd; Le Mans, with carburettor engine (E4005-9), taken as spare car but used for race after XKD 606 damaged in practice, Frère/Titterington (race number 2), crashed; front subframe fitted to XKD 602 tub during works rebuild to create one car numbered XKD 603; 1957 sold to Ecurie Ecosse; painted metallic blue and registered RSF 303; Buenos Aires, Sanderson/Mieres, 4th; Spa, Sanderson, unplaced; Nürburgring, Flockhart/Fairman, unplaced; Two Hour race, St Etienne, Flockhart, 1st; Le Mans, Sanderson/Lawrence (race number 15), 2nd; Monzanapolis, Fairman, 4th; Kristiansand, Sanderson/Fairman, ret'd; Spa, Fairman, ret'd; 1958, Sebring, Flockhart/Gregory, ret'd; Spa, Fairman, unplaced; 1958 Nürburgring, Flockhart/ Gregory, crashed; St Etienne, Flockhart, 1st; works prepared for Le Mans, with 3-litre engine (EE1207-10), Sanderson/ Lawrence ret'd; works prepared for 1959 Le Mans, Gregory/ Ireland ret'd; TT, Goodwood, Flockhart/ Bekaert, 6th; Silverstone, Flockhart, 2nd in class; sold to James Munro (USA), with 3.4 carburettor engine; now owned by Sir Anthony Bamford (Uttoxeter, UK).

XKD 604

Engine number E4003-9 **Registration number** n/a **Colour** BRG **History** Long-nose 1956 works car; March/April built with PI engine and de Dion rear suspension; Silverstone, Titterington, crashed; dismantled by works; chassis frame allegedly sold to Ecurie Ecosse; sold to Jim Tester (Scotland) who built up a car with frame, a de Dion rear axle and some original parts; sold, via Terry Larson, to Tom Armstrong (USA).

XKD 605

Engine number E4001-9 **Registration number** Le Mans trade plate 393 RW **Colour** BRG **History** Long-nose 1956 works car; built with PI engine; Silverstone, taken but not raced; used for testing at Reims; Reims 12 Hour race (engine changed to E3005-9 in practice), Hamilton/Bueb, 1st; Le Mans (engine changed to E4007-9 after practice), Hawthorn/Bueb (race number 1), 6th & fastest lap; first works 3.8-litre engine fitted & car painted white with blue stripes; 1957 Sebring 12 Hours, Hawthorn/Bueb, 3rd; lent to Cunningham/Momo team, initially for racing and then for display; 1961 shipped back to works & painted BRG; then on long-term loan to Biscaretti Museum, Turin; mid-1980s returned to works; displayed for period at BMIHT Museum (Syon Park, London); 1995 light restoration work being carried out; Jaguar Daimler Heritage Trust (Coventry, UK).

XKD 606

Engine number E4006-9 **Registration number** Le Mans trade plate 032 RW, later RSF 301 **Colour** BRG **History** Last long-nose 1956 works car; Le Mans, was to have been race car but damaged by Titterington in practice; repaired at works;

November, delivered to Ecurie Ecosse with 3.4 carburettor engine (E4004-9); painted metallic blue and registered RSF 301; 1957 Buenos Aires, Argentine, Flockhart/ Galvez, crashed by Flockhart; rebuilt at works with new frame and bonnet; works prepared for Le Mans, with 3.8 PI engine & 2.69:1 axle, Bueb/Flockhart (race number 3), 1st; Monzanapolis, Lawrence, 5th; Kristiansand, Lawrence/Scott Brown, ret'd; Spa, Fairman, unplaced; 1958, Aintree, Bueb, 4th; Spa, Bueb; Charterhall, Flockhart, 1st & 2nd; 1960, Silverstone, Flockhart, unplaced; 1960 either this car or XKD 603 taken to Le Mans (Whyte states in text that it was 603 and in Appendix that it was 606; David Murray states in his book that the 1960 car had done five Le Mans, which suggests it must be 603; however car carried registration RSF 301 which *may* suggest that it was XKD 606; Graham Gauld in his book *The Story of Ecurie Ecosse* states it was 606.); 1961 sold to Jack Wober (Glasgow); sold to Richard Wrottesley; 1962 Silverstone, crashed heavily; tub re-skinned over original skin; 1963 sold to John Coundley and rebuilt; sold to Pierre Bardinon (France); 1975 stated to be owned by Moët et Chandon (or member of Chandon family); early 1980s sold to Victor Gauntlett; Lynx fitted '57 style sliding throttle PI; mid-1980s sold to Jacques Setton (France); 1992 sold to Mr Louwman of Dutch National Motor Museum (Raamsdonksveer, Holland); 1994 car restored by Prowess Racing; car in care of Robert Brooks (UK).

XKSS 722 (XKD 539)

Engine number E2045-9 (E4509-9 according to log book) **Registration number** 4 DPD **Colour** Carmen Red **History** Supplied to Henlys, London; 29/5/57 sold to Coombs of Guildford; 'road-tested' by Basil Boothroyd for *Punch* with illustrations by Brockbank; Brighton Speed Trials, John Coombs, 1st in class; 29/6/58 sold to F. English Ltd, Bournemouth; 26/1/60 sold to Gibson Jarvie of UDT finance company and re-registered UDT 100; 19/10/60 sold to Laystall Engineering; 3/1/62 sold back to UDT (it has been stated that car was next owned by Col. Ronnie Hoare but the above information, and subsequent information, complete with the precise dates taken from the log book, was written up in an article, presumed to be by Bill Rigg, in *Jaguar Driver*, June 1964 issue, and makes no mention of Hoare); re-registered 548 ARX; sold to Chequered Flag, London; 18/9/62 sold to Bill Rigg; early 1963 car sent to works for top-end overhaul and replacement diff unit; March, massive accident on road when one front brake locked on at 80mph and, 'one of the local corporation's concrete lamp standards was demolished backwards without any sensible diminution of velocity'; according to *Jaguar World* the car was rebuilt using last new monocoque; Whyte states that Rigg converted car to D-type; in fact Rigg states, 'As no XKSS monocoque shell was obtainable, the car was rebuilt as a D-type'; raced during 1963

ABOVE **The long-nose XKD 606 won Le Mans in 1957 in Ecurie Ecosse colours, with Bueb/Flockhart driving.**

in Martini 100, Leinster Trophy, Six Hours Relay, Five Hours Relay and a number of shorter events; 1000 trouble-free miles covered until last race at Brands Hatch when, 'an exhaust valve decided it had lived long enough'; winter 1963/64, engine rebuilt as 3.8; 'by now, the car had neither the original engine, body or chassis, so it was decided to re-register the vehicle under its present number AWP 816B, and it is once more competing in all suitable events on the circuits'; car damaged at Silverstone and Rigg crashed another car fatally a fortnight later; part repaired, the car was sold to Nigel Moores who rebuilt it as a D-type; 1988 the D-type and original monocoque sold to Yoshijuki Hayashi (Japan); parts reshuffled to restore XKSS; February 1989 sold to Mr Louwman (Dutch National Motor Museum).

XKSS 754 (XKD 542)
Engine number E2054-9 **Registration number** n/a **Colour** Cotswold Blue **History** Supplied to Jaguar Cars North America; no history known until owned in 1963 by Henry Black (Illinois); 1966 owned by John Scherer who damaged car at a hillclimb event; sold shortly after to current owner, who is rebuilding car which has covered only 11,000 miles; William Culbertson (Dayton, Ohio, USA).

XKSS 728 (XKD 547)
Engine number E2051-9 **Registration number** n/a **Colour** BRG **History** Displayed as D-type at 1956 Barcelona Fair; then converted into XKSS; July 1957 shipped to Jaguar Cars North America; displayed at 1957 Chicago Auto Show and sold to Don Perkins from Winnetka, Illinois; September 1961 sold to John Norsym, Chicago; used sparingly until 1967; laid up and kept in storage until 1998; incredibly original and complete car in superb time-warp condition, with unusual tan interior; 1998 sold at Christies Pebble Beach auction to Gary Bartlett (Indiana, USA).

XKSS 769 (XKD 550)
Engine number E2062-9 **Registration number** n/a **Colour** BRG **History** Displayed as D-type at Appleyards, Leeds; then converted into XKSS; supplied to

Jaguar Cars New York; sold to Tosie Alex who was known still to own it in 1961; June 1964, advertised by Dr David Beiver (New York); later owned (1971) by Frank Opalca (Illinois); sold to Jeffrey Pattinson; 1991 sold, via Terry Larson, to Gerald Nell (Wisconsin, USA).

XKSS 701 (XKD 555)
Engine number E2060-9 **Registration number** SJ 9729 **Colour** BRG **History** First car to be converted from D-type into XKSS; work done in Experimental Dept and completed 14/1/57; given new 7-series number to denote car built in 1957; supplied to New York as demonstrator & repainted Sherwood Green; March, Mansfield race meeting, Louisiana, C. Gordon Benett (Vice-President Jaguar USA), 1st; sold to Robert Stonedale (Houston, Texas); July 1957, Galveston, 4th; September, Mansfield Races, Louisiana, 2nd x 2; by this time full-width screen, bumpers & luggage rack had been removed and a roll-over bar added, car looked more like a D without head fairing; September, Aggie Sports Car Race, Oklahoma Airport (owner had his left leg in a plaster cast!), 5th; November, Galveston, 3rd; later owners included Delmo Johnson, Bob Reedy, Bob Guest & John Hancock; at some stage a Chevrolet V8 engine was fitted & frame cut & altered to suit; 1968-72 owned by John Ridings Lee (Texas); acquired by Herb Wetson, who started rebuild by Ali Lugo of Connecticut, including fitting un-numbered subframe that came with XKD 536 to replace damaged V8 frames, and possibly original rear suspension from XKD 560; sold to Robert de Lano Sutherland (Colorado); "There was never much that I could remember that physically identified the car as XKSS Number 701, but Walter C. Hill Jr had examined everything and was convinced that it was this car," states Sutherland; as Lugo was making no progress & parts were disappearing, Sutherland got "most of the car back to Colorado"; some work was done by Mike Dopudja and Rodney Green; then decided to ship to Lynx; the car broke loose in the container and was damaged; Lynx wished to start the full restoration afresh and Sutherland decided to sell the car; he traded it with Coys of Kensington; November 1981 sold, via Lynx, to Takahashi (Japan), who had Lynx rebuild car in D-type form; 1992 car rebuilt by Lynx in XKSS form.

XKSS 760 (XKD 557)
Engine Number E2074-9 **Registration Number** n/a **Colour** Cream **History** Supplied to Jaguar Eastern Canada; sold to Peter Hessler (Quebec); believed sold to A.H. Iler (Montreal); 1957 raced at Bridgehampton by Peter Templar; later rebuilt by Bill Strohm (Pasadena); early 1970s sold to musician James Dale (Toronto); c1983 sold to John Mozart (California, USA).

XKSS 757 (XKD 559)
Engine number E2071-9 **Registration number** XX 120 **Colour** Cream **History** Supplied to Gilman Motors, Hong Kong; sold to K.Y. Cheang; registered XX 120 and covered 1400 miles on road; 1959 possibly sold to Ron Hardwick; November, Macau GP, Hardwick, 1st; sold car back to K.Y. Cheang; sold to Martin Redfern; rebuilt at some stage, after accident, with new front subframe & other parts, now more akin to D-type in appearance; 1960 Macau GP, 1st; sold to L.C. Kwan, Hong Kong; 1962 Macau GP, Redfern, ret'd having led; 1963 for sale; 1966 sold to Nigel Moores (Liverpool, UK); rebuilt as XKSS & painted BRG; 1988 sold to Yoshijuki Hayashi (Japan); 1995 sold to Peter Rae (UK); 1996 offered for sale by Symbolic Motors (USA).

XKSS 725 (XKD 562)
Engine number E2077-9 **Registration number** n/a **Colour** Cream **History** Supplied to Jaguar Cars North America; sold to Fausto Gonzales de Daiez (California); subsequent history unknown until discovered in Cuba by Colin Crabbe; shipped to UK; rebuilt by Hall & Fowler for Donhoff collection, Germany; sold to Burkhard von Schenk (London); currently for sale with Gregor Fisken, London.

XKSS 704 (XKD 563)
Engine number E2072-9 **Registration number** n/a **Colour** Cream **History** Supplied to Jaguar Cars North America; sold to David Causey; 1960 owned by Ronald Scranton (Hoopeston, Illinois); later owned by Walter Hill (Florida); Hill stated in a letter published in the February 1976 issue of the *XK Bulletin* that he was converting this car to a D-type, however it seems that he subsequently chose to do this to his other XKSS instead (see XKSS 710); 1991 Hill stated, 'it is in good running condition, restored to its original specification and form. It has all matching numbers'; summer 1990 featured in *Jaguar Quarterly*; Walter Hill (Florida, USA).

XKSS 707 (XKD 564)
Engine number E2066-9 **Registration number** n/a **Colour** Cream **History** Supplied to Jaguar Cars North America; believed sold to Lou Brero, but he was killed in Hawaii prior to taking delivery; sold to Sammy Weiss; Weiss killed a few months later at Laguna Seca; 1958 car sold by Oxford Motors (Wiess's company in Sacramento) to Sidney Colberg (San Francisco), who owned it until 1972;

shipped to UK and owned by Geoffrey Marsh, Chris Stewart & Campbell McLaren; now registered JAG 1; 1992 sold to Allen Lloyd (UK).

XKSS 763 (XKD 566)
Engine number E2068-9 **Registration number** n/a **Colour** Carmen Red **History** Supplied to Jaguar Cars North America; believed sold, via Momo Corporation, to E. Colasante (Long Island), but alternative information gives Anthony Rugerio as first owner; 1983 sold to Bob Baker as 'one-owner car'; 1985 sold to Richard Freshman (Los Angeles); 1986 sold to Deitrich von Boetticher (Munich, Germany); Nuremberg, damaged when hit guard rail; sold to Tom Mittler (Indiana, USA).

XKSS 766 (XKD 567)
Engine number E2067-9 **Registration number** n/a **Colour** Mist Grey **History** Supplied to Jaguar Cars North America; sold to J.B. del Cueto, a Cuban living in New York; after initially keeping car in New York, it was taken to Cuba; mid-1958 sold to unknown Cuban who entered local race meetings and other competitions until Castro revolution in 1959; subsequent history unknown until discovered in Cuba by Colin Crabbe in 1980; 1987 sold to Crabbe and shipped to UK; sold to Hubertus Graf Donhoff (Germany); rebuilt by Hall & Fowler; evidence of some accident damage discovered and aluminium skin and frames had been crudely repaired, also some metal fatigue & corrosion; new frame therefore constructed & fitted, but original frame kept with car; painted BRG with black upholstery; registered CSX 436; 1992 for sale at Coys of Kensington; 1995 sold to John Coombs (UK); sold, via Adrian Hamilton, to Dean Meiling (USA).

XKSS 710 (XKD 568)
Engine number E2073-9 **Registration number** n/a **Colour** BRG **History** Supplied to Jaguar Cars North America; sold to Don Horn (Memphis); sold to H. Hempstead (Long Island); sold to Bob Grossman (New York City); sold to Larry Fine (Toledo); sold to Harry T. Heinl (Toledo), who stated that car was "in perfect condition when I sold it"; c1966 sold to Delavan Lee; c1970 sold to Walter Hill (Florida), who stated in 1991: 'Restored several years ago to short-nose D-type configuration with all matching numbers and in good running condition. Re-restored fairly recently to long-nose 1957 Sebring form (copy of XKD 605), in all respects authentic in that form and specification, including early Lucas (Jaguar 1956/57) fuel injection, etc. All XKSS 710 components, matching numbers, are saved. The body panels, engine, brakes and so on, as now installed, are new or old original Le Mans works components, or original XKSS 710. Let me stress that this alteration was a pleasurable technical exercise done solely for my entertainment and interest, and is not mis-represented as a works car. The engine is full race 3.8 by Martin Morris/Bryan Wills (Lakeham). PI head, etc, by me. The block is not an early

works 3.8 block; it is a regular production 'garden variety' block altered as necessary to meet the 1957 works PI specs'.

XKSS 713 (XKD 569)

Engine number E2076-9 **Registration number** n/a **Colour** Cream **History** Supplied to Jaguar Cars North America (despatched 16/4/57); sold to James Peterson (Altadena, California); August 1957, San Fernando Drag Strip, FTD; Tom Groskritz, who was given a run in the car by Petersen, reports car next sold, in 1958, to radio & TV personality Bill Leyden (Beverly Hills), and that he "used to see that white car with its red interior frequently parked in a studio parking lot off Sunset Boulevard in Hollywood. In the early '60s Bill sold the XKSS to rising actor Steve McQueen' – but the subsequent owner states that Peterson sold the car to McQueen in late 1958; McQueen painted car dark green to avoid attention; the seats were retrimmed in black leather by noted show and race car trimmer Tony Nancy, and the wheels were polished; "Otherwise," states Richard Freshman, "it remained in stock condition throughout his ownership, 'terrorising' the local police and 'midnight road race sports-car set" until October of 1967. McQueen made a sale of 'convenience' to the William Harrah Automobile Collection in Reno, Nevada, with the understanding it was to be displayed in the collection and would not be driven by anyone, nor sold. During the spring of 1976, McQueen approached Harrah's to re-purchase and was initially rebuffed. Finally, in February 1978, after a lengthy legal exchange, he managed to re-purchase the car for substantially more than his original sale price"; mileage then 25,273; after standing for 11 years, the brakes and other minor details were refurbished; 1984 auctioned following McQueen's death; sold to Richard Freshman, a friend and neighbour of McQueen's; mileage then 39,396; extensive mechanical overhaul then carried out by Lynx with Freshman visiting every 6-8 weeks; 1992 mileage 41,200; Richard Freshman (California, USA).

XKSS 719 (XKD 572)

Engine number E2082-9 **Registration number** n/a **Colour** White **History** Supplied to Jaguar Cars North America; sold, via Jaguar Midwest, to James Grove (St Louis); later owned by Stephen J. Earle, who may have sold it and bought it back twice; c1970 sold to Robert Danny; c1982 sold to Robert Baker; rebuilt by Lynx; 1983 sold to Bill Tracy (Virginia), but soon sold; Norb Schaefer (Indianapolis, USA).

XKSS 716 (XKD 575)

Engine number E2080-9 **Registration number** n/a **Colour** BRG **History** Supplied to Jaguar Eastern Canada; sold to Stanley McRobert, Montreal; St Eugene race meeting, 1st; raced and hillclimbed in Canada for several years with some success; later owned (1968) by Peter

Kalikow (New York); c1980 sold to John Harper, converted into D-type by Lynx and raced; sold to John Pearson (Whittlebury, near Silverstone, UK); sold, via Brian Redman, to Don Marsh (Columbus, Ohio, USA).

E - T Y P E S

NUMBER 1

Chassis number S850006 **Engine number** RA1343-9S **Gearbox number** EB126CR **Body number** R1015, later R5859 **Registration number** BUY 1, later 4 WPD **Colour** Pearl Grey, Dark Blue upholstery, Blue hood **History** Supplied to Henlys, London (despatched 14/4/61) as steel-bodied roadster; sold to Coombs of Guildford as demonstrator; Oulton Park, debut race, Roy Salvadori, 3rd; car became works development car and increasingly prepared by works; Norbury Cup, Crystal Palace, Salvadori, 1st; Peco Trophy, Brands Hatch, Salvadori, 2nd; Silverstone, Salvadori, 5th; British GP meeting, Aintree, Sears, 2nd; Scott-Brown Trophy, Snetterton, Salvadori, 2nd; Peco Trophy, Brands Hatch, Salvadori, 3rd; Molyslip Trophy, Snetterton, Salvadori, 2nd; 1962 Oulton Park, Graham Hill, 2nd; Easter Goodwood, crashed heavily by Salvadori, rebuilt with lighter gauge steel body; Silverstone, Hill, 3rd; Mallory Park, Hill, 2nd; TT, August Bank Holiday Brands Hatch, Hill, 5th; Goodwood, Salvadori, 4th; winter 1962/63 became prototype for Lightweight E-type, extensively rebuilt with many modifications, principally aluminium shell and aluminium block engine; Snetterton, Hill, 1st; car homologated under Appendix J; Sussex Trophy, Goodwood, Hill, 1st; Loton Park, MacDowel, 1st in class; *Daily Express* Silverstone, Hill, 1st; Grovewood Trophy, Mallory Park, Hill, 1st; British GP meeting, Salmon, 3rd in GT class; TT, Goodwood, Sears, 4th; 1964 *Daily Express* Silverstone, practised by Jack Brabham, raced by Dan Gurney, 8th?; Pontin Trophy, Crystal Palace, Jackie Stewart, 1st; British GP meeting, Brands Hatch, Stewart, 2nd; sold to Charles Bridges, Red Rose Racing; raced by Brian Redman, many successes, 21 firsts, 1 second (to a 250LM) & 5 club circuit records, and launched Redman's career; sold to Gordon Brown; 1994 crashed heavily during Silverstone demonstration; 1995 being rebuilt by John Pearson with monocoque repaired rather than sections replaced; Gordon Brown (Preston, Lancashire, UK); 1998 for sale.

NUMBER 2

Chassis number S850659 **Engine number** RA1345-9S **Gearbox number** EB9376CR, later ZF number 73 **Body number** R5860 **Registration number** 5115 WK (may have been registered 5114 WK originally, see below) **Colour** White with blue stripes **History** First 'Lightweight' supplied to Briggs Cunningham; 1963 Sebring 12 Hours, Hansgen/McLaren, 8th; Le Mans, ret'd or 9th (see below); raced in USA; displayed at Cunningham Museum;

later owned by Anthony Bamford, Geoffrey Marsh and, for many years, Nigel Dawes; driven on several occasions by the author and written about in various magazines; c1991 auctioned by Coys of Kensington and sold for around £1.2m to unknown British buyer. **Note** There is considerable confusion between this car and Number 7, not helped by bonnet-swopping at Le Mans. The car presently registered 5115 WK is now fitted with the engine from Number 8 (5116 WK). There appears to be an unhelpful lack of body and chassis numbers on the monocoques of either of the two remaining Cunningham cars. This situation was not helped by the car presently registered 5114 WK having a racing accident in the 1970s. I possess a sheet of paper with the JCB logo in the top left-hand corner which states: 'Lightweight E-types for home delivery to Mr B. Cunningham on 4.3.63 with invoice numbers 14182, 14954 and 14955'. The chassis, engine, body and registration numbers are grouped as: S850659, RA1345/9S, R5860, 5114 WK; S850664, RA1349/9S, R5865, 5115 WK; S850665, RA1350/9S, R5866, 5116 WK. Regrettably it seems impossible to establish whether or not the above is correct, as Jaguar does not appear now to have records which would verify or disprove. One can only state that it appears to be impossible, at present, to distinguish between these two cars, but that both are equally desirable ex-Cunningham Lightweights; 1996/7 sold to Allen Lloyd (UK).

NUMBER 3

Chassis number S850660 **Engine number** RA1344-9S **Gearbox number** EB9375CR **Body number** R5861 **Registration number** n/a **Colour** n/a **History** Sold to Kjell Qvale, San Francisco, USA; Sebring 12 Hours, Ed Leslie/Frank Morrill, 7th overall, 1st in over 3-litre class; Laguna Seca, heavily damaged in practice; repaired and displayed in Qvale's BMC showroom in San Francisco; 1963 sold to Howard Gidovlenko (Santa Ana, California) and whereabouts unknown until his death in 1998; recorded mileage just 2600; sold at Monterey Classic Car auction to Lynx on behalf of British client.

NUMBER 4

Chassis number S850661 **Engine number** RA1346-9S **Gearbox number** EB9813CR, later ZF number 72 **Body number** R5862 **Registration number** 86 PJ **Colour** Metallic Green **History** Sold to C.T. 'Tommy' Atkins (early April); raced during 1963 season by Roy Salvadori; *Daily Express* Silverstone, 2nd; Grovewood Trophy, Mallory Park, 3rd; TT, Goodwood, 3rd; 1964 *Daily Express* Silverstone, 5th; c. May sold to Roger Mac; 1964 TT, Goodwood, ret'd; *Autosport* Three Hours, 2nd; many more successes during 1964; early February 1965 advertised, with new engine fitted, at £3500; sold to Peter Mould; sold to Guy Griffiths; late-1960s sprinted and hillclimbed by Penny Griffiths; Penny

Woodley (Stratford-upon-Avon, UK).

NUMBER 5

Chassis number S850662 **Engine number** RA1347-9S **Gearbox number** EB9642CR **Body number** R5863 **Registration number** 4868 WK **Colour** Silver **History** Sold to Peter Lindner, German Jaguar Importer (registered 3/5/63); Nürburgring 1000Kms, with Peter Nöcker, ret'd; Avus, 1st; 1964 works prepared for Le Mans & fitted with Low Drag roof; March 1964 fitted with 5-speed ZF gearbox no. 75; Le Mans, with Nocker, ret'd; steel block fitted; Montlhéry, Lindner crashed fatally; car impounded by French authorities; many years later written-off remains acquired by Philippe Renault; sold to John Harper; sold to Guy Black, then of Lynx; sold to Howard Cohen; Lynx rebuilt new car using spare monocoque obtained from works & almost all mechanical components & many repaired body parts from original car; sold, via Lynx, to Peter Schack, Germany; sold to Peter Kaus (Aschaffenburg, Germany) for his Rosso Bianco Collection.

NUMBER 6

Chassis number S850663 **Engine number** RA1348-9S **Gearbox number** 455-1 (all-synchro) **Body number** R5864 **Registration number** 49 FXN **Colour** BRG **History** Sold to Peter Lumsden & Peter Sargent (early May 1963); Nürburgring 1000Kms, crashed at Flugplatz by Lumsden while lying 4th; rebuilt by works with new monocoque; TT, Goodwood, Lumsden, 9th; Silverstone, Sargent, 1st x 2; extensively modified by Playfords to revised 'low drag' body design by Dr Samir Klat and car considerably developed in many areas by Klat and colleague Prof Harry Watson; 1964 Le Mans, ret'd; February 1965 advertised for sale for £3000, but not sold; Lumsden continued to race car in 1965; later owners included a Mr Drane, John Scott-Davies, R.A. Gibson, David Cottingham, Brian Classic, John Carden (car then yellow), Howard Cohen; sold to Jerry Rosenstock (USA); 1997 sold, via Terry Larson, to Lee Munder (Michigan, USA).

NUMBER 7

Chassis number S850664 **Engine number** RA1349-9S **Gearbox number** 455-2, later ZF No. 68 **Body number** R5865 **Registration number** 5114 WK (may have been registered 5115 WK originally, see Number 2 note) **Colour** White with blue stripes **History** Sold to Briggs Cunningham; 1963 Le Mans, ret'd or 9th (see Number 2); raced in USA; displayed at Cunningham Museum; sold to someone who worked at Paramount Studios; sold to Anthony Bamford (UK); sold to Michael Fisher; crashed in historic race, rebuilt; sold, via Adrian Hamilton, to Bill Tracy (USA); sold to a Mr Oglesby; sold to Campbell McLaren; sold to Richard Freshman (USA); restored using iron engine block, but aluminium block retained with car; sold back again (and aluminium

ABOVE **In 1964 the Lindner Lightweight E-type (Number 5) was fitted with 'low drag' bodywork and the most powerful 3.8-litre engine ever built by the works.**

block reinstated) to Campbell McLaren; 1995 sold to David Vine (UK); 1997 sold to Hong Kong based collector.

NUMBER 8

Chassis number S850665 **Engine number** RA1350-9S **Gearbox number** 455-4, then ZF No. 68 **Body number** R5866 **Registration number** 5116 WK **Colour** White with blue stripes **History** Sold to Briggs Cunningham; 1963 Le Mans, Salvadori/Richards, crashed by Salvadori when he hit oil at around 170mph on Mulsanne Straight; car very heavily damaged and caught fire; engine fitted to Number 2; car no longer exists.

NUMBER 9

Chassis number S850666 **Engine number** RA1351-9S **Gearbox number** EB162CR, later ZF No. 77 **Body number** R5867 **Registration number** YVH 210 **Colour** n/a **History** Sold to Peter Sutcliffe (July 1963); Grovewood Trophy, Mallory Park, 4th; Scott-Brown Memorial Trophy, Snetterton, 1st; British GP meeting, 5th in GT class; Snetterton, 4th; 1964 Spa 500Kms, 10th; Montlhéry, 1st; Nürburgring

1000Kms, rolled car; Reims 12 Hours, with Bill Bradley, 14th; Limburg GP, Zolder, 2nd; TT Goodwood, 15th; *Autosport* Three Hours, 5th; Kyalami Nine Hours with Dickie Stoop, 3rd overall & 1st in class; 5th Rhodesian GP meeting, Bulawayo, two races, 3rd & 2nd; Rand GP meeting, Johannesburg, 2nd; 1965 South African GP meeting, East London, 3rd, David Brown Tractor Trophy (same meeting), 1st; Killarney, 2nd x 2; 1965 sold to Red Rose Racing (or Richard Bond) & driven by Charles Bridges & Richard Bond, 9 firsts & 2 seconds; sold to Bob Vincent and raced by him; sold to Bob Jennings and hillclimbed by owner and Mike MacDowel; sold to Bryan Corser (Shrewsbury, UK); painted Tyrolean Green and fitted with certain non-standard items of external trim; sold to Walter Hill (Florida, USA).

NUMBER 10

Chassis number S850667 **Engine number** RA1353-9S **Gearbox number** EB9813CR **Body number** R5868 **Registration number** n/a **Colour** White **History** Supplied to Brysons, Australia (despatched 30/10/63); sold to Bob Jane; 8/12/63, Australian GT Championships, Calder, 1st; February 1964, Australian TT, Longford, 2nd; March, NSW Sports Car Championship, Bathurst, 3rd; April, Victorian Sports Car Championship, Sandown, 3rd; taken to Europe by Bill &

Bob Jane for part of season and raced in several events; July, British GP meeting, Brands Hatch, 10th; shipped back to Melbourne; registered JAG 038; 1965, Bathurst, timed at 150mph & set class lap record; November, Australian TT, Lakeside, 4th; February 1966, Australian GP meeting, Lakeside, crashed; raced by Spencer Martin at Sandown, Warwick Farm & Mallala; October 1966 advertised for sale, but not sold; used for display at Jane's tyre depots for several years; during 1970s bumpers, bonnet motif bar and headlamp trims fitted; 1980 offered for sale at $80,000; sold at Australian GP auction to Peter Briggs' York Motor Museum; 1984, raced at Wanneroo Park; owned by York Motor Museum (Australia).

NUMBER 11

Chassis number S850668 **Engine number** RA1354-9S **Gearbox number** ZF number 73 **Body number** R5869 **Registration number** 2 GXO **Colour** Silver **History** Sold, via Coombs of Guildford, to Dick Wilkins (December 1963) and used as road car; sold to Neil Corner; sold to Phil Scragg; painted light blue; sold to Tony Harrison; hillclimbed at Shelsley Walsh; author remembers Harrison commenting "it may be a very historic car but it doesn't handle"; on display at Birmingham Science Museum for many years; c1987 sold at Rick Cole auction, Monterey, USA; sold to Nigel Corner; still with remarkably low mileage and extremely original; now silver; raced in historic events by owner; Nigel Corner (Yorkshire, UK).

NUMBER 12

Chassis number S850669 **Engine number** RA1355-9 **Gearbox number** ZF number 69 **Body number** R5870 **Colour** Old English White **History** Sold to Phil Scragg (January 1964); used extensively and very successfully in sprints and hillclimbs; sold to musician & broadcaster Antony Hopkins; sold to Brian Classic; sold to Bob Vincent; sold to Michael Dawes (then Dark Green); sold to Michael Fisher;

sold to Brian Classic; sold to Chris Drake; sold to Yoshijuki Hayashi (Japan); 1995 sold to Peter Rae (UK); 1997 sold to Nicolaus Springer (UK); 1998 sold to anonymous international collector.

LOW DRAG COUPE

Chassis number EC1001 **Engine number** E5033-9 **Gearbox number** C7513 **Body number** R2181 **Registration number** CUT 7 **Colour** Grey **History** Project Number ZX 537/30; first of an intended team of cars for international GT racing; lighter gauge steel body with Sayer-designed 'low drag' roofline; project proceeded very slowly and car was first run on 9/7/62; after gathering dust in the Experimental Dept, car sold to Dick Protheroe in mid-1963; Reims, 2nd & 1st in GT class; TT, Goodwood, 6th; Snetterton, 5th; 1964 *Daily Express* Silverstone, 6th; Spa 500Kms, 12th; Nürburgring 1000Kms, crashed in practice; Reims 12 Hours, with John Coundley, 8th & 1st in class; *Autosport* Three Hours, 10th; Paris 1000Kms, Montlhéry, with Coundley, 7th & 1st in GT class; February 1965 advertised at £3200; sold to David Wansborough; TT, Oulton Park, went off into lake; then believed owned by Messrs Gordon, Ramsay & Fellowes; sold to Mike Wright who campaigned it in hillclimbs & sprints; sold to Robbie Gordon; 1973 sold to Adrian Hamilton for £1850; sold to Robert Danny; sold to Walter Hill (Florida, USA); driven by author at Hill's ranch; c1990 sold to Paul Vestey; rebuilt by David Cottingham & RS Panels; c1994 sold, via Adrian Hamilton, to David Pennell (UK); 1995 sold to Viscount Cowdray (UK).

The XK Club's monthly magazine, the *XK Gazette*, has regular updates on the Cs, Ds and Lightweight Es, features, columns by Chris Keith-Lucas and Terry Larson, and is edited by Philip Porter. The Club is for owners and enthusiasts, and has members in 26 countries. Membership information from: XK Club, PO Box 2, Tenbury Wells, WR15 8XX, UK.

INDEX